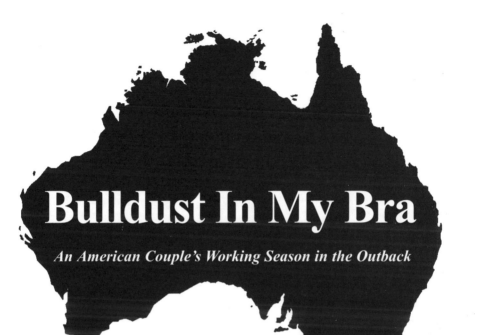

Bulldust In My Bra

An American Couple's Working Season in the Outback

Arlene,
Life's challenges often
turn into opportunities!
God Bless,
Rebecca Long Chaney

Rebecca Long Chaney

ISBN 1-57087-609-6 soft cover
ISBN 1-57087-616-9 hard cover

Library of Congress Control Number. 2002110198

Front and back cover photos by
Jan Glenn of Ashburton Downs Station, Australia.

Professional Press
Chapel Hill, NC 27515-4371

Manufactured in the United States of America
02 03 04 05 06   10 9 8 7 6 5 4 3 2 1

First Edition

To Lee

Thank you for inviting me on
the adventure of a lifetime.

Dedicated to the memory
of two very remarkable men we met
on our trip who made a profound impression on us.

Jack Harvey
of Mininer Station, Australia
May 13, 1929—October 1, 2001

Fred Hutchings
of Dalemere Ayrshire Stud, New Zealand
September 16, 1907—July 22, 2000

And to the memory
of some very special people
who we lost while we were away
and since we've been back home:

Shirley Eader
Evelyn Schildt
Estella Long Harbaugh
Dr. Giuseppe Santus
Milton Cole
Betty Sayler
Gail Cissna

Acknowledgments

There are many people who made our trip possible and others who helped make the book a reality; I'll do my best to remember all of them.

First and foremost—Thank you to the many friends and acquaintances in California, Tonga, New Zealand, Papua New Guinea and Australia who not only invited us into their homes, but welcomed us into their hearts—we are blessed by their love and friendship.

A special thank you to Jan Glenn of Ashburton Downs Station who photographed some of my cattle station work which is featured on the front and back cover of this book. Photography was only one of her many talents. She is an incredible bush woman who I admire greatly and hold dear in my heart. Thanks for making such a difference in our lives.

And much gratitude to the folks who hosted us, especially Mick O'Brien, Andrew Glenn, Tricky Hockley, the Blackburns, Days, Harveys, Quills, Giglias, Minsons, Davises, Loudens, Hutchings and Luaus.

We are forever indebted to the unconditional love and support of our parents, Harold and Peggy Long and Bonnie Chaney. They truly are wonderful individuals. Hugs and kisses to all of our friends and family who e-mailed us on the road and sent packages reminding us of our support team in America.

My daily journal entries were sent bimonthly via e-mail to my best friend, Kelly. She printed every correspondence knowing it would be the basis for my book. Her inspiration during our trip and over the past 30 years sums up the words—true and devoted friend—thanks Kel!

Sincere appreciation to the Randall family, especially George and Betsy, owners of the *Frederick News-Post* and The Job Shop. I am grateful and overwhelmed by their continued support of this special project. Thanks to Tony and

v

Maureen Wheeler, founders of *Lonely Planet* travel guides. Their vision in helping travelers see the world has been a valuable travel aid for backpackers worldwide.

This book would not be a reality without the committed hours and expertise of my four initial editors/proofreaders—Kelly Hahn Johnson, Nancy Luse, Maryrose Welch and Lee Chaney. Thank you for reading every word of my draft and for your input and encouragement. Much thanks to Fran Mears who planted the seed to write a book—at the time she was the Maryland/Delaware Bureau Chief for the Associated Press.

Hats off to the veteran farm broadcaster of all time, Orion Samuelson, who wrote my foreword. Orion has interviewed every U.S. president since J.F.K and has dedicated tireless hours to report and promote global agriculture through his nationally syndicated radio and television programs—thanks Orion.

I can't forget my friends and former co-workers at the *Frederick News-Post* for their time, talents and continued support, especially Lyle Millander, Kathy Moser Stowers, Denise Hope, Bob Harper, Linda Gregory, Mike Powell and Eric Fogle.

And thanks to the committed team at Professional Press, especially Ginny Turner, Michelle Winslow and Austin Kemp.

I would be remiss without thanking my very patient husband. During days of discouragement, Lee always had a kind smile and gentle word to motivate me to write. Thanks Lee for your thought-provoking poems which made a special addition to this book—you truly are amazing!

My family and friends, near and far, and my dog Bode, of course, make me the luckiest lady on earth. Thank you God for my many blessings.

Rebecca Long Chaney

Foreword

Let's just leave our jobs and careers and head off in a totally different direction...in a different place on this planet; let's just get away from it all. I suppose nearly everyone at one time or another has had that feeling of making a total change in lifestyle. But, in most cases, it's a fleeting dream that is quickly replaced by reality. I must admit the thought had never entered my mind, but then for 42 years I have been blessed with the best job in the world...traveling to all 50 states and 43 countries to cover the world of agriculture and agri-business for radio and TV giant, WGN in Chicago. My father, a hard-working Wisconsin dairy farmer, gave me the best job description I've ever received, when, after watching me do my noon-hour radio broadcast in the studio said, (serious as a heart attack) "It must be nice to look at all that hard work and then just talk about it."

So when I met Rebecca Long Chaney there was an instant rapport because we both had dairy and journalism backgrounds and her husband Lee, had a lifetime of dairy experience. But that is where the similarity ended! Their decision to leave successful careers and close family ties and head for the Outback and deal with the extreme hardships that our pioneers experienced in the 1800s went far beyond my idea of a change in lifestyle in the 21st century.

But I'm glad they did, because I now have the opportunity to experience all of this through them without having to leave the comfort of my favorite reading chair. And thanks to Rebecca's ability to paint word pictures I can see and feel the unforgiving land of the Outback, the aching muscles, the grime of the cattle station, the dangers of the cattle musters, the lifestyle lacking all the comforts of home in America and the people of the country who survive and seemingly thrive in the Outback. I found the chapter entitled "I'm Going to Die" especially vivid; and then there was the side trip to Tonga where, indeed, they became real-life "Survivors" without the benefit of the network TV coverage.

I interviewed Rebecca on my radio show and found her life story absolutely fascinating...she talks as well as she writes. She sparkles when she talks about being the first lady from the College of Agriculture to become Homecoming Queen at the University of Wisconsin; her courtship and marriage to Lee; her work as a journalist covering agriculture; and her love of the dairy industry. She talked openly about the times she wondered why they embarked on this adventure? Would the marriage survive? What career path would they follow when they returned home?

She is not alone in the family as a writer. Lee is a poet and you will enjoy his work throughout the book. I especially liked his "Don't Worry" and I think it really answers the "why" in their minds. So sit back and let Rebecca and Lee walk you through the Outback. You may want a bottle of liniment alongside because I know you will feel some of the aches and pains of this adventure.

Orion C. Samuelson
Agri-Business Services Director
WGN Radio/Television
Chicago, Illinois

Preface

Before our adventure, my husband, Lee, and I had been married for two years, preceded by a four-year courtship. For the most part, we had a great marriage—no small feat considering the limited time we spent together. Many of my friends were envious of our special relationship, but they had no idea how taxing our careers had become.

I worked for a daily newspaper in Maryland as the agricultural editor, covering night meetings, weekend cattle shows and other agricultural events, plus I spent countless hours volunteering with youth in the farming community. Lee was a dairy farmer and herdsman, not exactly a five-day-a-week, nine-to-five career.

Sometimes it seemed we were married more to our work than to each other. Stress from my job and the fact I had entirely too many irons in the fire always had me on edge. Lee and I enjoyed what we did, but our shared quality time had a lot to be desired and we feared it could eventually destroy our union. We both agreed things had to change.

Little did we know, however, that our newfound togetherness would be shared with deadly spiders, poisonous snakes, and thundering herds of bulls with horns as sharp as knives. We didn't realize that our marriage bed would be in a tin shack with no electricity or running water, or that our sweet, romantic pillow talk would be replaced by discussions of the best way to string barbed-wire fences or stop a cattle stampede. While our friends had spats over who had control of the TV remote, we argued over whose turn it was to collect wood so we could at least have an occasional hot shower.

It was Lee's idea to trade our typical, predictable lives for a year of the unknown in the Australian outback. The funny thing was, I was always the world traveler. I had a passport filled with stamps and a willingness to go anywhere, anytime. Lee was content just to stay on the farm. I once planned a weekend for the two of us at a hotel in downtown Baltimore, less than 30 miles from home. By Saturday he was chomping to go back to the farm.

Gradually he came around to my way of thinking and got a passport so we could fly to Switzerland for our wedding and honeymoon. But a wedding is one thing and ditching our jobs, family and friends for a year on the other side of the world was quite another.

The idea sprouted when Lee read a 1998 Christmas card and letter sent to us from Mandy Day. I'd met the Australian woman at a rural conference held in the United States that year in July. Her letter described life on a cattle station in the outback. Up until then we had kicked around the idea of moving to Wisconsin, but then Lee got another idea.

"I want to go to Australia," he said.

I humored him and made him promise we would keep the screwball plan to ourselves until we could work out all the details. We would need to save money, unburden ourselves of excess belongings and line up work in Australia. We also didn't want to risk having people talk us out of the adventure.

After Christmas we celebrated the New Year with our friends Kelly and Blane Johnson in Bedford County, Virginia. I spilled the news over a few beers by the bonfire. Kelly and I, friends from childhood, had taken off nine months in 1992 to travel around the world so I knew she wouldn't think we were crazy. We continued to talk about our plans over the three days we spent with them. It was the longest stretch of time during our six-year commitment, other than our honeymoon, that Lee and I together had been away from home and the responsibilities of the farm. That, if nothing else, was enough to convince us we would be doing the right thing by readying our backpacks.

A few days later Lee, who was surprising me with his itchy feet for travel, wowed me again with a poem he had written about the visit with our friends.

Mistress of Bedford County

He anticipates their rendezvous to be warm and fulfilling,
But was not discouraged to find his mistress cold, tired and
    unwilling;

With the attention he paid her as so often before,
She blossomed like a flower, fingers clutching for more;

He fed her lustful hunger at an unwavering pace,
Basked in her glow, hot breath on his face;

Well after sunset, they both must retire,
He bids a reluctant farewell to his mistress—The Fire.

Lee Chaney

That was the first of a series of poems Lee would write before and during our year abroad. I would constantly be amazed not only in what we experienced in our travels together, but also in what we discovered in each other.

Contents

Poems by Lee Chaney

Dilemma Darkens Dream

On January 24, the heart of Australia's summer, my husband, Lee, and I were headed to one of the most unforgiving landscapes in the world—the Australian outback. The thought was rather daunting.

The Lada Niva four-wheel-drive vehicle we bought was small but functional. It was christened the Road Toad because of its brownish toad-like color and rounded roof. We hoped it would get us to the end of our 1,000-mile journey before we were cooked from lack of air conditioning.

Our destination was Juna Downs Station, a 900,000-acre cattle ranch supporting more than 5,000 beef cattle. It was located in the northern part of Western Australia. Juna Downs, managed by Mandy and Shane Day, would be our transition station before we proceeded to our next jobs in the outback. I'd met Mandy in 1998 while covering the International Conference for Women in Agriculture in Washington, D.C. for the daily newspaper I'd worked for at the time. Mandy and I kept in touch. Her letters fascinated Lee and sparked a newborn spirit in him to live life differently and pursue new horizons. Never in a million years would I have guessed Lee would travel halfway around the world to find what he was searching for in his heart.

I couldn't believe we were really there and beginning our outback conquest. I sat up, readjusted my baseball cap and waited for Lee to turn the ignition. I twitched in my seat—

tense, nervous. Once we passed through Perth, we hit the Great Northern Highway, although "great" and "highway" were misnomers for the stretch of two-lane traffic with potholes and no shoulders. This was the major highway system through Western Australia?

It was warm when we left Perth; the farther north we drove the more stifling it became. The harder we pushed the Road Toad, the hotter the engine boiled, turning the interior into a sauna. By early afternoon it was suffocating; our sweat glued us to the vinyl car seats. Perspiration dripped in rivulets.

The alternator light came on. "Oh no, not a problem already," I groaned.

We were passing through little towns about every 50 to 100 miles and were able to pull into a small tractor dealership. While the mechanic and Lee examined the Road Toad, I found relief in the air-conditioned farm store. I chatted with the folks across the counter. One of the women noticed my sweaty red face. "You do have air conditioning in your vehicle, don't you?"

"No, but we do have water," I said brightly, trying to dismiss my discomfort. They couldn't believe we were driving up north in that kind of heat without an air conditioner. But it would be the first of many unbelievable things we would do as a result of limited resources and funds.

"No worries," the mechanic said slamming down the bonnet, as it's called in Australia.

I was miserable. I traded my hat in for what my friends and I called a "do rag." I dipped my bandanna in the cooler of ice, which had been reduced to cool water, and tied the dripping rag around my head. It kept the hair and sweat out of my eyes and offered a little relief. Every ten minutes I dipped the bandanna and tied it back on my head to fight off heat-induced nausea. Perspiration continued to roll down my legs.

A never-ending expanse of bushland, hills, spinifex, and rock ledges was a welcome change to the hustle and bustle of cities and towns. As we inched northward, blades of grass waved with a deeper green hue, a sign of a good season of rainfall. Spinifex bushes, the most common desert shrub in Australia, shot up like the elongated stiff bristles of a brush reaching two to four feet in the air. Their clumped masses marked the countryside, interrupted only by patches of grass and natural boulder clusters and formations.

I was typically a chatterbox, but the scenery left me speechless. I was hypnotized by the stunning changes in the vista as hundreds of miles melted away. I'd always thought the outback was dry and barren. While some regions of Australia were hammered with hot and rainy weather, others were plagued by drought.

It was the country's mystical Aboriginal legends of "Dreamtime," pioneering stories of cattle and sheep drives across the continent, and its climatic and topographical mixes that drew Lee and me farther into the isolation of the outback. After visiting friends for two months in Tonga, New Zealand and Papua New Guinea, Lee and I were ready to work. Our goal was to experience firsthand the challenges of outback life on a remote cattle station. It was our dream, but was I ready?

Western Australia was the largest of the country's seven states and it covered one-third of the nation's total landmass. We had a real introduction to its immense size during our trek to Juna Downs Station.

A menagerie of kangaroos, road trains and rugged countryside filled the landscape. The marsupials grazed lazily alongside the road at dusk and dawn. The two- to four-sectioned tractor-trailers nearly blew us off the road. Road trains, as much an Australian icon as windmills, were introduced decades earlier to save time and fuel on the country's endless highways. The oversized truck and trailers could be 175 feet long. They carted livestock, food, gas and other products to and from outback towns and stations. The trucks were remarkable sights rolling down the highway.

Like the road trains, the Road Toad was equipped with a 'roo bar to protect it from total destruction if a kangaroo unexpectedly pounced into its path. But a road train's bar was larger and called a bull bar to safeguard the cab when a cow or bull wandered into the road in the middle of the night. With no boundary fences on the half-million-to-one-million-acre stations, cattle often meandered on the highway after dark in search of a cool road surface to lie on. Stations were so big, in fact, they were identified on official Australian maps like major landmarks, towns or cities.

Drivers had to be mindful of straying cattle, prolific kangaroos and the wild emus that zigzagged through the scrub. The flightless birds' antics were comical and engaging. A pack of dingoes, Australia's wild dog, stood tense in the bush with ears alert. They posed little threat near the road, but were predators and dangerous. Bungarras, the enormous lizards resembling something from prehistoric times, slowly crossed the road sniffing the ground for the day's meal, usually a decomposed bit of road kill. Lee drove 12 hours straight. 'Roos invaded the lush green grass near the bitumen making driving conditions hazardous. We pulled off the road at 11 p.m. Without the proper camping equipment, we tilted our front seats back and nestled in our sleeping bags.

"Lee, please put your window up and lock the doors," I asked.

"Excuse me?" he said.

"Someone could come along and murder us," I pleaded.

"We're hundreds of miles from civilization and you're worried someone is going to kill us," he said. "Well, I'll put my window up and we won't have to worry about getting murdered because we're going to suffocate to death."

"Okay, you can crack your window, but not enough to get an arm in," I surrendered.

Lee knew I was a worrywart and probably questioned how I was ever going to survive outback life.

The rising sun glared in the window and we were on the road by 6 a.m. Lee drove. He said the Road Toad wasn't the easiest vehicle in the world to drive and suggested I continue to navigate. I most happily obliged and entertained him as the miles between us and Juna Downs Station disappeared. We arrived in Newman about 9:30 a.m. and phoned Mandy and Shane Day.

"Hello, Shane?"

"Yeah, mate."

"This is Becky."

"How ya goin'?" he asked.

"Good, we've made it to Newman. How does the road look into Juna?"

"We just got another couple of inches of rain last night, but if you have a four-wheel drive you shouldn't have a problem making it in."

"Okay, we'll see you in about two and a half hours." Click.

"Lee, Shane said he thought we'd be able to make it," I said with an anxious smile as I jumped back into the passenger seat.

We knew we were taking a chance going to the outback that time of year when weather and road conditions were very unpredictable. There were two seasons in Australia—the wet and the dry. The wet season was during the summer, November through April, when intense heat and torrential downpours made roads impassable and station work nearly impossible. The dry season, May through October, was Australia's winter, when months were cool, windy and provided little to no rainfall.

Excitement surged through our veins when we finally came to the Juna Downs Station sign directing traffic left to a dirt road. After the first three miles I looked at Lee and said, matter-of-factly, "This isn't bad, this will be an easy drive."

First rule in the outback: never assume anything. It was only a half mile afterward we faced our first obstacle—a flooded creek bed. The water was swift and the meter-reading pole measured about one meter. The poles, we learned later, were at most locations where floods were prevalent.

For the past two weeks Lee had been like a caged animal that had to get to the outback to start working, to do physical labor. There was nothing that was going to stop him from getting to Juna Downs, not even the flooded creek. He looked over at me and didn't have to speak, his eyes said it all: *Hang on, honey, here we go.*

I braced myself, unbuckled my seat belt and rolled down my window to escape if necessary. Lee had much more confidence than I did in the Road Toad, the 18-year-old Russian-made automotive marvel he thought he had found. Lee threw the Road Toad into four-wheel drive and we slowly drove into the flooded creek until the wheels were completely submerged. Lee, no doubt, was doing the "man thing" and had to test the Road Toad's road and water abilities.

Rushing water made me nervous—I was scared. The water forcibly pushed underneath our vehicle and attacked the sides with its violent wet fingers. It gushed up against the bottom of my door. All I imagined was the Road Toad slowly drifting downstream, tipping on its side and trapping us in a watery grave. I tightly clutched our laptop computer, Clyde, knowing if we were swept away I'd have to try to save myself and him, our most important cargo.

Tires sank into the mud, but the Road Toad miraculously made it through. At that point Lee figured if the Road Toad made it through that flood, it could make it through any flood. We crossed four more flooded creek beds. My body tensed at every crossing and I readied Clyde for escape.

We rolled into the Juna Downs Station homestead, the Road Toad spattered with water and mud. Mandy and Shane walked out of the house and looked a little bewildered.

"What's wrong?" I asked, as I stepped out of the battle-stricken vehicle.

"We thought you said you had a four-wheel drive," Shane said.

"This is a four-wheel drive," Lee proudly insisted.

The Days assumed we had a huge four-wheel drive like a Toyota or Dodge, not a little Lada Niva. Had they known, they assured us they never would have asked us to attempt the drive out to the station in the wet season. Lee was pleased with the Road Toad's performance.

It was hard to comprehend where we were, but we were finally there in the remote outback with so much to learn and discover. My feelings of apprehension, unsureness, nervousness and yes, even fear, had transformed to excitement and anticipation. We had arrived and hoped we were mentally and physically prepared for our outback challenge. The new chapter of our year-long adventure abroad had begun.

The modest one-story house was made of siding and tin. A stationary trailer had been added a few years earlier and provided additional living space. There were three outbuildings. The largest was utilized as a shop and a small shed contained horse tack. Four small units that looked like a long mobile home provided accommodations for employees during mustering season when cattle were rounded up and sent to market. A windmill erected 100 feet from the main house was the central focal point. There was little question about its importance. Windmills were the lifeline of the outback, the difference between life and death.

A fertile lawn surrounded the house and was enclosed by a fence. Fuchsia flowers cascaded down a lattice along the side of the veranda in the front part of the house. Bushes bursting with white and yellow blooms marked the trail along the slate path to the dwelling's side door.

We settled into our temporary home at Juna Downs. The Days had managed the property for the past eight years for Hamersley Iron, a multi-million dollar business that boasted the richest iron ore deposits in the world.

Shane and Mandy shared colorful vignettes of station life, outback hurdles and memories of days gone by. Juna Downs was two hours from the closest town and was in the Pilbara Region, the largest shire in the world. With such a distance to the closest town, there wasn't any such thing as a quick trip to town or slipping in for supplies. Biweekly trips were reserved for mail runs, picking up necessities and buying groceries in bulk. Those trips were often interrupted by more rainfall and flooded roads.

Mandy and I reminisced about our initial meeting in Washington, D.C., nearly two years earlier. Who would have guessed our common link to agriculture would bring our worlds together?

The Days had purchased a property 950 miles south and would be moving in a month. We helped them pack and prepare for their big move. Mandy and Shane attempted to turn Lee and me into a genuine jackaroo and jillaroo, respectively, the names given to those folks seeking temporary employment on cattle and sheep stations.

When it wasn't raining, Mandy broke horses. Lee and I watched her technique closely, her horsemanship skills and the round-pen method she utilized. I stared in awe at Mandy's talents. I had never watched anyone break in a horse, certainly not a woman as brave as Mandy.

Our days at Juna continued to be full of station duties. The 32 windmills located on the property required frequent maintenance checks. Horses had to be wormed and young stallions were castrated. We assisted with all aspects of the daily routine.

Although difficult at times, we adapted to our new outback lifestyle—100-degree plus heat, an invasion of black flies, limited electricity fueled by a diesel generator, and isolation. I had gotten used to the huge spiders with bodies the size of small mice with three-inch legs. As long as they respected my space, I respected their space and we could live in harmony.

The epidemic of nasty flies plagued the outback during the summer months. They dotted our faces and backs and exhausted our swishing efforts. Finally, we just allowed the winged insects to crawl around on our faces. If we had swatted at flies all day we wouldn't have gotten anything else accomplished. After several bouts of gagging when I unwittingly sucked in a fly, I learned to keep my mouth shut. And keeping my mouth shut, as Lee would say, was a huge challenge for me.

Mandy and Shane, our outback mentors, had taken great care in restructuring our Australian slang and developing our knowledge and skills of station life. Lee and I were sad the day Mandy, Shane, and their 11-year-old son, Stuart, departed for their new property, but we were ecstatic to leave for Wallareenya Station which was located nearly at the northern tip of Western Australia to start our next job. We were in the midst of good-byes when the Days' phone rang.

"Hello, Juna Downs Station," I said.

"Is Becky there?"

"This is Becky."

"Hi, Becky, this is Moya from Wallareenya."

"Oh, hi, Moya, how's it goin'?" I said with a bit of nervousness in my voice, expecting the worst, as every drama queen does.

"It's too wet up here for anyone to get in. I'm really sorry but you won't be able to work here at Wallareenya."

I got off the phone almost in tears. "We can't go to Wallareenya to work, what are we going to do?" I asked Lee and Mandy.

It was a nightmare. Our dream was crumbling around us. Our six and a half years together, three of them as husband and wife, had been committed more to our jobs and volunteer work than to each other. Lee was a dairyman and had bred or developed some of the top Brown Swiss dairy cattle in the United States. He had sold the national prize-winners to pursue his dream of working in the Australian outback.

I had won regional and national writing awards during my ten-year stint with the *Frederick News-Post,* the second-largest daily newspaper in Maryland. Appreciation certificates and plaques had lined our walls at home reflecting the hours devoted to 4-H, FFA, Farm Bureau, Grange and other civic, agricultural and youth organizations.

Lee was dedicated to a life on the farm and I was committed to serving others. We were happy, but had little time to spend together. We knew there was more to life and we were determined to find it. It was a bold move to leave our successful careers, family and friends to embark on a life-changing expedition, and that vision was threatened by one discouraging phone call.

For the next hour I frantically called cattle station after cattle station searching for employment. Over and over again, my memorized speech was, "Hi, my name is Becky. My husband, Lee, and I have been working at Juna Downs Station for a month. We both have agricultural backgrounds and we're wondering if you needed any help?"

And the repeated answers were the same, "Sorry, we have our crew lined up. No, we don't need any help. It's just too wet for you to get in."

It didn't look good. My stomach tightened, I felt sicker after every call.

"If you come with us and Lee helps me break some horses in, I will just give you a horse," Mandy said. "Then you could sell it for one to two thousand dollars."

It was a really nice gesture, but we wouldn't impose like that on the Days. They had already been wonderful hosts.

Moya felt so bad that we couldn't come to Wallareenya to work that she gave me her parents' phone number in Western Australia's southern region. She said they were dairy farmers and was sure we could work there. Having driven 1,000 miles north to the outback four weeks earlier, we had no aspirations to head south again. Lee had spent the past 14 years of his life milking cows. He certainly hadn't traveled halfway around the world to milk cows again. It was the intrigue of life in remote Australia that still tugged at our curiosity. We wanted to venture deeper into the outback, where thrills and adventure awaited us.

In a matter of one phone call our world had changed. I had spent nine months planning every detail of our trip abroad, organizing every stop, every visit. We had just completed our third month on the road and our first major crisis had hit. Where had I gone wrong? Was it my fault that our dream was lost? Where were we going to go? How would we make money?

Don't Worry

Don't worry about me, I'll be just fine,
Haven't lost my way, my will or my mind;

Simply time to move on, no sense in suspending,
No deep regrets, no tearful ending;

Been a good ride, but now is the time for change,
Turn from the familiar, explore the strange;

Not on a crusade to find greener pastures,
A little time for discovery is all that I'm after;

I'll take full advantage of the chance I am given,
Not looking for a way out, just more time for livin';

No cause for alarm, I'm not running away,
Just looking around, enjoying each day;

Where I hang my hat, part of you will always be,
If that part was ever lost, I wouldn't be me.

Lee Chaney

Chaneys Go Walkabout

F or the moment we were two lost souls. All I could do was reflect on what we had given up for the trip. I hoped our efforts for life change were not in vain. It was all too much for me to comprehend. I needed to escape that discouraging afternoon and my thoughts quickly drifted to our trip preparation, departure and the three countries we visited before Australia.

Okay, I admit it. I get worked up over the silliest things. My tear ducts fill when I read a sentimental birthday card and just forget about keeping my mascara from running when I watch a sappy movie. It was not for nothing that my friends call me the Drama Queen.

That was the case when I began the rounds of coworkers, friends and family, telling them about the plans Lee and I had for quitting our jobs and heading to Australia for a year. The general manager at the newspaper where I had worked for nearly a decade was momentarily dumbfounded. The head of human resources had a box of tissues handy when the tears started spilling down my cheeks. I think the assistant managing editor wanted to join Lee and me, if nothing more than to get away from the piles of papers on his desk.

With no kids, no mortgage, no debt, and a world of contacts, it was the perfect formula for adventure, a new way of life, discovery of unchartered waters and a chance for changes in our daily routine that we believed we needed.

Lee's objective was to work in Australia, but I told him it was ridiculous to travel halfway around the world and not make some stops on the way. I sent faxes and e-mails to my friends in Australia to line up work. I organized our stays in Tonga, New Zealand and Papua New Guinea. The two months prior to our departure proved to be exhausting, both mentally and physically. They took a heavy toll on me. I took Tylenol P.M. for my chronic headaches and to help me sleep. Time ticked away until finally there were only two weeks until departure and I left for my last assignment for the *Frederick News-Post.*

Lulled by the conversation of thousands of agricultural education students seated around me, I remember how I quickly had a reality check and thought, *It's Friday, October 29. I'm covering the 72nd annual National FFA Convention and I'm set to leave the country in two weeks. Not for a couple days or a week for another business trip to cover agricultural news, but overseas for a year.*

I remember how the anxiety built up in my chest. I was 35 years old. Could I handle the challenges that lay ahead? I had been at the paper for nine and a half years. I loved my job, I loved the people I worked with and I was finally making great money! So why was I giving it all up? His name is Lee. It's amazing what people do in the name of love. Call me crazy, but in my heart I knew it must be the right thing.

The flight home allowed me a little time to reflect on the student function. The FFA convention had always been a highlight of my year, ever since I had attended the national gathering in 1985 in Missouri to receive my American Farmer Degree, the highest recognition possible in the organization. During the 1990s my journalistic career took me back to the event. I had wonderful memories, not only with the FFA, but with all the agricultural groups and individuals I wrote about.

As the plane taxied down the runway, I slumped down in my seat, closed my eyes and before I drifted off to another time, I recalled the most memorable moment of my final convention. At Maryland's FFA delegation breakfast, the state's FFA executive secretary, Mark Adkins, introduced me.

"Becky, please stand," he asked. "I'd like to thank Becky for all of her support and coverage over the years. We're really going to miss her."

The more than 150 members of the delegation rose to their feet, applauding. I was overwhelmed with gratitude and tears. I'd miss those kids. I'd miss all the folks in the community who made my career so rewarding.

Once the plane touched down in Maryland, my emotions soon drowned in a sea of final trip preparation. Selling stories from our experiences abroad would be critical, both professionally and financially. But how was I going to do that? Enter Lyle, the paper's computer guru. He researched and purchased our iBook laptop and digital camera. That was only the beginning. Software was downloaded, Lyle instructed us on the finer points of computer wizardry and last, but not least, we had to register with an Internet provider.

We needed an e-mail address. I wanted it to be something different, something to symbolize the trip, but didn't have a clue. I figured with Lee's poetic genius, he'd come up with something catchy. At home I caught Lee on his way to the barn for evening chores. "Lee, we have to come up with an e-mail address and I need to pass it on to Lyle tomorrow."

He looked back and said, "Okay, I'll work on it." Halfway across the lawn, he stopped, whirled around and yelled, "I've got it!"

"What's your idea?" I inquired skeptically.

"Chaneys' walkabout."

I smiled, liking the sound of it. "You amaze me. It's perfect, I love it." So chaneyswalkabout@aol.com was born.

Through Lee's trip research he discovered that the Aborigines, Australia's indigenous people, often went on walkabout, a spiritual retreat into the bush for days, weeks and even months. We hoped our year-long walkabout would be as fulfilling.

We chipped away at final trip details. Visas were picked up in Washington. Supplies were purchased. Bank accounts were closed. More good-byes, packing and boxing, then more good-byes and packing and boxing.

I made little headway boxing up our belongings, so I summoned the aid of girlfriends, Kelly and Mitzi. They were aware of my heavy involvement in the community and the fact I was a real pack rat. Armed with bags and boxes the duo started making piles—things Becky might want to keep, things she really needs to throw away and items for Becky and Lee's yard sale.

The trash pile grew, but there was little on my to-keep piles. They told me it was okay to finally throw away the napkin and favor from somebody's wedding, the wine corks from special occasions, and the more than 100 Christmas cards I still had on the wall from two years earlier.

The girls threw things in trash bags when I wasn't looking and when I tried to retrieve the extra rubber bands and paper clips that were tossed, they said, "Becky, you don't need them." There were still things I couldn't part with and didn't part with.

We loaded our vehicles and delivered all the to-go items to Dad and Mom's farm for our upcoming weekend yard sale. The newspaper advertisement read: "Moving sale, couple moving to Australia, Saturday and Sunday, Nov. 6-7, 8 a.m.-6 p.m." More than 30 borrowed tables from the Graceham Fire Department were lined with useful items, plus a lot of junk I never knew we had. I hated to part with my beach chair, but I only used it two days a year for the girls' annual beach weekend. It was easy to slap a price tag on my iron, practically new from its limited use. Our low-price offerings, along with my half-price sale of Princess House crystal, added up. The extra $1,000 came in handy on the trip.

It was a week and a half before our departure. My last day of work was Nov. 4 and Lee was irritated I had worked until the last minute. We only had nine days to pack for the year, pack up the rest of our worldly possessions for storage and clean our home. Plus, I needed to finalize our one-week visit to California, ten-day stint in Tonga, one-month stay in New Zealand, 12-day excursion in Papua New Guinea and ten months in Australia. It was no wonder I was close to a nervous breakdown.

I vividly recall November 10—three days before departure and we weren't packed, organized or close to having everything boxed for storage. "I need more help," I said to Lee as I did a quick mental inventory of what needed to be done.

"You work until the last minute and now you're not ready and it's my fault," he said as he glared back at me.

I collapsed in a chair, dropped my head in my hands and cried uncontrollably. I'm the Drama Queen, remember, but tears rarely intimidated Lee. He gave me a stoic look. "I don't care if you cry until your goddamn eyes fall out," he said.

I was nearly paralyzed by the abrupt statement. His comment floored me, pretty much a first for the Lee Chaney I'd met six years earlier. It was always his kind words, endless compliments and loving nature that attracted me to him. I certainly didn't like his reaction to my brief mental lapse, but in minutes he apologized profusely. The stress of departure worked on us both.

It was a hectic week. Dinner engagements with my best friends from work, high school and college filled most evenings. Lee and I made the rounds to visit family. The hardest good-bye for me, undoubtedly, was my parents. They had always been supportive of all my crazy adventures and more than anyone knew how dedicated I was to my career and volunteer work. They had instilled in me a strong work ethic, a passion for agriculture and, most importantly, the guts to pursue my dreams. The night before we left, Lee and I were up all night packing for the trip and boxing the remaining things to be stored. Like always, there was nothing like procrastinating.

On departure morning, Lee's mother picked us up at 5 a.m. We weren't ready yet, but it was time to go. We literally pitched the rest of our travel supplies and clothes into our backpacks. Mrs. Chaney assured us she would finish packing up the house and put the final cleaning touches on the trailer we had lived in for almost four years. We headed to Baltimore-Washington International Airport.

Well, we're off! That was the first entry in my journal dated Nov. 13, 1999. I wasn't nearly as nervous as I had been the entire 11 months since we had made the decision to leave the country. A peaceful calm embraced me. I wasn't sure if it was the anxiety pill my doctor prescribed or the realization that Lee and I were engaging in what could be a transformation of our lives and our relationship. As flight attendants gave their two-minute safety lecture, Lee grabbed my hand, gave me a reassuring glance and kissed me softly. We were both so exhausted, even the excitement of the trip didn't keep us awake.

Since the farthest west Lee had ever been was Colorado on a hunting trip with my Dad a month earlier, I wanted to share some of my special places and people in California. I didn't know how Lee would react to finally getting off the farm. I feared he might go through work withdrawal. The hunting trip was the first non-cow-related trip for Lee in six years other than our honeymoon, and even our wedding day and honeymoon had included cows.

Our first stop was Modesto. Our long-time friends Edwin and Della Genasci welcomed us to their Brown Swiss and Holstein dairy. Their Swiss-Italian roots made them fun and generous hosts. We explored Californian's initial hub of gold rush fever; slugged back beers while stuffing ourselves with polenta alongside the animated men of the Swiss-Italian Club; and marveled at Modesto's famed vineyards and 1,000-cow dairies. After three jam-packed days, it was time to bid our friends farewell, but not before Edwin and Della had to don my infamous Statue of Liberty sunglasses for photos. The unique red, white and blue sunglasses, arched in the front like the madame's crown itself, were purchased on a road trip to New York City years earlier.

(Kelly, my other traveling partner, Nancy, and I had escorted our mate from Australia, Mikey Blackburn, to the Big Apple for a sightseeing venture. We had hoped to give him a look at the Statue of Liberty, but cold, damp fog blocked our vision. We did the next best thing, ducking into a junk shop filled with tacky souvenirs, and buying the glasses as a me-

mento. A tradition evolved of taking along the glasses wherever we went, getting people to wear them for pictures. Most people didn't have to be asked twice to slap them on. Our collection of pictures spans the globe.)

Our visit to the West Coast was filled with stops to see friends from San Francisco to Los Angeles. I believed our California stop would be good for both Lee and me. It gave us the chance to get used to spending 24-hour days together and an opportunity to see how really compatible we would be before hitting a third-world country or difficult circumstances in the outback. Some people had said, "This trip will either make you or break you." I never even imagined it could break us, but time would tell.

We drove through Sequoia National Park and hiked to the peak of Moro Rock at 6,725 feet. We sat at the top of the dome-shaped granite monolith, literally absorbed in the clouds and trying to catch a glimpse of the horizon as the soft, cotton-like clumps occasionally cleared. There was so much to see in the world and Lee was beginning to get his first taste. For someone who had hardly explored life outside of Carroll County, it was obvious he was changed by the Moro Rock experience. His somber outlook had already transformed into a new appreciation and a zest for life.

An American couple quitting their jobs to work overseas for a year is pretty much unheard of. It was a great time in our lives—we had our health, energy, enthusiasm and most importantly, we had each other. My one inner fear was if our relationship could truly withstand the trials of the trip and the constant companionship. What would happen when we meshed the worlds of the globe-trotting wife and the stay-at-home hubby? We knew we would encounter hardships along the way—ones that would not only test our physical and mental stamina, but our marriage as well. No matter what, we planned to make the most of the incredible journey. A journey of our minds, hearts and souls—a journey of our love and life together. I hoped the 380 days together would bring us closer and not tear us apart.

It was time to leave our friends, time to leave our family, time to leave America. I thought all my butterflies had fluttered away, but nervousness consumed my body as we drove away in the rental car toward Los Angeles to catch our international flight. We returned the rental car, checked in, then I was flooded with relief, excitement and still a touch of anxiety. Lee and I had a farewell toast in the bar. I slowly savored my drink as I knew it would be the last Coors Light for a year. We had checked our backpacks, but still had two carry-on bags.

The carry-on bags weren't stuffed with emergency clothes or makeup, but rather all of our computer and camera gear. I had my old reliable Canon AE-1 35mm that Mom and Dad had given me. It was a graduation gift when I completed my courses at the University of Maryland's Institute of Applied Agriculture. We had a Canon Sure Shot which was the greatest little camera we'd ever owned. Our new Kodak DC280 Zoom digital camera, specifically purchased to e-mail photos home to accompany my feature stories, was tucked away in its own bag. And the most valuable investment of the trip was our Macintosh iBook laptop, affectionately referred to as "Clyde."

Clyde would be our only real connection with friends and family while we were away. He and all the other important equipment were secured under our seats and in the overhead compartments. The past few weeks had been draining and Lee and I fell asleep, but not before Lee devoured both of our meals. Seven hours later we had a layover in Hawaii. While we stood in line to have our passports cleared, a curious woman in front of me turned around.

"Why are you going to Tonga?" she asked.

"We're going to meet with a girl from Maryland who's there serving in the Peace Corps," I answered.

"Really?" she said, "My husband is the Peace Corps director in Tonga."

I thought, *What a small world. Kelly just won't believe this.* She always jeered me and said I must carry a horseshoe up my butt because of the way things fell into place for me. I didn't realize at that moment just how I would depend on that horseshoe.

Look Beyond

Am I crazy? Have I lost my mind?
Traveling so far, for a thing I may not find;

A reckless adventure or a promising trek of revelations?
Don't know if it will destroy or exceed my expectations;

Will I recognize what I seek at first glance?
No guarantees, but now is the time, here is my chance;

Not a complete change of direction, but a passing season,
For each choice I make, I have my own reason;

If you don't understand I cannot explain,
This choice is so basic, so simple and plain;

I choose to pursue happiness to see what it brings,
Not to clutter my life with material things;

Looking beyond what many want to what I already possess,
If I can be true to myself I will be a success.

Lee Chaney

There's a Horseshoe up my Butt

A s we stepped off the plane in Tonga we were blasted by the island's tropical humidity. My leggings, which had kept me warm on the plane, were now glued to my sweaty legs like plastic wrap molded over a container that has been microwaved on high. My biggest question, *Was Lee ready for his first third-world experience?*

Armed guards were stationed by the entrance to customs and a drug-sniffing dog examined all carry-on luggage as we walked through the double glass doors toward the counter. They asked all the typical questions, "Why are you in Tonga? Where are you staying? When are you leaving?" We passed the inquiry, passports were stamped and we proceeded around the corner.

Clyde weighed down my shoulder, but I couldn't complain—he was our most precious belonging. It didn't matter what was lost, stolen or damaged, but it couldn't be Clyde. Insurance would have cost as much as Clyde's price tag, which was totally idiotic. There was no economical reason to have it, so we didn't. As the only link to enable me to send stories for publications in the States, Clyde was our lifeline and we treated him with respect and care. We guarded him as we did our passports. He was a sharp-looking laptop. In a see-through body trimmed in a stunning fluorescent-ocean blue, Clyde always drew attention when he was out of his carrier. For two computer-illiterate people like us, we were blessed to have him.

We walked down the narrow corridor of the small international terminal of Tonga and arrived in a room half the size of a basketball court, if that. The room was shoulder to shoulder people, nudging one another, pushing through the crowd. We were unaware at first, but soon realized it was baggage claim. Bags weren't carefully delivered on a conveyor belt to be plucked off one by one. Rather, they were strewn everywhere. It was total mayhem, like a feeding frenzy. I affixed myself to the wall while Lee disappeared into the hysteria in search of our three bags. We each had a backpack, plus one bag was completely stuffed with gifts for the Tongan kids being taught by Diann, the Peace Corps volunteer I'd be interviewing. Diann was from back home and the editors at my old newspaper thought she'd make a good story.

I barely kept track of Lee's progress in the turmoil of travelers—deployed like a heat-seeking missile in search of a target, our backpacks. I lost him. I looked vainly to spot him in the colossal confusion. Finally, I saw the top of his baseball cap, heading toward me. Lee was out of breath and sweat dripped down the sides of his face, rerouting through his scruffy facial hair from two missed days of shaving.

"This is crazy, but really kind of cool," he said and without another word, he handed me the bag and disappeared again in the jungle of passengers to find our other backpacks. He delivered another bag, we laughed, and he dove back in again like a football player ready for the next play. I continued to melt into the wall and survey the room, trying not to stare, but people intrigued me. Guards surrounded the room, keeping a watchful eye for any potential trouble. One guard stood next to me. I looked at him, smiled.

"Is that the only way out?" I asked as I pointed across a mob of people toward an exit sign. He smiled back and, in broken English, tried to explain the departure route. He finally just motioned for me to follow him. I started pushing our luggage cart after him, hoping Lee would soon show up with the last piece.

I kept my eyes peeled for Lee while I stuck to the heels of my newfound friend. I wasn't really sure where he was leading me. Then it occurred to me that he was moving everyone out of the way and making a path to get us out. Why was he doing this for us? My girlfriends, Kelly and Nancy, would say it was that "cow queen" smile I gave him, the smile they always ribbed me about that goes back to my days as Miss Brown Swiss and assorted other coronations.

Without speaking, I simply nodded to Lee and he followed my lead and placed the last bag on the cart. The guard motioned for people to move, practically pushing them out of the way. Finally out, we were like little kids fighting our way through a group of students to recess. Hundreds of eyes stared at the two white folks escorted out. Feeling a little intimidated, we stopped to catch our breath and to make a plan, if that was possible in a place like that. But we had no plan, only to find transportation to town and seek accommodation at Sela's Guesthouse. Arturo, the Tongan Peace Corps director whom I'd met during our layover in Hawaii, told us most Peace Corps volunteers stayed at Sela's upon their initial arrival. It was reportedly a clean, reasonably priced guesthouse. So Sela's it was, but how to get there? There were no buses in sight, only taxis which we were sure would be overpriced as they seem to be all over the world.

A long line of yellow cabs stretched for half a mile and the drivers were poised to pounce.

"Which taxi should we take?" I asked Lee.

Suddenly, a man approached. He was only about five foot five, stocky in build with a succession of tattoos running down his left arm. He wore a gray T-shirt, navy blue sweat pants and a delightful big smile. "Ride?" he asked. "Taxi? Please come."

For lack of a better idea, we followed him. It was so hot, I felt sick, no doubt, from being overdressed. I'd have to shed my leggings soon or be soaked in sweat. Our taxi driver loaded our gear in the trunk and we were off to town. I sat in front trying to ward off car sickness, as warm air blew on my face. Lee seemed overwhelmed with the moment. He sat in the backseat, a cheesy grin plastered his face like a kid on his way to see his first circus.

Ali introduced himself and for the next 20 minutes we stumbled over words doing our best to communicate. Language always seemed to be a barrier, but with a little patience, hand signals and gestures, barriers soon dissolved. Our new Tongan friend helped us unload our gear at Sela's Guesthouse and offered to pick us up the following day to go sightseeing. We were so busy organizing last-minute travel details and making sure all of our finances were in order, we'd had no time to research *Lonely Planet's* Tonga guide to pencil out a program. A guided tour sounded super.

We checked into our simple room—a desk, three single beds, a ceiling fan and three nails hammered in the wall for hooks. The first order of business was brushing my teeth. It seemed we had been traveling for ages. We left the States on November 20, had a 14-hour flight with a layover in between, and this was November 22. The additional time was lost when we crossed the International Date Line. I grabbed my toothbrush and paste and found the communal sink near the two communal showers. A woman in her mid-20s stood by the sink. Garbed in over-sized island dress, she looked like a seasoned traveler. Previous overseas trips had conditioned me to the many health risks of third-world countries. I typically brushed my teeth with bottled water to limit my exposure to bacteria and parasites harbored in local water. But I thought, *What the heck, I'll ask.* "Do you think it's all right to use the tap water to brush my teeth?"

"Oh yes, it's fine," the traveler said. "Where are you from?"

"Maryland," I replied.

Her eyes widened, "So am I."

I couldn't believe it. Could this be the Peace Corps woman from back home?

"Diann?"

"Yes."

We laughed. I had corresponded with her for several months prior to our departure and had several chats with her parents in Frederick. Diann was the main reason we were in Tonga, but I hadn't had time to organize how we'd find each other. That horseshoe was working overtime. Diann had taken a few days off from her Peace Corps assignment and was on the main island of Tongatapu getting material at the official Tongan Peace Corps Office. Diann and I made arrangements for Lee and me to visit her in four days on the small island of 'Eua, where she was stationed.

Noted for its walking treks, dive sites, coral gardens, reefs, rain forest and white-sand beaches, Tonga was our home for two weeks. Ali arrived at Sela's bright and early the next morning to fetch us. We had taken some time to read about Tonga the night before, learning that the South Pacific island was colonized by European powers with the first contact in 1616. The Kingdom of Tonga, represented by only a few dots on the world map, was being promoted as one of the first places in the world where people would see the sunrise in the new millennium.

For the most part, the archipelago was unspoiled by Western influence. Considered one of the poorest of South Pacific countries, Tonga was a developing country, therefore had received help from Peace Corps volunteers for 32 years.

Our first stop was the famous Mapu'a 'a Vaca blow holes, or chief's whistles as the locals called them. They stretched four miles along the South Shore, near the village of Houma. The blow holes were shooting fountains or geysers of sea water reaching heights of 90 feet. We caught a glimpse of the tree that explorer Captain James Cook took a rest under during his third Pacific voyage in 1777. He became good friends with the 30th Tu'i Tonga (king) and presented him with a full-grown tortoise that lived nearly 200 years. At the time of its death in 1966, the tortoise that was named Tu'i Malila enjoyed a seat at the royal kava circle and free run in the palace gardens.

We saw the terraced tombs of former kings and the Ha'amonga 'a Maui Trilithon, one of ancient Polynesia's most intriguing structures. Archaeologists believe that the 11th Tu'i Tonga, Tu'itatui, who reigned at the turn of the 13th century, was responsible for its construction. The structure consisted of three large coral stones, each weighing about 40 tons, arranged into a trilithic gate. The monument reminded me of England's famed Stonehenge.

Our tour included a visit to the Botanical Garden Bird Park where we saw some of Tonga's native birds and wildlife. We were introduced to an eight-inch giant centipede on display. "Don't worry, their bite isn't fatal, it's just very painful," the park's guide said.

When I found out that centipedes frequent bathrooms and showers, I spent as little time as possible in them. Sometimes at night I made Lee come to the bathroom with me to hold a flashlight so I could watch out for the creepy-crawly things.

The Flying Fox Sanctuary in Kolovai was both fascinating and eerie. Hundreds of flying foxes, actually enormous bats with wingspans of up to three feet, hung upside down from the huge casuarina trees. I imagined the flying predators attacking like in Alfred Hitchcock's *The Birds.* Although the nocturnal creatures could be found throughout the South Pacific, Tonga was the one place they were considered taboo, or sacred. They were eaten unsparingly by gourmet islanders in other locations, but they remained protected in Tonga and only members of the Royal family were allowed to hunt them for sport.

We ran out of daylight and missed the "Fishing Pigs of Talafo'ou." The village of Talafo'ou was known for its smart pigs. At low tide the domesticated animals ventured out on the tidal flat looking for shellfish. The Fishing Pigs were the most interesting of Tonga's epidemic of swine. Pigs were everywhere. They roamed freely. Cars often had to stop, and occasionally the little oinkers weren't fast enough to get out of the way, which as far as I was concerned, was a real waste of some tasty bacon. Locals told us the pigs went into the bush to eat or down the road, but they always returned home. After seven hours of taking in the hot spots of Tongatapu, our tour came to an end. Ali was fun and wasn't shy about putting on the special Statue of Liberty sunglasses for a photo.

The following day marked our first excursion on our own and our first disagreement on the trip. After ten days together, 24 hours a day, I felt really relaxed, finally. I was happy how smoothly the trip had gone so far. Things had fallen into place and Lee and I got along beautifully. Well, that was until we walked to town using a local map. The first problem was that most of the street signs were missing, which made our afternoon stroll anything but delightful.

"According to the map, we go this way," I said.

"I'm pretty sure it's this way," Lee said, examining the tiny sketch and pointing in the opposite direction.

"Honey, that's back toward Sela's," I replied.

"No, dear, Sela's is that way. We need to make a right here," Lee declared.

After a series of "honey and dear," our direction debate soon deteriorated until I gave Lee my usual silent treatment for the next ten minutes. We compromised and took a different street, and our planned 15-minute walk ended up being an hour of heat, sweat and tension by the time we reached the town center. I thought, *This is going to be a really long year if this disagreement crap continues.*

We spent a Sunday on Tongatapu, interesting to say the least. Most of the day we kicked back at Sela's. She and her husband were friendly, but a little reserved. We sat and talked for hours to other travelers from Australia, England and Scotland. We shared traveling tales and the folks from Australia made sure they scared me with their true snake dramas. In the afternoon Lee and I walked downtown again, argument free and without getting lost. It was like a deserted town from the wild West. I expected incoming tumbleweeds rolling into the island ghost town. I had seen many abandoned towns in the movies. It was spooky. Perhaps it was the aftermath of aliens who had snatched up everyone overnight.

No tumbleweeds or extraterrestrials—it was Sunday. Tongans strictly observed the Sabbath and, by law, no one was allowed to work on Sunday. People were not allowed to open stores, do laundry, mow the lawn, swim or fish. All work and recreation was forbidden. If anyone was caught, it was a $10 *pa'anga* fine or three months hard labor. We were warned about Sundays and told that life pretty much stopped and to just do as the natives did—eat, visit and rest.

Our friends in the guesthouse told us about a bakery that opened up at 5 p.m. every Sunday. That was sweet music to my ears, or should I say my belly. We were out of food and only had a few things to snack on until the bakery opened. A 1982 cyclone devastated Tonga and people found it difficult to survive day to day. During the crisis the government allowed bakeries to open at 5 p.m. on Sunday to help families. The law had never been reversed and locals and visitors continued to enjoy the homemade treats every Sunday afternoon. Thank goodness—we were so hungry.

Going into a bakery nearly famished was a bad idea. We walked out with a huge ring of pizza bread and eight other sugar-packed delicacies, all for $2. It was so cheap I wanted to buy more, but I knew we couldn't eat it all, even if we shared with our friends at Sela's.

When downtown was open, life boomed in the tiny metropolis. Nuku'alofa, the hub of activity on Tongatapu, had German cuisine, Chinese, Italian and several other specialty restaurants. One night we ate at the Chinese restaurant Fakalato. I ordered beef and cabbage, being conservative and safe. Lee was more daring and ordered steamed fish.

When his ocean catch was set in front of him, I thought his eyes would bug out of his head, or at least I knew mine did. It was the entire fish—body, head, eyes, tail. It looked a little gross and its mouth was pried open, I guess for dramatic effect. Lee enjoyed it to the last bite.

Lee had heard the story before, but I couldn't help but share my best fish story again from a '92 world trip with Kelly. She and I spent four days with a family in a remote mountain region of Fiji. They had no electricity, indoor plumbing or modern conveniences. The family prepared a special meal before our departure. We sat on the floor, Indian style, waiting for the first course. A bowl of fish soup was presented to each of us. Not an appetizing-looking fish soup, but rather a bowl of warm clear water with a disgusting fish submerged in the liquid. It was the entire fish. How could we eat something when it seemed to be staring us down?

Kelly nudged me. "Please help me eat this fish," she whispered. Kelly and I knew how important it was to eat whatever the family served, out of respect and appreciation, no matter how bad we thought it was. It was proper travel etiquette. I knew Kelly detested fish. I had to help her. After I ate my soup, I nonchalantly switched our bowls. I was sure there would be a time or two on that trip for Kelly to reciprocate. It was fun to reminisce about a past trip, but it was time for Lee and me to make our own memories.

Following supper we made it a real night out. We paid $3 pa'anga each, or $2, for the movies. We couldn't beat that, but we soon found out why. It was a little frightening as we poked our heads in the theater door. It was like stepping back in time. The chairs were dark green and ragged, springs were exposed. It took several minutes to find two chairs together without springs poking us in our bums. Trash covered the floor and a film of dust and dirt layered the entire theater. Shredded drapes hung around the theater trying to prevent sunlight from drifting through the cracks and large brownish smudges dotted the movie screen. It was less than first rate, but actually had a flare of ambience about it.

I was just excited to be at the movies. At home we rarely had the time to go, but it was our favorite pastime. We relaxed, even if a few uncomfortable springs still poked our behinds. The lights dimmed, the feature film rolled. It was *Runaway Bride,* which, ironically, had been filmed in our hometown just a few months earlier. About halfway through the movie, it started splicing.

"Figures the movie is damaged," I whined. Then the screen went blank. There were only a few other Tongan teenagers in the theater. We looked around to see what their reaction would be to the movie interruption.

"I think they are as fascinated with us as they are with this movie," Lee whispered.

Noticing we were a bit miffed, the teen-agers wandered over. "Hof tiimme, moovay braake," one said in a decipherable English.

We followed them out and purchased some very stale popcorn and flat Coke, all very fitting for the atmosphere that we couldn't help but be enticed by. We returned to the theater for the second part of the film.

Our visits to third-world nations would not only bring unbelievable adventures, but allowed us to explore and experience a new culture, people and each other. Our greatest Tongan adventure was about to begin.

Thank You for Running Fast

Thoughts of the chilly November our friends and family in Maryland would be enduring did little to relieve the Tongan sauna we were thrust in. The tropical climate, with its humid sunny days and early morning and afternoon rain showers, was a severe weather change for us.

The more we learned about the Kingdom of Tonga, the more fascinated we became with the country and its people. Tonga consisted of 171 islands, but only 40 were inhabited by people. We flew into the largest island, Tongatapu, but were heading to the third-largest island, 'Eua. To get there, we boarded what looked like an ancient ferry and set out for our two-hour epic voyage across open sea. Wasn't that a two-hour cruise that got Gilligan and his companions in trouble?

Thank goodness I had taken a seasickness pill! Twice the ferry climbed waves, became airborne, then crashed down, knocking some people from their seats. I wanted to watch for whales, but the enormous swells hitting our bow worried me. After locating the emergency exits and the life jackets, I closed my eyes—praying we'd arrive safe and dry.

It was hard to believe 'Eua was the third-largest island—it was very small with only one main road running through the center. The majority of the island was covered by native bush and virgin rain forest. The remainder had been cleared and farmed by the nearly 5,000 Tongans in 14 villages who called 'Eua home. One of the only two taxi drivers on the island picked us up and delivered us to our home-stay family, arranged by Diann.

Heilala and Fineone Peau, our hosts, lived in the village of Ha'atu'a, home to 80 families. Many still lived in thatched-roof huts, reflecting the rudimentary lifestyles of its citizens. Mrs. Peau was in Tongatapu caring for her daughter-in-law, who was having a difficult pregnancy. Her oldest daughter, Kafoatu Luau, returned home to care for us. Although most travelers preferred the pampering of hotels and restaurant cuisine, we lived in a modest five-room home with five other people. Family members slept on the floor and insisted we sleep in one of their only two beds.

There was an outhouse and primitive showers, complete with 100 percent cold, cold water. Those cool mornings and early showers under the frigid water were almost more than I could take. Although the showers were a challenge, we were quickly warmed up by a cup of hot cocoa. Fresh banana, coconut and pineapple just picked from our family's plantation in the bush were other morning delights. Many breakfasts included an egg sandwich. Eggs were either cooked on a small one-burner gas stove that sat four inches off the floor or fried outside in a pan over a fire.

Sundays were devoted to the *'umu,* an underground oven. Meat was wrapped in leaves and then foil, and placed in the 'umu before the family left for church. The 'umu was the traditional way for Tongans to cook and most natives on outer islands continued the practice.

Kafoatu, or "Atu," as she was affectionately called, was a sweet, robust host with a beautiful smile and shiny long black hair. Atu's English was limited, but her jovial personality was all she needed to communicate.

When we first arrived I recall being a little alarmed when I saw how food was prepared and noticed there was no refrigeration. What strange and new bacteria would make it into our systems? But the reason for adventure travel was to live as the locals lived. And that was just what we intended to do. We were taking a chance, but it hadn't killed them yet, so I figured we'd be okay. Our farming backgrounds had made Lee and me pretty resilient.

Photos covered the walls, some just adhered with tape and others wrapped in plastic wrap to protect them. The windows and archways were trimmed with red-and-white frilly lace as makeshift curtains. Bedspreads covered the furniture. They didn't have fancy decor or expensive furniture, but instead offered a warm, alluring home. I was surprised, however, that the family had a TV and VCR when so many other necessities were missing.

Their lawn was meticulously manicured, with bright-colored flowers and a rock path that led to the front door. A fence surrounded the perimeter of the lawn to keep out pigs and any other uninvited guests. Not only did families on 'Eua have limited household conveniences, most didn't have a vehicle, and our family was no exception.

Tongan families marketed their extra produce, as well as selling their *tapa.* To me tapa sounded like some exotic fruit I couldn't wait to sink my teeth into, but my taste buds were disappointed when I found out it was homemade cloth. Tapa signified the wealth of a family and large pieces were often made and exchanged at weddings, funerals, graduations or royal events. We had the opportunity to watch locals strip bark and then pound it as flat as paper. The pounding started early in the morning and was usually our wake-up signal, unless the 5 a.m. church bell beat them to the punch.

Tapa was made from hiapo, the underbark of the paper mulberry tree. Mature trees, a little more than an inch in diameter, were cut near the base and the bark was removed. The soft inner bark was beaten with an iron-wood mallet. After the pounding process, pieces were pasted together, placed on a woven base and stenciled designs were hand painted in black and rich earthy reds and browns.

When Sunday rolled around, Lee and I wondered how locals on 'Eua spent the Sabbath. Our host sister, Atu, gave us a *tupenu* (skirt) and a *kiekie,* a decorative waistband with dangled strips of pandanus, strands of seeds, bits of cloth or fiber cords which was worn to church and other important occasions. It was an important sign of respect.

Diann let me borrow one of her long dresses and I put on the kiekie Atu had given me. It was difficult to look at Lee in his tupenu without cracking a smile and thinking, *If people see these pictures at home, they will have serious questions.* His white skinny legs were testament that the sunlight rarely hit them. Atu turned Lee slowly, tying on his kiekie, getting it just right, like she was putting the final touches on her little girl before the first day of school.

Once Atu had Lee all set in his ankle-length skirt and kiekie, we walked to church. Everyone left their shoes outside and entered the church barefooted. In the Wesleyan church it was customary for women and children to sit on the right side and men to sit on the left side of the aisle. Although we didn't understand a bit of the Tongan service, it was still a wonderful experience. The minister welcomed us, which was really special, but made us feel like fish out of water. If you think white folks stick out at the Tongan airport, try a little village church. I spent most of the service peacefully pondering our trip. I thanked God for the wonderful opportunity he had provided for us. I prayed for family and friends, hoping they knew they were in our hearts.

My peaceful meditation was soon distracted when I couldn't help but notice a huge cockroach scurry down the aisle like he was late for church, sneaking in before the minister detected his vacant seat. The roach cut in on the men's side. In a frenzied race of confusion, it scampered back and forth between two aisles like it was checking out hairy legs. Finally, it stopped and seemed to say, *This looks as good as any.* At that moment the insect crawled up a man's leg until it disappeared beneath his long tupenu. I wanted to jump out of my seat and go squash it or warn the man of the intruder under his skirt. The man didn't move. Could it be these people had such tough skin they didn't feel roaches crawl on them? Or maybe they were sacred, making them insect untouchables.

Immediately following church, we sifted through the pile of shoes, sandals and flip-flops—ours were easy to find and quite different from island footwear. We took photos with some of the local children. They made funny faces and hand signs for the camera. Getting their pictures taken thrilled them.

We were about to start walking home when we were invited to a one-year-old's birthday party, which we found out was a really big event in Tonga. It was right up there with 21st birthdays, weddings and funerals. The village was relatively small. We walked around the corner and a tent was erected on a lawn for the celebration.

On the ground, stretched beneath a 100-foot tent, were woven mats for sitting. The middle of each mat was lined with banana leaves and food was piled the length of the tent under a white netting, which protected the massive array of chow from flies. The meal featured eight roasted baby pigs carefully placed down the spread. I don't think I'd ever seen so much food at a feast. Nearly 75 people sat on the ground for the "pig out." We were asked to sit up near the head of the feast where the dignitaries were sitting. We sat with the village chief, the minister and the school superintendent.

It was customary in Tonga to eat with your fingers so we started to pluck this and that and get a "taste" of a real Tongan feast, known as *kai pola.* The birthday boy's aunt, Meleane, sat beside me and tried to introduce us to all their specialty foods. She was another beautifully bronze-skinned Tongan woman with an amiable persona. Meleane sat near the head of the feast because as the eldest aunt, she was very important, much like a godmother's role.

She peeled some of the pig skin off and laid it on my plate. I gave her a funny look. "We just eat the pig skin like this?" I asked, slightly wrinkling my face.

"Yes," she answered.

I picked it up, examined it for pig hair and then popped the greasy skin in my mouth. As it crunched between my teeth, I wiped the extra grease from my chin. I ignored the fact I was eating the skin of a suckling piglet. Earlier in the week Diann gave me a heads-up regarding a kai pola. "The pig skin looks disgusting, but it tastes really good," she said. "At my first feast I didn't have a choice, they loaded my plate with it. I loved it."

I recounted that story over and over again in my head and continued to chew. To my surprise, I even had seconds.

We had lobster, mussels, chicken curry, root crops, pudding and horse meat. It was our second serving of horse meat on the island. It wasn't our typical fare, but at least we tried it. I was happy not to see a horse head decorating the spread of vittles—the two huge hog heads overshadowing the eight piglets were bad enough. Whole steamed fish, head and all, was also featured. I passed on the fish. I considered myself an adventurer, but figured I had satisfied my limit in the food category for one day.

Growing up on my parents' Maryland dairy farm helped prepare me for my less-than-glamorous experiences and escapades. I thought, *What could be worse than running through manure barefooted? Or watching maggots doing their job in the cycle of life? Or being completely covered in afterbirth while assisting a cow deliver her calf?* Although rural drudgery was one thing, horse meat and fish heads were quite another. Farming had built my character, taught me responsibility and, in my mind, nurtured me into a pretty tough farm girl— or, at least, I used to be. Because I'd worked behind a computer for the previous ten years, my country roots had faded like my laptop faded when the power was low.

While waiting for the feast to begin at the birthday celebration, I noticed a giant, well, maybe not giant, but a *big* cockroach. The nearly three-inch pest crawled up the minister's leg under his tupenu. The minister didn't flinch. I sat quietly, cross-legged, enjoying the tranquility of the moment. I said a little prayer to myself. Unfortunately, it wasn't Thank you, God, for this wonderful day or Thanks, God, for providing this incredible feast and fellowship; rather my prayer was *Please, God, don't let that damn cockroach make its way near me.* I'd hated cockroaches ever since one crawled on me in bed at college.

Well, I certainly believed in the power of prayer, but I guess I didn't pray hard enough. In minutes I felt something enter my tupenu. I jumped halfway up, almost causing an international incident. It escaped. Lee just laughed at his psychotic wife. Ten minutes hadn't gone by and the pesky creature found its way under my tupenu again—this was going to be a serious battle. I thought, *Why couldn't this cockroach find another place to hang out, there was certainly enough food for all of us.* What surprised me and also pleased me, it was the last roach I saw during our entire visit in Tonga.

We presented gifts to Epeli, the birthday boy. He really enjoyed his little cow toy and his *Frederick News-Post* balloon. Lee played with Epeli for a long time, entertaining the adorable round-faced child. It was truly amazing to spend time with people and actually communicate without speaking a word. Yes, there were times when the language barrier was an issue, but with patience and smiles, nothing was impossible. As usual, Lee's gentle nature with children was expressed by the heartfelt giggles of the little one-year-old.

We returned to our home-stay house and were magnetized to the setting sun as it drew us closer with every step. The clouds were tinted with pink and purplish tones made vibrant by the sun's rays and deepened as the sun lowered behind the horizon. It made our little home look even warmer and more charming.

Later Sunday evening, Lee and I enjoyed the meal that Atu and her sister, Leni, prepared in the 'umu. Atu's broken English and her willingness to talk continued to provide laughter. She wanted to visit her husband, Makai, and daughter, 'Asu, who lived in a village about a half-hour walk away. We escorted her because women were not allowed to walk alone. On the way I thought I would practice my Tongan lingo.

"Malo e lelei," I said flipping my tongue just so, trying to perfect my Tongan hello.

Many people went for an *'eva*, a Sunday afternoon amble after a full day of eating and sleeping. We passed lots of locals. I continued to stumble my way through my Tongan greeting.

"Malo e lelei," I repeated. "Malo e lelei." Atu burst into hysterics. "What's wrong?" I asked with a confused look.

She composed herself, but still couldn't hide her grand smile. "You are not saying hello, you have been thanking people for running fast," she said cracking up again, along with Lee chuckling beside her. I was embarrassed, but roared with cross-your-legs laughter anyway. I decided to leave the greetings up to Lee, who seemed able to wrap his tongue around the language much better than I could.

Lee and I discovered why our host family had a TV and VCR. The tiny island had very few businesses, but smack dab in the middle was a small thatched-roof hut renting videos—the dwarfed version of Blockbuster, no doubt, with pirated copies of movies. We rented one of the *Rambo* adventures and, of course, some chick flick. Diann, Atu, Lee and I got situated in the living room for the evening's entertainment. Little did we know that it wouldn't be the movie.

It was hot, stuffy. A storm brewed to the west. Atu opened the front door and a fresh cool breeze cut through the muggy stillness. Something dashed in the front door right across the living room floor. *What was that?* I thought. It was quick. I wasn't paying attention to the floor, my eyes were affixed to the TV screen waiting for Rambo to take on bullets, cuts and near-fatal trauma and then save the day.

No one said anything. Another flash across the floor. But that time my eyes did focus, it was a goddamned rat. I rarely cuss, but it was a goddamned rat. That crispness in the air was a sure sign of an approaching storm. The nasty rodents had no intention of being caught out in a thunderstorm and sought refuge in the living room—with us. Another rat rushed in the front door. What did I think—they were going to stop and knock? One ran right over top of Atu, who was lying on the living room floor. It didn't faze her, unless she hid her fear so we weren't alarmed.

I couldn't believe it. I thought, *No way, absolutely no way, would anyone at home believe this!* I wasn't freaked out with disgust, it was all rather comical. Rats and mice are commonplace on a farm and I even caught a rat in my house one time. I accepted, but still detested them. I kept my knees tucked right under my chest on the couch. There was no way I wanted a rat running over or up my legs.

One rat repeatedly ran around the corner from the kitchen, always detecting at the last minute Lee's feet, which blocked his path. Just before crashing into his feet, the rat skidded around Lee's chair like a little race car sliding around a turn of a NASCAR final. The rat back-paddled its tiny feet in a frenzy on the linoleum floor until it got its traction and scampered to another escape route. The 20-plus geckos on the ceiling didn't bother me, as I knew they ate spiders and other scary things. But rats, they were another story. Lucky for us, after about an hour of rat invasion, they disappeared mysteriously like the passing storm.

I had to get down to business, the reason we stopped in Tonga. Of course, I wouldn't trade the experiences to that point for anything, not even the roaches and rats, but it was time to begin my research on Diann and the Peace Corps for my article. On Monday I met with her. Diann was passionate about her job and often expressed her enthusiasm. She told us the Tongans were very receptive to Peace Corps volunteers and her students were usually very willing to learn.

"I love coconut milk and sometimes my students climb a nearby tree and bring me a coconut to school," she said. "In America, teachers get apples; I get coconuts."

She introduced us to one of her students, 14-year-old Tevita Moala. We said hello.

"Like coconut?" Tevita asked.

"Yeah, I love coconuts," I responded without thinking of the circumstances of my statement. Tevita shimmied up a tree. Only his hands and feet gripped the trunk like a monkey. He stopped halfway to rest and proceeded to the top. No small feat considering he didn't use any ropes. He knocked down three coconuts, then backed down the tree, careful of his footing. Once on the ground he whipped out a 16-inch bush knife and chopped the coconut tops off.

"Here, see if you like," he said handing us the milky green-colored fruit. The coconut milk was clear and sweet. After we finished the coconut juices, Tevita gave it another whack, splitting it in half so we could eat the coconut flesh.

Diann was 26 years old and lived in a small three-room house, 12 feet by 12 feet, on the Hofangahau Middle School's campus. She taught English to students in form one (seventh grade). Diann was one of 53 Peace Corps volunteers serving the Kingdom of Tonga and one of more than 200 Marylanders serving around the globe that year. She told us she would recommend the Peace Corps to anyone.

"It's been the most rewarding adventure of my life," she said. "If you really want to challenge yourself and make a difference in the lives of other people while also having the experience of a lifetime, the Peace Corps is a unique opportunity."

Although she loved teaching, she said the kids sometimes exhausted her patience. "Because I'm a *palangi* [foreigner], they test me a lot more than other teachers. It's definitely a challenge. The best part of teaching is when I can be creative and make the lesson really fun. It's rewarding to see my students enthusiastic about learning and also to see them proud of the work they've accomplished."

She had cleared many hurdles educating the young islanders and had overcome many obstacles adapting to Tongan life and culture.

"I've adjusted to boiling my own drinking water and I share my bathroom with a huge land crab that is territorial. I also have a rat, but as long as we can all live here comfortably, it's okay. Sometimes if I'm really tired, I don't boil my water, I just drink it, mosquito larva and all."

She also tired of subjecting herself to cold showers so she resigned to taking cold sponge baths out of a bucket. According to Diann, some of the local customs or *faka Tonga* (the Tongan way), had been very trying.

"Last week I told my principal that I really needed my lawn mowed. He brought a cow and calf and tied them in my backyard to a tree. The pigs, that roam everywhere, were rooting under my house and finally they put tin around the bottom. Now the pigs only mess up my yard. And one time I was visiting a family and the daughter put a huge live worm in her mouth. It was gross and the worm wiggled as she ate it. I ran out screaming because the worm juices were running out of the sides of her mouth."

Diann felt she had been enriched by her Peace Corps experience and still had more than a year to go. As Diann recounted story after story, I scribbled half sentences in my reporter's notebook using my own created shorthand that no one else would be able to read. I didn't want to miss a word. One minute we'd laugh, the next I'd be blown away by another shocking story.

"I wandered over to where I saw smoke one day and I thought teachers were cooking a pig," she told me. "I looked a little closer and it was a dog. It tasted like tender roast beef, just a little stringy."

Diann's worst experience was during the infancy of her service when she was stationed on a nearby island. She came home from teaching one day and noticed the baby of her host family playing in the yard. He was sucking on a long object. To her horror it was the plastic tampon applicator she had thrown in the trash container earlier. Somehow it had been retrieved. She grabbed it from the child's mouth and tried to explain to the mother. "It okaaay, Deeana, baby just find toy," the mother responded, not realizing what her baby was really playing with. Since most village women had never even seen female hygiene toiletries, she had no idea why Diann was so upset. After that incident, Diann said she took great care in storing and disposing of her personal belongings.

"Living here has taught me patience, flexibility and that there are many different ways to go about something to get a job done," Diann said. From all the good and bad experiences in Tonga, she added that she wouldn't trade it for the world. She had learned to deal with different situations, eat with her hands, chase chickens and pigs out of her house, do laundry in buckets and destroy weeds growing through her floor.

"The Peace Corps is an excellent way to make yourself more marketable when you return to the United States," she said. "Many people join the Peace Corps to enhance their resumes, make a difference in peoples' lives by helping them, experience another culture, learn a new language and, of course, for travel and adventure."

If Lee and I survived our year-long odyssey, maybe the Peace Corps would be next. I'm sure it wouldn't surprise anyone.

We ventured out on our own one day and our proposed short walk turned into a four-hour daymare. We hadn't packed any water, which we knew was completely stupid on our part. We thought we were going for a half-hour walk to a nearby guesthouse and hoped a sudsy cold beer awaited us. We walked and walked, following the dirt road we thought led to the guesthouse. We had no idea where the hell we were. Finally, a utility truck drove by and stopped.

"Can you speak English?" I said with an urgency of hope.

"Liddle bit," the driver answered.

"Does this road go to guesthouse?"

"Naw, naw, dis road go to prison," he said.

Lee and I looked at each other in bewilderment, then thanked the gentleman for stopping.

"Lee, how'd we get out here?" I asked. "We have a two-hour walk back and I'm so thirsty."

"You'll be fine," he said trying to reassure me.

No cold beer, no water—what a dismal day! We turned and started trekking back.

"It's no wonder we got lost with all the damned signs in Tonga missing, falling down or pointing in the wrong direction," I complained. "But this is all part of the experience, right?"

"That's right, dear, now pick up the pace," Lee ordered.

"Wait for me, I can't go any faster," I pleaded. "Hey, Lee. Hoist me up to pick that funny-looking fruit. There will be moisture in that."

"It could be poisonous, ya know," he said.

"Are you serious?" I asked hoping at any minute I'd be biting into a juicy delight.

"We better not take a chance, let's just keep walking."

"Okay," I said, pouting like a kid who had candy taken away.

We walked and walked and walked. A farmer came out of his plantation pedaling his bike loaded with the day's harvest. We certainly couldn't get a lift from him. We waved and smiled. We made it to the main road with still an hour's walk ahead of us. And then, we were blessed. A truckful of locals, sitting amongst piles of bananas, pineapples, papayas, tara and yams, stopped for us. We didn't try to hitchhike or even try to wave down a vehicle. Tongans always stopped to pick up locals walking, but we didn't realize the protocol included *palangi.* Maybe we looked lost, thirsty, exhausted—hell, we were! The man in the front seat jumped out and motioned for us to take his spot. The driver handed us each a papaya. From hell to heaven—the day was good.

Most residents in 'Eua were farmers or had a plantation in the bush. A few farmers had trucks or tractors, but there were many farmers who only had horses or bicycles as their sole mode of transport. Farmers took much pride in their large gardening plots. And after a hard day's work, for many, it was off to the daily *kava* rituals.

Kava was an intoxicating drink and a popular age-old custom for most natives on South Pacific islands. During a *fai kava,* men sat around and drank the liquid produced from the root of the pepper plant. It was a main social event in villages. The fai kava, or kava circle, was traditionally for men, but women were sometimes invited to serve. Nearly 25 men crowded into the principal's home. A man submerged the powder of the pepper plant in water. He dipped and squeezed, dipped and squeezed, until the murky liquid was ready to transfer to the ceremonial bowl. Served in halved coconut shells, the liquid actually tasted like muddy water, or what I imagined muddy water tasting like.

Many men sometimes gathered in kava circles five nights a week until the early hours of the morning, not going home until 2, 3 or 4 a.m. And then they did it all over the next night. Well, all I had to say on that was—*Better the Tongan women dealing with that than me. Tradition or not, my husband better be home before 4 in the freakin' morning.*

I continued to interview Diann, learning more and more about the Peace Corps and faka Tonga. Lee felt like a fifth wheel and decided to leave us girls to chat. He told us he was

going back to our host family's house. I finished my interview and Diann walked me home. Lee wasn't at the house. I
assumed he probably had taken a walk to explore the village. Diann and I walked up the dirt road to find him.

"Man at minister's house," a Tongan said from his front
lawn as we passed. Well, there was only one reason he was
at the minister's house and it certainly wasn't for Bible study.
We walked to the minister's home, conveniently located across
from the church, and were invited in. There Lee was in all his
glory, sitting on the floor with a stupid little smirk on his
face, flanked by the minister on his right side and the village
chief on the other. The three were having in-depth conversation, no doubt, as they sat around the kava ceremonial bowl
slurping down the intoxicating fluid. The minister often had
fai kavas and usually had one on Sunday mornings before
church. I guess it stimulated his sermon.

After we left the minister's home, Lee started laughing.
"Don't tell me you're inebriated?" I asked.

"No, but I have a funny story for you and Diann," he
said. "We watched both of you walk by the house on your
way home. The village elder said, 'There goes the police.'"

Diann and I were a little surprised, but not really. Didn't
matter how men put their pants or skirts (in this case) on in
the morning, they were pretty much the same the world over.

• • •

A special graduation celebration for the Wesleyan Church
School where Diann taught was held to recognize students
for advancing to the next form (grade). Following the award's
ceremony, a concert was held featuring traditional Tongan
dancing. After being coaxed, villagers helped Diann into her
wraparound woven costume and she performed the *fisa
pa'anga,* or money dance. Dancers were oiled down and during their dance money was stuck to them. The dances were
often used as fund-raising events for schools and communi-
ties.

When Diann first arrived in Tonga, Peace Corps trainees
were required to make or do something demonstrating what

they had learned about Tongan life and culture. Diann chose to do the fisa pa'anga at the Peace Corps gathering. She said some of the village women were getting her dressed with all the necessary garb and lathering her in oil. The ladies were chitchatting back and forth in their native tongue and assumed Diann could not understand them. Little did they know, Diann translated their entire conversation.

"The funniest remark was when one of the women said, 'If the oil drips, she's not a virgin.' I almost burst into hysterics, but kept my composure so the women didn't know I could understand them." She learned later that there was a myth about the oil dripping off the fisa pa'anga dancers. If oil dripped they weren't supposed to dance because only virgins were allowed to perform the fisa pa'anga.

Our last night on 'Eua was very memorable with our home-stay family. Mom Peau had returned from her main island crisis. She delivered good news. Her newborn grandchild was doing well. She and her daughters prepared an incredible kai pola for our going-away feast, complete with a roasted piglet right in the middle of the floor. The food was delicious, but it was the people we'd remember.

Atu's husband, Makai, stood up and began a speech, which was customary at special events and I guess our departure was a special event. We were shocked because we didn't even know Makai could speak English which made it all the more personal.

"Although we are very poor, we offer you what we have, you are our family now and are welcome back anytime," he said.

Emotion overcame me as my eyes glazed over with tears. It was wonderful to make friends in a developing nation. The family had so little, but offered much love and friendship. It made me really appreciate the things at home that I took for granted sometimes, like family, friends, a car, the freedom to work or play on Sunday and let's not forget a warm shower and indoor plumbing.

We'll always remember our host family, as well as the excitement of school children when I took their pictures and the sheer delight of nearly 200 primary students nearly bombarding Lee as he handed out "got milk?" stickers. We'll treasure our new friendship with Diann, and yes, we had new names to add to our ever-growing Christmas card list—a list my friends needled me about, insisting I tried to keep in touch with every acquaintance. Maybe it was time to axe my fifth-grade teacher and the nice lady I met on the train in Switzerland 14 years earlier. Well, maybe just one last Christmas card.

"Nofo a," good-bye from Tonga.

Family Circle

Wrapped in the warmth of the melting sun,
The circle of friends has only begun;

Hours are spent sharing song and story,
Breath of the sea carries voices with glory;

The circle is full of giving and caring,
A stranger is welcomed to join in the sharing;

Language and words have little in common,
But in this circle of new friends it presents little problem;

Time to return to my new family's home,
With their gracious invitation it feels like my own;

Last evening in 'Eua surrounded by family and friends,
Wish my time on the island would not so soon end;

I bid fond farewell as I leave with the sun,
But my family circle on 'Eua has only begun.

Lee Chaney

Poor Bastard

Stirred by memories of a magical visit with Jim and Lorraine Davis on their sheep station in the backblocks of New Zealand in '92, I knew the country still held fun and perilous possibilities for Lee and me. I had written "Mr. Jim" several months earlier and told him of our travel plans. I made one request in the letter: "Mr. Jim, it's your job to turn Lee into a cowboy before we get to the Australian outback." Lee had only ridden a few times when he was a small boy, but he did have guts and a strong ambition to learn all that he could.

We arrived at the Davis's new 130-acre cattle and sheep farm near Taumarunui on the North Island. I got out of the car and instantly threw my arms around Mr. Jim and planted a kiss on his cheek. Annual Christmas letters were our only correspondence, but it was the only communication necessary when a powerful bond existed regardless of the thousands of miles that separated us.

He hadn't changed much, other than the fact he was now 60-something as opposed to 50-something. He had a little more gray hair that swept down close to his shoulders. Mr. Jim's rugged-looking skin was a sure sign of the harsh weather and stress associated with farming. I introduced Lee to Mr. Jim—greeting formalities followed and then there was a moment of silence. Mr. Jim looked at Lee inquisitively. "So you're the poor bastard I have to turn into a cowboy," he said.

We all laughed and headed to the house. One might feel intimidated by Mr. Jim's straightforward manner, but Lee was immediately comfortable. Mr. Jim was direct, but had a heart of gold. A few years earlier the Davises acquired Tawa Ridge Farm and had been making improvements ever since. Lorraine's plush lawn was beautifully groomed. It was the beginning of New Zealand's summer and many of her perennials adorned their country home with an array of colors. An old tree stump on the lawn was decorated with old shoes and purple blossoms grew out of them.

Mr. Jim's job was caring for the animals and keeping the pasture in order. He was also the co-manager of Feltrim Grazing, a station accommodating 36,000 sheep and 2,000 head of beef cattle. The sheep were scattered on 10,000 acres and over the next five days it was our job to muster the sheep in for seasonal shearing.

"Okay, Becky, you're on Flute," Mr. Jim said. "And Lee, you're going to be riding Tammy."

Lee climbed aboard the paint-colored mare. The saddles, traditional in New Zealand, were like a cross between an English saddle and the old U.S. military saddles. There was no saddle horn to hold on to, typical of western saddles, but there were two thigh pads to help support the rider when going downhill, spinning or stopping quickly.

Sporting around on his four-wheeler (all-terrain vehicle), Mr. Jim gave us our instructions as he headed on an eastern route with his dogs and the rest of us headed west in pursuit of thousands of sheep. His grandson, George, was part of the mustering team and was the essential member who kept Lee and me from getting lost in the heavily forested area.

The mob of sheep, numbering about 3,000, took the wrong path—just our stupid luck. The sheep crowded to the top of an extremely steep mountain. *What now?* I thought. Mr. Jim had the dogs. It looked impossible, even deadly, to attempt by horseback. I guess I knew the answer already, but was hoping I was wrong. George, Lee, and I, on our hopefully steady mounts, had to push the mob down the other side of the mountain. That day I learned just how much Kiwi cowboys must trust their horses—many times with their lives.

It was crazy. For the first time on the trip, I asked myself, *What the hell am I doing here?* My legs shook uncontrollably. I didn't know if it was the pressure I was applying to my legs trekking down the face of the mountain leading Flute, or was I just really scared that Flute, at any second, was going to crush me. It was certainly my vertical limit and that was even if my horse and I survived.

Just weeks earlier a Kiwi galloped up the side of a mountain to move sheep and his horse lost its footing—they both tumbled to their deaths. They were professionals with years of mustering experience and were skilled at scaling mountains and ridges that looked suicidal. I was simply a "wannabe" Kiwi cowgirl, so I asked myself again, *Where did I come up with the insane notion that this would be fun?* Wishful thinking, obviously diluted by the fact I grew up tough on the farm and thought I still possessed those qualities after working behind a desk for ten years. I was really going to be pissed if we were hurt our first week in New Zealand doing what seemed to be idiotic equine stunts.

Step by step I progressed, trying to monitor every stride as I repeatedly looked behind me, attempting to control Flute's gait. Several times she slid in to me, knocking me to my knees twice and once almost over the mountain. We had considered navigating the treacherous 1,000-foot embankment on our horses, but thought we stood a better chance at making it on foot. But with Flute's hooves pounding down on my heels, I wasn't so sure. I slipped a few more times and thought it was only a matter of time before Flute's hoof smashed my foot, my leg or my body. Finally, we neared the bottom. It had seemed an eternity to get there. I patted Flute and thanked her for not plowing me over on the way down. Lee seemed to handle the challenge much better than I did, and I was supposed to be the experienced horsewoman. Mr. Jim laughed at our story later.

"You probably only had two words at the top and bottom of that mountain," he said. "'Oh God,' at the top and once you were at the bottom, 'Thank God.'"

He was so right—I was just happy it was over. It was truly remarkable the places the steeds went, the hills they climbed and slopes they descended. George's horse not only knew the mountains, but was also a polocrosse horse. Rated as one of the best polocrosse players in New Zealand under 16 years of age, George instituted his mustering skills and talents on the polocrosse field. He tried to show me the technique of the game, but after my poor polocrosse debut I knew I better stick to mustering. Catching the ball was pretty easy, bouncing it and scooping it up again in the racquet was a little more difficult, but just forget about me trying to throw the ball from my racquet's net.

During my '92 stint at Mr. Jim's, I had ridden a very spirited mare named Ugly. She was destined for the slaughterhouse until Mr. Jim saved her. He plucked the skinny, rough-looking animal out of a pen packed with horses on their way to becoming top canine protein. He quickly recognized the horse's potential, but her original nickname, Ugly, stuck. Seven years later, Ugly was still one of Mr. Jim's favorites. A leg injury forced her early retirement from mustering. Ugly's only job evolved into raising quality foals. Mr. Jim showed us Ugly and her new foal. He looked at me endearingly and motioned me over.

"She's two months old, but I haven't named her yet," he said. "I saved that job for you, Becky." I always knew my friend Kelly and I shared a special connection with the Davises, but I never knew to what extent until that very moment. I welled up with that feeling I get right before tears start to stream down my face. It was an unexpected gesture.

"I'll have to think about a name," I told Mr. Jim. "I want it to be special."

Our daily musters continued to be a challenge. One morning it was so chilly, my toes were going numb. I took my feet out of my boots one at a time and rubbed them, trying to get the circulation back again. I typically was not a cold-weather person.

Mustering was often difficult, but certainly made easier by Mr. Jim's dutiful sheep dogs. Each dog had a particular purpose. The huntaway barked and moved the sheep or cattle, while the heading dog subtly kept animals controlled. As Mr. Jim's whistle commands echoed through the forest valley, the amazing dogs knew exactly what needed to be done.

As usual, Mr. Jim went in one direction taking the dogs and sent the horsemen in another. For a novice rider, Lee was quite courageous, taking his horse everywhere George and I went. In fact, in many cases, Lee was the first one up a hill, through a clump of trees or down a slope. He was either really brave, really stupid or showing off. Showing off was my guess.

On our final day, we moved a group of 44 bulls. Mr. Jim was on Tammy and I rode Flute. We took to the high ground to start moving them down. Mr. Jim told me to watch the bulls closely because they would charge if provoked. I had no desire to tangle with a bull, but knew it would be good practice. As we galloped across the field to cut off the herd, it was like a scene out of an old John Wayne movie—*Yippie, ki-yay, here we come.* It was the most physical work I'd done for a while and I got pretty tuckered out. Although my body and bones seemed exhausted, I carried the biggest sense of pleasure from our visit with the Davises.

Mr. Jim reminded me of a stunt rider from the wild West, the difference, however, was that it was Mr. Jim's job. His crafty maneuvering up and down steep terrain, zigzagging in between trees and other obstacles to herd livestock was not engineered by props and directors, but was simply a sample of what the man had done for a living his entire life.

Our time with the Davises dwindled down. Lee mastered the saddle and I might say, truly surprised me with his quick ability to pick up riding. He wasn't ready for the Olympic trials, but I was proud of him for being so willing to give it a try.

"I've decided on a name for Ugly's foal," I told Mr. Jim. "How about Whisper?"

"I like it," he said.

To me, Whisper was perfect. The whole reason we were at Mr. Jim's was because he was Chris Hutchings' brother. We knew Chris because she married Tony Hutchings, whom we knew because our Maryland friend, John Morris, had met Tony at a World Ayrshire Conference in 1980. Whisper was the name of my favorite Ayrshire calf when I was a kid. The reason I had the opportunity to spend time with the Davises was because of that initial dairy industry connection.

Evenings at the Davises were always spent crowded at the kitchen table, first to devour Lorraine's delectable gourmet creations and then to chat about life. One day before evening tea, as supper is referred to Down Under, Mr. Jim walked by me and kissed the top of my head while I was seated at the kitchen table. "What's that for?" I asked.

"Because I love you," he said. He told me he always kissed his grandchildren and asked them, "Do you know what that's for?" His grandchildren always answered, "Because you love us." I truly felt like part of the family and my spirit was always inflated when I thought of our Tawa Ridge hosts.

It was not an easy good-bye, as I knew it wouldn't be. There wasn't a dry eye. Even 15-year-old George was choked up. Not all acquaintances and visits were to be remembered, but that one will not only be remembered—it will long be treasured.

• • •

We also had the chance to spend five days with the Hutchings. Tony and Chris had picked us up in Auckland, the capital of New Zealand and home to one million people—nearly one third of the country's entire population. Tony was a man in his late 60s with the energy of a 30-year-old, who always seemed a step ahead of everyone. Ten years his junior, Chris matched his energy and often left us in her wake. We exchanged hugs and kisses. It was as if they had already known Lee for ages when Chris embraced him for the first time. Chris and Tony had lost their first spouses and found love again with each other. The Hutchings had a passion for the outdoors and shared their activities with us.

But before our country jaunt began, our city tour included an impressive view from the Sky Tower, Auckland's highest structure. We roamed through the America's Cup Village and hoped for an invitation to spend the afternoon on a visiting multi-million dollar yacht. That horseshoe didn't always work, so we left Auckland and headed to the place we liked most—the quiet, the quaint, the country.

As soon as we were outside of city limits, the rolling pastures were an immediate reminder of the country's beauty I remembered so well. Homes and farms were sculpted into the hillsides, cattle and sheep dotted the meadows, and wildflowers burst with color. New Zealand, once visited, usually topped a person's list for the most beautiful country. The small nation was packed with natural wonders. Other than the people and the sights, my favorite part of New Zealand was no snakes or poisonous spiders.

Our Kiwi hosts, now retired from dairying and enjoying their busy retirement schedule, took us to Miranda Springs, a natural hot springs area. New Zealand is famed for literally being a hot spot and had numerous areas with boiling mud pools, shooting hot geysers and the distinct smells of sulfur, or should I say, rotten eggs.

Miranda Springs was a welcome stop. Although we'd had a delightful experience in Tonga, it felt mentally and physically sobering to travel in a country with modern conveniences. (I look back and think, *Yeah, right, I thought Tonga was tough, little did I know what awaited us in the Australian outback.*) We checked into our dormitory-style room and changed into our bathers, New Zealanders' name for swimsuits. Learning the Kiwi lingo was another challenge we had to tackle. New Zealand's official language was English, but many of their descriptions differed from those in the United States. We quickly learned that a flashlight was a torch, a cookie was a biscuit, trash was rubbish, a sidewalk was a footpath, the trunk of a car was the boot and if something was really cool, it was wicked. And as far as I was concerned, Miranda Springs was wicked! Tony was under the weather, so Chris, Lee and I headed to the natural pool.

Ahhhhh! My entire body went limp as if someone had just given me a sedative as I slipped down the side of the pool into the therapeutic liquid. The warm mineral pool was a luxury for our weary traveling bodies. I watched Lee with delight. He had never in his life experienced anything like it. I can't ever remember being in a swimming pool or hot tub with him during the previous six years. Lee could definitely be a born backpacker. He had the aptitude and the attitude of *I'll do anything, eat anything—you only live once and I'm here to experience it all.*

Relaxing in the mineral pool didn't actually make us work up an appetite, but we were hungry just the same. It was time to introduce Lee to one of New Zealand's most loved fast-food treats. The pool-side deli was opened and we each ordered a steak and cheese pie. Resembling a small American potpie, pies were a favorite food Down Under. I savored every bite as memories came flooding back of all the pies Kelly and I consumed in our travels. Pies came in a variety of choices including meat or vegetable or combinations baked in a small crust-covered shell. It only took one bite for Lee to become addicted.

We retired to our tiny room with bunk beds and I read aloud a few highlights about New Zealand's trails that Lee was very eager to hike. As I read, Lee, masked with a bright smile, pulled out his new sleeping bag for the first time on the trip. It had been too hot in Tonga to break it out, but the coolness of New Zealand nights provided the perfect opportunity. It seemed a little thing, but Lee was like a little kid climbing onto his first bicycle when he crawled into his green insulated sleeping bag.

Chris and Tony lived by Lake Okataina and had a beautiful view of a nearby island that Chris often kayaked to. Their lakefront property was peaceful and serene. They were caretaking a friend's summer house next door, which became our temporary home during our visit. Tourists paid a fortune to stay right on the lake, but we were guests and had the whole house to ourselves. My horseshoe was working.

The view through our front bay window was breathtaking. The deep-green, almost blue-tinted, grass was recently mowed and led to the lake's shore where small waves lapped onto a short beach. Beyond the lake, small forest-covered islands popped up out of the water. We carried our things into the living room and I began to unpack, or "explode," as Lee liked to describe it. He often laughed at my ability to clutter an entire room with our things in a matter of minutes. He was indeed right. The room was in total disarray, not in minutes, but seconds. Piles of clean clothes, piles of stinky clothes, piles of material for my stories and piles I had questioned my reasoning for packing in the first place.

Our first evening with Chris and Tony was spent making a game plan for the next few days. While we chatted I hooked up Clyde and got online. After 16 days of no communication with family, goose bumps erupted on my body when I heard Clyde say, "You've got mail." We had 21 messages. Correspondence from family and friends was already making the transition a little easier. We didn't have time to miss anyone yet, every day was packed with events.

The Hutchings lived outside Rotorua, a traveler's delight, full of sights, smells and activities for the young and old. It is most renowned for its thermal area and has been nicknamed "Sulfur Springs," a reference well earned from the odors emitted from its pools of boiling mud and steaming waters. Our visit to Rotorua was not complete without a night out to a traditional Maori program. Maoris were the first inhabitants of New Zealand and many of the main towns and cities provided special presentations as a way to educate the public and to preserve their interesting ancestry.

In Rotorua, two Maori brothers with a vision to protect and promote their nation's heritage and culture, sold their Harley Davidson to develop Tamaki, a living Maori village experience. The venue offered visitors the unique opportunity to see firsthand the customs, traditions and life of the Maori people before they were colonized by Europeans. What started out with one van and a work force of ten Maoris had evolved into a fleet of 30-passenger buses and a staff of nearly 100 Maori descendants. Once on board the bus, our driver, Darren, shared many Maori stories with us and explained several of their indigenous customs.

If a Maori experience was what we had hoped for, well, Lee got the close-up and personal version. The 35 passengers nominated Lee as the chief of our bus, or the chief of our "war canoe." Lee, along with six chiefs from other war canoes, was required to meet the fearless warrior at Tamaki's village gates to see if all had come in peace. Following the peace offering and *haka* or war dance, we enjoyed a cultural show. Chiefs were invited on stage to give the hosting village chief an official greeting, the *hongi*, two presses of the nose. The visiting chiefs were warned not to press noses three times as it was a sign for marriage proposal.

It was probably much more entertaining for Chris, Tony and me, since Lee was singled out as a chief. Lee was laid back and pretty conservative, some might even say a little shy. At Tamaki, poor Lee was thrown into the limelight, being thrust on stage with the other chiefs in front of more than 300 people. Probably not his number-one idea of a good time, but he enjoyed it. Lee was a great team player. Although he was a bit reserved at times and hadn't gotten off the farm much, his greatest virtue was his ability to communicate with people. I was finding out his natural people skills were going to be a real asset during our time away.

We enjoyed a traditional *hangi* feast which was cooked in an underground oven using a certain type of wood. The feast included meat, vegetables, salads and seafood. It was followed by a traditional dessert—custard over cake. Yummy! I'm such a sucker for sweets. I'm sure my sweet tooth was attributing to my weight gain. If I didn't soon curb my eating and drinking habits, I'd grow completely out of my clothes. The evening was capped off by special presentations to the visiting chiefs, and Lee received a small Maori carving. The *tiki* symbol was said to give its owner good luck and reproductive powers. That was all Lee and I needed—not! I could barely carry my backpack, let alone an infant.

Rotorua was not only famed for its deep-rooted Maori history and its thermal activity, but was world renowned for its trout fishing, attracting anglers from around the globe to its pristine waters. Lee was an avid fisherman in the States, but mostly limited to small catches in the farm pond. We visited Brian and Val Blewett, owners of Waiteti Lakeside Lodge, and operators of local trout expeditions. The couple's quaint lakeside accommodation provided top-notch troll fishing capped off by samples of delicious smoked trout.

Troll fishing was a new experience for me. We boarded the boat and Nick, our troll guide, showed us where to sit. As soon as we were out in deeper water, Nick cast my line, put it in a holder, pointed to it and said, "Becky, that's your line." Troll fishing, I soon discovered, was fishing by trailing a line in the water behind a slow-moving boat. I was lucky enough to get the first bite. "Pick up your pole and reel it in," Nick instructed in his Kiwi accent.

I was so excited, but was such a rookie. As I reeled in slowly, Brian and Nick gave me directions while Nick held the fish net ready to scoop up my catch. "Steady, steady," Nick said. "If the fish starts to pull or fight just let your reel go."

Well, with that vague instruction I almost tossed my pole into the lake because I thought that was what I was supposed to do. Thank goodness common sense knocked me like a huge wave and I thought, *How silly to pitch my fishing pole into the lake and lose it.* What Nick meant, as I soon found out, was to release the line and let the trout take it out a bit to prevent a struggle. "If you fight trout they just break the line," he explained.

I continued to reel in and Nick dipped down in the lake to ladle up my fish. Of course, my trout was under the minimum regulation of 35 centimeters so we had to pitch it back to freedom. Lee was elated with his catch of the day, a four-pound brown trout.

The following day we were on the water again, confined in the shell of a kayak. Never in our lives had we attempted kayaking, not by choice, but rather by limited time and resources. Chris was excited about the arrival of their friend, Jim Fleming, who was on his annual 11-day quest around Rotorua's 13 lakes. The 70-year-old gentleman paddled in and we all enjoyed morning tea on the deck. Chris, Lee and I joined Jim on a short length of his journey across Okataina Lake.

I climbed into my small canoe-like object, nervous about the whole idea of trying to balance the water vehicle over waves. I wiggled down into the correct position, Velcroed the skirt-type thing around my waist to prevent water from going into the kayak, and gripped my paddle. Lee gave me a push. The kayak almost tipped over as I maneuvered over the first shoreline ripple. It was much more difficult than I had anticipated. I finally got the hang of it and managed to stay upright despite the lake's waves that hammered my sides. We paddled with Jim for an hour then said our good-byes, wishing him luck on the remainder of his expedition. It took all the energy I could muster to go against the tide and make it back to shore. It was fun, but I thought, *My kayaking debut would satisfy my water sport desires for a while.*

A highlight of our visit with Chris and Tony was meeting Tony's 92-year-old father, Fred Hutchings. Fred immediately puckered and pecked me on my cheek. "Becky, Fred's ninety-two, but he's still a big flirt," Chris said.

Fred was healthy and sharp as a tack. He was tall, thin and distinguished looking. He reclined in his chair and shared many tales of his life and experiences. I enjoyed his stories and learned about the Hutchings' family rise to fame in the dairy industry. Their humble beginnings flourished into one of the top Ayrshire herds in the country. Fred and his brother, Giff, arrived in Rotorua in 1930. Rotorua at the time was overgrown bush country. Fred drove their Model-A Ford while Giff drove the three-horse dray loaded with plow, harrow, slashers, axes and what was deemed as necessary tools at the time. The siblings lived in a tent for six months while they worked tirelessly, carving a life for themselves out of the bush and scrub. They built a two-room house to accommodate each of their wives and two children each. Two years were spent clearing the land before the pioneers purchased their first dozen crossbred heifers. They milked them by hand and sold the milk, raising just enough money to pay for the heifers.

By 1933, the brothers were able to buy their first Ayrshires, which would be the beginning of the Hutchings' family dynasty with Ayrshire cattle. They bought eight heifers and added five more in 1934. The Ayrshires were purchased from Mr. Douslin, somewhat of an eccentric character, according to Fred. He was a diamond miner from South Africa and moved to a lake in Rotorua in 1920 with his American wife. Mr. Douslin's passion for Ayrshire cattle and trout fishing made Rotorua an ideal location for his two loves.

Long, difficult years laced with both triumphs and trepidation finally yielded the Hutchings the top herd for milk production. They also established Dalemere Stud, a tradition spanning five decades. Fred's walls were adorned with black-and-white photos of champion Ayrshire cattle and his much-loved days on the farm. He reminisced about the past, but was sparked by the future and proud that his great-grandchildren were carrying on a family legacy. For 58 years, Tony continued dairying at the original Dalemere location until he dispersed his Hilltop Farm herd.

Today, Tony's son, Graeme, manages Fred's original farm on Mangatete Road near Ngakuru. Dennis, Fred's grandson, oversees Fred's second farm and he carries on the famous Dalemere herd, which is still shown successfully throughout the North Island. Fred's son, Malcolm, also owns a prominent Ayrshire herd. With the noted distinction of being the eldest of five generations, Fred lives for the day and appreciates all of his yesterdays. He said he owed a lot of his success to the love and support of his late wife, Edna, and his incredible family. As we were leaving, Fred hugged me tight, kissed me twice and with a sweet but subtle, mischievous smile on his face said, "At ninety-two, I'm pretty safe."

He turned his attention to Lee. "Take care of her," he said. Lee nodded his head, accepting the wise man's advice.

"Life is what you make of it, so make the most of it and enjoy it," Fred said as he wished us luck in our travels. I took those words to heart and knew I would long remember our special visit with Fred Hutchings, an incredible person, the family patriarch, a world-class dairy icon.

Familiar Stranger

Familiar stranger why do I bare you my soul?
Share my dreams freely, detailed and whole;

Reveal plans for the future, fresh and unbroken,
Occupants of my mind, alive but unspoken;

With interest sincere and manner polite,
Opinions exchanged no matter how slight;

Each word sculpts my thoughts as they flow from my mind,
Somehow telling this stranger lends them dimension and
        design;

This chance encounter confirms one simple notion,
Dreams only become real if I set them in motion;

No progress is made if no effort is spent,
Actions speak louder than words of intent;

No place for excuses, they just cause delay,
Plans not backed by action will soon slip away;

Thank you, familiar stranger, for your patience and time,
I wish you luck in your endeavors as I pursue mine.

                                        Lee Chaney

Holiday Time Down Under

"We have to switch sides," Lee whispered to me, half asleep.

"Why? I'm quite comfortable," I responded as I curled up on the seat and nestled my head into his lap again.

"My butt is asleep and we have to get into a different sleeping position."

"How does your butt fall asleep?" I asked, giggling, then switched sides with him.

Similar conversation went on throughout a long chilly night crammed in the front seat of the ute, as four-wheel-drive pickups were called. We were parked along the road somewhere about 100 miles south of the northernmost point of New Zealand that we had visited earlier in the evening. "I'm dog-ass tired and we better stop," Lee said, struggling to stay awake.

Playing it safe seemed the sensible thing to do, especially since we were driving a friend's farm truck. David and Elaine Louden lived near Whangarei, two hours north of Auckland. They couldn't leave their dairy farm to show us around so they offered us their ute. It was Lee's first experience with the steering wheel on the right side and driving on the left side of the road. That coupled with the fact we were so tired forced us to pull off the road. It was not exactly a peaceful night of slumber. I woke up what seemed to be every half-hour from the tapping of rain hitting the windshield, cramps in my arms and legs and scary noises in the dark. Lee thought I was silly as I locked the doors and surveyed the area.

"Who do you think is out there?" he asked.

"You never know," I said. "Didn't you see the movie *Children of the Corn*?"

He always knew I had issues with darkness and that I often jumped at the drop of a pin. I just cuddled up close to him in the front seat, closed my eyes and hoped that daylight would come quickly. We hadn't packed our sleeping bags and cool air seeped in the cracks of the door all night. The morning sun finally peeked beyond the hills.

Rain was pouring buckets when we started out. We weren't well rested, but we were alive. During our drive home we had a chance to finally talk about our incredible few days of seeing some of New Zealand's spectacular scenery. The evening before, we had arrived at Cape Reinga just in time for a breathtaking sunset. A magnificent hue of pink stretched across a light blue December sky like a swift and steady glide of a painter's brush over canvas. A cobblestone path led to the lighthouse, one of many lighthouses located around New Zealand's shores, helping boaters and fishermen find their way home. Waves crashed against titanic-sized rocks. The air grew chillier, giving me goose bumps. The day's warm weather was finally choked away by darkness.

On the way to Cape Reinga we stopped at the Bay of Islands, noted for its cluster of small islands, dolphin and whale sightings, unique features and picturesque setting. A day on the Cream Trip Cruise took us to the famed "Hole in the Rock," as well as islands, inlets and coves with interesting history. The Cream Trip Cruise was named for the route, years earlier, when Captain Lane picked up dairy farmers' milk around the bay. That route continued in present day, but rather than daily milk pickup, mail and provisions were delivered and collected.

I'll never forget the tragic saga about one of the small bay islands. It looked lush, fertile and inviting, but as the story unfolded to the 30 passengers, it transformed to an eerie landscape of mystery and danger. A widow who had lost her husband at sea decided she and her children would still make a go of it. It was unheard of back in the 1800s for women to strike out on their own. The hard-working widow finally met her demise when a hired farm boy with psychological problems murdered the entire family.

Many of the small islands were tainted with tales or enchanted by historical data and heightened by legend. The first Christian mission was established in 1823 on Paihia. Russell, the oldest town in New Zealand, was headquarters of the South Pacific whaling fleet in the 1830s. In 1772 Marion du Fresne and members of his crew were massacred and cannibalized and so the place was dubbed Assassination Cove. American author, Zane Grey, camped on Otehei Bay in 1926.

Cruising back to shore, we were treated to hot tea and scones, a traditional snack in New Zealand. The scones were warm and smothered with jelly and homemade whipped cream. I devoured my first and second servings.

It continued to rain on the drive back to the Loudens'. A few miles from their farm we stopped at Longview Estate, a vineyard and winery. My interest, of course, was the winery's name. I simply wanted to check out the Kiwi namesake of my parents' Long View Farm and since I was there, a souvenir bottle of wine was at the top of my list.

Many things throughout the trip often reminded me of days growing up on Long View Farm or "The Farm," as it was always called. The Farm is located one hour northwest of Washington, D.C., and provided many opportunities during my youth. It seemed long ago, but I cherish those childhood memories.

After the not-so-pleasant night sleeping in the front of the Loudens' ute, we finally made it back to their farm. The Loudens milked nearly 100 Holstein cows and enjoyed exhibiting at local competitions. We enjoyed pre-Christmas activities with the Loudens—Christmas tree selection, decoration and gift exchange. David and Elaine's two daughters, one-year-old Madison and two-year-old Sophie, were excited about the holiday.

Sophie always cracked me up and to this day, Lee and I still use one of her favorite sayings. If Sophie was discontent, she would say, "Sophie tired now." That simply meant she didn't want to deal with the issue at hand or cooperate with her parents. So for the remainder of the trip whenever Lee and I were at wits' end, we simply looked at the other and recited, "Becky tired now" or "Lee tired now."

Elaine helped David with most of the milkings and kept the girls at the barn during chore time. Madison was either in a crib or strapped in a swing. Sophie was old enough to stand in the milking parlor with her parents. They worked hard and opportunities were limited due to their commitment on the farm.

Oh, how true that was! It was not easy leaving the dairy when cows must be milked twice a day, every day. I recalled Lee's horrific schedule that forced me to attend many gatherings by myself. Many people didn't know I was married, because more often than not, I was always seen by myself. Time spent with our host families always gave us a new outlook on marriage, children and relationships.

The beautiful thing about people is that everyone is different, all relationships are different and all people handle situations differently. Some visits gave us insight in what we hoped to aspire to, while other stops influenced us to avoid certain relationship issues or actions or at least helped us to see how we could handle it differently.

We were quickly running out of time and flew to the South Island. The airport was buzzing with activity, just three days before Christmas. We landed in Christchurch and were picked up by Jenni Minson. Jenni had visited my parents' farm in 1990. Jenni and her husband, Ian, owned Crauford Holstein Farm, our home for a week. I got a little homesick during the holidays, but tried to make the most of our Christmas experience overseas. Folks at home knew we would be at the Minsons over the holidays and we received many Christmas cards and packages. The words of love and encouragement inspired us. I shared some of our Yankee traditions and holiday dishes. "Mom would be so proud," I often said after I created one of her favorite dishes.

We had spent Thanksgiving in Tonga and were invited to join a small group of Peace Corps volunteers for the pilgrim and Indian homage. I was the oldest in the group and was pleased they needed so much advice. I told them how long to leave the turkey in and I was the only one who knew how to make gravy. Mom had taught me well and would have been especially tickled with the onion and cucumber salad I created from fresh vegetables out of our Tongan host family's plantation. Mom's cucumber salad was always a requested dish at family gatherings. Of course, mine probably wasn't up to spec, but our new friends enjoyed it just the same.

A month later in New Zealand, it was time to take in another holiday away from home. Mark, the Minsons' eldest son, lived and worked on the family farm. Mark was inquisitive by nature and very involved with his motorized toy car collection. His passion and experience earned him a trip to compete as far away as Europe. Two other sons were also involved in the operation. Ross helped on the home farm and Craig managed a dairy across the road. We were truly blessed to have a family open up their homes and hearts to us during Christmas. It's a busy time and many people wouldn't have bothered.

On Christmas Eve we went to a local church service. As usual we were a few minutes late, but quickly found a seat in the back pew. The old rustic church had ceiling beams visible and the lights were dimmed, pulling us into the spiritual event. Christmas Eve services had always been very moving for me. My Aunt Fran was born on Christmas Eve. She had lost her battle with cancer in 1988, and I missed her. Aunt Fran was special, I guess because of her sometimes wild and uninhibited nature. She reminded me of myself. She was adventurous and had traveled the world. She's my Dad's sister and was one of ten children. I always think about Aunt Fran at Christmas and thank God for the times we shared. She's a great source of inspiration.

Earlier that evening Lee helped Ian position the Christmas tree. It seemed a little unusual to have a tree in the middle of New Zealand's summer. Typically, New Zealand summers were very warm, but it was unseasonably cool. Their seasons are completely opposite to our seasons. Ironically, it was so cool on Christmas morning I asked them to light a fire in the wood stove. I woke up early Christmas morning, not by choice and not because I couldn't wait to see what was under the tree, as Christmas mornings always came early when I was a child.

The ding-aling-aling of the phone ringing at 4 a.m. immediately stirred my sleep. I quickly thought, *I hope that's not anyone calling us and getting the time confused.* It was the first morning in ages Ian had the opportunity to sleep in. Someone knocked on our bedroom door. "Come in," I said.

It was poor Ian, who looked like he was sleepwalking. He handed me the phone. "It's for you," his groggy voice spit out.

"Hello," I said as I pressed the receiver to my ear.

"Merry Christmas," an excited voice answered. "This is Patty."

"Patty, do you know what time it is?"

"Oh yeah, it's four in the afternoon."

"No, Pat, it's four in the morning here."

"I'm sorry, I'll call back."

"Oh no! I'm awake now. It's Christmas, of course you don't have to call back."

It was so good to hear her voice. Our departure from America was probably the toughest on my sister Patty. I was close to all of my brothers and sisters, but Patty had taken it the hardest. Lee and I talked to my brother-in-law Lance and my nephew Jimmy. One-year-old David didn't have a lot to say yet. Patty told me there were troubles with the family, but she wouldn't elaborate, she didn't want to upset me. But it did upset me. It upset me that the adults in my family couldn't get along. I could only pray for them and hope that life would someday be better for the Long clan. I never took sides in the past and I wasn't about to take sides in the future. I loved my family dearly, but there was only so much mediation one could do. I resorted to leaving it in God's hands. Worrying would only make me crazy, spur a lot of headaches and be responsible for many sleepless nights. I knew very few families without problems, so I reckon my family was pretty normal.

Lee and I usually spoiled each other on Christmas, but we were on the road and had nowhere to pack things—nor did we have money to buy them. After all, we didn't need anything, we had each other and were on the trip of a life-time. Things were going really well and we hadn't managed to kill each other yet.

I did miss one thing on Christmas—getting up before sunrise and driving a half-hour to The Farm to help Dad milk. It had become a tradition the past several years. Lee had to milk with his partner, Brad, and I didn't want to be by myself on Christmas morning. Mom preset the coffee pot so it would be ready at 4:30 a.m. for Dad and me to enjoy a cup before heading out to get the cows in. He was a quiet man, but those holiday milkings often proved the best times for talking about life, family and things we could not change.

Something new we experienced with the Minsons was Boxing Day, celebrated on December 26. It was another day for people to eat, drink, sleep and be merry. As the story was told to us, Boxing Day derived decades earlier when the royal family in England had servants. The servants were allowed to "box" up all the leftover holiday food and take it home for their day off, which was the day after Christmas.

For the 17th year, the Minsons hosted five other couples for a friendly lawn tennis competition. We gave tennis a try, but decided it was a sport we should stick to watching, not playing. One of the couples we met on Boxing Day told us they knew a friend's daughter driving to Queenstown who might be able to give us a ride. How perfect—opportunities just seemed to present themselves when we needed them the most. "Opportunity or horseshoe?" Lee teased.

It didn't matter, we were simply lucky. Lee and I had thrown around the idea of hitchhiking to Queenstown to save money, but fortunately we got a ride. Sarah was friendly and full of information as she drove us south. It was great to be able to drive with someone and not be held captive by a bus. I could request to stop anytime I needed to, unlike tour buses that only made scheduled stops. (Many New Zealand tour buses had no bathrooms. On one ride I had to go so bad Lee told the driver I was sick and needed to stop because it was an emergency. I wasn't going to die, but I was seconds from wetting my pants. That's what I get for drinking two beers before I hopped on a bus for a three-hour ride.)

We arrived in Queenstown, the adrenaline mecca of the world. From bungee jumping and sky diving to jet boating and white-water rafting, the South Island resort town had it all. A.J. Hackett, famous for his jump off the Eiffel Tower in 1986, established the world's first bungee-jumping business in Queenstown in 1988.

I'd had my bungee-jumping debut in '92 when I dived 142 feet off the Kawarau Bridge in Queenstown, and decided at that time: never again. It was a horrible feeling, free falling until the bungee cord bounced me back up. Once was certainly enough for me. But by no means was my frightening experience going to deter Lee from taking the terrifying leap.

Lee jumped off the Nevis High Wire, New Zealand's highest bungee at 402 feet and the second highest in the world. He told me that halfway down he said to himself, *What the hell am I doing here?* But it wasn't enough of a scare to stop his next 171-foot jump off The Ledge, which towered above the hillside overlooking Queenstown. On The Ledge, he bravely jumped off backward for more of a rush.

For a little less excitement we took the gondola up to the Skyline and raced down 2,400-feet slopes in luge carts. Since I hadn't driven for a while, my steering was slightly off and I crashed twice, once almost taking Lee out with me. We laughed as we dashed around hairpin curves and up and downhills. I saw yet another side of the man I had been with for six-plus years. I saw a much more relaxed Lee Chaney. Someone who was finally taking time to "smell the roses."

Our next day was spent on the "Barbecue Bus" to Milford Sound, one of New Zealand's most popular tourist destinations. The bus made frequent stops at scenic views during the four-hour drive to the Sound which culminated with a cruise. We were in awe of the breathtaking ocean inlet with cascading waterfalls spilling down the sides of enormous mountains. The cruise was complete with a visit by a pod of bottle-nosed dolphins. There was something really special about seeing marine life close-up in the wild.

The biggest challenge for me to date was our final Kiwi adventure, a day on the Routeburn Track, one of the country's most famed rain-forest hiking trails. At the halfway point, the small group of five hikers had lunch. Our guide told us to be back at the van by 4 p.m. He stressed the importance of starting back at 2 p.m., no matter where we were on the trail. Lee and I started our ascent to the waterfall. Two miles uphill probably wasn't a big deal to someone fit, but I wasn't fit. For a non-hiker like myself, it was tough. After about a quarter of a mile, I stopped.

"Go on without me, I just won't make it, Lee," I said between heavy breaths as tears filled my eyes. "Please, keep going without me. I'll just take my time and turn back at two or wait for you on your trip back down."

"Come on, I'll wait for you," he said.

"No, really, please keep going," I said.

He kissed me before his manly pace picked up. I watched him get smaller and smaller until he disappeared in the heavy foliage. He didn't want to leave me, but I insisted. I knew he really wanted to make it to the waterfall. I was so pleased with his initiative on the trip and his willingness to experience as much as he possibly could, I dared not hold back his spirit.

Shoot, pretty soon I wouldn't be the traveling goddess any more. At Lee's rate, he would become the seasoned traveler in the family. I plodded along at a slow, but steady, pace. It didn't get any easier, but I forced myself to continue. I could have given up and just waited for Lee to fetch me on his way back down, but I wanted to try, I wanted to push myself. Part of the trail was very difficult, more like mountain climbing than hiking. Sweat ran down my face, my legs ached and my knee wraps did nothing to alleviate the pain in my arthritic joints, a condition I obviously inherited from my mother. I drudged on, picking up my hiking boots one foot at a time, scaling the rocks until, at last, I saw a break in the forest.

It was 1:45 p.m., I could see the top. I couldn't believe it. As I crested the final boulder, I almost burst into tears. I made it! I really made it! I was so proud of myself and I knew Lee would be proud too. I saw him hiking down from the top of the rocks he had climbed for a better look at the waterfall. His eyes widened, I think he was a little shocked to see me.

"Good job, you made it," he said, walking toward me. He gave me a big hug.

Lee might have been more pleased with my performance than I was. He knew hiking was not my forte and that hills especially challenged me, but I had made the ten-mile hike. The initial group of hikers joined up for our walk back. Kathy was a native of New York and her boyfriend, Bob, lived in California. Silke hailed from Germany, spoke good English and was probably the most fit. It never ceased to amaze me how enchanted people were with our story. The fact we left behind successful careers and were traveling and working abroad for a year. Kathy and Bob were full of questions. They couldn't believe we had quit our jobs to venture into an unknown world. The positive feedback reaffirmed our decision and our commitment to make the most of our year away. We knew what we were doing was unusual, for the most part, but I guess we didn't realize how unusual until we shared our story with other travelers.

The van dropped us off in town. The hour drive back did little to reduce the stiffness that consumed my legs. My body felt drained and I was simply exhausted. There was no way I'd have enough energy to bring in the New Year. That night the entire world would be drinking, shouting and ringing in the new millennium. My weariness repressed any desire to whoop it up downtown.

Clouds rolled in, the sky turned gray, there was a stillness in the air. In fear of a downpour Lee and I bought a bottle of wine, cheese and crackers and decided to celebrate in the privacy of our room, even if it was just a dormitory-style unit with two single beds. We also opted to ride the bus home, as my legs couldn't take any more walking and I wasn't about to tackle the two-mile walk uphill to the backpackers' lodge in a rainstorm.

By the time we arrived back at the lodge it was raining cats and dogs. The rain was going to put a serious damper on many of the festivities scheduled around New Zealand to usher in a new century. Gisbourne was dubbed the official site of the first sunrise in the world. Thousands flocked to the small coastal town along the eastern seaboard of New Zealand's North Island for the event. It would have been neat to be there, but Lee and I typically preferred the quieter atmospheres and one-on-one conversations with new friends from far-off lands. It wasn't always like that. I had liked big parties, packed with people. Lee and I had one of our first dates at the Western Party held at The Farm. Hundreds of people drifted in to drink, sing karaoke and to try to avoid being put in the makeshift jail made from Dad's old hay wagon. I'd always have a touch of that wild side, but I guess with age, my priorities had changed, and, of course, my level of energy. The days of staying up late, partying, and then putting in a full day seemed ages ago. Although the new millennium seemed a great reason to party, my body revolted. There was no way we were going to go out in the rain to celebrate. First, it was disgusting out; second, we were on a serious budget and knew drinks at downtown bars would cost a fortune; and third, we just wanted to relax. The backpackers' lodge accommodated more than 100 travelers and there were no vacancies. We were lucky we had reserved a room.

The lodge offered happy hour in its spacious bar and commons area every evening. Beverages were priced for poor backpackers like us. It was fun meeting people from all walks of life and finding out why they were traveling and what they did for a living. Lee and I visited with folks until 8 p.m., when the majority of guests boarded the bus for downtown to bring in the New Year in style. Well, our style was going to be small, quaint and quiet. We sipped our New Zealand wine, nibbled our brie cheese and tried to outwit each other with the card games the Minsons had taught us. Right before midnight, we heard a lot of commotion. Seven people were hooting and hollering on the banks of the lodge, reacting to the explosive fireworks lighting up the sky as rain trickled down lightly. The two bartenders from the lodge passed out glasses of champagne.

Five more enthusiastic partyers arrived. They were from the Isle of Guernsey, a channel island off the coast of England. I was excited to talk to them because Guernsey cattle, one of the six major U.S. dairy breeds, originated there. (You know the saying, "You can take the girl out of the country, but you can't take the country out of the girl." Well, that's me, up and down. I always discussed the dairy industry with friends and strangers. I loved talking about cows, probably because of all the opportunities in my life as a result of my involvement in the rural community. I'd traveled to most U.S. states, stayed with families in more than 20 countries, and organized and chaperoned three groups overseas—all because of my agricultural roots and contacts.) Were my newfound friends interested at all in my cow musings? No! They may have been from the Isle of Guernsey, but I'm not sure they even knew where milk came from, let alone what a Guernsey was.

It was 2 a.m. when Lee and I called it a night. We had to catch a bus in four hours. The morning came pretty fast. We had a few minutes in Queenstown before departure, so we did a little window-shopping. I spied a furry bra with a sign that read, "Nipple Warmers." I showed Lee and we both laughed. I had a strange condition of my extremities getting really cold. Usually it was my fingers and toes, but occasionally I suffered from severe cold breasts. On The Farm when I milked in the wintertime, I often had to excuse myself to go in and warm my boobs over the wood stove. Sounds crazy, but it was very painful. I thought those nipple warmers would have been the greatest remedy for my chilly bust, but the store didn't open for two more hours and we'd be well on our way by then. No nipple warmers for me. I'd have to continue to put tiny heat packs, like hunters and winter-sports enthusiasts used, in my bra during my frigid outings.

Our bus ride back was long and uneventful, other than the number of backpackers who had celebrated the millennium a little too hard. I was so happy I wasn't one of those people who were nursing very bad hangovers. They were crouched in their seats, hoods pulled over their heads, staring blankly—that's if their eyes were even open.

New Zealand's incredible landscape, friendly residents and our Kiwi host families would always be a highlight of our days on the road when we decided to reclaim our lives.

Answers

Make a choice, choose a direction,
Dare to be wrong, so little learned with perfection;

Mistakes are not failures, but teachers of lessons,
Conclude your own answers, ask your own questions;

Each life is different, each is unique,
No single book contains all the answers we seek;

So find your place in the world, where you truly belong,
Think for yourself and dare to be wrong.

Lee Chaney

Terror in the Ocean

V ast, serene, peaceful all came to mind when I boarded our passenger boat for a day of exploring the Great Barrier Reef. We were spending three days in Cairns on Australia's northeast coast. It wasn't a lot of time, but sufficient to see one the world's seven natural wonders. Cairns' claim to fame is the Great Barrier Reef. Along with its extensive 1,200-plus miles of reef system, its 400 different types of coral serve as home to 1,500 species of fish, 4,000 kinds of clams and snails, 350 varieties of sea urchins, starfish and sea cucumbers, and thousands of species of sponge, worm, crab and shrimp.

To experience the fascinating ocean haven, we took the Passions of Paradise Cruise, along with 43 other travelers, to Paradise Reef for some spectacular scuba diving and snorkeling—or was it? Warm air blew through my hair as I relaxed on deck, willing myself not to be seasick. A clear deep baby blue sky gave way to the blinding sun. It was a gorgeous day, but I dreaded the fact I had to wear a swimsuit. I had lost my tan from Tonga and had grown another size in New Zealand. I was going to give "bikini" a bad name. I'd always been self-conscious of my body and worried about my weight. I was so relieved to be rid of the day-to-day hassles in America that my newfound freedom and solace seemed to pack pounds on my figure like someone took a butter knife and literally spread the creamy delight on my thighs.

Bikini or not, I wasn't going to fret about it that day on the reef. The fish wouldn't care and I couldn't be bothered about what other people thought. I put on my bikini and practically fell out all over the place. My breasts pushed out of the cups, nearly showing my nipples. My poor swimsuit was stressed, but I had no intention of starting my diet that day and was determined to make the most of our time at one of the most captivating places on earth.

My snorkeling was sensational, but my dive had much to be desired. It was more or less a half-hour of terror on the ocean bottom. First, we had 20 minutes of instruction on deck. Next, I had to squeeze, and I do mean squeeze myself into a rubber-like diving suit. I held my breath, sucked in, and Lee zipped me up. The staff handed out equipment and we learned how to use our breathing apparatus. We had to hawk a loogy on our facemask, swirl it around with our finger, and dip it in water to clear the mask.

I grunted as I stood up with the oxygen tank as it pulled my shoulders back. Then I had to be brave and leap into the ocean with 75 pounds of extra weight. There was an underwater deck to hang on to while we tried to adjust to breathing with an oxygen tank. Submerged, I tried to get a good seal on my mask, but my ears would not clear. I couldn't equalize the pressure, probably because I was nervous and feared my head or ears would explode.

I clutched the deck. The weighted waist belt helped keep me beneath the water, but I just wanted to surface. I hated being under water. I wanted to do it for Lee, but I was uneasy. Just the thought of being underwater to depths of 30 or more feet took my breath away. My heart palpitated like a flickering candle I couldn't control. *Relax, breathe, relax, breathe,* I kept telling myself. *The instructor certainly wouldn't let me die. Let go, let go, it's time to descend with the rest of the class. Relax, breathe.*

I looked at Lee through my fogged-up mask—guess my loogy wasn't big enough. Lee was like a fish, completely comfortable with scuba diving, it seemed. *I can do this, I can do this,* I repeated again as I finally peeled my hand from the underwater platform and let the weights drag me down. I equalized the pressure on the way down, swallowing, trying desperately to relieve the pressure in my ears. Lee and I hungered for adventure together, but this wasn't adventure, it was hell—I hated it.

I just wanted to have fun. I wanted to float to the top, have someone pull my heavy, soaked body out of the cool water and offer me a glass of wine. I wanted to kick back in the sun and take in the beautiful surroundings. I knew the Great Barrier Reef could be incredible, but I couldn't relax. Then, I bit my upper lip and decided *I can do this!* I descended a little more. I really didn't see anything interesting in the murky waters. I'm sure anxiety blurred my vision. As divers' flippers glided across the gritty ocean floor, clouds of gray and brown silt filtered through the water.

During our lecture on deck, we learned different hand gestures. We knew the signals for going up or down and for being okay or in trouble—all very important when diving and equalizing body pressures. Everyone seemed to be okay. We knelt on the sandy bottom in all of its ghostly calm and passed around a sea cucumber. The creature had a velvety black skin and it resembled a fat, foot-long worm. I handed Lee the sea cucumber and he very rudely and quickly pitched it to the next person kneeling beside him. I wanted to sock him for not appreciating it and taking time to hold it. *I was the one freaked out,* I thought, *he could have been a little more considerate.*

Suddenly, I realized he was in trouble. He started with the thumbs up sign, signaling to the diving instructor he was having a problem and needed to go up. The first thing we learned was not to panic and ascend to the top or we'd risk bursting our ear drums or doing something weird to our heart. In seconds, the instructor was in front of Lee trying to determine his plight. Lee made it quite apparent he was running out of air and breathing in water. Lee was the one in trouble, but I felt like my oxygen was being cut off. My heart sank even deeper than I already was—*My God, Lee was in trouble!* I was helpless.

I had no idea how to help or what to do. I tried to remain calm and watched intensely as our instructor tried to help Lee empty his mask and breathe. *That little jerk better not leave me yet, I need him,* I thought as I fought back tears. I had to pull myself together. The instructor didn't need me to go into shock and have two rescues on his hands. The whole ordeal was less than a minute, but it seemed like an eternity. It was the worst feeling. I could do absolutely nothing, except watch life be sucked from the most important person in the world to me. Lee's mustache had prevented a good seal and water continued to ooze into his mask until water was level with his nose and literally drowning him.

Even though the instructor had given Lee plenty of Vaseline for his mustache on board to assure a proper seal, it wasn't enough. Lee panicked but, thank God, had motioned to the instructor for help. He responded to Lee's anxiety attack quickly and calmly. I was immersed in the hand-to-hand commentary waiting for the instructor to either save Lee or for Lee to lose it.

Finally, I saw the instructor pinch his thumb and first finger together in a circle, the signal for 'Are you okay?' My heart missed a beat when Lee also gave the oval gesture indicating he could breathe again.

The scare wasn't enough to prevent Lee from diving again. That time he gobbed so much Vaseline on his mustache that it was smashed to his face. He looked like a grease ball, but at least he'd have a good seal, saving us both from a nervous breakdown. I decided to snorkel the rest of the day. I was all for Lee taking a second dive, but I couldn't bear to have anything to do with it. I'm sure certified divers have incredible underwater experiences, but I was never going to strap on an oxygen tank again.

Our reef expedition was highlighted by the extraordinary and sometimes bizarre-looking fish that swam right by our faces. They brushed by our skin, often stopping right by our masks to examine the large figure intruding into their water. Fish were like cutout paper figures dipped in cups of paint on an assembly line. They were long, short, fat and puffed out like they were holding their breath underwater. They donned bright tones and were laden with spots, stripes and unusual marks. Upon closer inspection, many fish tails were actually heads, a defense tactic to confuse their enemies. I thought, *What a peculiar and wonderful world—an aquatic circus complete with characters, colors and crazy performances.*

The enormous clams, many larger than a wheelbarrow, spewed bubbles, and made me think I was in some kind of underwater science fiction movie about to be sucked in by the colossal mollusks. The real climax of my day was swimming next to a giant sea turtle. It was almost intimate to glide through the water like two beings competing for the gold medal in the synchronized swimming event of the Olympics. Every graceful stroke was made with precision and care. Its long-webbed fins hardly made ripples in the water as we floated side by side on a steady course. No one else was around—it was just the sea turtle and me. Stunning shades of green, blue and brown accented its shell. I made smooth arm sweeps to keep parallel with it. I was sure that I'd probably never have another sea turtle encounter in my lifetime. With little effort I could have latched onto the ancient-looking treasure, but feared I'd frighten it.

I wasn't sure if sea turtles were even dangerous. I knew the snapping turtles on The Farm could easily take a finger or toe off. Comparing the sizes of The Farm pond snappers to the titanic sea turtle, I reckoned the sea turtle could have snatched off an entire limb. I had no mistrust, only curiosity and the desire to be lost in the moment, lost at sea, lost with one of the most beautiful animals I'd ever seen in its natural habitat. It was magical.

Lee recovered from his first diving disaster only to have adrenaline shoot through his veins with another diving episode. He had a good seal on his mask and bebopped around the reef's ominous, but brilliant, coral system, checking out strange marine life. He remained calm when he encountered a shark. Instead of swimming in the opposite direction, his curiosity got the better of him and he swam toward the predator for closer inspection. I had a shark story too, but Lee's shark, of course, was bigger and more vicious. The white-tipped shark I saw only measured about three feet, but a shark is a shark and I got the heck out of Dodge, swishing my flippers as fast as I could to distance myself from the flesh eater. Lee swore his shark was a six-foot-long man-eater.

"Yes, dear, of course you saw the bigger, meaner shark," I retorted, letting him believe he was king of scuba diving.

The Passions of Paradise reef trip certainly delivered fun and adventure. The staff made a special effort to help guests make the most of their reef excursion. On the way back to port, the hosts poured complimentary wine and did face painting. We met Ron and Kevin, two gentlemen from Las Vegas. They were on a two-week holiday to Australia and said they had enjoyed every minute of it. We took our underwater cameras to get film developed right away and the four us shared photos over a cold beer at a waterfront restaurant.

Other than experiencing the reef's amazing ecosystem firsthand, we attended a special program in Cairns the following evening called "Reef Teach." We learned that the Great Barrier Reef was the world's largest structure made by living organisms. The two-hour class highlighted all aspects of the reef, most notably its reproduction. A few nights after a full moon in late spring or early summer, the vast coral reef system spawns with trillions and trillions of sperm and eggs released, which are visible to the naked eye. The event is described as a gigantic underwater snowstorm. The instructor was quite a character and turned simple information into the most fascinating trivia. It was well worth our $5 admission fee. We learned so much and could really appreciate the water world we had experienced.

We had one more day in Cairns and wanted to do something interesting and keep it within our budget. We scoured dozens of promo brochures at our backpacker lodge for full- and half-day trips in the area and decided on the Billy Tea Bush Safari. We were picked up at 6 a.m. for our Daintree and Cape Tribulation tour. The all-day four-wheel-drive tour took us to where the rain forest meets the reef, a few hours north of Cairns. Our first stop was the Daintree River. We boarded a boat to float down the tributary through the mangrove forest. We got a peek at the elusive green tree snake coiled around a tree limb and a baby estuarine crocodile sunning himself on a fallen branch by the river's shore.

It was the rainy season, so we had periodic downpours throughout the day. During one river crossing, flood water crested the tops of our tires. The drive was scenic and our tour guide was fun—all in all, it was a good day. Later that evening we were going to go to dinner, but Lee couldn't find his credit card. It would really be bad if it was stolen or lost—it was for emergencies or when we hadn't exchanged enough money. After backtracking our day, Lee realized it must still be in the Billy Tea Bush Safari credit card machine. He was right. Someone was watching over us. The tour operator dropped the card off later that night. It was a good lesson always to double-check that we had everything.

We were packed again and ready for our next exotic adventure, 12 days in Papua New Guinea (PNG). But first a quick call home to check in. "Hi Mom, how are you?" I said, excited just hearing her voice.

"How are you and where are you?"

"We're fine," I said. "We're in the northeastern part of Australia getting ready to go to Papua New Guinea."

"I have some bad news for you, Becky—Shirley Eader died," Mom somberly said.

I couldn't maintain my composure, tears flooded down my face. Shirley was one of my most loved people in the dairy industry. "What happened Mom?" I asked between my blubbers.

"She got pneumonia and with her black lung she just couldn't fight it."

"Mom, please give my best to the Eaders. I'll call in a few weeks. Give Dad a hug and kiss. I love you."

I couldn't get Shirley out of my mind. How senseless. How could God take one of his most devoted shepherds? She was special and always put everyone else's needs before her own. There hadn't been anything over the years that I asked Shirley that she didn't do. She helped with food stands, fund raisers—you name it, Shirley was there in flying colors. She was only 64 years old.

How could life be stripped from such an incredible person? Shirley and her granddaughter, Adriane, came to the yard sale we had before leaving the country. I'll never forget that chilly November day.

"We'll miss you," Shirley said hugging me tightly. "Please keep in touch, I love you."

"I love you, too," I said hugging her back just as tight. Little did I know it would be our final good-bye.

I had a restless night, thinking about Shirley and nervous about leaving for PNG in the morning. We loaded our things into the taxi before the sun was up and headed to the airport.

"Where are you flying to today?" the inquisitive taxi driver asked.

"We're going to Papua New Guinea," Lee answered.

The taxi driver looked shocked. "Do you have a death wish?" he asked with disbelief in his voice.

"No, why would you say that?" I asked with an uneasy tone nearly matching the driver's skepticism.

"Don't you know people get killed there? They use machetes," he responded as if subtly saying we were the dumbest travelers he'd ever met.

I was already nervous about going to PNG and the taxi driver was not helping at all. I told him we knew it was dangerous, but you had to be a smart traveler and not take unnecessary risks. Of course, as the words departed my lips, that's just what they were—words, meaningless words. My gut feeling was reaching into the depths of indecisiveness and treading on the skirt tails of fear. I was supposed to be the world traveler, the one for Lee to look to for guidance. So why was I feeling vulnerable? I think I had talked Lee into stopping at PNG so I could overcome my fear of the country and to prove I was a global veteran—I could travel anywhere, blend in anywhere, be safe anywhere. Was I just kidding myself?

Where Are the Penis Gourds?

C ontrary to belief, there were not wall-to-wall penis gourds in Papua New Guinea. Lee thought my only interest in PNG was to see the magnificently painted and shaped genital sheaths. Today, the natives typically only strapped the decorative gourds on their privates during special cultural shows or other native performances. The traditional costume could also be seen in really remote areas. I was a bit disappointed, but penis gourds or not—the country captured my imagination.

It was an exotic land, still uniquely untamed and mysterious. PNG offered a new experience for even an avid traveler. Considered to be the last frontier for travelers, the island nation is located just north of Australia's east coast. Densely populated at 4.5 million people, PNG gave us a fascinating look at village life and a chance to experience its rain-forest trekking, mountain hiking and snorkeling.

We were apprehensive about our visit and had no idea what to expect. We knew it was a country most travelers didn't visit due to its negative publicity and its dangerous reputation. People thought we were nuts venturing into such an unpredictable place. I admit I was scared, but wanted to disprove the horrible stories dramatized by the media. I'm certainly not downing the reporters—after all, I had worked for a daily newspaper for a decade. But I was well aware of the "power of the press." That's our job—right? Reporting

---

the news, dramatizing a bit to make the story pique the readers' interest. I hadn't always agreed with everything my comrades had written, but certainly respected the profession.

PNG stimulated my curiosity. I hoped to discover a people willing to embrace us, make us feel like friends and family rather than visitors. I wanted to experience something special. I hoped to tell other travelers not to judge an entire nation because it gets a little bad coverage. As we flew to our exotic destination, I studied the guidebook to be as familiar as I could with the country. I memorized proper traveler etiquette, the dos and don'ts in PNG—we had to be safe. We landed at Port Moresby, the capital. According to the guidebook, this was PNG's most dangerous city. The day's headlines were "Five rascals die robbing bank," and "Tucker shop owners killed with machetes." I guess that taxi driver wasn't bluffing—people were still murdered with machetes.

My anxiety level multiplied in seconds. I was more nervous than ever. Rascal was the common name for a troublemaker, thief or murderer. The rascals had landed a helicopter on top of a bank. The police killed all of them. PNG authorities had no patience with law breakers. There was no such thing as innocent until proven guilty—police had a zero-tolerance policy. Perhaps the "No Tolerance for Violence," campaign helped curb crime—we could only hope. We realized we had to use precautions and not put ourselves in potentially dangerous situations.

We sat in the airport reviewing the local newspapers, waiting for the connecting flight to Mt. Hagen in the central Highlands. It was only 20 minutes before our flight and we hadn't heard our boarding call. Finally I asked, and to my astonishment we were told the flight we wanted was out of another terminal down the street. Panicked, we quickly gathered our bags and lugged them down the stairs. My heart pumped like a tire taking on air, heavy and labored. We ran with our bags. Outside the international terminal it was hot and muggy. The streets seemed to brighten the sun's rays. I squinted.

Our flight was out of the domestic terminal. No longer protected by the armed soldiers inside, my chest tightened with more anxiety. *Oh God, please don't let there be any rascals hanging outside the airport,* I nervously thought as I clutched my backpack tightly, looking like a helpless beast thrust in a den of lions. People lined the sidewalks, some standing, some sitting. They stared at the crazy white folks with all their gear in tow. Some looked despondent while others looked curious, almost threatening. Maybe it was in my head. It wasn't fair to judge them by what they wore or how they looked at us. If we missed our connecting flight we would have to spend the night in Port Moresby, a fate I feared.

Luckily, we found our departure gate with just ten minutes to spare. We boarded our questionable 16-seat passenger airplane. On the way, the plane rose and fell through air pockets. My stomach was queasy. I closed my eyes and concentrated on happy times. We landed in Mt. Hagen. It was the smallest airport I'd ever seen. There was no baggage claim area or a revolving belt. All luggage was piled on a cart in a tiny room. Everyone grabbed their bags and departed, except us. The owners of Haus Poroman, a lodge that was supposed to have backpackers' accommodations, had our flight information and promised to pick us up. No one showed. There was no one holding a sign or even anyone who looked like they were searching for someone. Lee and I turned to each other with that abashed look of *What the hell are we going to do now?*

We strapped on our backpacks and went outside of the so-called airport. Our money belts were hidden in our pants and our camera gear was safely tucked away in our day packs. It was as tropical in Mt. Hagen as it was in Port Moresby. Monsoon season was at its height when temperatures soared, humidity peaked and rain typically fell daily. We waited ten minutes. No one came. We started to walk eastward, but had no idea where the road would lead. I prayed someone would rescue us. I had no ambition nor the energy to walk anywhere with our bags. Still, no one came.

"This is good for me, this is good exercise," I said trying to psych myself up, but already felt the weight of my backpack cutting into my shoulders. That mind over matter stuff just didn't work sometimes, but I did believe in the power of prayer. We hadn't taken ten steps until a man jumped out of a vehicle.

"Americans? Beeeeky and Leeeee?" he said. The little man before us was a godsend. Who knew where we would have ended up on foot?

Thomas was a short man, very polite, and he spoke pretty good English. He was about 50 years old with dark brown skin and wore old-looking, but neat clothes. Once at the lodge's town office we met Keith Wilson, the owner. He told Thomas to take us wherever we needed to go before heading up the mountain to Haus Poroman.

Keith was a hearty white man with fair hair and a reserved disposition. It surprised me that someone involved in the travel industry was so withdrawn. Thomas took us to the bank and accompanied us inside. I started to count the colorful paper bills the teller had given me when Thomas quickly rushed to my side. "Put money away quickly, put it away safe," he said. "Many travelers robbed when leave bank."

Just freakin' great, I thought. Just when I started to feel a little more comfortable, I was blasted with the prospect of danger again. I didn't feel any safer in the country and had certainly not overcome my fear yet. I found myself trying to be friendly. I smiled a lot, while at the same time continually looking over my shoulder and searching for potential threats.

Thomas drove a vehicle with two seats up front for the driver and passenger. The back was equipped with two long seats parallel to the sides of the vehicle rather than from side to side. The design allowed more passenger room. We stopped back at the office and picked up Stacey, a young national, as PNG natives are referred. Stacey was from New Britain, one of PNG's outer islands. Her family owned a hotel and she was working at Haus Poroman to gain additional experience. She was cute, petite, versed in English. Her amiable nature mellowed me.

Our ascent up the mountain was not just a ride, it was an adventure. The six-mile journey was the bumpiest trip of my life. We held on tightly to the ceiling bars as we were tossed completely off our seats. The heavy rains had taken their toll on the dirt roads. Crevices and holes dominated the path. One vehicle had the misfortune of falling into a hole and had been abandoned. Another had a flat tire and was left as well. In many cases the owners didn't have spare tires or the resources to repair their vehicles. It created a sort of makeshift auto graveyard alongside the back roads as many were never retrieved.

Different cultures intrigued me. Their beliefs, their way of life—I was always engrossed with the tales and information people shared. Some stories were heartwarming, but others were hard to digest, making me really happy I lived in America, a land of choice and freedom.

We rounded the last corner and almost collided with a villager and his hog. I guess he was out for a late afternoon stroll with the family pet. The man paraded his massive porker by a rope attached to its right front hoof. I learned later that swine were highly regarded in PNG.

Keith and his wife, Maggie, had landscaped a peaceful and beautiful retreat that attracted numerous dignitaries to its quiet mountainside haven. The Haus Poroman lodge was built in the village of Kunguma, Maggie's family's tribe. She had met her Australian husband, Keith, years earlier while he was working at a Mt. Hagen bank.

The lodge's hosts, Jack and Barbara and several others, made sure we received the full PNG experience. The main lodge was a large log structure. A fireplace in the center gave it a cozy atmosphere. We spent many evenings by the shadows of flickering flames, talking about our diverse backgrounds.

Our little bungalow, a circular hut made of bamboo and grass, had a double bed, and a wooden patio overlooking a meticulous flower garden. Tall red blooms reached to the base of our little balcony. A variety of leafy variegated ferns reminded me of vertical growing hosta-lined paths. Eight-foot trees with large green palm fronds shot up throughout the landscape. A dandelion-colored ground cover surrounded the opposite bungalow while dainty carnation-like reddish-purple flowers climbed down another front lawn.

Warm showers were fueled by wood because electricity was limited. Every day a generator turned on from 6 to 9 a.m. and from 5 to 11 p.m. Haus Poroman had a dedicated staff. A frail, barefooted elderly woman welcomed us daily with a toothless grin and tight embrace. Her tiny stature made her seem like a descendent from the land of little people. She helped make sure flower beds were well groomed and lawns were raked. She didn't speak a word of English, but warmed us daily by her generous squeeze and innocent giggle.

I was amazed that we felt so comfortable with people we couldn't actually communicate with in words. Intentions were translated through simple smiles, handshakes, hugs or nods. I realized it with Lee as well. In certain traveling situations, speaking to one another was impossible. There were times when our eyes met, we exchanged a silent, but reassuring glance. It was often during those wordless gestures when my heart tingled with a sort of calm, knowing we were together and hoping it was for the long haul. Marriage doesn't just happen and anyone who thinks it does, well, that's probably why they have a miserable marriage or are divorced. We knew we would face uncertainties and difficulties on the trip and in our relationship, but we believed we'd handle them, for better or for worse. We didn't realize how worse it might get.

Jack was the epitome of bachelorhood. He was in his early 20s, working in the travel industry and obviously wowing the female gender. He was thin, kept his long black locks pulled back in a rubber band and spoke very structured English. His receptive personality made us feel safe. During evenings at Haus Poroman, Jack's specialty was entertaining guests, answering questions and discussing sightseeing possibilities.

Sheer palatable ecstasy was the only way to describe Haus Poroman's cuisine. Homemade soup was the starter, nearly tantalizing our taste buds beyond limits. The following courses were nothing short of gourmet euphoria. Every morsel, every bite, was swallowed in absolute pleasure. My clothes got increasingly tighter. I had no intention of dieting and missing out on all of that wonderful food. My philosophy was, *We've already paid for it, so eat it and worry about losing it later.* I was going to enjoy every aspect of the enchanting country, from its people to its breathtaking landscapes and from its cultural experiences to its food. However, my weight gain did bother me. I looked at Lee with a depressing puppy-eyed goggle. "I'm a chubby girl."

"But you're really cute," he said with a soft smile and kind voice.

The great thing about traveling with a friend was the other person's capability of cheering you up, making you laugh and, most of all, someone to share experiences, good and bad. Lee had been a pretty good traveling partner, but not like traveling with a girlfriend. I had to train him to detect things the way my girlfriends did. If there was something in my teeth, or a booger hanging out of my nose or if my makeup was smeared—it was Lee's job to inform me. But men just don't think of things like that, so more often then not, I walked around with snot under my nose, food stuck between my teeth and mascara smudged around my eyes. I would either have to keep nagging him or send him to a class of Wife Detection 101.

In PNG I wasn't worried about my appearance, but told Lee he had to practice his duty so he wouldn't slip up when we went back to Australia. Most nationals working in the travel business were well groomed and excited to talk about their country. Jack was a very knowledgeable host and shared much information about PNG culture and history. The country was originally inhabited by Asian settlers more than 50,000 years ago. The first European to set foot in the daunting place was Portuguese explorer Jorge de Meneses in 1526-27, who named it Ilahas dos Papuas or Island of the Fuzzy Hairs. Spanish explorer Inigo Ortiz de Tetes later called it New Guinea because he thought the people were similar to those of Guinea in Africa.

The lodge employee chronicled highland life, enthralling us with every anecdote. What fascinated us most was that highland inhabitants didn't see their first white man until the late 1930s. The Leahy boys, three Australian brothers, ventured into the Highlands in 1938, the first white men to explore PNG's interior. They not only struck gold, but found nearly one million nationals. Until then, the very primitive highland people had no idea a world existed outside of their isolated mountain home.

In addition to discovering gold and introducing the highland people to a life unknown, the brothers fathered many offspring during the next several decades. We had the pleasure of meeting two Leahy descendants, Maggie Leahy Wilson, proprietor of Haus Poroman, and her cousin, Joe Leahy. Joe was featured in two documentaries that depicted the hardships of a half-white, half-PNG coffee plantation owner and the local tribespeople who worked in the rural enterprise. We watched the film *First Contact*, remarkable live footage of the Leahy brothers' initial meeting with the highland people.

We hiked through the Napilayer Valley where the Leahy brothers made their riches. The brothers didn't do it on their own, though; much of their success was credited to the help they received from nationals who searched for and harvested the gold. The Leahys paid the nationals in kina shells from PNG's shores, along with axes, picks and other modern Australian tools of the '30s and '40s. The kina, PNG's official money, was named for the significant role the kina shell played in the country's early development. I was curious about the anthropologists in PNG during our visit. They were filming and interviewing community elders before they died and the information was lost forever. We weren't elders, but were interviewed just the same. Perhaps our mugs would show up in some PNG documentary.

Typically tourists only have the opportunity to see the sights and main attractions, while travelers tend to learn more about the people, mingle with the natives and experience their culture firsthand. That's what traveling meant to me, a chance to meet new people in timeworn lands, to make friends by their fire and to do as the natives did.

During our half-day hike through the Napilayer Valley we met farmers working their land. No tractor, no rototiller, no oxen—only a barefooted, shirtless man with a hoe. We admired the woman who took great care in sweeping the dirt areas around burial plots. Half-clothed and naked children played with toys made from vegetables and tree branches.

It had rained that morning making the hike muddy and challenging. Lee and I, our guide and a German couple in their 50s, slipped and slid down mud paths, crashing through overgrown vegetation. In some areas we had to form a line, holding on to the next person firmly to get up or down the slope safely. I wore my hiking books, but the caking sludge made traction impossible. Our stop for lunch was a welcome break. A cheese sandwich and fruit provided by Haus Poroman was a treat. With bulging eyes I watched the German woman pick out her cheese slices and pitch them to the ground.

"Don't you like cheese?" I asked.

"No, I daant," she said.

"Do you like any kind of cheese?" I continued, probably being a real pain in her butt.

"I hata all cheeses," she confessed.

I was shocked and couldn't think of anyone who hated all types of cheese. I thought, *Poor woman, missing out on all that good cheese.* Of course this was the dairy farmer's daughter coming out in me. I couldn't help myself, I always endorsed dairy products and milk. It was in my blood. Agriculture was the one thing, no matter where I was in the world, I could promote. It was my love, my passion.

I had a real appreciation for farmers in PNG. Eighty-five percent of the country's population were subsistence farmers, growing produce merely for survival. Many nationals grew extra crops and marketed the surplus or traded it for other main food staples like milk and bread. Nationals farmed on all available land, often resorting to very difficult and deadly terrain. Sometimes their farm plots were on such steep slopes they tied a rope to their leg and secured it to a rock or tree to prevent a fall to their death. I looked in astonishment at the farming parcels on vertical mountainsides. Women scaled hillsides heaving huge *bilums* that hung from their heads and clutched infants beneath their arms.

We praised their resilience, their determination to farm every available space. They worked hard in order to display their best produce, livestock or handicrafts in the town market. We visited the daily bazaar dumbstruck by the scents, sounds, colors and contagious smiles. We strolled through the crowd, zigzagging between playful children and piles of root crops, nuts and fruit.

Women sat on the ground in front of their perfectly stacked selections. They continually washed each piece and restacked them. Sun glistened off the wet rinds of the inexpensive food. Presentation was important. Whether it was produce or homemade ropes to tie the family hog, everything was neat and tidy. Women occupied the chicken pens, sitting right on the earth's floor stroking their prized birds. They took such pride in their goods and services. I asked why most of the people working in the gardens or staffing the market spots were women. We were told it's just part of their culture, women were just expected to be a majority of labor in PNG.

Once we took in all the local charm, it was time to venture out of our comfort zone, away from the protection of Haus Poroman and into the chaotic rat race of local existence.

Tic Toc

Our master the clock, it disrupts our morning,
As it shouts out its warning;

We wake from our sleep, feet hit the floor,
Limited time to get out the door;

Make it to work just under the wire,
Long for the time we can retire;

Our day begins with a mountain of work,
We glance at the clock, it gives us a shirk;

Attack your tasks at a feverish pace,
You're not going to win, just finish the race;

Check on the clock, its hands start to quicken,
Head starts to ache, heart starts to sicken;

Stop...Smell the roses, The clock's not your master, it's there for
*   you,*
To let you know there is time for what you want to do;

Like floating down a river or talking with a friend,
Time just keeps moving, no beginning...no end.

Lee Chaney

Reaching the Summit

More than 10,000 natives and visitors are killed in vehicle accidents on PNG highways and back roads annually, but those statistics didn't dissuade us from trying the local mode of transportation. Our funds were limited, so we couldn't afford the luxuries of first-class travel and top drivers. The locals used public motor vehicles, referred to simply as PMVs.

PMVs covered the gamut of pickup trucks, vans, buses and even large farm trucks, with people squeezed in alongside goats and hogs. We walked to the Mt. Hagen plaza. Drivers shouted the names of destinations. It was prodigious confusion. We looked at each other and laughed, not knowing what we were getting ourselves into.

"Kundiawa, Kundiawa!" a man shouted in a deep, rapid manner. "Kundiawa, Kundiawa."

After bartering for the best ride, we climbed aboard an 18-passenger bus and found seats. More and more people boarded, but the seats were full. A ridiculous 32 people jammed onto the bus. Kids sat on their parents' laps, adults squeezed on the edge of seats or sat on the boarding steps. No seat belts, no nothing.

The close proximity enabled me to examine people's scars, breathe in their interesting odors and wonder where they were going. I tried to enjoy the scenery, but soon closed my eyes and prayed that we would arrive safely. The drivers were borderline crazy and their road skills left a lot to be desired. I cringed every time the bus fell off the shoulder or seemed to balance on two tires negotiating a turn or swerving from an oncoming vehicle.

Every town and city had a designated area where PMV drivers parked and yelled their sometimes indecipherable destinations. Depending on locals for directions always worried me. Years earlier on a seven-week trip alone in Europe my host family, who spoke very little English, whisked me away to the railway station in Parma, Italy, to catch a train. I remember it vividly.

"Are you sure this train is going to Fribourg, Switzerland?" I asked.

"Si, si, mea sura," my host mother said, nodding her head.

"Not Freiberg, Germany, but Fribourg, Switzerland, right?" I asked, still with a questionable look.

"Si, si, ciao Beeecky," Mom Mutti said and kissed me on both cheeks.

"Ciao," I said. "Grazie."

I dragged my bags onto the train and sat by a window for the long train ride. A conductor examined and stamped my youth Eurail pass.

"This train is going to Fribourg, Switzerland, right?" I asked.

"Si, Fribourg," he answered.

I curled up in the side of my seat to sleep, knowing the seven-hour journey would pass quicker. I woke and wiped my sleepy eyes. Every half-hour there was usually a stop when the conductor announced the train's arrival. Something didn't sound right. I looked out my window and to my disbelief we had bypassed Switzerland and indeed were headed to Freiberg, Germany. I couldn't believe it. What were my options? No one was waiting for me in Germany, they were waiting for me in Switzerland. I had one choice, to get off the train and wait for a train going the other way. It was 1 a.m., just about the most dangerous time for a young woman to be out at night alone in a foreign country. I was so scared.

I prayed for the next train to get there quickly. Finally, after what seemed forever, a train rolled down the track headed back toward Switzerland. I was so careful to get what I thought was the correct information. My supposed seven-hour train ride turned into a 14-hour epic through three countries and then backtracking. It was a good travel lesson and a test of patience and bravery.

So if I was a little weary of our PMV ride I had good reason to be. The bus was so full the walls looked like they might split at the seams if the bus hit one more pothole. After four hours of surviving road rage we arrived in Kundiawa. After a few deep breaths and Hail Marys (and I'm not even Catholic), we found another PMV to take us up the mountain to the village of Kegsugl.

A short-bed pickup truck was the only PMV heading to Kegsugl. I searched for a place to sit, the truck was packed. Our two backpacks joined two other duffel bags, three huge sacks of vegetables, eight boxes of supplies, a tire, plus 14 other people. We were practically sitting on top of each other.

Two of the women had umbrellas trying to shield their small children from the sun's harsh rays that felt like fingers probing our skin with stinging heat.

They stretched their arms to share their umbrella with me. I smiled and thanked them, but with hand gestures encouraged them to protect their children as my baseball cap protected my face. PNG people were kind. They didn't have much and shared what they had. How did they acquire such a bad rap around the world?

Lee sat in the rear corner of the truck on the tailgate and I nestled in the center, my legs straddling a sack of vegetables. The next three hours were somehow both frightening and invigorating as we ascended the deadliest dirt road I'd ever experienced. No guard rails, no shoulders. Drops plummeted several miles. My heart raced with excitement, fear. My legs were cramped and they fell asleep. I repositioned them, only to be poked in my bum by whatever veggies I was sure I was smashing.

The other passengers' kind gestures and smiles made me feel a little more at ease like we were on a Sunday drive without a worry in the world—right, tell me another one. The driver got dangerously close to the edges. I made the mistake of asking the man sitting beside Lee about road safety. "Do any trucks go over the edge?"

"Oh yessa, yessa," he quickly answered. "No one surviva, toowa fara down, peoples everywhere."

One of these days I'd learn to keep my big trap shut. Did I really want to hear that—hell no! I was already a nervous wreck. Several sections of the road were washed away by heavy rains leaving a narrow path to navigate. I held my breath as we crossed one washed-out area, knowing the slightest movement could mean death. Again, I asked myself, *Why am I here? I'm too young to die.* Lee saw the horror in my face.

"Many timme, slips notta fixed fora weeks," my tailgate buddy said. "Sometimes da whole road washed daway and peoples trapped up mountain fora longa timme."

Oh great, I thought. *The road is going to disappear and we'll be stranded for weeks on a remote PNG mountainside.* During dangerous or literal breathtaking occurrences, I often conjured up worst-case scenarios in my mind. My vision that day, of course, was us plunging to our deaths because our nutso driver went too fast around a turn. He was psychotic and if I thought being on foot was any safer from the lunatic, I'd have walked. "It's a good thing our family can't see us now," I muttered to myself. They'd totally freak and wonder why we were trying to get ourselves killed.

Scaling the 57-mile road was slow and dusty, but we were delighted with the opportunity to visit with other passengers. Many times Lee and I exchanged that silent glance, that reassuring look of love, that sparkle of excitement mixed with a tinge of "Oh my God." *This is really cool, no one would believe this,* I thought, still filled with fear, but reveling in the real-life fantasy.

We were headed to the farthest guest lodge up the mountain which served as the starting point for travelers hiking to Mt. Wilhelm, PNG's highest mountain. I didn't know what the hike would hold, but I did know the vehicle excursion just to get to the base was an adrenaline rush like slow-cooking candy reaching its boiling point.

Passengers were dropped along the way and more were picked up. As we waited for the transition of passengers at one stop, a little old lady approached the PMV carrying several bunches of strawberries for sale. Her frailness was overshadowed by the inner pride glowing from her wrinkled face as she held up her neat display of strawberries. Small, red berries hung from braided stems—she smiled confidently. An elderly man in the back of the truck purchased four bunches. He handed each of his two little grandsons a bunch and then handed the other woven creations to Lee and me. I was overwhelmed with his thoughtfulness. How lucky we were to experience the true spirit and soul of PNG. Their humanity inspired us.

Lee and I were the last two passengers. The truck stopped, but there wasn't a lodge in sight.

"Last stop," the driver yelled.

"But where is the lodge?" I asked.

"Two mora mile," he said pointing to a steep incline up the mountain. I looked at it, then looked at Lee.

"Please, Lee, after this three-hour drama, please see if the driver will take us to the top," I begged. "I can't do it, I just don't think I can carry my backpack two more miles. It's going to be dark soon." Thank God, Lee bartered with the driver and for an additional $2 each, he took us to the top, to the lodge's front door. I threw my backpack out, toppled over the side, sluggish and worn out, but relieved. "Lee, had I known the last two miles were like that, I would have paid that man $20 each to get us here," I said.

Lake Pindi Yaundo Trout Farm, also known as Betty's Place, was in the village of Kegsugl. "Hi! I'm Betty. Welcome," a woman barely five feet tall said, but wearing a smile that elevated her short stature. Born and raised in PNG, Betty was a jovial and informative host. She had light bronze skin and a soft head of curly graying hair. Betty and her Australian husband, Kent, and many nationals spent years clearing rain forest and jungle to carve the farming and floral paradise out of the mountainside. They raised trout, pigs, ducks, rabbits and goats, provided work for many of the local villagers and took in travelers who had hopes of climbing Mt. Wilhelm.

The guest lodge was homey and provided a peaceful atmosphere for travelers to relax, read or have intellectual conversations. A veranda circled halfway around the lodge and overlooked the entire property, which was meticulously landscaped. Dozens of little ponds were scattered throughout the oasis of perennials, and green and flourishing ground cover. Many types of brilliant-colored flowers provided beautiful table centerpieces.

In the midst of cooking us trout that we later dubbed the best we'd ever eaten, Betty explained the complexities of PNG culture. She told us that a week earlier she had accompanied a friend for negotiating a "bride price." "One family offers a few thousand kina and several hogs to another family in order to acquire a bride for their son," she said. "Men stay in their native tribes and daughters are expected to be exchanged for money and hogs. Some men have many wives. Typically when the bride price is negotiated the bride to be is 15 to 18 years old, while the groom is 25 years old or older."

"It's hard to believe that is still practiced," I said, surprised but intrigued with the local custom.

"Many, many old traditions still our life," Betty added.

Pigs in paradise or so it seemed. It was Betty who finally explained the importance of swine in PNG. The prestige of a family was largely based on the number and size of their hogs, a great status symbol in the country. No wonder many villagers proudly escorted their prized pigs around the village.

Other than the delectable baked trout, Betty and her cook prepared a vegetable dish with sauce. The meal was topped off by a bowl of strawberries smothered in cream. All my traveling experiences in third-world countries had taught me one critical rule—"If you can't boil it, cook it or peel it—

don't eat it. And under no circumstance do you eat anything that has been washed or has ice in it."

Most bacteria and disease is harbored in water. So there I was staring down at a scrumptious bowl of plump red juicy strawberries peeking out beneath mountains of cream saying, *"Eat me, eat me!"* My common sense said, *"Don't eat it you fool,"* but my tummy said, *"Yum, yum, go for it. So what if I get a little food poisoning in the middle of nowhere and almost die."* I devoured the entire bowl. My iron gut prevailed, but it was risky.

We were the only guests and were definitely getting the first-class treatment. Betty visited with us for hours. "Before the times changed, mothers and children slept in one hut and all the men slept in another hut called the men's house," she said. "When a boy was old enough to do chores, he was moved to the men's house. Today men and women can share the same hut, but not the same room." Naturally, I wanted to ask, *Well, then, how do they make babies?* But, surprisingly, I kept my mouth shut.

Bedtime came early in anticipation of our big hiking day. The generator turned off, light faded. The cold mountain air sieved in through windowsills. We snuggled close and drifted off to sleep. In the middle of the night, Lee and I both woke up at the same time—the bed shook, nearly bouncing off the floor.

"Are you having one?" Lee asked, referring to the intimate impulses I occasionally feel in my sleep. His tired eyes were half opened; he was dazed.

"No!" I yelled as my eyes practically bugged out of my head. "It's an earthquake!"

We didn't know what to do. Before we could jump out of bed and run to safety, the bed stopped shaking. It was over. "Wow, that was pretty exciting," I said as we both lay there trying to comprehend what just happened.

The following day we found out the earthquake registered 5.6 on the Richter scale—I guess we were lucky. In the morning we departed with our porter and guide, Arnold and Joe, respectively, to hike to Pindaunde Lakes at 10,500 feet.

The idea was to arrive at the lake to allow enough time in the afternoon to climatize our bodies to the altitude before attempting Mt. Wilhelm's summit, a powerful 14,789 feet. That's higher than Pike's Peak.

I'm not sure if it was altitude sickness (or "attitude" sickness, according to Lee) but I felt sick. Maybe it was due to the fact I had eaten breakfast right before I started hiking or the reality I was a tad out of shape.

After the first 25 minutes my nauseous stomach coupled with my weary body slowed me to a snail's pace. Even frequent stops didn't help. Arnold carried my day pack. I had two camera cases strapped on, but the five pounds of gear felt more like I was lugging 20 extra pounds. It got to the point where I walked a few steps and planted my butt on a rock or fallen tree—I had to rest, slow my heart palpitations. Perspiration dripped from my brow. I couldn't go on.

"Come on, baby, you can do it, just take your time," Lee coached. Along the path, Lee often told me to sit and rest. His words encouraged me to trudge on. I didn't want to let Lee down. He had looked forward to hiking PNG's highest mountain. I pushed myself as I'd never pushed myself physically.

"We almosta dere," the guides repeatedly said, but we never seemed to get there.

Finally, I collapsed on the verge of vomiting—I was totally beat. My rapid breaths sucked more energy from my body. I felt defeated, my legs ached. I wanted to give up, but my inner spirit wouldn't allow it. I needed Lee to give me one of his alluring smiles, an inspirational gesture or one of his poetic verses to pick me up and push me on. That's when my loving husband looked down at me and said, "Dear, you look like a sick horse that needs to be shot and put out of its misery."

Not the motivational words I was looking for, and at the time, I found no humor in it at all. Somehow I found the strength and struggled to my feet—I made the conscious decision to get to the midway point without taking another rest. I was going to make it or die trying. It was the most exhausting thing I'd ever done and was much more difficult than my Routeburn Track hike I'd thought was such a challenge.

I battled for every step, battled for every breath; finally, I made it—drained and delirious, but with a quiet and overwhelming sense of accomplishment. I expired to the ground like the wicked witch in *The Wizard of Oz* after she's splashed with water. The witch melted but I felt triumph as I basked in the sun's glimmering light bouncing off the lake's calm surface. My victory break made me realize there was no way in this lifetime I could attempt the summit. I sat back on Lee's backpack, my muscles pierced with pain—tears filled my eyes.

"Lee, I'm really proud I made it this far, but I won't attempt the summit. You'll have to do it without me."

It was very difficult for me to give up. We had planned to do it together. But it was Lee's dream and more like my reverie. If I couldn't make it, I would be destroying his dream. The guide's rule was if I had to turn back, we all had to turn back. No one was left on the mountain trail alone because several climbers had lost their lives. Twelve people had already died hiking to the summit and I didn't especially want to be number 13. So it was decided that Lee would attempt the summit with Joe. We relaxed the rest of the afternoon. Lee and Joe's departure was set for 2 a.m.

A gutted cabin at the lake provided shelter for hikers before their summit attempt. It was a modest, single structure with wooden boards for beds, a one-inch foam mattress pad, and a little gas stove for cooking. Arnold and Joe, along with the hut's caretaker, Prans, and his nephew, David, lit a fire outside to cook their dinner. They cooked potatoes while Lee and I boiled water for Oodles of Noodles. (I remembered Oodles of Noodles was a main food staple when I was a college student. My roommate and I slurped down the cheap food in order to afford quarter beer nights.)

Jack had taken us shopping to prepare for our hike. We needed to buy water, salt, soup and nuts. He also suggested chocolate for energy boosters. Heck, I didn't have any argument there—if we had to have chocolate, well, all righty then.

We also bought gloves and wool socks. It was very cold on the mountain. Arnold had no coat. Lee let him borrow his thermal L.L. Bean hooded jacket. We got in bed early and played cards from the bit of light illuminated by a tiny candle. We blew it out by 8, but Lee was very restless. I'm sure he was a little nervous and anxious about his climb.

The alarm rang its irritating jingle at 1 a.m. We finally pulled ourselves from the comfort of our sleeping bags at 1:30 a.m. Water was boiled for hot tea. Joe had a pair of rubber boots, but no socks. The temperatures at the summit were said to dip well below freezing. I found my new pair of wool socks and gave them to Joe since I wasn't going. His mouthful of big white teeth almost blinded me with his excitement. He thanked me and immediately put them on. But he didn't pull them on his feet, he slid them on his hands. I guess his feet were tougher than his hands. The people had such resilience. I was impressed by their strength, their character and above all, their unselfish personalities.

Donning only head lamps, a windbreaker and gloves, Lee and Joe walked toward the door. "Joe, take care of Lee," I said as they opened the door to leave. Joe turned and nodded. He and Lee both gave me the thumbs-up signal and walked out the door. Lee also had his day pack with hiking essentials—water, snacks, emergency batteries, matches and two cameras. They left the lake hut at 2:30 a.m., a half-hour late, but still anticipating the summit at sunrise.

Lee had to retrieve his coat from Arnold for the hike so I gave my coat to Arnold for the rest of the night. I retired to my empty room and curled up in my sleeping bag and threw Lee's over me. I took my flashlight and scanned the walls reading the graffiti left by the hikers before us. Messages of love, sex and triumph with the dated climbs of success were scribbled on the walls and on the hardwood bed. I tried to sleep, but it was hopeless. I lay there thinking about the long, dark climb. I prayed Lee would come back safely. Plus, I was a real fraidy cat. I was alone and nervous and kept Lee's Swiss army knife opened and ready in case I needed it—a side of the Drama Queen coming out in me again.

Horror stories of backpackers being robbed, raped and murdered invaded my dreams. Maybe the fact I was in the middle of nowhere like the folks in *Friday the 13th* when they were all slaughtered by psycho Jason. Chances were slim that someone would hike through the cold to a remote mountain lodge, but it wasn't impossible. Desperate people execute desperate measures.

As daylight burned away the morning mist and dried the dew-covered grass I carried my sleeping bag down by the lake and sat there waiting and watching for a sign of life coming down the mountain. I was suspended in time like a helium-filled balloon floating endlessly in the distance with little hope of being grounded anytime soon. I nervously peered toward the mountain face. Lee was fit, he was strong, he was smart—but then so were the other 12 adventurous hikers who had lost their lives. If anyone could get worked up with worry, it was me.

"Miss, Miss, I sees zem!" Prans yelled as he ran toward me with a pair of binoculars. He handed them to me. I closed one eye trying to focus.

"I can't see them, Prans. Are you sure?"

"Me shure, me shure," Prans said, helping to point the binoculars in the right direction.

"I see them, I see them!" I said with much elation and relief.

Two tiny dots moved down the mountain. What a weight off my heart! It took two hours for those little dots to materialize in actual eyesight on the other side of the lake. The mountain reflected beautifully in the still green water. I walked around the lake's bank to meet them. As they got closer I had a huge welcome grin, but Lee wasn't smiling at all. In fact he looked distraught, even distracted.

"So how was it?" I asked.

"It was the most physically and emotionally draining experience of my life," he said in a serious, almost grim manner.

At that moment I thanked God for getting Lee back to me safely and for helping guide me to the decision to stay at the lake hut. Lee raved about Joe's performance, remarkable for a 54-year-old man. "He just put his hands behind his back like it was an afternoon stroll in the park and kept a steady pace," Lee said. "Most of the time all I could see were the soles of Joe's boots. I had to stop several times to catch my breath, the altitude sucked oxygen away. I couldn't believe how difficult it was, especially near the top."

It was exciting for me to relive the climb with him as he told me of the challenges along the way and his determination to conquer the mountain. "On about my tenth stop I thought to myself, 'What kind of fucking death wish do you have coming up this mountain?' We crested the summit just after sunrise. It was an incredible view. You could see for miles and miles in all directions. It was unbelievably frigid and, after taking a few photographs, both cameras froze up."

He described the trek, the difficulties and the rough terrain that made the hike more like mountain climbing, concluding with "You should really be glad you stayed back." After hearing those words I was happy I remained behind, but was so proud of Lee for making the summit. Bandages were still wrapped around his aching knees. He was exhausted, but had acquired a new sense of achievement— exhilarated by his performance.

Back at the lake hut he lay on the ground to recoup his strength and energy. After three hours he sat up, still groggy. "You don't have to worry about me attempting Mt. Everest anytime soon," he said.

That was certainly a relief. Unlike the hike to the lake hut, the descent back to Betty's Place was much more enjoyable. To Lee's surprise, I led the group.

"You have a good pace on there, you must think a cold beer is waiting for you," Lee teased.

"There's no cold beer, but there is a Diet Coke in Betty's refrigerator," I said as my stride quickened.

We made it down the mountain in two hours as opposed to the four-hour hike from hell the previous day. We were welcomed by Betty's bright smile and bouncy personality. She served us scones with strawberry jam and cream, then excused herself to attend to yet another village emergency. To the villagers, Betty was the matriarch, the one they respected and looked up to. The one they sought out for guidance and assistance in times of crisis. After we consumed our tasty treats, it was time for a much-needed nap. Lee was still functioning on very little sleep. I was tired, but when we went into our room, I mustered up a little energy to tell Lee I knew the exact remedy for him to rest comfortably. With a big smirk stretched across my face, I looked into his eyes.

"Pretend I'm just another backpacker you just met," I whispered. "Pretend you picked me up and I speaka no English."

I caught him off guard and we ended up having a fun afternoon rendezvous. Later we heard voices and knew other backpackers had arrived. We joined them in the dining area. There was a German couple, a husband and wife from Austria, and two young German women traveling together. Betty burst into the kitchen. "I apologize, but dinner will be late this evening," she said frantically. "We have another emergency in the village and a baby is dying."

She disappeared out the door. While we waited for Betty's return, we backpackers shared travel stories. I always relished hearing other people's travel tales, their exotic and sometimes dangerous destinations, the characters they met and the things they experienced.

A year ago Ingrid had taken an 11-day trek in Nepal. Everyone in the group had dropped out along the way due to exhaustion and altitude sickness. Ingrid was one of three people who made it to the mountain top. "We had a great view of Mt. Everest," she said. "It was really tough, but a personal best for me."

Biorne and Brigitte had been traveling for several months. They had dated for eight years, and suddenly took their life savings, flew to Guatemala and bought a sailboat. With no sailing experience, they bravely took to the seas and sailed to PNG. They had a few mishaps along the way, but had enjoyed every leg of their voyage. When their funds ran short they did street performances in different cities and towns.

Professionally, they operated their own stilt-dancing company in Germany, so entertaining came naturally. The Austrians looked like a health-conscious, fit couple, who probably wouldn't have a problem with the Mt. Wilhelm climb. They left the cold weather of Europe to take in the tropical wonders of PNG and were set to hike to the lake hut in the morning. We continued to wait for Betty and sipped warm tea.

She returned hours later. As she prepared dinner she told us of her ordeal. They arrived at the hospital to find no beds and no lights. Women were having babies by candlelight on the floor. Betty wished people in outer villages could get better medical attention. The biggest problem, according to Betty, was the fact that the PNG government was corrupt. Many men in the political arena were getting richer while the people of PNG suffered. It was a sad story, but one that was true in many third-world nations.

"When tribal leaders are voted into parliament, the quick rise to power is so overwhelming that they don't know how to handle it," she explained.

Evening tea was ready and well worth the wait. We started with a water-based soup that looked tasteless with onion and green pepper floating around. It was quite good, but not as delicious as Betty's milk soup with onions, carrots and butter we had had when we arrived. Our final meal was topped off by baked trout with garlic and other herbs. Fried potatoes, carrots and cabbage was our side dish. I'd miss Betty's humor and I'd miss her cooking. We called it a night and hoped to have an early start. Every place we stayed held significant memories. At Betty's I'd remember the seeds balanced on a plate on a ceiling beam that she was drying for a cousin to take back to Europe. "It's illegal," she said. "I hope he doesn't get caught."

I'd recall Betty outside with her gumboots up to her knees feeding hogs and ducks and then wading in waist-deep water to scoop up a few trout for the evening meal. Dust bunnies adorned every bookshelf and item in the guest house, but was proof that Betty's priority was keeping the outside picture perfect. She said it took years of hard toil to craft the mountain into the floral oasis. The development and operation of Betty's Place provided many jobs for local villagers.

We finished breakfast and visited with Biorne and Brigitte on the veranda. Brigitte looked at us strangely. "You're American?" she queried.

"Yes," I said, nodding my head.

"It's very unusual for American couples to backpack," she pointedly said. "We hardly ever meet American backpackers in our travels."

I told her that was probably true because travel was not promoted and encouraged in America like it was in other parts of the world. As far as I could tell, U.S. industry and production took priority over quality family time and travel. Brigitte and Biorne were excited about attempting their Mt. Wilhelm climb, but Brigitte woke up with a swollen arm. She held ice on it and they abandoned the climb.

It was time to depart Betty's Place, time to leave behind the achievements of Mt. Wilhelm, and time to go in pursuit of the next challenge. Our descent down the mountain was a little less dramatic because we didn't have to pile in the back of a PMV. We rode in the front seat with Robert, a gentleman from the state's horticultural department, who had also stayed at Betty's Place. He worked with local farmers in the area, trying to market their produce for better prices. Robert told us the program was successful until some of the middle men started taking more of the profit.

"That really discouraged the farmers from participating in the program," he said. "I'm investigating it now and trying to regain the farmers' trust."

Robert stopped for me to take a few photos of the mountain gardens. The farming plots amazed us, and from a distance the cultivated ground took on an impression of the threaded patterns and designs of a patch-work quilt.

"In America, if you can't drive a tractor on it, you don't farm it," Lee told Robert. We all smiled, but Lee and I knew the statement was true.

Part of the Stone

The past is in stone, where it will remain,
But the future is a frontier waiting to be claimed;

Your way is not marked with obvious signs,
It's a faint mountain trail, a challenge to climb;

Break camp at the base, searching your soul,
Survey the summit, that is your goal;

Prepare yourself well for what to expect,
Dangers and wonders to treat with respect;

Time passes quickly day after day,
Up a hill 'round a hill, well on your way;

A steep rocky ledge slows your pace to a crawl,
Make sure of your footing, the mountain won't care if you fall;

The summit is reached, true colors have been shown,
Your adventurous journey is now part of the stone.

Lee Chaney

Madang, Topped Off by Mumu

P*NG continued to seduce us with its surroundings, cul-*
ture and people. Bright poinsettia trees with blood-
crimson blooms lined many dirt roads; dark brown-
ish-red coffee beans dried on blue tarps; nationals dressed
in feathers, bones, shells and paints to demonstrate traditional dance; the fields of green fertile tea leaves were cut by
hand; and the pigments and personalities of the marketplace
were vivid reminders of the country's exotic charm.

It was hard to believe there were more than 750 native
languages. To combat the communication barrier between
tribes, Pidgin was developed decades earlier. It was a mix of
English, German and Dutch dialect. The official language,
however, taught in school and used in the government, was
English. Even though the official language was English, very
few people were fluent, which made communication for us
more of a challenge.

We had three ideas for our last six days. We could snake
down the Sepik River, visit the Tari Region to see the famous
wigmen or check out coastal life. Warned about tribal unrest
in the Tari Region, it was easy to axe that off the list. Two
clans were fighting, making it unsafe to even drive through
the region. A dignitary had been killed in an auto accident.
The public official's tribe proclaimed war on the region where
he was killed. Clans wouldn't think twice if visitors got caught
in the crossfire. Tribal fighting was still conducted with spears,

arrows, and machetes. The introduction of firearms had greatly added to casualties.

Since our arrival we had learned more and more about potential dangers. Our speculation was reinforced by the barbed-wire fence that surrounded most businesses. One of the biggest risks was "payback." It was an indigenous custom when people typically took the law into their own hands. If something happened to someone in one tribe, the tribe retaliated against the person or the assaulting tribe as they were doing in the Tari Region. Visitors became easy targets for crime because they were usually not associated with a clan, therefore, the criminal had no fear of payback.

The Sepik River Tour sounded captivating, but it was too pricey and mosquitoes were worse near the river. They carried deadly viruses, most notably malaria. We had taken our malarial tablets religiously. I knew the rewards of preventative medicine and planning ahead.

I promoted the practice as a kid in a 4-H public speaking contest. "An Ounce of Prevention is Worth a Pound of Cure," was the title of my blue-ribbon speech. For me, the philosophy had worked my entire life, so why change? Precautions were extremely important and could be the fine line between life and death, whether traveling abroad or in your backyard. Many countries required inoculations for yellow fever, typhoid fever and other conditions before they allowed you into their country. Lee and I had to get several shots.

The unfortunate thing was preventive shots didn't always assure an illness-free trip. On my '92 trip I became gravely afflicted with some mysterious virus in a remote town several hours from New Delhi, India. First, I was nauseous and then severe diarrhea literally erupted. I vomited in a rusty bucket simultaneous to what felt like Mt. Saint Helens spewing from my rear end. I lost control of my bodily functions.

Kelly helped me back to the bed, held a cold compress on my head and talked to me, trying to keep me conscious. She read the guidebook aloud as we tried to diagnose my condition. I went downhill fast. I hallucinated, then my mind went blank. The last thing I remembered was the relentless pain. I groaned, half delirious, lifting my legs in the air as if I were riding a bicycle upside down to eliminate the pain. Nothing helped. I shook with chills and then sweated. I was too sick to even think of death. Kelly stayed by my side all night. In the morning, my condition had stabilized. Kelly ventured out to see if she could find a doctor. Although she reassured me throughout the night that I would be fine, she later confessed she was extremely scared and thought I might die. I recovered in three days and was able to travel again.

That illness was enough of a fright to last me a lifetime. I hoped Lee and I would never have to endure such a sickness or accident in our travels. I prayed a lot and members of St. Paul's Utica Lutheran Church at home prayed as well, keeping us on the church's prayer list the entire trip. I believed our families' and friends' prayers kept us safe.

The Sepik River Tour was out and the wigmen were out. We boarded a small airplane for the north coast. After difficult rain-forest hikes and exhilarating mountain drives, it was time for a few days a little less physically and emotionally taxing. We landed in Madang, billed as the most beautiful city in the South Pacific. Our passenger plane wobbled up the runway and stopped beside another very small terminal. One medium-sized room draped with a few stimulating posters of PNG beach life and filled with two tables and eight chairs, welcomed us to arrival, check-in and baggage claim. We slipped on the straps to our backpacks and hoisted them in dreary anticipation of our five-mile walk to town. Lee threw his backpack on quickly and effortlessly. I was still suffering post-Mt. Wilhelm trauma—and I hadn't even attempted the summit. I didn't try to whisk my backpack up from the ground, but rather steadied it on the table, reluctantly slipped into my shoulder straps and stood up. We had to keep a fast pace in order to beat sunset. Two-tenths of a mile from the terminal gates a truck driver pulled over, disrupting our march. A soft-spoken man peered out his window. "You need ride to town?" he asked.

Stunned for a split second, Lee and I both responded, "Yes, thank you," and hopped in the back of the truck. We looked around and discovered we were in the back of a mail truck. Packages were strewn everywhere. I glared at the small, large and oddly-shaped parcels, dreamily hoping I'd spot one addressed to Mr. and Mrs. Lee Chaney. We leaned back on the sides, relieved and each let out big sighs. "It's that horse-shoe working for you again," Lee said with a snigger.

We both laughed and held on tight as we bounced our way to town. The gentleman dropped us off at the Lutheran Guesthouse. The guesthouse had a main dining room beside of the kitchen. It wasn't a place where we cooked for our-selves, typical of many backpacker accommodations. Break-fast was included in our $15 per person fee—not bad for a warm, clean room, hot shower, plus a meal. There was a sitting area with shelf after shelf of books. Fliers were pinned to the wall announcing programs and activities. Converging at breakfast helped us meet some of the locals as well as other travelers.

We met a German family that had been living in PNG for more than ten years serving as missionaries. The mid-30s couple had three children and lived out in a village, but made periodic trips to town to gather supplies. During their visits, they called the Lutheran Guesthouse home. I admired people who gave up their home country to devote their lives to mis-sionary work. I had hoped to meet up with another mission-ary family my Aunt Libby had written to us about. They were friends from her local church in Ellicott City, Maryland and were with the Summer Institute of Linguistics (SIL) serving in PNG. The SIL was a worldwide missionary organization. Members were usually husband-and-wife teams and spent 15 to 20 years in a country learning the language, develop-ing an alphabet and translating the Bible. It sounded fasci-nating. I wanted to meet them, but they were hundreds of miles from us.

After we were settled into our room we walked into the tiny metropolis of Madang to the marketplace. It buzzed with activity. One man stood on a small platform preaching Chris-tianity while most nationals worked fervently, cleaning their vegetables and fruits and carefully bagging, counting and stacking them. Others urged us toward their offerings neatly arranged like miniature pyramids. I bought a bag of peanuts and some mystery fruit I'd never seen before. Lee purchased some smoked fish that looked completely disgusting and certainly not digestible, but he chewed and swallowed it without blinking an eye. I often swore the man had an iron gut. Little old ladies sat cross-legged, many holding rainbow-colored umbrellas to shield them from the sun. The market reminded me of my childhood days selling sweet corn along our little county road. But the PNG market was much more than a little farm kid selling a few dozen ears of Silver Queen—it was the literal lifeline for locals.

To our surprise, we bumped into Biorne when we left the market and we asked about Brigitte.

"After you left Betty's Place, Brigitte's condition worsened," Biorne explained. "Her arm continued to swell, she developed a fever. Her arm was all red from infection."

"Oh my goodness," I said with the Drama Queen tone I was known for. "Is she okay? Did you get help?"

"We got a ride down the mountain to Kundiawa," he told us. "The doctor in Kundiawa said Brigitte had a very serious infection. They had to medevac her to a better hospital to get the treatment she needed."

I was momentarily speechless. Brigitte could have died. I was shocked by the reality of traveling misfortunes and hoped we didn't become a statistic.

"Brigitte is recovering slowly on our sailboat," he added. "It is anchored off a small island across the inlet from Madang. Would you like to come this evening for a visit? I think a visit would be good for Brigitte."

That evening Biorne picked us up in his motorized dinghy to deliver some social medicine to a weak and recovering Brigitte. After he scooped out the excess water, we boarded the circular ocean craft and set sail, you might say, toward his sailboat, the *Sy Mi Columpio*. Brigitte was pale and moved slowly on deck, but did her best to be a good hostess. We told her to sit and rest, but she was so excited to have company. It had been a difficult and lonely time for her. Our peaceful little powwow lasted until the sun slowly set. The yellow and orange rays of sun cut through the clouds as shades of blue turned to tints of red and pink reflected atop the inlet waves. From the last hints of daylight to the stillness of dark, we discussed cultural differences in PNG, life on a sailboat and traveling mishaps. Biorne carted us back to the mainland in his leaking dinghy.

The following day we walked to the town's little bay inlet where ocean-savvy PMV motorized canoes waited to take locals and visitors across the inlet. The trickiest part was stepping off the dock into the boat. The day before I watched as a woman lost her footing and splashed into the inlet's dark and dirty waters.

The boat rolled with the short choppy waves while we climbed in. We arrived at Kranket Island, scaled over the side and steadied our balance on land. Our dilemma was which way to walk. The guidebook suggested one path going partway through the island and another that encircled the island. We had a short discussion. I was irritated again by Lee's indecisiveness. I was sick of organizing the daily schedule. I wanted Lee to determine the course of the day. We started walking to the north. It was beautiful, serene. Brilliantly shaped and colored plants lined the path. I stopped often to admire them and tried to guess the species.

We were visiting PNG during the off-season. No other travelers were on the island. The serenity and harmony relaxed me, but I ached for conversation. Not conversation with the locals, but for conversation with my husband. We had a good marriage, I thought, but I wished Lee talked more. He was quiet and reserved at times. Perhaps that was my fault as probably I talked too much. I was sad that day—sad that Lee didn't talk to me more. Why is conversation so important to women? We crave it like pregnant women crave ice cream. As a young adult, I recalled my mom once telling my sisters and me how quiet Dad was, that he hardly ever talked to her.

"Your father isn't a good conversationalist, but he is good in bed," Mom confessed. Too much information, but Mom needed to get her frustrations out. Lee had many good qualities, as my Dad did, so could I really hold it against Lee for being quiet natured?

"Just talk, say anything," I begged.

"What do you want to talk about?" he queried.

"I don't care what it's about, just talk to me."

He chatted a little as we plodded down a tropical path, trying to appease me. Conversation was a small request. It shouldn't be too painful on his part. We stopped to snorkel and got in the water near a fallen tree. Even though I had flippers on, my feet got tangled in debris on the bottom. I sank in the sand and mud. I thrashed about, knowing I was disturbing sea snakes and at any moment I'd see a long curved creature slithering toward me. From what I had read, almost all sea snake bites were fatal. I immediately retreated to the large tree branch above the water and perched on it like a scared cat. "Can we go snorkel at a safer place?" I asked as my legs shook.

We wandered farther down the path and joined a group of local children swimming in a lagoon. They took great humor in our funny-looking goggles as they jumped and splashed around us. Wearing only big smiles, their naked brown skin glistened as the sun caught the droplets of water that clung to their bodies. The shores for the most part were undisturbed. The white sand met the crystal turquoise water in a ripple of tiny swells, breaking around the small feet of our little friends.

As we headed back to the mainland via PMV water taxi I was hypnotized by the low mist enveloping the trees and hilltops. The alluring clouds were like majestic angels spreading their wings over creation. Spiritually lifted by the scene, I sat back in the boat, closed my eyes and thanked God for the natural blessings of the world and for giving us the opportunity to experience them firsthand. *And God, could you maybe get Lee to talk a little more to me?* I asked.

We arrived back on the mainland and returned to the Lutheran Guesthouse, where we showered, changed and were off again. Every night we frequented the Madang Club, one of the only eateries in town. It was good and cheap. We got large seafood specialties for less than $5 each. For three nights I treated myself to Szechuan lobster. It was the most incredible seafood dish. I was never a fan of lobster, but that dish was sheer taste-bud magic. Our table on the restaurant's veranda was in a perfect people-watching location. Locals fished off the dock while kids played, laughing aloud without control. Families piled in PMVs, hands full of bags, going to their home islands. It was a busy little utopia and we were part of it.

Walks back to the Lutheran Guesthouse were dark and daunting. The streets were cloaked in blackness. I guess the town couldn't afford streetlights. It was a good 15-minute hike. Lee and I carried only enough money for dinner and left all of our camera gear locked up at the guesthouse. Every night we walked into the guesthouse we felt safe behind its 12-foot locked gate. Tension dissolved like instant Jell-o.

Our flight from Madang back to Mt. Hagen was on the smallest passenger plane yet. We were in the first seats directly behind the two pilots. The plane was so small there was no door separating the pilots' compartment from the passenger seats. We stared right into the cockpit. There were so many instruments, gauges, gadgets and dials.

"I sat there watching the pilot and co-pilot spin wheels, flip switches and pump levers," Lee told me later. "I wondered which one was going to start pedaling to get that bird in the air."

We flew through clouds blindly for an hour and then, all of the sudden, a mountain appeared right in front of us. My heart seemed to drop to the floor and I raised in my seat hoping to will the plane to rise with me above the mountain top. The pilots steadied their course, rising just above the mountainous peak, circled and descended on Mt. Hagen's airstrip.

Thomas picked us up and delivered us to Haus Poroman. It was our third time to check into Haus Poroman during our PNG visit and each time we were put in a different bungalow. The final accommodation was smaller, but closer to the main lodge and had a well-groomed garden around it. We were not alone in our little humble abode. Daily droppings and night-time scurrying made it evident of the mice or rats that shared our hut. I detested the little rodents for the most part, but my third-world experiences had conditioned me to accept such roommates. And it wasn't like I hadn't grown up with them on The Farm.

On our last day Jack invited us to hike to the hilltop where the Leahy brothers had built their home so many decades earlier. I still wasn't in the best of shape and struggled. Mountain children rushed to our sides, held our hands. The curious youngsters were clad in dirty mismatched clothes. Thick greenish-yellow snot clogged their nostrils, their eyes were pale, but their friendly bright smiles were contagious. They giggled and sometimes three children tried to hold my hand at once.

It was Sunday and we passed the village church shortly after the final benediction. Families visited outside the church; kids played. Roadside entrepreneurs fired up their make-shift grills and offered roasted corn on the cob and boiled potatoes. The kernels had been blackened on the grill. It was delicious and memories of biting into those first sweet corn ears on The Farm came surging back. During hay season, the crew at Long View often went through three or four dozen of the white tasty cobs at one sitting.

That afternoon Jack, Stacey, Lee and I hiked through a nearby rain forest. Jack talked us into climbing down a wa-terfall. I hated peer pressure, but it was a challenge and I loved a challenge. Off came our shoes and down the rocks we descended. I slipped, but caught myself. I was obviously trying to break a leg before leaving PNG the next day. It was the dumbest thing I had done yet. I continued to climb down, trying to place each foot and hand securely on a rock. The rocks were wet and slimy. At one point Jack took one hand while Lee had the other to help guide me between two ledges that I didn't think I could make without falling to the rock ridges below. Finally at the bottom it was time to celebrate. Jack and Stacey took out their little pouches of betel nut, the plant that locals chewed, giving them a mild narcotic feeling. They were not allowed to chew it back at the lodge while they were working, but it was Sunday and they had the day off. "Have you tried betel nut?" Jack asked.

"No, but we've watched a lot of people chew it," I said.

Jack and Stacey insisted we give it a go. Betel nut or *buai* derived from the areca palm. Jack instructed us to pop the nut into our mouths, discarding the husk of the nut. Then he showed us how to dip the mustard stick or *daka* into the crushed coral lime which was called *chumbung.* "Chew it up good, then hold it in your mouth, in your cheek or bottom lip and just spit. Then tell us how you feel," Jack coached.

We did as instructed and soon had the characteristic blood-stained mouth. Streams of bright ruby-red saliva escaped our lips, often dripping down our chins. "I think I feel a little funny," I said with what I felt were half-glazed eyes.

"That means it's working," they laughed.

Betel nut was sold at all the markets and usually took up at least half the space. It was a main staple in the culture. Children started to chew the discarded husks of *buai* as early as five years old.

After hiking up a mountain, climbing down a waterfall and experimenting with betel nut I was ready for a much-needed nap. We returned to our bungalow for a short rest before evening festivities. It was our last night in PNG and it was my 36th birthday. In honor of my special day, our friends at Haus Poroman prepared a traditional feast in the *mumu,* an underground steam oven. The pit in the ground was lined with banana leaves followed by layers of fire-heated stones. Meat and vegetables were wrapped in herbs and leaves and piled on top the hot stones. Henry, the *mumu* master as I called him, carefully constructed the multi-layered food unit, topping the creation off with final layers of leaves and branches.

His hands were rough from his many years of physical labor. Henry's feet were also worn and calloused from a lifetime of no shoes. His older sister also helped with the *mumu* meal. Her hardened hands and feet also told the story of her difficult years. Difficult years did not, however, taint their zest for life. They were happy people, always sharing smiles, handshakes and hugs. It was a birthday I will never forget. I helped put the hot rocks in the *mumu*. As smoke filtered out of the open hut, a national strummed his guitar. After four hours, Henry unwrapped the top leaves—browned and curled from steaming. Platters were brought out from the kitchen: one for the chicken, one for the *kaukau* or sweet potato, one for the bananas. Everything was placed on a table, buffet style. The owners, Maggie and Keith, invited their families and the entire staff.

The real guest of honor was Maggie's stepmother, a petite, delightful lady who was in her 90s. Although she couldn't speak a word of English, her delicate chuckles and mannerisms charmed us. I noticed several of her fingers were missing, as I had noticed on several other women. Curiosity got the best of me and I asked Jack. PNG women often chopped off a finger as a sign of mourning or to make a profound statement to an abusive husband. More missing digits meant a more difficult life the woman had endured. I sure had ups and downs in my lifetime, but I wasn't about to chop off a finger.

Joe Leahy also attended the party. He was featured in two very popular PNG historic documentaries. Joe was like a local celebrity. I asked everyone to sign our little black book to help us reflect on the special evening. I blew out my candles and the evening culminated with a three-clap birthday salute customary in PNG. We returned to our bungalow. It was a mess. Dried grass fragments from the bungalow's structure were everywhere. Evidently, mice had been busy running about our little guesthouse in our absence. I brushed away the debris and zipped up my backpack.

Everything was packed and ready to go the next morning. On our way to the airport we passed a truckload of people covered in mud. I asked Jack what it meant.

"When a loved one dies, relatives and friends mask themselves in mud for several days to reflect the loss they feel," he said.

I sat back in my seat, shut my mouth for once, and took in the final sights, sounds and smells of PNG. That's what I loved about traveling—the indigenous customs we learned. Traveling in a strange land gave us the opportunity to witness and experience everyday life. For the adventurous soul, PNG was a must visit. Whether it was to catch a glimpse of some of the hundreds of species of wildlife and birds, photograph some of the 9,000 species of plants, or take in a local sing-sing or cultural celebration, PNG had a world of spellbinding displays for all types of travelers. Although time and money probably wouldn't allow us another visit, it would always be remembered as a favorite stop. It was definitely not an easy country to travel in, but was a challenging and enchanting place to explore.

Lukim yu bihain (see you later), I thought as our aircraft speeded up for takeoff. Good-bye to the warm receptive smiles, the firm handshakes and the fraternal hugs. After nearly two months of visiting friends, sightseeing in three countries and having little responsibility for the most part—it was time to enter the next phase of our trip. Time to work in Australia, the original basis for the trip.

No End

It is not right, it is not wrong, it is simply the way,
Traditions that have carried from the past to today;

Some have been forgotten, some have been replaced,
Some you seek for comfort like your mother's warm embrace;

Much change has occurred in such a little time,
Ideas now cross back from your culture to mine;

The world is by no means perfect, it's an ever-changing place,
Adapting to these changes makes us part of the human race;

So go in peace my brother and if ever you need a friend,
I will remember our time together; our bond has no end.

Lee Chaney

Stowaway

It was time to give up the dangers and untamed mystique of PNG and head back to the comforts of civilization. I reveled in third-world cultural experiences, but was ready to get back to a more cosmopolitan routine. Little did I know, we didn't leave PNG completely behind.

Before heading to our jobs in the outback, we spent ten days on the Blackburns' dairy farm, Burnvale Holsteins. The farm was one and a half hours south of Perth, off Australia's west coast. Mikey, his wife, Josette, and daughter, Kiana Rose, entertained us and started to break us into Australian slang and humor. Sheilas are females, blokes are men, mates are friends and, of course, a bottle of beer is a stubby.

First on the agenda was completely cleaning out our backpacks and washing all of our clothes. One inconvenience about extended visits to underdeveloped countries was the limited laundry services. Clothes are either washed in the river or in the sink, if you are lucky enough to have a sink. Our soiled and smelly garments were evidence of our neglected laundry duties.

I hadn't opened my large backpack for days and was living out of my small carry-on bag. I picked piece after piece out of my backpack and started different piles—light-colored clothes on one pile and darks on another. As I grabbed one of the last remaining shirts in my backpack I literally fell back, my jaw dropped—I was voiceless. I wanted to scream, but nothing came out. To my horror, a large dead rat lined the side of my backpack. I ran out of the room appalled at the intruder in my luggage. Lee, Mikey and Josette came to investigate. "Don't you know it's illegal to smuggle animals into this country?" Mikey said sarcastically.

I could have died—I felt violated. I couldn't believe the rodent had been living or I guess dying in my backpack for several days, unbeknownst to me. Not even the airport's keen canine had detected the stowaway, but it did nab the woman standing next to me in baggage claim who innocently had two apples in her purse. They were confiscated. The rat must have gotten into my backpack in our PNG bungalow. The incident taught me a very good lesson—always keep my luggage zipped up and bags closed!

I told Lee weird and goofy stuff always seemed to happen to me. At times I thought it was a curse, but usually it provided days and days of laughter. I remembered calling him one evening when I was covering the National FFA Convention in Kansas City, Missouri. I had finished my feature story and quickly changed to go to the hotel's bar to catch happy hour. I sat by myself, and made three trips to the bar to take advantage of reduced prices. After final call at 7 p.m., I got on the elevator. "I looked down and my fluorescent green striped thong underwear were hanging out of the bottom of my jeans," I said, recounting the story to Lee. "I was alone on the elevator and couldn't stop laughing. Ya know, that shit always happens to me."

The rat was just one more for my list of unbelievable episodes. The stowaway was not forgotten.

The Blackburns were fun hosts. Mikey had visited the States eight years earlier and was still as I remembered— tall, cute, completely full of himself. He was always like a brother and we took every opportunity to pick on each other. He was packing on a few extra pounds (beer weight, no doubt), a sign he wasn't 20 years old anymore, but rather nearing the 30-year-old plateau. His bride of five years was gorgeous inside and out. I often praised her for her years with Mikey.

"It's beyond me how you can live with that man," I wise-cracked.

Kiana Rose inherited both of her parents' blond hair and beautiful smile. Mikey thought she was the perfect child. "She never cries and when she was a baby we could take her to the pub," he boasted. Kiana was 11 months old when we met her and she immediately was smitten with us, especially her Uncle Lee. There was a special connection and Kiana adored both her daddy and Uncle Lee.

The Blackburns took us to Albany, a popular tourist town on the south coast of Western Australia. Whale World introduced us to whaling, formerly one of Australia's most prestigious industries. The photos and information about products produced was interesting, but personally, I was most fascinated with the whale pizzle on display. At first, I thought it was a uniquely shaped anchor, but boy was I wrong. It was at least 18 feet long and weighed some 300 pounds. Now, I call that a "package."

We stopped at the Valley of the Giants where the famous Tree Top Walk, a nearly 2,000-foot-long ramp structure, allowed us to roam through the canopy of the giant tingle trees. Some of the magnificent trees towered more than 130 feet above the ground and had a 52-foot circumference.

Our three days of sightseeing were great, but Lee was anxious to head north to the outback to start working. Back at the Blackburns, the first order of business was finding a reliable vehicle for the thousands of miles we planned to traverse. Armed with the newspaper's car section, a detailed map of Perth and telephone numbers in the event we found ourselves completely lost, we struck out in search of an automobile that would hopefully serve its purpose during our ten-month stay.

We arrived in Perth and met Frank, Mikey's brother-in-law. Frank was a security officer at Perth's international airport and was also mechanically blessed. The idea was for Frank to take charge of our car visits to prevent a slick Aussie bloke from selling us a lemon. We went to a few homes and to a used-car lot. Our quest for a dream car never materialized. I was no help during the car-hunting ventures. I knew nothing about vehicles. I never had to change the oil or change a tire. Not because I lacked the initiative, I just never had a flat tire. I'm not ashamed of my automobile ignorance, I could do things other people wouldn't know how to do. I could milk a cow, deliver a calf or do a headstand on a horse (well, I could as a teen-ager, anyway).

We had no success finding wheels and we're running out of time. Our funds dwindled. We needed to get to the outback—we needed to work and make money. Finally, Mikey took off one day from the dairy and he and Lee went car shopping. I was relieved not to have to go, but on the other hand, who knew what trouble Lee and Mikey would find themselves in. They had just met a week earlier and were already good mates. They loved to talk, look at ridiculous things on the Internet and above all, they enjoyed drinking a few stubbies together.

Seven o'clock rolled around and there was no word from the blokes. Josette and I were sure they had given up the search and had stopped at a pub somewhere and were proceeding to get stupid drunk. Anxiously we waited. I counted the minutes—the worrywart coming out in me again. I wasn't concerned about the possibility of a new vehicle, but more for their safety. We had just put Kiana to bed when we heard a rattley engine come in the driveway. We walked out to the front lawn.

Mikey pulled into the carport as another "thing" rolled in behind him. The thing was a dull tan vehicle similar to a Ford Bronco II. It was one of the most ugly vehicles I'd ever seen. Lee informed me proudly that it was a Russian-made Lada Niva four-wheel drive. I thought, *I don't care what the hell it is, it sure doesn't look like it's going to get us from point A to point B, let alone thousands of miles.* The fading tan frame was trimmed with red and yellow racing stripes. Probably in its glory days, the little puddlejumper had some real lively stories, but it was 18 years old and the aging bundle of scrap metal looked a bit pitiful.

"How many stubbies did you blokes have before you purchased this prize?" I asked.

Lee assured me that he and Mikey had made a sound buying decision. I hoped Lee knew what he was doing. The blokes did, however, stop and have a beer on the way home to celebrate what they believed to be the ultimate acquisition. After careful intellectual consideration during their cocktail hour, the duo dubbed the new vehicle the "Road Toad."

The Road Toad needed a few adjustments and Lee spent hours making improvements down in the farm's shop. Lee cut, welded and bolted until he had created a classy jerry-can holder on the rear of the Road Toad. There were sometimes 300 or more miles between gas stations and it was critical to carry extra water and extra gas. Lee was pleased with his new contraption. He bought two jerry cans, a red one and a light blue one, at the Cookernup store.

"Do you have a black permanent marker I can use?" he asked. I dug in my day pack and pulled out a handful of highlighters and markers.

Like a painter carefully putting the final touches on a work of art, Lee wrote Road on one jerry can and Toad on the other. I was seeing a totally different side of Lee. A man free of pressures for the first time in years. He was even more laid back and was absorbing every aspect of the adventure. The personalized jerry cans would, no doubt, attract unusual glances as we traveled to the outback.

The Road Toad was a favorite of Kiana's. She didn't know many words yet, but she always managed to say, "Road Toad, Road Toad." Her sweet little smile and voice would melt her Uncle Lee's heart and he'd take her right to the Road Toad to play. When play time was over, it was back to the shop.

Lee didn't stop with the jerry-can holder. The Road Toad was his special project and he was determined to make sure the vehicle had everything we needed. He showed off the new wheel carrier he welded and bolted on the front of the Road Toad. Lee attached it to the 'roo bar which was standard protection on most Australian vehicles. Kangaroos were as overpopulated as deer were in the States and caused thousands of accidents annually, as well as crop loss and environmental damage. I was proud of Lee's engineering talents. It seemed that every day on the trip I learned something new about the man I had been with for over six years.

We crammed things into every available nook and cranny in the Road Toad. The *eski,* as Aussies call coolers, was easily accessible to retrieve ice, water and sandwiches. The Road Toad was ready, but were we? Hugs and kisses were exchanged. Photos were snapped. Everyone just shook their heads at Lee's handiwork with Road Toad majestically printed on the jerry cans. Tacky? Yes. But personalized and a valuable component of our upcoming journey.

We backed out of the driveway, waved, blew more kisses, and then proceeded up the dirt road to the main highway. Out of the Blackburns' driveway, my emotions burst like a bottle that has been shaken, with pressure building up until the cap is popped off. Tears rolled down my big cheeks. "Are you going to be okay?" Lee asked. He knew I was a sensitive person, it was a trait that he was both drawn to and at times was very irritated with. But on that occasion he was very supportive. I tried to get my words out between sniffles.

"I'll really miss Josette and Kiana—and Mikey too, even though he's a little shit sometimes," I said, trying to gain my composure, but tears still washed down my face. "I'm scared too!"

"Scared of what?" Lee asked.

"I'm scared of what lies ahead, our jobs in the outback—I'm just scared."

"Don't worry, dear, everything is going to be fine," he said, placing a comforting hand on my leg, looking at me with reassuring eyes. I cried a few more minutes and finally pulled myself together. What was my problem? Adversity was part of my life—family illness, rejection, tough times on The Farm. I needed to be brave and look at this as a new challenge—an opportunity for personal growth. I could only pray that what lay ahead was the zenith of our long-sought dream.

Our first destination was Juna Downs Station in the Pilbara Region, about 900 miles north of Perth. The Road

Toad had no air conditioning and we were in the dead of summer. The drive was suffocating in 100-degree-plus heat. Following hair-raising and butt-raising flooded creek bed crossings, the victorious Road Toad delivered us to Juna, home to Mandy and Shane Day and their son, Stuart. I was still a nervous wreck, but hoped I didn't disappoint the Days. Most of all, I hoped I didn't disappoint Lee.

Flat-out on Aliza

J una Downs was just one of four stations owned by Hamersley Iron. Ethel Creek Station, Rocklea Station and Hamersley Station completed the two million-plus acres the company had snatched up to provide access roads for transporting its iron ore. Every ranch continued to function as a working cattle station. In addition to Shane and Mandy Day managing Juna Downs, Mandy was the safety director for all four Hamersley-owned stations.

I knew the Days would be unique characters. I guessed that from the letters I'd received and the few conversations on the phone. Mandy was a tough, outspoken woman from the bush, or back country. She was quick to render a "goddamn this" or "goddamn that."

Short in stature, Mandy was one massive construction of muscle. Her rugged persona and sternness often melted into kindness, even charm. Her humor, witty personality and bush mannerisms repeatedly had us in stitches, as did Shane's off-the-cuff remarks. At first Shane was quiet. That soon changed as he felt comfortable with us. He was about five feet 11 inches, a bit taller than Lee. Shane always wore his bush hat to protect his balding head, which he blamed on years of putting up with Mandy.

The Days' only child was an odd duck. Stuart was a great 11-year-old kid, most of the time. Not odd so much, as unique, but the freckle-faced, strawberry-blond-haired youngster was growing up in an adult world. His friends were on other stations two or more hours away and they rarely were able to visit. Most of Stuart's world orbited around his parents.

He had pale skin. His days were spent indoors reading and playing Nintendo. Stuart had been a bookworm, but his Nintendo fetish had taken over. Stuart was educated through the School of the Air program, checking in daily with his teacher at the Port Hedland School of the Air headquarters via two-way radio to receive his assignments. The program depended on the commitment of parents monitoring the work. The Days had a special room devoted strictly to Stuart's schooling. Mandy shared her frustrating stories of days in the private little classroom.

"Stuart, do your goddamn homework before I throw you out the goddamn window," Mandy recalled. "I brought you into this world and I can damn well take you out!" Her stories amused us, often shocked us.

Many station owners hired the services of a governess to live at their station and assume the role of nanny and educator. The School of Air was the only way to educate outback kids without sending them to boarding school at an early age. Most stations were more than two hours from the closest town, making it impossible for children to attend a regular school. When kids hit 12 or 13 they were sent to boarding school for their high school education.

Lee spent many days helping Shane check windmills. Windmills were the only way most remote areas of Australia had water and could accommodate livestock. Lee walked into the homestead most evenings covered in dirt, but lit up by the biggest smile. He was working with his hands and loving it. It was no secret he was a workaholic. He had enjoyed the previous two months of traveling, but he was ready to get dirty.

Mandy spent her days breaking in young horses. She asked Shane to come give a green horse its first ride. Shane hesitated because he didn't have his proper riding boots on, but Mandy insisted. Finally, Mandy's eyes shot daggers in

Shane's direction. "Come on, Shane, get in the goddamn saddle and ride the goddamn horse," she shouted.

Shane crumbled to her wishes. Mandy proceeded to chase Shane and the yearling around the small arena as the young horse bucked. "Ride the goddamn horse, ride 'im," she yelled repeatedly.

Lee and I stood silent, watching the commotion. It was only our second day on the station, and we wanted to laugh, but we were still getting to know the Days. I sauntered over to Lee's side and stretched up to his ear. "Lee, if Mandy tells you to get in the goddamn saddle and ride the goddamn horse, then you better get in the goddamn saddle and ride that goddamn horse," I whispered.

Careful not to break a smile as it may have offended Mandy or Shane, we were consumed with hysteria inside. After a few days when our personalities clicked, we recalled the horse-breaking incident. I confessed what I had whispered in Lee's ear. Although Shane found no humor in the story, Mandy was in merriment.

In between rain showers we went on long rides, Mandy on the green horses, me on Aliza, a seasoned station horse. I came to trust Aliza, not only as my mount, but with my life. We spent hours riding the vast bush wilderness to get the green horses comfortable under saddle. Mandy broke the yearlings for other station owners.

It was the wet season and undetectable marsh areas often trapped horses in its sucking mud. The ground appeared to be fine, but the water saturation made many spots on the station death traps. Aliza refused my commands twice and they were times we entered a high-risk area threatening horse and rider safety. "Aliza will let you know if it's bad and if she refuses to go forward it's because it's dangerous," Mandy said.

The 11-year-old bay mare was full of vigor and power. She obeyed the slightest pressure of my legs and turned on a dime. I did a lot of the riding while Lee worked horses on the ground. With very little equine experience, other than his five-day stint in the New Zealand backblocks a month earlier, Lee was a real greenhorn. Not only had I seen a special connection between Lee and children, but he also had that same aura of nurturing that attracted animals to him. We could be standing in a paddock and if any horse walked up, it would walk to Lee. It was incredible.

Another young horse was delivered to the station. Lee helped Mandy a few days with the filly, but then heavy rains forced us to let all of the horses out. The mud in the horse yards made it hazardous—little did we know releasing them to roam the homestead's 500-acre fenced-in paddock would be even more risky. We thought the young horse would join the few other horses in the paddock and be fine. We quickly learned danger was synonymous with the outback. Unfortunately the filly ran through a barbed-wire fence and ripped the top of her front leg open. By the time the horse was found the following morning, the wound was already too old to stitch up. Mandy and Shane had performed minor operations on their stock horses. It was too far and too expensive to get a veterinarian out, so most station owners did their own surgical procedures and routine vet work.

Lee took on the filly as a special project. He cleaned the six-inch gash daily, treated it and walked the animal. He massaged the filly's leg until she was ready to be exercised more aggressively. In two weeks he was lunging her. It looked like Moe, the name Lee gave the young horse, would make a full recovery.

"Here Lee, this is yours. You broke that filly in and you deserve it," Mandy said, handing Lee the $300 breaking fee she had received.

Mandy was an accomplished horse trainer. The gesture meant a lot to Lee. I was really proud of him. Unbeknownst to me, Lee even rode the filly. He was going to be an outback cowboy, yet. He was reading his third horse-training book, so I guess he figured he was an expert. He often made me nervous with his "I can do anything" philosophy. Not that I questioned his ability, I just knew 1,000-pound horses were unpredictable.

Our next introduction to the outback was castrating three colts. The Days had constructed a round pen using discarded tires. It was small and specifically designed for the beginning stages of breaking horses. We needed a compact, confined area to work. We ran the first young colt into the round pen. He pranced around with all his dignity and even arrogance, completely unaware we were getting ready to strip him of his manhood, so to speak.

Mandy lassoed his head, then she and Shane slipped a halter on his head. With little to no previous handling, the colt was unruly. The off-side legs were roped and the ends were handed to Lee and me to wrap around the bottom of the gate. The colt reared with a vengeance before leg ropes were wrapped. The swift movement ripped the rope from our grip. My gloves saved my hands from getting split open. Lee wasn't as lucky. He tried to hold his rope, but the force of the 600-pound yearling jerked the rope, burning his hand as it slipped away.

"If the colt pulls before the ropes are wrapped, just let go," Mandy said. "People have lost hands and fingers."

They forced the colt back to the gate, where Lee and I were stationed. Leg ropes were tossed to us again. We both quickly and carefully wrapped them around the gate and held tight. Next time the colt reared to escape, he bounced onto his side with a thud. Shane lassoed the other rear leg and tied it as tight as he could, stretching the animal's rear quarters to make the operation safer. Mandy's job was critical and demanded strength and stamina. She covered the colt's head with a sack and held it steady. The horse was secure.

Shane sterilized his knife. It was all pretty cut and dry, no pun intended. Sedatives were not used. Shane cautiously grabbed the colt's doodads and squeezed the scrotum firmly to the end. We checked the ropes to make sure they were tight. He made his first incision. The horse tried to kick. It was impossible to escape, unless, of course, the ropes snapped. Following the incision, Shane popped the testicle out of the scrotum, pulled it out and carefully cut it from the horse. Blood ran down the horse's belly and leg as the horse lay helpless on his back. Shane picked up the emasculators (testicle clamps) from the sterilization bucket and closed them tightly on the horse's incision. The tool clamped the blood veins and would aid in the healing process. The clamp was removed and the procedure was repeated on the other testicle.

At that point, the colt seemed to be consumed with pain. It was important to get the operation completed as quickly as possible. The animal was restless and made futile attempts to move its head. Squeeze, cut, pop, pull, slice and clamp—the last one was out. Shane drenched the bloody area with an anti-bacterial solution. It was critical that we all released the animal at the same time and not get our fingers caught up in the ropes or get them crushed between the colt's powerful hooves and the gate. I nervously removed my rear leg rope as fear surged down my spine. I knew if the animal gave one last mighty struggle, my hand would be smashed.

We had been at Juna two weeks, but still had more than nine months left in the outback. I couldn't exactly work with a crippled hand. I didn't let on to Mandy and Shane that I was afraid—I had to prove myself. I had told them of my many arduous years growing up on a farm—I couldn't fail. Castration day was my opportunity to conquer my self-doubt. I did and I successfully released the animal's rear leg without succumbing to fear or injury.

Mandy and I continued to compare childhood experiences. I told Mandy about my rough riding as a kid—the early years of playing cowboys and Indians in the Catoctin Mountains behind our Springfield Dairy Farm. And later galloping fearlessly across the fields and through the woods at The Farm where my pony ran me between two narrow trees, slashing the skin off my knee. Twenty-five years later, I still had the scar.

We laughed about our crazy youthful years, when danger seemed more like a game than a life-or-death situation. I told her how my brother, Doug, and I used to practice back-to-back bareback on Shotgun, our Shetland pony. We were determined to take the first-place blue ribbon at the next Thurmont Riding Club Field Day. We rode hard at The Farm, but I hadn't owned a horse for 18 years and for the previous decade I worked in an office.

I had only gone trail riding a few times with my high school best friends, Becky and Kim, over the years. Those rides were at a slow pace so our beer didn't shake up. I wasn't sure if I still had the roughneck attitude I grew up with on The Farm. Was I going to be a softy, embarrassing myself and Lee? Only time would tell and that time came sooner than I expected.

A few evenings later Shane, Mandy and I were on a long ride around the station. They were both on green horses and I was on Aliza. As we departed the homestead we trotted for a few miles so Shane and Mandy could get their young horses used to the saddle and new surroundings. They looked over at me and their faces glowed with amusement.

"What's so darned funny?" I asked.

"If you're not careful, you're going to give yourself a black eye," Mandy responded, chuckling with laughter.

What did I expect? I had been teased about my voluptuous anatomy since high school, when all of the sudden something erupted into large mounds on my chest. The fact I'd been traveling for two months and doing nothing but eating and drinking hadn't helped the situation. My once 38C cups had exploded to 42D. My decaying bras from the trip's wear and tear offered no support, whatsoever, which was quite evident when I trotted my horse.

Shane and Mandy ribbed me, but I took it all in good fun. I kept one hand on the reins and held my other hand across my chest to eliminate the horrific bouncing. It still didn't stop Shane from giving me the nickname "Big Boobs Becky."

We were more than an hour from the homestead. The green horses were going pretty well. A small mob of cattle were grazing and a huge Brahman bull looked like he was the big daddy in charge.

"There's Amy," Mandy said, pointing to a particular cow. "We'll have to try to find her before we move south. She goes with us."

I thought, *With more than 900,000 acres to roam, how would we ever find her again?* That's when my cockiness, or should I say "stupidity," took over. "I reckon I can draft her out," I said, confidently alluding to the ridiculous notion I could cut her out of the mob and herd her back to the homestead.

"Go on then," Mandy said, giving a supportive nod. She knew I was a competent rider, but for the most part she had no idea of my ability other than the stories I told her of my teen-aged cowgirl days. Riding was like pedaling a bike—once you've done it, you never forget it—right? I squeezed Aliza's sides gently and proceeded near the mob. I knew the effort was completely up to me because Mandy and Shane's horses were barely ridable, let alone ready to chase cattle.

The cattle ran in all directions. I kept my eyes fixed on Amy and occasionally glanced at Big Daddy bull to make sure he wasn't making a sneak attack. Amy was easy to pinpoint—she was the only Holstein, or Freisian as Mandy called her, in the mob. I separated Amy and another beast. Their hooves dug into the soft ground. Clumps of mud and grass flew in the air. They ran with one thing on their minds—escape. I took off after them, but held Aliza back. I was still a little unsure of her full potential and still a lot unsure of my reborn ability to ride fearless. My legs tensed. Perspiration bubbled by my temples. Amy was getting away. My pride would be crushed if I let the animal beat me.

"Let her go, let Aliza go!" Mandy screamed. It was obvious I was holding Aliza back. I didn't have time to think. I couldn't let Mandy down. My determination to prove myself and stop Amy from escaping clouded the reality of safety. There was no way I could retreat. I let Aliza go. We were flat-out in hot pursuit of Amy as she ran through the scrub like a convict who had no intention of being taken back into captivity. My heart pounded, both from excitement and from the immense concentration and control it took to chase the bolting cow. Adrenaline swelled through my body as we seemed to go even faster. Aliza jumped fallen trees, stumbled through boggy areas and leaped over creek beds—she was Super

Horse. I couldn't believe what was happening. It wasn't another mustering story Mandy was sharing—it was real—it was dangerous—it was my first attempt at bringing in a half-crazed animal.

Finally, Aliza and I succeeded and not only stopped Amy, but had her traveling up the fence row toward the homestead. For the next 15 minutes, it was great. I had drafted out my first beast and she was heading home. But you get nowhere with an over-confident attitude—Amy bolted for the scrub. Mandy and Shane tried to assist.

"Be careful!" Mandy yelled. "There's a strand of wire between two trees somewhere around here."

We were galloping toward a clustered forest of mulga trees and I had to worry about a damned wire stretched between two trees. *Just great!* I thought, *The sun is setting, I'm chasing a dumb cow and I'm about to be decapitated in just my second week in the outback. Lee certainly will not be happy about this.* My dear husband would be distraught by my demise—I hoped. He'd have to leave the outback before he experienced everything he came to Australia to experience.

I reined with one hand while holding the other hand around my neck just in case the wire surprised me. Aliza and I were once again on what I described as a "death run." We hurdled fallen debris or simply vaulted through it, forcing shattered pieces of dead wood in all directions—nothing could stop Super Horse. We crashed through spinifex as tall as Aliza and every time we cut Amy off, the baffled cow bolted the opposite way. My entire body trembled, I was exhausted and we still didn't have Amy under control. I was losing my patience.

"You're doing one hell of a job, but I'm going to switch with you," Mandy said as she rode toward me.

I was a little disappointed, but more relieved than anything. Darkness had nearly swallowed up all remaining signs of daylight and I was worried about the suicidal wire. Mandy took off on Aliza like a bolt of lightning. I held the green horse for a moment contemplating my situation. I either could ride the young horse in or risk walking it and stepping on a snake in the dark. I decided to take my chances in the saddle.

"Gee," I said to myself aloud, grabbing the horse's mane and sliding my foot into the stirrup to mount. "This will be interesting."

It was the horse's first ride away from the homestead and I had to continue his education. I hoped that he didn't turn into a bronco scene from the rodeo finals. I carefully threw my leg over the animal and positioned my derriere. He backed up into a bush, then leaped three feet forward in one effort from fright. That was enough of a jolt to question my decision, but I stayed in the saddle. Shane and I found the dirt road and headed toward the homestead. Mandy had been gone a half-hour. I prayed she hadn't found that nasty wire. We neared the outer gate of the homestead. I saw a shadow cast by the moon's brightness coming toward us. It was Mandy and Aliza.

"Did you lose Amy?" I asked.

"Hell no! That goddamn cow is in, but I knocked her down once before she started cooperating," Mandy boasted. Like Aliza, Mandy was a seasoned mustering machine. They both knew the intricacies of gathering bush cattle and their combined experience defeated Amy. It had been a long time since I had had such a wave of physical exhilaration. I had an overwhelming sense of pride from almost successfully rounding up my first beast.

• • •

The family was packing to move south. Mandy went through filing cabinets and drawers making piles to keep or piles to burn. It was about as much crap as I had gone through before leaving the States. Stuart and I picked up the discarded piles to take to the trash barrels. We found some cool stuff. Mandy told us not to draft anymore out of the trash, but Stuart and I couldn't help it. It was hard enough to get Stuart away from Nintendo for a half-hour so I had to make the project fun. It was like a scavenger hunt. My brother, Dennie, and I always dug in dump holes at The Farm in search of old bottles, crocks and coins. Dad and Mom thought we were digging up trash, but Dennie and I thought they were treasures.

The Days continued to entertain us with their Aussie slang and just plain funny remarks. My favorites were, "I was mad as a cut snake"—Mandy; "Don't make me crossthreaded"—Stuart; and "It doesn't taste real good, but it'll build a turd"—Shane.

In the afternoon, Ken Walker visited from Newman. It was a treat to get visitors. He brought wine, beer and munchies. Ken once operated Eco-Tours and took tourists on educational overnight bush outings. "I cooked them real Aussie tucker, complete with kangaroo and camel meat," he said. "Camel meat is delicious and I have a special way to cook it."

Lee, Ken and Mandy fed horses while Shane and I worked on evening tea. During the day I made lentil soup that turned out to be enough to feed a small army. It was difficult to make things in small amounts. I was used to making big portions, a trait definitely inherited from my mother who cooked for Dad, six kids and at least a half dozen more. That was probably why I had a weight problem—I always made too much food and then tried to eat it. Speaking of weight, I had lost five pounds. I still couldn't squeeze into my jeans, but progress was progress.

When Lee, Ken and Mandy joined Shane and me in the kitchen, Ken said, "Lee has a real way with horses." Even a visitor recognized Lee's special connection with horses. Maybe he'd work with horses instead of cows when we got home.

Ken was quite a character. Our casual banter turned lively after the fourth bottle of wine. Lee wasn't used to drinking wine. I'd never seen alcohol affect him so quickly. He had the weepy-eyed syndrome and was almost talking chickapee, a name my friends had given me the occasional times when I couldn't quite pronounce my words after a few drinks.

The visit with the Days was a lot of fun, but my diet really went to hell in a handbag. I should have eaten less during the previous two months. I was certainly not obese, but was carrying an extra 20 pounds over my normal weight. The holiday was over. I was in the outback to work and hoped that between my responsibilities and the hot weather, the pounds would melt off. If the pounds didn't start to disappear, Mandy would continue to call me a wolfer, the alias for big girls Down Under. My weight gain hadn't been a real issue for Lee. It bothered me more.

"You can either be fat or you can be ugly, but you can't be fat and ugly," he always kidded. It wasn't what I wanted to hear, but Lee wanted me to see humor in my anguish. I had to face the facts, I had grown out of my clothes and I had to get back into them.

February 16 was Lee's 32nd birthday. Stuart and I made a chocolate cake with chocolate icing. After supper we surprised him with balloons, the cake and his birthday presents. I had gotten him a carved wooden pig from PNG. The pig represented many things—their importance in PNG and our visit there, as well as Lee's friends back home. (Years earlier our Brazilian mate, Ricardo, stayed at my parents' farm. We often went out with Lee's cattle friends. "Yousa guys are all pigs lika me," Ricardo said. "I love yousa guys." A black-and-white pig yard ornament given to us by Ricardo graces our Maryland front porch.)

We ran low on meat and outback hunters Lee and Shane went out to kill the fatted cow. That was one great advantage of living on an outback station: When the food supply was depleted, you could always count on another beast to provide protein.

Our conversations usually turned from jokes to world news to family heritage. I told them my parents' farm had been in the Long family for 100 years. My seventh grandfather back, Philip, had come over in 1749 from Germany on the ship *The Nancy*. I enjoyed genealogy, no matter whose family or farm I researched.

Both of Mandy's and Shane's parents operated huge sheep stations in the south. Mandy's heritage dated back to the Ponton brothers, who were convicts from Britain. They were sent on the ship *Sultana* to Australia for their punishment and were imprisoned from 1859 to 1863. Mandy said it used to be "hush, hush" to be descendants of convicts, but today it was the "in thing." (Nearly 170,000 convicts were shipped to Australia between 1788 and 1868. Following the American Revolution, Britain was no longer able to transport convicts to North America. With jails overcrowded in the United Kingdom, Australia was the alternative location. British colonization of Australia was based largely on convict labor.)

After the Ponton brothers served their sentence for a minor crime they were the first white men to explore the southern region of Western Australia. They developed Balladonia Station, a successful sheep station that has been in their family for 120 years. Balladonia continues to be an operating sheep station and Mandy's parents, John and Jackie Crocker, have opened up a museum at their remote location 100 miles east of Kalgoorlie on the edge of the Nullarbor Plain. The museum features more than 300 original paintings by Amy Ena Crocker, John's mother. She died in 1989 just four days short of her 87th birthday. Her paintings are well known in Australia. Mandy's grandmother was infamous for saving and preserving small animals and plants. The jars are also displayed at the museum. Balladonia Station made international headlines in 1979 when the American space station Skylab crashed there.

Family history intrigued me. I listened silently as the tales were retold. Mandy said her great-great-grandfather's brother was stolen as a child from the family's yard and eaten by the Aborigines. Legend or not, it seemed most white folks Lee and I encountered had little respect for Aborigines. I was not about to engage in a debate about the right or wrong treatment of the country's indigenous people. I would not be swayed by anyone's views. I was fascinated with Aborigines and hoped we would have the opportunity to get to know some of them, but first we'd have to secure our next job in the outback—it wasn't easy.

Simply Aware

The fury of the storms I sought, but didn't seem to find,
Has diminished in importance and faded from my mind;

Replaced by simple pleasures like the rising of the sun,
Setting eastern skies on fire, a fresh day has now begun;

Red sea of the Pilbara, slick calm in every direction,
Mosaic rippling ranges break the tide of mulgas with exception;

On this arid sea; life has a simple meaning,
With the fresh burst of rain; pools of spinifex begin their greening;

A lazy rainy day to put some thoughts together,
No sense in getting crossthreaded—can't control the weather;

Nothing is for certain, so little can be predicted,
I know my plans for the future will often be conflicted;

Don't mistake me for apathetic or think that I don't care,
I revel in wonder at the gift to be aware.

Lee Chaney

Lee, The Snake Slayer

W e had two weeks left at Juna Downs—two weeks that I prayed would continue my no-snake streak. I questioned Lee's decision for selecting to work in a country that had nine of the world's ten most deadly snakes.

"Always look where you walk," Mandy warned us. "And at night, if you think you need to get out of bed, grab your torch and scan the floor before you step out." Okay, I was really scared!

My great fear of snakes had been fueled from childhood. When I was five I lived on Springfield Dairy Farm, home of my great-grandfather, Pappy Leatherman. I often spent days wandering about the 200-year-old plantation-style homestead in search of pets or flowers to pick for Mom. One day I re-called standing on my tippytoes trying to retrieve beautiful blossoms from a dogwood tree. My hands were almost full when I sensed something very strange. I looked down and an enormous black snake was coiled up beside my little feet. I screamed bloody murder and dashed to the house in uncon-trollable fright. My ever-brave mother came out, as I toddled behind her apron string. She picked up the snake with a pitchfork and carried it to the chicken house.

"Mom, why are you putting the snake in the chicken house?"

"Don't worry, the chickens will take care of it."

And then there was the time my brothers put a baby snake down my shirt—brothers were supposed to terrorize their sister—right? It was no surprise I had a snake phobia.

I scanned the ground before each step at the cattle station. My steps were forceful. I hoped the vibration of the ground would make any snake retreat. We had a large box of extra clothes sent from the States and had all of our belongings scattered across the floor near our bed.

"Becky, you might want to get all that stuff up from the floor," Mandy said with a concerned look. "When it's hot snakes come in the house in search of a cool place to find solitude. I reckon a snake could find a pretty good hiding place in all your stuff."

She didn't have to say another word. I moved every last box and bag from the floor. Then to add to my fear, Mandy shared a few snake stories to really get my attention. During the Days' eight years at Juna there had been 15 large snakes in the house—none of which saw the light of day again. On one occasion, Mandy had just gotten out of the shower and saw a venomous six-foot mulga twisted up in the corner of her office like a donut. With no time to think, the bold bush woman slipped on her cowboy boots and grabbed the shotgun. She walked toward the snake, still naked and dripping wet. Stuart was only a little boy at the time and snakes were dealt with immediately. Mandy aimed and fired. She blew the critter to pieces.

"The snake was as thick as a horse's doodle," she said. "And if you haven't seen a horse's doodle, it's pretty darn large."

I heeded Mandy's warnings and was almost neurotic about looking out for snakes. The only snakes I'd seen were ones that crossed the highway. I knew our luck would run out some time! Lee and I stayed in one part of the single-floor home while the family slept in an addition across the center veranda. One night the Days had gone to bed and Lee and I were in the kitchen checking e-mails when the most unusual sensation prompted me to look over at the kitchen sink.

"Lee! Lee! Go get Mandy and Shane!" I said in a nervous, but controlled tone as I climbed on top of my chair. On the floor in front of the sink a small snake slithered. I had read the venom of small snakes was sometimes as deadly as that of large snakes. My research had also provided the descriptions of many of Australia's dangerous creatures. It was a king western brown, distinguishable by the black ring around its neck. King western browns were very prevalent in the Pilbara and were considered one of the most poisonous. When you said "snake" in the outback, people moved. Mandy was in the kitchen in a flash armed with a broom.

Mandy swirled the broom handle down on the snake. The force partially dismembered it as it squeezed between the counters, where there was little question the animal would die. That was all the excitement I needed for one evening. We had a very slow connection online and continued to download e-mails. There were two doors in the kitchen that made me very nervous. I maintained eye contact on the bottoms of both doors, which were an inch off the ground, making them easily accessible by a snake.

A half-hour after the first sighting, I gasped, "Oh my God, Lee, it's another snake." Its tongue flickered as it poked its head under the door.

"We can't go through the door to get Mandy and Shane," I said, on the verge of losing composure. The snake was shimmying under the door between us and the veranda. There was no way to get help. The snake seemingly rendered us helpless until my "Crocodile Dundee" husband burst into action. He grabbed the "snake-killing broom" and moved slowly forward. My heart raced. "Lee, be careful! He can easily strike you."

It was another king western brown. Lee Dundee lowered the "killing broom" to just about three inches above the snake, then quickly crushed the head between the floor and the broom handle. As it fought to escape, its tail whirled wildly.

"Oh my God, Lee! It's pulling back—kill it, kill it, before it gets away, kill it!" I screamed.

I was worried about Lee getting bitten, but I was more worried about him missing it and it coming back later that night and getting me. Always the ever-concerned wife? Two king western browns in one night seemed like a dreadful dream. I thought, *Where there are several baby snakes, there are a big and deadly momma and poppa snake, and now a pissed-off momma and poppa snake.*

The days that followed were anything but calm. I had nightmares of stepping on snakes or being trapped in the bathroom with one. My imaginary scenarios went on. It would be our only snake sightings at Juna, but certainly not our only snake clashes in Australia. I was both entertained and frightened by the many snake stories we heard. Some people were in the dunny (outhouse) and had to flee with their pants around their ankles because a snake was behind the toilet. Mandy and Shane had often just missed stepping on them by inches. Mandy's friend, Michelle, was bitten the week we were leaving. She was hospitalized and required an I.V. drip until she recovered. Snake danger was real and I prayed my demise would not be by the fangs of a king western brown. I'd heard snake venom was painful and I hated pain.

There was never a dull moment at Juna, but that made our visit all the more interesting. I watched a legless lizard maneuver around the house in a frenzy. Another small lizard found refuge on the floor by our bed. What really worried me were the nickel-sized beetles and warty frogs in the house that made perfect snack food for snakes. My wishes for a rodent-free house were futile.

Stuart got crossthreaded at me for making him work. The boy was a brain, but when it came to work he was, in my own father's words, "As worthless as tits on a boar hog." Strenuous activity was not his forte, but his intuitive nature made him likable. Every night I went into Stuart's room to terrorize him. I tried to give him a good-night kiss and he always pulled the covers up to hide.

"Missed me, missed, you didn't get me!" he'd yell. He acted like he hated it, but if I didn't go in, he'd ask his mother why I hadn't said good night yet. So I continued to pick on him, to his delight.

It rained a lot those final two weeks at Juna. Flooded roads trapped us at the station for days. The rains made it impossible to do too much outside and the lack of exercise did nothing for my weight-loss program. I had gotten into a pair of Mandy's strides, but they were so tight I could hardly breathe. I forced myself to wear them all day—good punishment for cheating on my diet. Lee had already managed to work off some of his excess weight. He had picked up 27 pounds during the first two months of our trip and was tipping the scales at 182. Now he was down to 170 pounds. He looked good. "Skinny," as his brother, Allen, often called him, needed some extra pounds anyway.

I resumed my strict diet, drank heaps of water and cut my portions back drastically, but it didn't seem to help. I'd even nearly eliminated beer consumption. I didn't have to drink, it was simply a social aspect I enjoyed. I hadn't suffered a hangover on the whole trip. Either a sign of maturity or a sign of low funds.

The end of February neared and rain continued to pound the Pilbara. We got more than four inches in three days. I didn't know Australia had monsoon season! I felt claustrophobic and wondered, *When the hell will we get out?*

Maybe the outback's remoteness started to take its toll on me. I still thought it was an incredible place, but the rains held us captive—we couldn't work or drive anywhere.

We were like horses in a round pen—I couldn't escape and went in circles all day from one room to the next. I was anxious to be more productive. I spent many rainy days on Clyde. Oh, what would I have done without Clyde? I worked on feature stories, typed in my journal and replied to e-mails. Clyde was my diversion, my solace, my connection to an outside world that I couldn't get to. He was my link to the people and places I missed and loved. I wasn't homesick, but eager for the rain to stop and eager to work.

Lee didn't do well either with nothing to do. Clad in his Drizabone and bush hat, Lee went out to check the horses.

He didn't want a repeat of another horse speeding through a barbed-wire fence. He was gone for hours; it was dark. I worried myself into a panic of awful thoughts. I pictured him suffering from a snake bite, struggling to get back to the homestead. Or maybe he was lost amongst thousands of acres, walking deeper into scrub or maybe he was attacked by a pack of hungry dingoes. I was the Drama Queen, after all. I told Mandy I'd give him ten more minutes and then I'd go look for him.

A dark figure walked through the door. Lee looked cold and wet, but he was so handsome in his long leather Drizabone, I almost forgot about being worried that he had gone off alone.

"Next time, I'm going with you," I said. "And by the way, if you weren't already mine, I'd have to have you."

His eyes lit up probably thinking he might get lucky. Lee was blessed with features that made him attractive whether he was in a suit or completely covered in dirt. When we started dating, girls often came up to me and said, "Are you dating Lee Chaney? He's hot!" Lee couldn't have cared less about his appearance and that made him even more appealing.

After five inches of rain had drenched the ground, the sun finally reappeared. We continued to help the Days pack up for their move. Stuart helped me carry boxes to the truck.

"Do you have a good hold of the damn end, we wouldn't want to drop the bastard," the brash youngster said. I just laughed—pretty much everything out of the boy's mouth shocked me. Although Stuart had a colorful vocabulary, he was years ahead of his peers and would, no doubt, be a professor or a scientist one day.

Mandy and Shane contemplated over their horse situation and wondered if all of them would fit on the semi.

"Well, if they don't all fit, we'll just have to shoot one," Mandy said. I was miffed and thought at first it must be a cruel joke, but she was serious. Any horse that didn't fit on the truck would be shot and left behind. That was life in the outback—not something I agreed with, but I understood and respected their decision.

We went to the big shindig that Hamersley Iron threw honoring Mandy and Shane. Lee and I volunteered to watch Stuart while they enjoyed their farewell party. We ate supper in the hotel's restaurant. I was incapacitated by a migraine headache and retired early to our family-sized hotel room. Lee and Stuart came in an hour later. They played cards for several hours in the adjoining room. Lee taught Stuart three new card games. I wasn't asleep and enjoyed eavesdropping on their game commentary.

"Stuart, ya little shit, don't cheat on me." Lee repeated.

It was 10:30 when they came to bed.

"Good night, Lee."

"Good night, Stuart."

They both assumed I was asleep. When Stuart pulled the covers up and closed his eyes I snuck over to give him a kiss good night. I nearly scared him to death, but Lee warned him. Stuart breathed a huge sigh of relief. "Thanks buddy, she almost got me," he said to Lee.

Stuart and I talked for another half-hour while Lee continued to tell us to be quiet and go to sleep. I said my prayers aloud and read my daily devotional. Stuart was very interested in God and Jesus. I tried to explain the best I could. He wanted to talk and talk and talk.

"Stuart, I'm sleeping now," I said, trying to end the conversation marathon.

Stuart was certainly never lost for words. I finally got into my own strides—a sign my new eating and drinking habits had paid off. The breakfast buffet in the restaurant was sparse. The Aussie selections were much different than the States. Where was the bacon, sausage, pancakes? Or the little blueberry muffins I loved so? Baked beans and spaghetti for breakfast? Was I seeing things? Did that migraine headache destroy some serious brain cells? I watched as folks piled baked beans and spaghetti on their plates alongside their toast and eggs. Once again I thought, *When in Rome, do as the Romans do.* I heaped the unusual assortment onto my plate. I recalled having baked beans for breaky one morning at Juna, but I thought it was because there was nothing else to eat. I realized it was actually a typical Australian breakfast served with eggs. Another day, another mystery solved.

I hadn't slept well the night before. I dreamt Lee was drunk and running around naked and licked a girl on the face during some national disaster. That morning I punched him in the arm.

"What the hell are you doing running around naked and kissing girls?" I asked.

"You know, you really have strange dreams," he said.

Back to reality and back to Juna to finish packing for departure. Jackie and John arrived with their huge semi, Crocker Transport.

It had been a year since Mandy had seen her parents. It was just four days until the Days would head south and Lee and I would head north to Wallareenya Station. We looked forward to going to Wallareenya, but heard the snakes were much worse. *Oh goody, I can't wait,* I thought sarcastically. *Maybe the spiders are baby-eaters too.*

It was hot and humid the day we loaded the semi. Amy and her calf loaded pretty easily, but the horses were complete idiots. The more stupid the horses acted, the more crossthreaded Mandy got. And when Mandy was mad, you shut up and stayed the hell out of her way. Mandy was really great, but you knew when to avoid her wrath. She was never verbally brutal to us, but Shane and Stuart did experience her bouts of fury. I must admit, the two of them usually deserved it. Sweat lathered the horses' necks and inner thighs. They were hot, nervous. As the steeds heated up, Mandy heated up. She exchanged some choice words with Shane. He piped back in frustration.

"Shane just don't argue with her," Jackie said. "Do what she wants and don't get her worked up anymore."

The strategy was insult the horses and maybe they'd load. "Go ahead ya slag bucket, get on the truck. I hope you don't fit so I can shoot you!" Shane yelled.

All rather comically, the loading was finally completed. Two cows and 21 horses positioned side by side. An older mare didn't make it on.

"I'll shoot the mare on Monday when I get back," Shane said. I couldn't believe it, but I knew it was more humane than letting the animal starve to death or be ravaged by dingoes.

Shane and John left at 2:30 for their 950-mile drive to Beverley to the Days' new farm. With Shane and John on the road, the rest of us branched out to do last-minute jobs. Lee dipped the six station dogs for ticks and kept an eye on Stuart, who was busy battling Nintendo's Pokemon and Pikachu. Mandy, Jackie and I climbed into the ute for a windmill run. Our main objective was to check a few windmills and retrieve five manure samples needed for nutrient testing.

We were 23 minutes from the homestead and noticed some cattle off to our right. It was important to get fresh samples. Mandy darted off the dirt road in their direction, yelling, "Shit!" We came to an abrupt stop, bogged down in the sodden field. For the next hour, as the unrelenting sun beat down on us, we worked hopelessly to get the ute out. We dug around the tires, placed old dried branches in front and behind the wheels and pushed the ute with every muscle we had.

"Get some dirt from the ant hills," Mandy told us. I had no idea what ant dirt would do, but I followed her orders. I kicked, pushed and prodded the giant mounds until cracks in the dirt made it possible to break off chunks. If the sturdiness of the ants' home was any indication, ants must be the best engineers in the world. We scattered the fragments of ant housing around the tires. It worked well. The ute had a little more traction. It rolled toward the top of the small crater the wheels had created in the ground, but it wasn't good enough. The wheels spun, gray stinking clouds spewed from the burning rubber and the gaping holes in the earth got deeper. We jacked the vehicle up in the front and tried to roll out. It was useless.

Sweat dripped. I felt sick from heat and exhaustion. Our clothes, shoes and hands were full of mud. Cuts on my hand were hidden by a smeared mix of blood and dirt. We dug and pushed, dug and pushed—no success! We were filthy, tired.

The sun was merciless. It was no surprise people died from exposure there. Rule number one in the outback—never leave the homestead without a water supply. I had grabbed two small water bottles. They were half empty. Mandy had to make a decision, either we wait for help that may or may not come, or someone had to attempt to make it back to the homestead—alive.

Embarrassed, frustrated and hot—Mandy knew there was only one choice. She must attempt the homestead. She took one of the half-empty bottles of water and before she started jogging slowly down the dirt road she looked at us one last time.

"Even if I don't make it back tonight, do not leave the vehicle," she ordered. "And if you get thirsty, the creek bed is about 300 yards through the scrub that away."

Jackie and I watched as Mandy got smaller and smaller until she had disappeared like an illusion in the baking sun. I was worried, but not scared—yet. We were mostly just hot and haggard. I prayed for Mandy's safe journey back to the homestead. It was ten miles and that was a long way in the middle of a smoldering summer day in the outback. Prepped in outback survival tactics, Jackie shared her knowledge of emergency skills.

"Never, never, under any circumstance do you ever leave your vehicle," she said, reiterating Mandy's instructions. "If you run out of water drink the water in the car's radiator." Gee, I'd never thought of that. That was a good tip. She told me many people had died in the outback because they tried to walk to get help and never made it.

"If you think your only hope for survival is to find help, then walk after the sun goes down," she said. "But that's only as a last resort."

So why was Mandy breaking all the rules? She left the vehicle, she didn't have enough water and she was jogging in 100-degree-plus heat. As the safety manager for all of the Hamersley Iron stations, she felt responsible for us. I knew Mandy was tough, but I couldn't help but think about the long trek in the scorching heat. As the hours passed Jackie and I sat in the middle of the road pondering our dilemma, but enjoying each other's company. We laughed when she told me how really "Australian" her husband was.

"John is a picky eater and bossy," she said. "He'll only eat meat and potatoes. And when his cup of tea is empty he simply taps the side of it with a spoon, that's my cue to get him another cup."

I couldn't believe John was so demanding, but it wasn't just John. Without stereotyping a whole nation, I'll simply say my experiences with Australian men revealed two hard facts—demanding and self-centered. Mandy once told me, "Mum always complains about Dad, but when they are apart, she pines away for him."

Jackie and I shared stories, not letting on that we were worried, but I could see it in Jackie's face. Since we were low on water, Jackie suggested we walk down to the creek and fill our bottle, if nothing else but to pass the time. We were about 100 yards from the ute, our steps crunching the tall dry grass. I stopped.

"Jackie, we're not dying of thirst yet. We still have a good 200 or more yards through very thick grass in which snakes hang out. If we get bitten we will surely die because there's nowhere to get help right now. What do you think?"

I didn't have to say another word, we did an immediate 180 and back to the truck we tramped. There was no need to risk a snake bite when we weren't parched yet. Jackie was 54 years old, had red hair and fair skin. She was only about five feet five, like Mandy. I knew Jackie felt the heat. But to be honest, she was more fit than I was. We waited patiently. It was still hot, but with the sun inching down behind the horizon, relief was minutes away. Idle chitchat continued to diminish our worries.

"When I went into labor with Mandy, John didn't make the two-hour drive to the hospital," she said. "I delivered Mandy in the backseat of the truck."

They had drama after drama on their station.

"Last year John was building fence and was bitten by a spider," Jackie said. "He got really sick and was in the hospital for ten days."

The bright sun dropped out of sight, darkness swallowed us up. There was no sign of Mandy. I glared down at my watch. More than two hours had rolled by since Mandy left and four hours since we left the homestead. Surely someone would be looking for us. Was Mandy okay? Should we start walking back? How long should we stay here? Why hadn't Lee started searching for us yet? Jackie and I had nearly surrendered to spending the night in the ute, then we heard a motor. Praise the Lord, help had arrived! Mandy was back with another vehicle. We hopped in the front seat and a great calm came over me as we drove home. The ordeal had been draining, but it provided much laughter—later.

"When I walked into the homestead I was drenched in perspiration," Mandy said, retelling her trauma. "Lee was still dipping dogs. He looked at me and said, 'Did you walk in or just get caught in a rainstorm? Could you keep an eye out for Chip? He disappeared after I dipped him. If you go in the house, could you check on the roast in the oven?' I felt like saying, 'Lee, I don't give a damn where Chip is and I'd like to shove that roast up your ass.'"

Lee didn't have a clue about our eventful day, but was filled in. The next morning we were up at 7. I knew Mandy was hurting because she was always up by 6. The freakin' mosquitoes usually woke me up every morning by 5:30 or 6. It was like some demonic ritual the winged blood suckers had planned for me. I'd gotten an average of six bites a day at Juna.

"I hope you don't get Ross River Virus," Jackie said. "It's a virus the mozzies carry and some of the station people have it. Once you get the virus you have it forever. It causes fatigue and other sluggish conditions for the rest of your life." I felt like saying, *Thanks Jackie, that's all I need.*

Shane called. He and John had arrived in Beverley. Shane flew back to Tom Price and Pat, the new Juna manager, picked him up. It was our last night at Juna. We were disappointed our time at Juna was ending, but ebullient about the next phase of our trip.

In the morning Lee and I were packed and ready to face what challenges Wallareenya had in store. We exchanged gifts and I asked everyone to sign our little black book. It was filled with special messages and sketches from people we'd met along the way. Some entries made me cry, some made me laugh, some I couldn't even read, and some just surprised me, like Jackie's message: "After talking to you on the phone, it was great meeting you. Although you sounded much smaller." What the hell did that mean? Did I have a skinny voice and a fat body? It was time for me to seriously lose weight. I wanted my body to match my petite small voice, after all. That was one thing you could count on Aussies for—straightforwardness and the God-honest truth, whether you wanted it or not.

Mandy, Shane and Stuart all wrote touching and hysterical messages. Mandy wrote, "I'm going to pine for both of you. Well, I'll pine for my wrangler, Lee."

She nicknamed Lee "Wrangler" during the first week to commend him for his newfound equine talents. It was the last night to irritate Stuart. I went into his room for the normal kissing formality. He screamed as though a two-headed monster had entered his dwelling.

"Stop screaming, Stuart, you know you like my kisses."

"You're right, I've always liked them," Stuart confessed with a sigh.

I knew Stuart was going to miss us. We said good night and Lee and I checked e-mails one last time. I had to go to the bathroom and couldn't find my torch. I walked slowly through the middle of the house, careful not to run into anything in the darkness. I had become much braver. Four weeks earlier I'd never have walked through the house without a torch. I made it to the bathroom, grabbed the doorknob and screamed! *Oh God, up-close and personal with a snake!* It was cold and clammy in my hand. I couldn't move. Then it leaped, I heard it hit the floor. Snakes didn't leap. It was a disgusting little frog. I scooted it out the side door. Lee heard me scream on the other side of the house and ran to my aid. Naturally, he thought it was funny.

On February 29, departure day, Mandy's friend, Tania, arrived to pick up the mare that Shane was going to shoot. The horse was saved. I took out the infamous Statue of Liberty sunglasses. Stuart's guinea pig, Jack, got in on the action, wearing the red, white and blue spectacles. We were all a little choked up saying good-bye. We had become family. We held off tears and snapped photos. Then, the inconceivable happened. The phone rang. It was Moya from Wallareenya Station. She told us the floods were so bad we'd never get near the station. She was sorry, but we couldn't work there.

I was frantic. Mandy gave me a list of station owners to call. No one needed help—it was the wrong time of year or it was too wet. Our dream of living, working and experiencing every aspect of the outback had come to a shattering impasse. I was struck with a melancholy sense of dizziness. We had come so far, spent so much money, had given up a good life in America and for what? For people to turn us away, to destroy our dreams. I was on the verge of tears when the phone rang again.

"Hello, Juna Downs Station, may I help you?" I said, pretending I was the happiest girl in the world.

"Is Becky there?"

"This is she."

"This is Jan Glenn from Ashburton Downs Station. You sounded like you were desperate when you called earlier."

"Well, we kind of are desperate," I answered, trying not to sound too pathetic.

"Are you willing to tear down old fence?"

"We'll do anything."

"Well, I haven't asked my husband yet, but I'm going to say it's okay. Call me when you get to Paraburdoo and I'll give you directions to the station."

"Oh, thank you so much." Click.

A job. She offered Lee and me a job. I wanted to jump, shout, but maybe my celebration was premature. Then I recalled our several acquaintances in the outback who had warned us about Ashburton Downs Station.

"It's rough-as-guts at Ashburton," one said.

"What do you mean rough-as-guts? Do you mean hard living conditions or that they are tough on their employees?" I remembered asking them.

"I just know it's rough-as-guts, so be prepared."

Rough or not, they were the only people willing to take us on—Jan Glenn was right, we were desperate.

We waved to the Days as they disappeared out the drive in their three-car convoy until the dust settled in their wake. Following a few last-minute chores and final checks, Lee and I stepped into the overloaded Road Toad for the next leg of our itinerary.

Lee pulled up to the homestead gate, I jumped out, opened it and then closed it behind him. I glanced back one more time, sad to depart our first outback post. I thought, *I'll miss Juna. I'll miss the family, the fun, the laughter. I'll miss the brilliant sunsets that pierced the evening sky, when hues of blue, peach, pink and canary yellow colored cumulus clouds in puffy swirls of magic.*

"Let's go Becky!" Lee yelled, interrupting my trance.

"I'm ready now."

Stone and Mortar

Great wall of security, wall of confine,
Not of stone and mortar, but the wall in my mind;

Foundation was set when I was a child,
Stronger I grew, deeper I piled;

Once comforting guardian, champion of order,
This wall I had built imposed stringent borders;

Held captive by the compound my own thoughts constructed,
Heard the world buzzing beyond but my view was obstructed;

Bold new ideas struggled with valiant persistence,
Their efforts refused by my mind's wall of resistance;

Was then I discovered of my self-imposed border,
Fear was the stone, ignorance the mortar;

I refuse to let this barrier grow one stone stronger,
Its restrictions I resent and can't allow one moment longer;

But how can I tear down a wall in my mind...?
The same way it was created...one stone at a time.

Lee Chaney

14

Rough-as-Guts

Distant rainstorms paraded across the horizon as we drove down the dirt access road to the bitumen. I continued to flash back to the antics at Juna, but was often interrupted by worries of the unexpected at Ashburton and what we might be getting ourselves into. Thoughts clouded my head as we drove toward Paraburdoo, the closest town to Ashburton.

Sweat again ran down my back. It was the end of February and temperatures soared over 100 degrees Fahrenheit. The Road Toad's lack of a cooling unit made the drive almost unbearable. Oh, how I missed the air conditioning in my little purple Plymouth Breeze at home.

We savored the views of Australia's landscape, fertile and green from the summer rains. Eight different walls of rain surrounded us, but not one drop of rain neared. There was no relief to the sun's penetrating blaze. Before arriving in the outback, I'd envisioned a dry, barren place. But it burst with blooms. My whole impression of the outback changed in that drive. It was the wet season and they were having a good year. In a few months I'd see the changes of the dry season, when cool air and winds ripped through the region.

We stopped in Tom Price at a caravan park for the night. Time alone was a rare treat which we hadn't experienced since we arrived in Australia six weeks earlier. I wasn't complaining about the shared visits—our farm contacts were the only way the trip was affordable in the first place.

Family stays provided first-hand interaction with a new culture and we saved thousands of dollars. But most importantly we established lifelong friendships. My Ohio friend, Esther Welch, once wrote to me that the agricultural community was like the "rings of an onion," never-ending circles of friends and contacts. She was so right. I had traveled to 25 countries and stayed with a farm family in most places. My rural roots were my foundation and the basis for the incredible opportunities in my life. The trip was Lee's first experience staying with families, all of whom he'd never met, many I'd never met. After our family stays in Tonga, PNG and New Zealand, Lee soon realized the tight bonds established. With greater lengths of time spent with families in Australia, that bond grew even stronger.

We kicked back in our little apartment and caught up on some needed intimate time. I updated my journal. We were up early, anxious to drive two hours to Paraburdoo and on to Ashburton. Lee pulled up beside the caravan park office to return our key.

"Don't you know you're not supposed to buy a Lada Niva?" the office clerk said.

"She's been tough so far," Lee said defending our bundle on wheels.

I was surprised the clerk's comment didn't hurt Lee's feelings. He was so proud of our 18-year-old clunker. It had taken us more than 1,000 miles in the burning heat of Oz, the country's given nickname.

Our first stop was the only gas station in Paraburdoo. We called Jan, who told us that recent rains made the 55-kilometer stretch of dirt road to the homestead impassable. "But don't worry," she said. "I've arranged accommodation for you. Call Nikki at 91-89-5579. She'll take care of you."

I was so relieved. Lee and I were running out of money and it was critical to start earning some wages. Being stranded in town didn't help, but at least we had a place to stay. I inserted more coins in the pay phone and dialed up Nikki's number. A cheerful voice on the other end answered. She had been expecting our call and instructed us to meet her at 1 Ashburton Avenue. I hung up, looked at Lee. My eyebrows raised and my head tilted in a confused manner. "Why are we meeting Nikki at a different address and not just going to where she answered the phone?" I asked Lee.

We wound through town, a small outback oasis boasting a population of 900 people. We crept down the street looking for the landmarks Nikki had given me and finally spotted the address and building.

"Welcome to Karingal Neighborhood Center, come on in," said a short, friendly woman with her brunette hair pulled back. "I'm Nikki."

We entered the air-conditioned building quickly, relieved to get out of the day's heat. After examining the walls and bulletin board, we realized Karingal was the hub of community activities, events, programs and social work.

"You'll be staying in our emergency shelter tonight," Nikki said. I thought, *We're backpacking and need to start work immediately, but to my knowledge, we aren't in dire straits yet.*

"This is for you," Nikki said, handing us a box full of supplies. "They are some emergency items you may need."

Lee and I took the box, thanked Nikki for her kindness and drove to the emergency shelter. We examined the contents of the box. Two cartons of shelf milk, toilet paper, cookies, bars of soap, instant coffee, tea bags and bread. After we pawed through the goodies I noticed the house rules taped to the wall and read aloud to Lee, "This facility is the emergency shelter for homeless people and domestic violence."

It really was a shelter. I couldn't believe it. We weren't homeless nor was I suffering from domestic abuse. It was a little weird, but a warm bed was a warm bed. I guess they thought we were two pathetic Yanks traveling on a shoestring—well, they were right. The lawn hadn't been mowed for ages and the house looked neglected. But the inside was homey.

The following day, we visited Karingal and asked if we could stay in the emergency shelter another night—the roads were still flooded. Nikki said it was fine. She worked with Shirley, a slim-framed woman with beautiful long red hair. Both social workers were passionate about their careers at the center. We downloaded our e-mail messages. During our time online, the women amused us with stories of Paraburdoo. Nikki said gossip was ridiculous in the small town.

"If there's not a rumor by noon, you start one," she said. "It's amazing when the rumor gets back to you, how much it has changed. There was a rumor about me sleeping with the town cop. I told them they could have picked a cop that was better looking. We call it the bush telegraph."

I reckoned the bush telegraph was no different than the gossip networks in most small U.S. towns, just that the outback had an interesting name for it. They told us to make ourselves at home and have a look in the op shop, their version of a thrift shop. Everything was $1 Australian (50 U.S. cents). We picked out a few T-shirts, long-sleeved shirts and two pairs of brand-new beach shoes, thinking at some point they just might come in handy. In addition to the $12 for our op shop treasures, we gave a $20 donation for our shelter stay in hopes that our money would help the next person in need. After two nights at the shelter Jan called and gave us the okay to make the attempt to the station.

"If you need anything, go to the post office and the ladies will give you some cash. They've done it before and I'll settle up with them later," Jan said.

"Thanks, that's really nice, but not necessary. Lee and I will be okay for a few more weeks," I answered.

Jan Glenn had never met us, didn't know us from Adam. Who was to say we wouldn't grab the money and run? During our brief phone conversations I looked forward to meeting the only person willing to hire us.

John, a man from the Ashburton gold mine, had also been stranded in Paraburdoo for three days. He was a typical outback character, navy blue shorts, navy shirt with the sleeves cut off. He bore the scars of a rough life—tattoos and leather skin. He drove a large ute loaded with three drums of gasoline. John told us that Ashburton was 60 miles from Paraburdoo as the crow flies but that our journey would be 100 miles, 60 on the bitumen and 40 on a dirt road.

"Look, there's the drive-in theater," Lee said as we drove out of town. It was a small screen, but it wasn't a drive-in, it was a walk-in theater. I'd never seen a walk-in theater. Chairs were lined up in front of the screen. We found out later that movie night was once a month with a double feature.

Finally, we made it to the sign that pointed left to Ashburton Downs Station. We turned and a five-by-five-foot yellow sign with black bold letters read, "Closed to the Public—Road not Accessible." Could the Road Toad make it? It was a four-wheel drive, but not like the heavy duty utes we'd seen in the outback. I didn't know if the Lada Niva could handle the extremes we faced.

We stopped and John got out to see how we were doing. He went back to his truck, stopped, opened his esky and grabbed an Emu Bitter. The green can of beer featured an emu on the label. It was Western Australia's state-brewed flavor.

The dirt road soon turned to muddy tracks. We came to the first flooded area. Lee stopped, put the Road Toad in four-wheel drive, and gunned the engine. We slipped from side to side.

"Slow down," I begged. "Do you think you're Mario Andretti?"

Mud splashed in on us. We couldn't put up the windows because the intense heat would have smothered us. I wiped mud from my arms, my face, the seat. Lee chuckled with sheer mischievous delight.

"You really love this, don't you?" I asked.

"Isn't it kind of cool. I told you the Road Toad would make it," Lee said.

I thought, *Men plus four-wheel drives plus mud equal a dangerous combination.*

Lee did what he thought were expert maneuvers to get through the swamp-like patches and flooded creek beds. We came to a deep tributary. I volunteered to put on my new beach shoes and walk through the water to see if the vehicles could make it. Draped with my camera bags I walked slowly through the murky waters, reciting nervously, "There are no snakes, there are no snakes, there are no snakes."

"No worries, mate. If there were any snakes we'd see them swimming on top," John answered.

I picked up my pace, heaving my legs through the thigh-deep water and sinking in the soft mud beneath my feet. "I think it's okay to make it through," I yelled across the creek.

John made the first attempt. No problem. He got to the other side and popped another Emu stubby. It was Lee's turn. He entered the water and moved pretty steadily until the Road Toad came to an immediate halt—the spark plugs were wet. Water was above the bumper and only half of the Road Toad was above water.

"Lee, make sure water is not going in the backseat," I yelled.

Lee opened the bonnet and John sprayed the ignition wires with WD40. They waited a few minutes. Lee started the engine and triumphantly reached the bank. He was even more smug over the Lada Niva's achievement. We continued to roll down the road, clumps of mud spitting from our tires. We swerved from 'roos and avoided areas that would probably swallow us in its quicksand-like sludge. We crested the last small hill and there it was, the powerful Ashburton River, in all its flooded glory. A torrent raged, spilling over the banks, uprooting trees and carrying debris with it. Somewhere beneath the waves of destruction was a cement road, one that we wouldn't actually see for three months.

Tricky, the station mechanic, and Mick, Jan's son, greeted us. Tricky was short, wore thick glasses and a worn black bush hat. Mick was a cute young man of 17, tall and a bit gangly. I was uptight contemplating the intimidating river crossing via motorized boat. It was a small metal boat, not much bigger than the canoes in PNG. What if it capsized? I could probably save myself, as I was a strong swimmer. But what about Clyde and all the camera equipment—we'd lose it all.

I nervously stumbled around the boat loading our gear. Mud oozed through my toes like cow manure did when I was a kid on The Farm. "That will make you grow," Dad often told me. "Put your shoes on before you get worms," Mom would warn.

Water gushed by. Waves licked at the boat trying to suck us in before we were ready. The Aussies held the boat steady as I apprehensively climbed in. I prayed I'd reach the other side. Tricky captained the first trip with just me and the gear. Clyde was strapped tightly around my neck and chest. That probably was not such a brilliant idea. If I fell overboard, Clyde's weight would drag me under. The boat skirted away from the shore and the current pulled the boat downstream until Tricky cranked the engine putting our little cruiser back on course.

Once across the river, I met Andrew Glenn, Jan's husband. He was a thin man, quiet, with a gray messy beard. The demanding outback lifestyle had aged his skin. He was probably younger than he looked. We loaded our gear in the back of the ute and I rode with Andrew a mile to the homestead.

"Welcome to Ashburton, I'm Jan Glenn," a tall, strong woman said. I was drawn to her immediately, probably because she reminded me of my own mother—energetic, tough, resourceful. After our time at Ashburton I learned that Jan's outer strength and stamina was matched by her inner courage and good will.

Lee rolled in next looking totally love stricken with the homestead, like a young man who realized he was about to get his first "root" as they call getting lucky in Australia. He wasn't taken with fancy property or decor because there wasn't any. Ashburton was a run-down station the Glenns were trying to resurrect. Lee was mesmerized with the location, the remoteness, and the fact he had finally arrived at his full-time job, at least for the three weeks Jan had promised to employ us.

"Would you like a cup of tea?" Jan asked.

"That sounds great," I answered.

Tea and coffee breaks were part of Australian culture. I asked Nikki the day before why people consumed hot drinks on blistering days. She said that actually tea and coffee had a reverse effect and could bring the body temperature down. I wasn't quite convinced of the theory, but went along with it. It was 3:30 in the afternoon, just about the hottest time of day.

"Follow me and I'll show you to the quarters where you'll be living," Jan said. *Ahh,* I dreamily thought, *Our own quarters where the jillaroos and jackaroos live.* I imagined it could be our private little air-conditioned unit located in a landscaped garden in the romantic outback. Flowers erupting with color and scent would greet me daily on my walk to the main house.

"I'm really sorry I couldn't get this place cleaned up for you," Jan apologized when she took us to the building.

"Don't worry, Jan. We appreciate the opportunity to work here," I said, totally giving her a line of bullshit.

"I'll go get some buckets, rags and detergent," she said as she disappeared back to the main house.

My first impression of our humble abode was that it was absolutely disgusting. There was filth everywhere—how could anyone expect us to live in those conditions? Containers of rat poison sat on shelves and in corners; spiderwebs strung from every possible nook and cranny; the sink was layered with mildew and rust. Dirt blanketed everything. The Quarters, as I called it from then on, consisted of a cemented area with roof and sink flanked by two three-foot walls. It was banked by two small rooms on the right containing a refrigerator and broken-down gas stove. A caravan was parked by the edge of the cement floor on the left. It was obvious no one had lived there for ages.

Reality check—the Glenns were the only people who would give us a chance. I had to suck it up and suck it up fast. It was an adventure, right? I could hardly comprehend the situation before me, but I knew I had to prevail, if not for myself, for Lee. It was a hell hole, but I was determined to make it our haven.

Jan returned, armed with cleaning paraphernalia. Where was my horseshoe when I needed it? It hadn't provided a five-star accommodation, but it did get us a job. Jan apologized again for the dreadful condition of our new home.

"No worries," I said flashing her my cow-queen smile. "We'll have it cleaned up in no time."

Before we were lost in the muck and misery of making the Quarters shine, Jan continued our tour. She showed us the shower facility. "Oh my God!" I said under my breath. It was almost enclosed; two sections of sheet metal were missing, which would expose the person showering to the world. The shower head was over a metal grate on a dirt floor. Later that evening I found out showers had to be quick before the shower floor turned to mud. It didn't seem real. We wanted an adventure, but I honestly didn't expect conditions to be this rough.

Jan showed us the *donkie,* or barrel of water that needed a fire lit under it daily in order to have warm water for a shower. The rusted drum was balanced on rocks with a tunnel for wood beneath it. A pipe ran from the drum into the little tin shed to the shower. Five yards from the open-air shower was the open-air dunny. The dunny was missing its door, but it did have a flush toilet—that was a bonus. Jan volunteered to clean the toilet. Other than the dunny door missing, the only problem was the intrusion of frogs, or damn disgusting frogs, as I grew to call them. Jan said they were a real nuisance and continually clogged up the toilets. Lee fished more than 30 of them out of our bowl. Not only did we have to scour the floor for snakes, but Jan warned us about the giant centipedes. She had just crushed a five-inch centipede on the dunny floor. It quickly became the main course for an army of ants.

Pictures of what I'd imagined colonial times being like swept through my mind. We were going to live like pioneers. I never knew it was that primitive in some areas of the outback. We had entered an alien world. We counted our blessings for the occasional electricity when the generator was on.

Lee and I took buckets of water, disinfectant, old rags and began the tedious task of removing the grime and grit. Lee swept and worked on the outside while I cleaned the caravan (house trailer). The caravan was muggy. My clothes stuck to my skin, sweat ran down from my armpits, tickling my sides. I tied on my do rag so sweat stopped burning my eyes. I scrubbed the counters, pushing clumps of dirt and foreign particles to the floor. Then, I dropped to my knees and wiped up the floor. It almost shined. We moved all of our gear inside the caravan. It was a great storage unit, but far too hot to sleep in.

We pushed the two single cots together outside on the cemented area. A tree growing just on the other side of the short retaining wall produced branches that hung over our beds. It was another one of those moments, when I said, "If our friends and family could see us now." I remained optimistic and turned my energies to trying to make the most of the situation. It wasn't complete poverty and we had been warned about Ashburton. Everyone has their own threshold of pain, discomfort or what they might deem "rough-as-guts." I hadn't met my threshold—yet.

The Glenns had only been at Ashburton for two years and other maintenance had taken priority over the workers' units. It was comparable to third-world conditions, but after all, the outback was another world. It was a long day. We ate with the family and retired to the Quarters at 9 p.m. Lightning illuminated the sky. Lee caught some of the spectacular lightning show on video. We crawled onto our separate cots and watched the flashes of electrical energy ignite the heavens. That was one advantage of sleeping outside—we could enjoy a lightning show or gaze up at dancing stars while we drifted off to sleep. We even saw two shooting stars, maybe a celebratory sign of our arrival to the outback where we hoped to find what we were searching for—hard work, solitude, quality time together—a renewed sense of being.

Before Lee was unconscious, we chatted about our arrival to Ashburton.

"It's rough, but I'm really glad to be here," Lee said. "It's actually really cool."

Lee's reaction didn't surprise me, and I did agree Ashburton was interesting. I lit a mozzie coil hoping it deterred the pests from seeking refuge from the incoming storm. The temperature had hardly fallen and the humidity had increased. It was my first night of pure hell in the entire three months of our trip.

That night as I battled insomnia, mozzies, heat and snake phobia, I couldn't help but compare it to a night I had spent in a backpackers' hostel in '92 in Sumatra, Indonesia. I remember it was stifling. Our room had a dull musky smell mixed with the odor of sweat other backpackers had left behind. What did we expect for $3 a night? Something kept biting me—it must be bed bugs, I recalled thinking. I'd never had bed bugs feasting on my tender skin. Between the heat and continuous bites to my hide, I was on the verge of a psychotic episode.

"Becky, what's wrong?" Kelly asked when she heard me sit up in my bed sniffling like a little kid who'd had a bad dream.

"These fucking bed bugs are driving me insane and it's so hot I can't stand it."

"Why don't you go take a shower and cool yourself off?"

At first, it sounded like a good idea, but as I entered the private little shower box, I soon realized it was all for naught. Indonesia didn't have showers, they had mandys, which consisted of a container of cold water with God only knows what micro-organisms and parasites. I took the small-handled pan, dipped out some cold water and poured it over my body. I continued the ritual, dip and pour, dip and pour, until the bites stopped inching and the cold water had soothed my sweaty skin. I returned to my room only to be overcome by heat and bites again. That night haunted me for a long time.

I thought I'd never face another night as challenging, but the first night at Ashburton came really close. The warm moisture in the air made it impossible to sleep and the mozzies were eating me up. I woke up and asked Lee if it was almost time to get up. He looked at the glow hands on his watch and reported it was only 1 a.m.

"Oh my God, Lee, one a.m.! I can't sleep, I'm miserable!" I said in utter grief.

"Sleep now, sleep now," a half-delirious voice said.

I believe it's a male trait that allows them to sleep no matter what. My dad could close his eyes anywhere and be quite comfortable to sleep. The same was true for Lee. The night didn't get any better. Finally darkness dissipated as the light of a new day appeared. Mozzies circled my head with their repeated singing in my ears, forcing me out of bed. I was tired, drained.

It was our first official day to start work. We were excited. Mick directed us to a fence row at 7 a.m. Clearing fence rows would keep us busy for days or weeks, but we were ready. At least I thought I was ready. Five or six strands of wire were cut and wrapped. We finished at 9:30 a.m. and went to another fence row.

The sun's blinding rays slowed my already fatigued body. I was sluggish and my face was flushed. That time Lee didn't say, "You look like a sick horse that needs to be shot and put out of its misery." Instead, he was concerned. He escorted me to the river, supporting my arm, fearing I was about to pass out. I splashed water on my face and neck until my entire upper body was soaked. My dripping shirt was glued to me, outlining every curve. The refreshing droplets revived me and I found enough energy to go back to the fence row. It was no secret the sun and heat in the outback often claimed lives, especially the inexperienced folks who traveled through its sparse landscape. By noon I begged to go in. I was nauseous. I doubled over several times gagging, but vomit never came. The heat was too much for me. I wasn't used to 100-degree-plus days yet. Even at Juna we rarely worked during the heat of the day. We trained horses early in the morning or late in the evening. At Ashburton there was too much to be done, regardless of the heat.

My workaholic husband insisted we work until 1 p.m. before taking a lunch break. *You're such a hard ass,* part of me thought. But part of me also respected Lee for being totally committed to his new job. I was physically ill, but still somehow enjoyed finally spending time with Lee. I'd always wanted to work with him on a farm as my parents had done since they were married. They had many difficult years, but persevered. It was 17 years before they took their first vacation—dairy farming is demanding. Mom and Dad developed a great farm, great cows and six great kids I might add (dysfunctional, but great). Long View Farm was a family affair— kids and cows achieving some of the top honors in the country. It wasn't easy, no family business ever is. It was downright brutal at times. The 1980s brought plummeting commodity prices—rural America was in a crisis. Farmers went bankrupt, committed suicide. Through the sea of ups and downs, our family stuck it out. I dreamed of working with Lee on a farm one day. The outback would be our test of compatibility.

Finally we stopped for lunch. I was careful not to eat too much. Large meals and heat were not a good combination. No doubt, I would look like a sick horse again. After lunch Jan told us to take a rest because it was 40 degrees Celsius (104 degrees Fahrenheit) and humid. There was no air conditioning at the Quarters; resting there was impossible. I sat on the veranda at the main house in the shade. Lee went down to the shop and helped Tricky. Heat or no heat, Lee was not about to take Jan's advice to do nothing. He was too antsy.

Every day we gathered with the family for smoko, the midmorning and afternoon snack break to enjoy a "cuppa" of steaming coffee or tea. According to Andrew, Smoko derived in the 1800s when cattle and sheep drovers took a break for a smoke and a cuppa on the trail.

Following smoko, it was back to fencing. I filled our water jugs. Dehydration could be a killer and I had other things to worry about—like poisonous snakes. It was hard to drink the water, almost unbearable. It tasted like dog vomit, at least what I'd imagined canine puke to taste like. Jan said calcium buildup tainted the water. Even tap water in Paraburdoo had the same distinctive nasty flavor. Jan gave me some citrus juice concentrate to add to the water to make it drinkable.

We headed back to the fence row, bumping along in the ute following dirt paths through the scrub. Wrapping wire was tedious, dirty work, but I could imagine worse jobs. Lee and I each had wire cutters and had to be careful the ends of the wire didn't jab us in the eyes. A slight breeze later that afternoon hit the sweat running down our faces and the backs of our necks, offering a subtle coolness.

"The most fun at the station so far is the different four-wheel vehicles I get to drive around," Lee said. Men and machines. Didn't matter how big or how small, they were always fascinated with utes, tractors and semis. It was a good thing Lee and I had agricultural backgrounds. Jan told me she wouldn't have even considered hiring travelers without a rural upbringing. It was because of our experience that they didn't have to hold our hands. They gave us a ute and sent us on our way.

When "Mario" (Lee) was racing through the scrub one day making his own path, we got lost. I was a little concerned. I had no fantasy of being lost on a nearly million-acre cattle station. We soon found the track and returned to the homestead at 6 p.m. Mick sent us back to the dump area to unload our rolled fence.

"Crikey!" I said to Lee. "What a dump pile."

Referred to as the "tip," it was the station landfill. Piles of junk and recyclable materials covered acres and acres of ground. Items were scattered everywhere, from old trucks to refrigerators and from rusty wire and pickets to ancient equipment. All stations had a tip. It was impossible to cart all the rubbish away or have it picked up.

The evening news featured Cyclone Norman off the west coast. He was moving out to sea. Cyclone Steve, near the Kimberleys, had lost his strength and had been downgraded to a tropical storm. That was a comforting thought. I ate a light dinner, determined more than ever to drop some pounds. My pants were still extremely uncomfortable, especially in the heat, and according to the Glenns, it could get much hotter.

"A year ago it got up to 51 degrees Celsius (126 degrees Fahrenheit) here," Andrew said.

Other than fighting sun poisoning, those first couple of days working together on the fence row were magical. Lee happily got grubby, worked up a sweat—he was enraptured by physical labor.

The Ashburton folks filled us in on other Aussie topics and Lee and I spent the evening laying disclaimers to several Yankee stereotypes, like all Americans have a big mouth, Americans are snobs, Americans think they're better than the rest of the world, and Americans drink a lot. We talked about work during the next few weeks. Jan told us how critical it was to clean up as much old fence and wire as possible.

"In 1994 at Meentheena Station, my horse got hooked up in some wire," Jan explained. "I went to dismount, but my horse reared up and fell back on top of me. I couldn't move. Andrew put me in the back of the ute and parked me under a tree in the shade. We were mustering and Andrew couldn't leave the mob. I remember smelling something really rotten. I looked up and donkey and 'roo legs were hanging from the branches for the dogs to eat. The pain got worse and Andrew finally called the Royal Flying Doctor Service (RFDS)."

"The doctor said to give her some pain pills and try to stand her up in an hour," Andrew interjected.

"Andrew tried to stand me up and I blacked out," Jan continued. "I think it really scared him. At 3 p.m. the flying doctor finally landed to take me in. Then the pilot said the airstrip was too short to take off so Andrew had to get the grader and lengthen the runway. I'd broken my pelvis bone."

Every story shared painted vivid pictures of harsh outback life, often disturbing and tragic, but also brilliant depictions of an incredible lifestyle. Jan told me that four people up North had been bitten by snakes that week. I'd

179

already encountered a few snakes in the outback and was still completely freaked out by them. On our initial arrival to Ashburton, I had one major question. "How long do you have to live before a snake bite kills you?"

"About two hours," Mick said nonchalantly.

"We're two hours from town so that doesn't make the odds of survival very good, does it?" I asked.

"Don't worry," he added.

But I was worried. I was downright terrified. Snakes came out at night to do their feeding. There were no lights on the station's airstrip; it was a pretty sure bet that a snake bite would result in death. And as usual a morbid thought entered my brain, *That's not going to please Mom and Dad to pick me up at the airport in a body bag.*

It was a scary walk in the dark from the main house to the Quarters. Even with a torch, I couldn't see very well. Every night when I needed to use the bathroom, I made Lee hold the torch so I could go right beside the caravan on the dirt ground. I was too afraid to use the dunny at night because of the long grass I had to trek through to get there. Lee didn't complain. Although he didn't share my fear, he accepted my almost deranged behavior. Ain't love grand!

No city lights, noisy highways or blaring emergency alarms—it was quiet in the outback. Unbelievably quiet and serene. Almost frightening except for the occasional breeding calls of frogs or the bawling of a lost calf.

"I really like it here," Lee said on our third night as he lay in bed looking out across the black sky lit up by glimmering stars.

We knew we were there for at least three weeks and maybe six if the Glenns wanted us to stay. I liked it at Ashburton, but didn't seem to have the connection that Lee seemed to have after just the first few days. I hoped I would find that same feeling, but only time would tell. I'd either learn to love it or hate it.

Why I Am

I live my life here and today,
Dream of my future, though it seems ages away;

A dream is a ship adrift, if it is just wishful thinking,
I must keep the wind in its sails, keep it from sinking;

I cannot dwell on storms from the past,
Though they hindered my progress and altered my path;

I will keep the wind in my sails, come struggle or strife,
I'm just a man, living my life.

Lee Chaney

Cyclone Steve

W e'd only been at Ashburton Downs Station a few days, but it was long enough to realize it wasn't going to be easy. A shadowy haze rose from the scorched ground as the sizzling sun threw its dagger-like rays. The mozzies drove me insane at dawn and dusk. The winged vampires would circle my head at 5 a.m. and by 5:30 their irritating buzzing forced me to get up. Lee and I spent the week working on the fence row. Every time I thought there couldn't be any more old wire to wrap, we found more. It was stifling by midday. We sometimes took breaks from 1 to 3:30. It was difficult adjusting to the outback climate; the heat made me dizzy and nauseous.

Wrapping the stiff, rusty barbed wire was no simple task. We conquered different techniques battling the wire. In some areas we wrapped it by hand, and in others we used a wire wheel attached to the back of the ute. The hand-cranked invention made the job faster, but more difficult. Days were long as countless silent hours were spent cutting and rolling wire. When we were in talking range, we'd drum up conversation to distract us from the intense heat.

"I like working with you, dear, but you're a pain in my ass to travel with," I told Lee in jest.

In a silly, even goofy kind of way, humor was my outlet. I had a gift for entertaining, making people laugh. My other outlet was Clyde. Any spare moment I had, I worked on our laptop, tapping out stories and updating my journal. The kitchen was my office, but people traffic and irritating noises made concentration nearly impossible. Frogs strategically staffed positions around the kitchen like soldiers on military patrol. The army of intruders delivered a symphony of annoying sounds. Australia's wet season brought an epidemic of the leaping amphibians. They invaded the kitchen and dunnies—everywhere there was moisture. I didn't really mind frogs. I minded their thin, short, black rolls of frog shit on everything. Their outbursts of song aggravated me and ruined my quiet time. I'd ignore them, then vault from my chair, swooping up a handful of the little orchestra of singers and toss them out the door.

When it was too wet to work on the fence row I prepared meals, landscaped and cleaned the main house and cold room. The cold room, or giant walk-in refrigerator, was quite literally the coolest job on a sticky hot Australian day. I organized foods that needed to be used soon and discarded the rotting provisions that looked like someone's science project.

We felt more comfortable with the family every day.

Jan talked and talked and talked. I couldn't blame her. She was isolated at Ashburton, devoid of female company and companionship except for occasional phone calls to family and friends. She had Andrew and Mick, but the fact was I had never met a man yet who could feed a woman's verbal desires. With little communication and no feminine contact, Jan ached for conversation and, of course, I gave it to her. It's not for nothing that Lee often asks, "Do you ever get sick of talking?"

With the absence of air conditioning and electricity, we continued to sleep outside. It left little opportunity for intimate moments, but it didn't bother us. We were so intoxicated with the adventure of finally getting to Ashburton to work that we thought about little else. Our tender moments were when our lips softly touched before we drifted off to sleep beneath the tar-masked heavens that exploded with thousands of sparkling lights, or mornings when we'd have a cup of coffee together before heading out to wrap fence, or times we didn't talk on the fence row, but our eyes met as if telepathically saying, "Wow, this is really special to be working together in the outback."

The closest I got to Lee that first week was when I nearly spooned him to death in bed trying to escape the howling winds of tropical storm Steve. The storm had gathered strength and was upgraded to a cyclone again. He whirled his ugly winds across the top of Australia. The storm system delivered sporadic torrential rainfall to the Pilbara. Cyclone Steve was a category two and we were on cyclone warning. He was traveling 18 kilometers per hour (kph) with gusts up to 150 kph. Rainfall in some areas had been up to 12 inches, producing devastating floods. Every few hours a fax transmission from the National Weather Center automatically printed out at the station. The eye of the storm was about 400 miles northwest of Ashburton. I was scared just looking at the printout and the round circles that formed the eye. It was getting closer every hour. The wind whipped and plump raindrops nearly blinded me as I ran between the Quarters and the main house. The saturated ground made it impossible to get to the fence row. All we could do was wait and continue to peel diagrams from the fax machine.

We were adapting to life at Ashburton and we liked the family. My bugaboo was with the dogs. The first couple of days I was ready to kill them when one of my flip-flops went missing. The damned dogs had pinched one of them and all I could think was, *My flip-flops have survived 20 countries in my lifetime and now, two stinking outback mutts have torn them up.* Lucky for the dogs I found my missing thong, as Aussies called flip-flops.

The wind grew fiercer. Cyclone Steve was getting closer. He was circling down around the northwest coast toward Karratha and was predicted to continue toward Exmouth. Neither town had recovered from previous cyclones that had wiped out most of their cattle and sheep stations. Cyclone Steve was technically still miles away, but we got belted with horrific winds, and sheets of horizontal rain that stung my face. The Ashburton River was well over its flood level.

After a few hours the rain stopped, but the wind continued to lash out like a circus performer's whip. Lee, Andrew and I wasted no time making rounds to as many windmills as we could reach. The winds were capable of spinning the grand water producers into oblivion. They had to be locked. We took the two working dogs, Frank and Bill, but I use the term "working" lightly—we never did actually use them on a muster or in the cattle yards. The other three dogs, Joy, Roy and Livingston, the "thong snatchers," were left behind. While Lee and Andrew locked windmills, I watched a flock of wild turkeys peck the ground as their feathers ruffled in the strong wind. Eight emus scurried through the scrub seeking a safe refuge from the storm. Passive red kangaroos ignored the cyclone's fury and nibbled on the crisp droplet-covered grasses.

The windmill run inspired Andrew to open up for the first time since our arrival. He talked about Meentheena Station, the previous station they lived on up north. The property hadn't been managed for quite some time before the Glenns took over ownership. In the first 18 months he killed more than 2,000 wild donkeys, camels and brumbies (wild horses). "The numbers had to be reduced because the wild animals were destroying the environment and eliminating the food resources for cattle," he explained.

Andrew told us about his days of droving cattle in Victoria. "We caught wild brumbies in the Snowy Mountains and sold them at the market," he said. "People were willing to pay big bucks for broken-in brumbies."

I told him one of my all-time favorite movies was *The Man from Snowy River.* He said his mate, Kenny Connelly, had been the stunt double in the movie for the main character, Jim Craig.

"You mean it was your friend who galloped that horse down the vertical slope?" I asked with an astonished look.

"Fair dinkum," Andrew said.

The Glenns were entering their third year at Ashburton. I thought it was still pretty rough, but when they arrived, Jan said it was unreal. All the windows were broken out of the house, the floors were caked with two inches of dirt and hundreds of rats had temporarily taken up occupancy. Difficult conditions were nothing new to Jan. She was raised on an outback station in Queensland where they milked cows by hand and farmed rice. "It's more remote and harder here in Western Australia," she said.

Lee, Mick and Andrew boated across the river to move the Road Toad and semi to higher ground in case Cyclone Steve brought more rain and flooding. A bloke called from Fossil Downs Station in the Northern Territory and said they were having the worst flooding since 1986. Crocodiles were floating in with the high waters and attacking livestock and had already killed two stock horses. Food was being airdropped to families who would be trapped for weeks or months. If Steve decided to turn inland, Ashburton lay right in his path. I'd survived Hurricane Agnes on America's east coast in '72, but our historic bank barn did not. I wanted adventure, but Cyclone Steve made me an emotional wreck— I was afraid of storms.

The heavens opened again, dumping buckets of cold rain. I got soaked sprinting to the dunny. All that rain would have been great collecting in a rain tank, but the Glenns didn't have one, as did many other stations. I adjusted to the unusual-tasting well water. Although my taste buds surrendered to the vomit-tasting water, my stomach rebelled and diarrhea hit me with a vengeance.

That evening I went into our partly open-air shower. As soon as I undressed and got under the shower, I was struck with an urge to poop. There was no way I was tramping back through the wrath of Cyclone Steve to the dunny in just a towel, plus I had to go and I had to go that instant. I went into the corner like a dog, squatted and defecated on the dirt floor. After my shower I cleaned up the slowly spreading pile before it became a hazard. I could hear the story, "Oh, yes, Lee sprained his wrist slipping in my diarrhea." Then I thought, *Jesus Christ, what was I being reduced to—shitting in the corner like an animal.*

The rain continued to confine us to inside jobs. I spent my time helping Jan and she shared countless horror stories with me about former employees. She told me about the manic-depressive cook, the lovesick German, the horny jackaroo and the half-dressed sheila. The crazy cook was about 35 and arrived with an injured hand. "The wrap was disgusting and soiled and all I could think was, This lady is going to prepare our meals?" Jan said. "I confronted her one day and asked if she was depressed. The cook snapped back and accused her husband of calling me. I told her that her husband didn't call, but I knew when someone had a problem and if she did have a problem, to take her medicine."

The husband actually had called and warned Jan that manic depressives were sexually active and employees should have a STD test. Jan was mortified. The cook had been spending time with Schultz, the German employee. Jan asked the cook to leave and Schultz volunteered to take her to the bus stop. Just over the river crossing Schultz ran out of gas. Luckily, Andrew was checking windmills and took him back to the station for petrol. "I think my superior German mind has left me," Schultz told Andrew.

Just when I thought she had exhausted her dispatch of misfits, I heard about the bitchy jillaroo, the adolescent-hormonal Aboriginal boy, blowup bloke and the flower-pot boys.

"Bitchy girl was horrible," Jan said. "She was rude and had no manners at all. She was a mate of the half-dressed sheila. Then there was an Aboriginal boy who was a 13-year-old stud and had several town girls always calling him. He was a good worker and I tried to set up a bank account for him, but his clan said that what he earned went to the clan. He wanted to come back this season to work, but I didn't want to deal with the clan issues. Conroy was a middle-aged bloke who managed to blowup our truck and shoot one of our family dogs while he was here. And then there were the two gay visitors who Andrew and I referred to as the flowerpot boys—they were really nice."

Jan's stories continued, every one more shocking and funny than the last. "Two Israeli visitors saw the sign for

Ashburton Downs Station and exited believing Ashburton was a gas station," Jan said. "They drove 50 miles out of their way, so we sold them some petrol. There was the dipstick environmentalist that arrived almost dead a few weeks ago on a push bike [bicycle]. He had gotten lost, ran out of tucker and water and was literally on his last leg."

Jan's station anecdotes often centered around men who had worked at Ashburton. "You know, guys have a hormonal problem," she said. "Anything with testicles. They just try to push and rush things and have to do the 'man thing'—I call it TMT."

"What does TMT mean?" I asked.

"Too much testosterone!" she said matter-of-factly. "All men suffer from it. It varies at different levels." I knew exactly what she meant and agreed wholeheartedly.

Upgraded to a category three, our cyclone warning had turned to cyclone watch. Steve's rage made a resounding visit to the station even though the eye of the storm was still a few hundred miles away. Rain from a dark, dreary sky drove into the already saturated ground. Slapping winds ripped leaves and fronds from the palm trees on the lawn, bark peeled off their trunks like a banana. The caravan we kept our things in nearly shook off its foundation. The cyclone was in circular limbo, teasing frightened residents when it turned a few degrees inland, only to straighten on its coastal track soon after. It didn't have to tease me, I was scared to death; but it was my demented fear—like half of me terrified for our safety and half of me thrilled by the prospect of experiencing a life-threatening cyclone up close and personal.

There was no fuel left to light our donkie. The storm made it impossible to find dry wood. I bravely got under the cold shower. Crikey! Goose bumps popped up on my body until I looked like a freshly processed chicken from "Perdue." Lee laughed as I jumped in place under the frigid streams. I tried to pretend it didn't bother me. Taking a cold shower in warm weather felt good, but quite another story when there was a cyclone blowing through.

"Cold showers are good for you," Lee said. "The more you shake the more calories you'll burn." I wanted to tell Lee he was a real jerk, but I knew he was only trying to help. I wanted to lose the extra weight I had gained, but I certainly found no humor in losing calories while I shook profusely in a cold shower.

Cyclone Steve was in his 14th day and finally classified as ex-Cyclone Steve and downgraded to a tropical storm, again. It was the longest cyclone in recorded Australian history. It had turned inland south of Geraldton and was headed across the interior. Carnarvon was in a state of emergency. The rivers were rising and the town braced for the worst floods in 40 years. They evacuated. Cyclone Steve was responsible for several deaths during its 6,000-mile-plus run.

Daily radio reports were crammed with news of the rain and wind's devastation. Travelers were stuck at roadhouses. Fourteen road trains full of food and supplies for outback settlements were stranded on the Great Northern Highway. Flood waters cascaded over low-lying areas of the bitumen making passage impossible. Sections of roads collapsed, sinking with the mud or simply ripped apart. The Great Northern and Coastal Highways were closed—the only ground lifeline into the top of Western Australia and the Northern Territory was cut off.

We were stocked with about three weeks of food and hoped we wouldn't have to have anything airlifted in. For the next ten days the ground was still too wet to get much done at the station. I helped Jan at the homestead. She exhausted her employee stories and shared tales of eccentric acquaintances.

"You would have liked my Aboriginal friend, Lizzy," Jan said. "She used to catch a goanna and cook it up and we'd eat it. It wasn't so bad."

"Yeah, it tastes like chicken—if you like chicken after its eaten a lot of dead stuff," Andrew chimed in with a mischievous smile.

He had a dry sense of humor, much like Lee's—not much to say, but when words were spoken, they made you think or laugh. I enjoyed Jan's company and was fascinated by her dispatches of station life. Mick was full of energy and plans for Ashburton and had just celebrated his 18th birthday. He was more motivated than any young adult I'd ever worked with over the years. Tricky, whose main role was the station mechanic, tended to get on my nerves at first. He tried hard to be friendly, but he irritated me with his directness. My reservations soon passed and Tricky, Lee and I spent many evenings exchanging banter.

It seemed I liked everyone at the station, but I hated one thing—Andrew's expectations of Jan. She waited on him hand and foot. She fixed his plate, got his tea—it was sickening sometimes. But then I remembered that was Australian culture. Aussie women were often subservient to their male counterparts. Jan told me Andrew was so spoiled by his mother that she felt obligated to continue the routine. "At first it was hard to adjust to because I'd go mustering and work hard all day and be just as stuffed as the rest of the crew, but I'd have to cook, clean up and do laundry on top of all the other."

Jan often talked about life at Meentheena Station. When the Glenns established Meentheena they had very little, not even a house to live in. They slept outside, cooked over a fire and squatted behind bushes for other important "business." They sounded like 19th-century settlers arriving to a wild frontier for the first time, but they were at Meentheena in the mid-1980s. Their homestead progressed slowly. After a year, they erected a bough shed to sleep in, nothing more than a wire structure stuffed with spinifex. Mick was only six years old and his classroom was the back of a horse float (trailer). His daily instruction was via the Port Hedland School of the Air. No wonder the conditions at Ashburton were no big deal to them; it was paradise compared to their humble Meentheena beginnings.

Every day I walked carefully in fear there would be a deadly snake stalking me. Once we left the main house at night, we only had 15 minutes before the generator shutoff. It was a race to use the dunny, brush our teeth and crawl in bed before our lights turned off.

During the cyclone I spent a lot of time inside. I worked on Clyde and served as the station's secretary, answering calls and taking messages.

"Hello, Ashburton, may I help you?" I asked.

"Who is this?" a curt voice asked.

"Becky," I answered. "Who is this?"

"Dorris, the next-door neighbor," she said. "Is Jan there?"

"Just a minute, please."

When Jan finished her conversation and hung up the phone, I asked, "Jan, how far does Dorris live from Ashburton?"

"About two hours," she said. I cocked my eyebrows inward and smiled. "What's wrong?" Jan asked.

"I just can't imagine calling someone two hours away my next-door neighbor," I said. The outback was a whole other dimension with its own perspective.

Jan and I started taking daily walks. It was relaxing and therapeutic. We walked and we talked, sharing more personal thoughts and stories. I admired Jan for the hard life she had endured and the sacrifices she'd been forced to make. Every day our friendship grew. Walking, along with my daily water intake, was my main weight-loss strategy. Since I refused to get up to pee in the middle of the night for fear of snakes, every morning my stomach ached. I'd either have to stop drinking water by 5 p.m. or conquer my snake and centipede phobia, and I knew that wasn't going to happen anytime soon.

Jan and I tackled the cattle yards in the afternoon. They hadn't been cleaned since the last muster in December, more than three months earlier. Gross, disgusting, foul, yuck! We picked up hundreds of rotten, maggot-infested cattle horns with our bare hands. The smell nearly made me gag. We took the barrel of decaying remains to the tip. The tip fascinated me. It was a great source of old and rustic items for my landscaping projects. The "Great Hole" that held the bagged trash and rubbish from the kitchen and other smaller discarded items was especially fruitful during my treasure-hunting digs. Two wooden fencing spools were perfect as plant stands and an old metal box was resurrected as a footstep into the caravan. My eye caught a rusty horse plow. The blokes moved it into the front lawn and I created a floral sanctuary around it. Old farm implements always made interesting additions to landscapes. Mom used antique wagon wheels, massive tractor tires and old livestock troughs at The Farm. I wanted to help make Ashburton into the showplace I knew it could be. If mustering season went well, the Glenns would be able to make the station improvements that had been put on hold.

During my quiet times at the station, I'd sit and stare. The land stretched forever, evoking a sort of alchemy that had already begun for Lee and me. It was like we were the only people on earth. It was no wonder Aussies called it the "Never, never" and the "Back of Beyond." Like a magnet, I felt drawn to the outback's subtle aura of acceptance, existence.

Sameness

It was March and our second week at Ashburton Downs. Every day we seemed to face new challenges or experiences.

"Lee, would you like to go up in the plane with me?" Andrew asked after breaky. "I need to check the property and flooded areas." Only a few stations had their own planes to check windmills and to use during mustering season.

"Yeah, that sounds great," Lee answered with the enthusiasm of a kid who had been picked by his teacher.

As usual, Lee was calm, I was nervous. Andrew's yellow two-passenger Super Cub looked safe enough except for the strips of gray duct tape secured on parts of the body and wings. I didn't think Andrew would fly unless he thought it was safe, but the duct tape offered little reassurance. I watched them taxi across the red-dirt horse paddock, turn and head back my way. The makeshift runway was typical of most outback stations, used by the RFD and cattle buyers. The plane rolled faster as the engine rumbled in full throttle. They lifted off, zooming right over my head and disappeared into the morning's light blue sky. An hour later they landed. A weary-looking Lee crawled out slowly. "That was really cool," Lee said with a big grin as his color started to flush back in his face.

Lee told me his first two-seater plane ride was fun except when Andrew dipped down suddenly to have a better look at the windmills and troughs. "That's when I think I felt a little funny," he said. "Looking down at the station was neat—it's so vast and green. I could really see all the flooded areas."

Even though the main house needed heaps of improvements, it had its own natural and historic charm. Part of it was built in the mid-1800s by Patrick Bresnahan, who helped develop Ashburton into a prosperous sheep station before his tragic murder. There were two reported stories. Legend had it that one of the area's stockmen was killed by the Aborigines. Bresnahan, along with a party of other station owners and stockmen, set out to find the killer. Unfortunately, Bresnahan met his demise at the end of an Aborigine's sharp spear. The other story stated that Bresnahan's organs failed as a result of alcohol abuse.

The house was an architectural symbol of the era. The one-story part-brick and part-white-stucco structure was situated on a small hill a mile from the river. The pioneer had probably hoped it would be high enough to protect it from flood waters. Since the Glenns had been used to living outside or in a bough shed for many years, house improvements were not a priority. They felt fortunate for simply having a roof over their heads. Many of the windows were cracked or broken out. Window shutters jiggled cockeyed off rusty latches. Wooden floors stretched across the three main rooms. Blotchy white painted doors hung crooked on their hinges—two were held shut with a rock.

The cathedral ceiling in the sitting room was meticulously painted with swirls of eggshell white. An antique chandelier was the room's focal point providing a certain ambience in the once-affluent parlor. A fireplace with mantel completed the mood. Its flames once glowed on the faces of drovers as they sipped their whiskey and exchanged outback yarns. Now, the mantel held a few framed photos of Jan, Andrew and Mick and Jan's other two mature children who lived on Australia's East Coast. Three pieces of furniture were strategically placed around the sitting room covered with blankets—mainly to protect their textiles from the dogs.

Mick's room also had a high ceiling, making it nearly impossible to sweep down cobwebs. With limited storage units, Mick's clothes were arranged in piles on a table. The six-foot-plus young man spent his summer evenings outside on a single cot pushed up against the side of the house. He lit a mosquito coil nightly, believing he had a better chance of getting rest battling mozzies rather than battling the muggy heat in the house. During the hot months Jan and Andrew also kept their double bed on the lawn where it was a few degrees cooler. Their room was smaller and had a storage cabinet built into the wall. I noticed something hanging from the ceiling around the light fixture. The black objects moved.

"Oh my God, they're bats," I shrieked as one swooped down to pay me a closer visit. I retreated to the kitchen. "I guess you know five bats have taken up residency in your bedroom," I said to Jan and Andrew.

"It sounds like 'The Addams Family' to me," Mick blurted out.

"I reckon the bats keep the mozzies away," Andrew said.

I never liked bats much before. They were scary and I've always feared they'd get tangled in my long hair. Before the trip I had written an article about local organic gardeners erecting bat houses that accommodated hundreds of bats. Every night each bat feasted on thousands of insects. The gardeners were pleased with their new biological insect control and had much appreciation for the nocturnal creatures.

Mick didn't share the same appreciation and he probably had every right not to.

"Damn, damn, damn!" Mick shouted as he angrily stomped into the kitchen the following morning.

"What's wrong, Mick?" I asked.

"First, there is bat shit all over my bed. Second, a damn bat plowed into my head when I got out of bed this morning."

I apologized for laughing, but couldn't help myself. I really was living with 'The Addams Family'!

The Ashburton River was still flooded. Water was swift, eroding the banks and uprooting weak trees. Jan and I dared a trip to town, first carefully negotiating the boat crossing in

197

the rapid torrent. We loaded two eskies in the ute parked on the opposite side. The eskies would prevent the perishable food from spoiling on the two-hour trek back home. Jan, Mick and I squeezed into the front seat. The ute made deep ruts getting through the flooded creek beds. At one questionable crossing, Mick got out and waded through the dirty copper-brown water to see if the ute could make it. We slowly drove through it.

We stocked up on groceries knowing the next trip to town could be two to three weeks away, as Jan was leaving for a bull sale in Perth that day. After the sale she was heading over east for a wedding and to cuddle her first grandchild. Jan's absence would leave me as head chef. I was looking forward to trying some of my tried-and-true recipes as well as some new Aussie specialties. Paraburdoo's grocery store didn't have the greatest selection. Maybe the shipment of supplies was still held up by flooded roads. The meat section had slim pickings. They did, however, have ox tripe, lamb's liver, and lamb's heart—all my favorites—not!

"I guess you know I'm not from around here," I said to the store manager. "Could you please tell me where I could find pie filling?"

"We don't have pie filling, but we do have canned fruit," he said.

"Okay, that will be fine. I'll just have to adjust my recipe."

No pie filling, what kind of a country was I living in? I was introduced to a host of new and unusual foods, but items I always used in my recipes were not available in Australia. We purchased $400U.S. in groceries. We pushed the carts out to the parking lot and packed the cold stuff in the eskies. Mick and I dropped Jan at the local hotel where she was spending the night before flying to Perth in the morning. She gave us hugs, but was reluctant to go. She had whined for days about all the reasons why she should stay home.

"You need to get off the station for a break," Mick insisted. "Mum, go and have fun. Look the bull in the eyes, if he looks back too hard, ya don't want the bastard!"

Mick had his occasional outrageous outbursts, but for the most part he was one of the most polite, well-rounded young men I'd ever met. Jan sauntered into the hotel and we started our long drive back to the station.

"Ya know, Mick, I'm 36," I said. "I'm old enough to be your mother."

"Are you really 36?" he asked.

"Yes."

"Well, Mum, I'm surprised to hear that," he said donning his perfect toothpaste-ad smile.

That was probably my first mistake at the station. From that day, Mick often referred to me as "Mum" or his "American Mum."

Our conversation came to an abrupt stop when a 'roo darted from the scrub. I heard a thud. The ute made out better than the 'roo. Mick bent the damaged wheel guard back into place. I thought a day off to go to town and get groceries would be fun. I was dead wrong. Thirty bags of groceries plus two full eskies was no walk in the park. It took several boat loads across the flooded river, then we trudged up a steep muddy bank. I was sweaty and tired.

I fixed steak for dinner, along with a corn bake and boiled carrots. Andrew and Mick liked their steak really well done or "really, really dead," as I put it. Andrew just sat at the table expecting me to wait on him hand and foot like Jan did. He wasn't my responsibility, but since we had only been at the station for two weeks I didn't want to rock the boat. I fixed Andrew's plate and placed it in front of him, cringing as I did so.

At dawn, Andrew left for Perth driving the road train. Every day the ground dried a little more until Lee and I were able to go back to work on the fence row. As usual, I got cut and scraped. It was like a war zone. I returned daily, nearly ravaged by new battle wounds from the rusty barbed wire.

"Here's dinner," Lee said as he walked in the kitchen carrying a blood-dripping 'roo leg.

"Excuse me," I said reprimanding him for getting 'roo blood on the cement floor I had just cleaned.

"It's for the dogs, but I wanted to show you," he said.

"Thank you, bye now," I said wanting the dog chow out of the kitchen.

"That was big fun—we all got one!" Lee said of his first outing to hunt 'roos.

'Roos were culled annually to keep the population in check. If numbers were not controlled, the environment suffered, as did the livestock in the area.

While Lee and I worked on the fence row, we were often at opposite ends. This meant I'd want to catch up on conversation at night. "Quiet now, quiet, sleep now, sleep," Lee softly chanted as he gently swept his hand repeatedly over my eyes trying to will me to sleep.

I could usually keep him responsive for about five minutes before his deep breaths told me he had fallen asleep. While Lee slept like a baby, the mozzies had nearly turned me into a monster. I cursed and retreated under my sheet trying to escape their blood-sucking frenzy. Their persistence wore me down. "Screw this, I can't deal with these mozzies!" I yelled as I jumped from my cot.

To my shock, Lee was still peaceful and content. Five mozzies circled his head buzzing in his ears like buzzards waiting to devour their prey. *How could anyone sleep through that?* I asked myself.

My lack of sleep slowed my pace the next morning, or I was "slower than other mornings," Lee would have said. He got very impatient waiting for me to go to the fence row. I had to put flavoring in my water, pack my Chap Stick, do rag, bush hat, gum and toilet paper.

"Are you ready yet?" Lee asked.

"You better start being nice to me and not rushing me so much—I'm PMSing!" I said as I climbed into the ute.

I was lucky, or should I say Lee was lucky that I wasn't one of those women who bitched a lot during their monthly cycle or "went on the warpath" as we used to tease my mom decades earlier. I did, however, get very emotional during my period.

It didn't take much to send me into a whirlwind of tears. Sometimes I wondered if Lee wished I was bitchy rather than being the emotional psycho he married.

We fell into the routine at Ashburton. Lee was loving station life. I guess to some people it was "rough-as-guts," but for us, rough or not, it was a great opportunity. Not only the chance to experience real Australia and a remote lifestyle, but to test our own relationship.

Work on the fence row got tougher with barbed wire mangled in bushes and piles of relocated dirt. I grunted, huffed and puffed, grunted, huffed and puffed, turning the iron wheel on the back of the ute, getting slashed by sharp barbed wire as it whipped around.

"That's really good for your stomach muscles," Lee said, thinking his comment was positive reinforcement. I felt like saying, *Screw you asshole, this is really tough,* but I knew he meant well. "I'm proud of you for hanging tough on the fence row with me," he added.

I didn't know how people lived in the outback. In some ways it was alluring and in others it was dismal. There were very few outlets for social gatherings or entertainment. It was as if stations held their residents captive. I understood why people in remote areas got depressed and why the outback had the highest suicide rate in Australia for men 18 to 24. It could be a very lonely place. Isolation took its toll on station people.

"You have to be a special breed of people to live in the outback," Jan often said. "Sameness, that's what we call the outback, sameness."

I knew I wasn't that special breed of people, but hoped I'd learn to adore the "sameness," not be made crazy by it. I didn't need anything else to test my sanity, the mozzies were doing a good job. The once dried-up billabong (pond) down from the house had finally filled from the recent rains, providing the perfect mozzie breeding ground. The billabong was a peaceful backdrop to the station. Horses often drank there, staring back into the pond at their reflections as ripples of water floated out from their muzzles.

Lee and I went to town for the biweekly grocery run. We stopped at Karingal to download e-mails. It was impossible to get a connection at Ashburton. We had 48 messages. The best message of all: my best mate Kelly announced her pregnancy. I teared up, both happy and sad. Happy that after nearly three years of trying she and Blane were finally pregnant, but sad because I wouldn't be there for her. We had been blood sisters since second grade when two silly little girls picked off scabs, smeared their blood and pledged a lifetime of friendship.

That was the toughest part of being away—missing special occasions and events. I got distressed on the trip a few times thinking about those activities or family members' health. Mom was a colon cancer survivor and Dad had survived a double bypass, but occasionally scared us with chest pains. Lee's mom suffered from lupus. Part of me thought we should have been home with them, but then I'd remember why we left the country in the first place. Our parents hardly saw us as a result of our hectic schedules and I knew how much they supported our overseas excursion. I stopped worrying and kept them close to my heart.

After stops at the grocery store, the hardware store, post office and the bottle shop for a six-pack of Emu Bitter, we started our two-hour trek back to the homestead. To my surprise, after one beer Lee turned into quite the talker.

"I'm glad I married you," he said.

"Why?"

"Because you're adventurous," he answered. "You came to Australia with me; you put up with my bullshit; you don't mind driving with me because it's the only time we have conversation; and you have your own language that keeps me in stitches."

"That's really sweet to say," I said.

"I feel really good right now," he said. "I never thought I'd come to Australia and now, I know I'll be back."

Jan called and reported they had bought six Hereford bulls and a Simmental bull. In between household duties I worked with Lee on the fence row. The heat didn't ease. Some days a slight breeze hit the sweat trickling down my face and neck and for a moment I found relief. After hours on the fence row the sun's powerful glare played tricks on me. The sun burned up the oxygen around me, choking the energy from my body. I took frequent water breaks, making sure I kept hydrated.

The days were incredibly hot, with temperatures soaring over 100 degrees Fahrenheit. After the day I almost had a sunstroke I started putting a drenched long-sleeved shirt in the freezer at night. By midafternoon when the sun and heat made me feel nauseous I'd put on the thawed, but still very cold shirt. It immediately brought my body temperature down. I tried to be tough and keep up with Lee. He admired my determination—after all, for the past ten years I'd worked behind a desk and did little work outdoors. I tried to put in an extra effort, knowing that every minute I spent working in the unrelenting sun, not only was the ball of fire burning me, but I was burning calories. Finally back in my jeans, though very tight jeans, I was committed more than ever to shed my unwanted pounds and inches.

Jan called again from Perth. She would be flying home in three days. That was good, it gave me a couple more days to clean and get things in order. I knew how Mom used to be when she was away and came home to a dirty house or hampers chock-full of laundry. Lee helped me get the lawn tidy by finishing my weed eating and mowing. It was amazing how nice a freshly mowed lawn looked and smelled, even in the outback. It was the only complete patch of green around. The rest of the station was mainly red dirt with scattered trees and bushes with no smooth fertile areas like the lawn. I got used to half-eaten 'roo legs lying on the lawn, skewered on metal pickets or dangling from a low branch. When the 'roo parts started to rot and smell we carried them to the tip.

Cyclone Olga hit the west coast. The eye of the storm stayed on the coast, but we were haunted again by fierce weather. The wind howled so loud it woke me at 3 a.m. Olga had blown in a cool front delivering sheets of cold rain. I crawled onto Lee's cot, snuggling close to steal his warmth.

By midmorning the winds had died down just in time for
Mick and me to drive to town to fetch Jan from the airport.
We stopped at Karingal Neighborhood Center to download e-
mails and learned they were sponsoring a community morning tea.

"Becky, will you be the international guest speaker?"
Shirley asked.

"Well, if you really want me to. What exactly do you want
me to talk about?" I asked skeptically.

"Tell everyone about your life in America and how you
ended up here in the outback," Nikki said.

All I wanted to do was send some e-mails and somehow
now was giving the keynote address. It was an easy job, really. I loved to talk and loved to tell people about our trip. I
met Fran, who had popped over from Tom Price for the morning tea.

"Write all of your adventures down," Fran said, "so you
can write your memoirs."

"Thank you, Fran," I said. "I'm hoping to write a book."

"That's exciting, just don't forget to write everything
down," she encouraged.

It was sometimes inconceivable the support and interest our trip generated both at home and abroad. I'm sure
there were people who thought and still think Lee and I were
crazy to quit our jobs to travel and work overseas. I didn't
blame them—sometimes on the trip I thought we were nuts.
Nearly everyone we'd met was fascinated with our story and
shocked to hear we'd left everything behind to pursue our
dream.

Jan was glad to be home. She asked me to take inventory of the Royal Flying Doctor Chest (RFDC), a green square
wooden box, 12 by 12 inches and just as deep. Due to the
distance to towns, all stations had a RFDC for emergency
situations because there was no such thing as calling 911 in
the outback. The chest contained surgical tools, medications,
injections and wraps for almost any medical predicament from
a simple headache to fractured bones and deep cuts. The
idea was to stabilize the victim until the RFDS could land

their plane on the station airstrip and evacuate if necessary. Established in 1927, the RFDS was developed to aid isolated families during emergencies. It was originally founded as The Australia Aerial Medical Service by Presbyterian minister John Flynn. His vision was to help people in remote areas of Australia's outback country. The name changed to the Royal Flying Doctor Service in 1942.

What the medical box didn't have was antivenin for snake bites. Antivenin was perishable and could not be stored at stations. *Crikey, that's just my luck,* I thought.

Following Jan's return she was still full of excitement about her big city adventure. "I didn't want to go, but it's good for me to get off the station sometimes," she said. "When I was in the city I was mesmerized by all of the things. I was goggle-eyed by everything I saw."

She was mesmerized all right. Jan returned with a new hair dryer, a microwave and an electric juicer. The woman didn't even have a mirror let alone any other luxuries. Jan only made it to the city once or twice a year and went hog-wild while she was there.

"You go, girl," I said. "Jan, you deserve to get yourself some nice things."

I swore it was like monsoon season at Ashburton. Sporadic rain showers and hot, hot weather had all the makings of a remote tropical South Pacific island. We just didn't have the crystal clear warm ocean to jump into.

Jan and I reinstituted our daily walks and admired the flourishing, healthy landscape. "When there is grass that means feed and a good season," Jan explained. "With a good season you have choices." She had a very good point. If Ashburton had a good season, the Glenns would be able to make business decisions that limited cash flow had prevented.

I enjoyed my walks with Jan. Lizards scurried across our path, leaving a squiggly trail in their wake. 'Roos leaped from hiding places in the scrub. The pink-and-gray wings of galahs waved in the air as the majestic birds took flight, allowing me a shadowed glance of their colored feathers in the setting sun. Curious white cockatoos perched on branches and atop windmills. What a wonderfully strange place.

Jan and I rarely had silent moments, but if we did, my thoughts drifted to family problems. Should I be home mediating the family crises as I'd done in the past? Is there really anything I can do? The answer was usually no. I knew I was where I really wanted to be—with my husband. We hoped to find what it was we were searching for—a new lease on life, a new outlook. Then I'd snap out of my trance to one of Jan's entertaining stories. I decided there was no sense in worrying about the what-ifs in life. All I could do was pray. Lee and I missed family and friends, but had developed a greater appreciation for those we loved and often took for granted. The feelings were reciprocated in the letters and e-mails we received. We never realized how much we'd be missed.

Lee worked on the fence row all day while I helped Jan in and around the house. We had lunch ready when the men came in.

"I was wrapping a wire and looked down and a six-inch centipede was crawling up my shirt," Lee said.

"Gross, what did you do?" I asked.

"I swiped it off and it got away," he said. I didn't know if I should be more worried about centipedes or snakes.

"It's mating season for snakes you know," Jan said. "So keep an extra eye out for them."

I had a revelation that day in the dunny. For weeks I blamed Lee for not lifting the toilet seat and pissing on the rim. But poor Lee was innocent—it was those damned frogs. Obviously, the snakes were too busy mating to worry about decreasing the frog population.

Andrew was still in Perth doing business and getting ready to head back with supplies and the new bulls. He called to tell us one of the $1,500 bulls broke his pizzle. They had insured the bull, but not for doodle damage—insurance companies get you every time.

It had been almost a month since our first snake sighting at Ashburton and two months since our snake ordeal at

Juna. I made it down to the homestead at 5:35 a.m. for breakfast.

"You missed it," Lee said.

"Missed what?"

"A snake!"

"Where?" I demanded.

"Jan found it in the bathtub."

"What happened to it?"

"Mick killed it."

I was disappointed I missed seeing the snake, but was glad Jan found it instead of me. Mick said he really wasn't sure what kind of snake it was, but hoped it wasn't a python. Pythons were not poisonous and were good to have around. They ate frogs and warded off poisonous snakes.

The fangs of a snake didn't impale me, but the barbed wire attacked me again, sinking its sharp teeth into my arm. Blood ran down my skin until it hardened into a dark black clump on my hands. I'd have a scar for sure, testament of my daily struggles with the damned fence. We moved on to uprooting pickets. It was more repetitions of my grunting, huffing and puffing as I wrestled the pickets out of the ground. Perspiration mixed with dirt dripped down my temples.

"Does it sound like my heart's in it, now, Lee?" I asked, referring to an incident the week before when he told me my heart just wasn't in it.

"Sure, dear," Lee said.

"I'm Xena, warrior princess," I added as I grunted and jerked to pull a picket out of the ground.

I'm surprised Lee didn't say, "Yeah, I'll admit you're a princess, just not a warrior princess."

For years Lee had called me "princess," reflecting my high-maintenance persona. I didn't demand glitz and glamour or expensive gifts, but I did crave attention. Even on the trip, Lee sometimes retorted back, "Is there anything else I can do for the princess?" Princess or not, there was no such thing as royal treatment in the outback.

All signs of Cyclone Olga were gone and the spectacular sunsets returned. Brilliant ruby waves emerged above the soft blue, the image seducing us to stay in the remote oasis forever. The temptation faded fast when something zipped by my head that evening as I changed for bed.

"Crikey, it's that damn bat!" I said.

Lee reiterated the fact that bats were good and not to worry. My only thought, *We're living with a bat—that makes us part of 'The Addams Family' too.*

Andrew, Jan and I drove to the two-mile bore (windmill). I met Baby, the camel. She was eight years old. Orphaned as a baby, she wandered into Meentheena Station where she grew up with the horses and thought she was one. Jan called Baby and she strode toward us, lifting her front feet high before setting them down on the ground. She sniffed around my cheek—either fascinated by her new visitor or overcome by my body odor. It was useless using deodorant in the sticky weather—Lee and I reeked at the end of each day.

Andrew asked if I wanted to go up for a fly in the morning. I wanted to fly, but I was edgy. Tourists paid big bucks for airplane rides. I had the chance to go up with the boss; I had to do it. I took my camera gear and a plastic bag in case I needed to vomit, but hoped my motion sickness stayed at bay. I climbed into the duct-taped Super Cub and wiggled down into my seat. I hooked my seat belt and put on the headphones so I could communicate with Andrew. Rains had made the property lush and fruitful. Cattle and 'roos grazed side by side. I looked in every direction in wide-eyed wonder with a speechless grin. The river didn't seem as threatening from the air. We landed and my plastic bag was clean.

After lunch I sat down to work on Clyde. Jan asked if I wanted to go across the river with her and the blokes. "Thanks, but I need to work on Clyde and get a story done," I said.

Five minutes later Lee walked in. "Jan told me to come ask you if you wanted to go with us before you get computer ass," he said.

I laughed and decided I'd catch up on Clyde later and join the crusade across the river—I certainly didn't want to wind up with computer ass. Jan and I got into one of our in-depth conversations. She told me Andrew was pretty boring when it came to food. That was an understatement. The man only ate meat, potatoes and beans.

"I reckon that food is one of the sensational things to enjoy in life next to sex," Jan said with a smile. I was surprised. Since our arrival Jan had been so conservative. She always had something interesting, profound or funny to say and I enjoyed getting to know her true self.

Lee fixed up the shower with new metal panels. So long to the once open-air shower. He also welded a door on the dunny so there was a little privacy. Things men do when there is a new girl coming to town. The following day Jan and I would be picking up a new employee. All I knew was that she was 26 and from New Zealand. My inner voice hoped she would be homely.

I didn't want to even think about the new girl. I lost myself in the outback's "sameness." The sameness had many different qualities. One minute it embraced us, intrigued us and the next minute it was frightening and trying to kill us. The surreal location was spiritually uplifting and allowed us the opportunity to think about life. It wasn't fuzzed with commercial lights, amusement or distractions. It was the outback—it was sameness.

The Journey

Emerging to consciousness, a journey of the mind,
Are we living in a real place, are we living in a real time?

The reality I have accepted, is in sight no longer,
Just a vast sea of opportunity with trade winds growing stronger;

A voyage of the body to enrich and enlighten,
Visiting new ports of call, cautious but not frightened;

Learning from others the reality of their lives,
Sharing experiences with them when opportunities arise;

Traveling uncharted waters navigating by points in the distance,
Will this journey guide future voyages? Will it make a difference?

No use for worldly fame, or riches untold,
For spotlights are blinding and silver is cold;

An open mind for the voyage is all I desire,
A chance to meet new faces and spend time by their fire;

Each leg of the journey carries me farther from home,
Or am I just getting closer to where I belong?

Lee Chaney

17

The New Girl on the Crew

My worst Australian nightmare came true. No, I didn't step on a snake; no, a centipede didn't bite me; but YES, the new girl was thin and cute. As soon as she and Jan walked out of the Paraburdoo Hotel, my heart sank to the pit of my stomach. I knew it was silly, but I couldn't help it. Toni was about five foot four with dark, shoulder-length brunette hair. Her skin-tight jeans molded her hourglass physique. Maybe it was my punishment for hoping she was homely. I smiled, said "hello" and helped throw her luggage into the back of the ute. We all squeezed into the front seat.

"Take her back to the airport, Jan!" I said. Toni's face whitened. She was miffed. "Jan and I already decided if you were pretty and thin, that you were out of here!"

We laughed and the brash joke broke the ice. I had two choices, I could like her or I could hate her for being born attractive. My personality wouldn't allow me to dislike her. Surely I'd have to add her to my Christmas card list. She was traveling alone in another country and didn't know a soul—I'd have to assume the big sister role and I do mean "big" sister. I had lost ten pounds and was really proud of myself. I missed my size-nine figure, but at least I was back in my size-11 jeans, even if they did cut off my circulation.

Jan dropped Toni and me off at Karingal Neighborhood Center. I got online, Toni checked out the op shop and Jan

went on to the grocery store. Lee and I had 32 new messages. I had sent a generic e-mail about our adventures to
more than 100 people in our address book. Responses were
encouraging and comical. We looked forward to hearing back
from folks. We almost depended completely on e-mails to
keep in touch and took turns at night reading the transmissions aloud to one another.

Toni quizzed me about the station. Without being disre-
spectful I warned Toni that the conditions were very modest.
I thought if she had an idea of what she would see that she
wouldn't be as shocked as I was when I had first arrived. I
packed up Clyde and browsed through the op shop for more
cheap deals. I handed Shirley $5.

"That's all for today," I said. "Thanks so much for letting
me check e-mails. You can't imagine how much we appreciate it. See you in a few weeks."

Toni and I helped Jan load $500U.S. worth of groceries.
Our mission—get the ice cream home before it was too melted
and ruined like it was the last time we went to town. The
drive home was interesting. A big goanna crossed the road.

"What is that?" Toni asked, startled.

"A bungarra or a goanna," I said, giggling at her.

Then a huge snake skimmed across the bitumen just
before it was flattened under our wheels. The snake didn't
bother Toni too much—her biggest concern was spiders. I'd
say from our spider discussion she suffered arachnidphobia.

"I think when I go over East I should get a bellybutton
ring," Jan said.

"Jan, you don't want to do that, they're disgusting," I
said.

"I have a belly ring," Toni sheepishly chimed in.

Once again I thought to myself, *Big mouth Becky—insert
foot.* A good thing I hadn't elaborated on what I really thought
of bellybutton rings. They're okay, but I personally believed
many women got them because they lacked self-esteem. Just
great, the little voices in my head chanted. *Thin, pretty and
now, she has a bellybutton ring to boot—one, no doubt, she'd
want to show off. It just keeps getting better.*

"I used to have a tongue ring, too, but when I ate ice cream it felt weird so I took it out," she added.

Oh, how I wished I could eat ice cream. I reckoned Toni would do wonders for my diet. I dreaded the ritual of unloading the supplies into the boat, crossing the river and carrying them up the muddy bank. We radioed ahead for Captain Hockley, as I often referred to Tricky, who always seemed to be in charge of the boat. Tricky waited patiently by the boat while Lee, Andrew and Mick sat lazily on the opposite bank, all of them curious to see the "new girl."

Toni probably sensed everyone staring at her, or should I say the blokes gawking at her. I kept my cool and pretended I was so freaking happy she was there. My instruction to Lee the day before was, "You get to have one good look, but after that I better not catch your eyes wandering." Part of me was kidding, but part of me was serious. It took two trips in the boat to get the groceries across. The third trip, Tricky fetched us sheilas.

"Becky, you and Jan sit in the middle, Toni is the lightest and she can sit at the end," Tricky advised.

I was mortified and faced Tricky. "Okay Tricky, Jan and I know we are not the lightest, thank you very much!"

As we neared the opposite bank, I looked at Lee, held up one finger and silently mouthed to him, "One look, just one look." He pretended not to notice me. While we unloaded, Lee turned his back to us, probably because he didn't have the willpower not to gaze at Toni.

"I told Toni when we picked her up that since she was pretty Jan and I were taking her back to the airport," I confessed to the blokes.

"Yeah, they were hoping you looked like a toad and couldn't ride a horse," Lee chimed in.

Husbands just had no idea sometimes. We dragged our tired bodies up the slippery bank to the ute. Toni jumped up front with Jan, my usual spot. I climbed on the back of the ute and held on tight as it rocked up the hill and down the dirt road to the homestead. Then, the real fun began. First, the soft ice cream was popped into the freezer with hopes it would refreeze to its original texture. Other groceries were sorted and I showed Toni where different foods and supplies were stored.

I took Toni under my wing and taught her the routine at Ashburton. In a diplomatic fashion I shared other information I thought would ease her transition to station life. I tried to be as helpful as possible, but held back my teacher-like manner. I certainly didn't want to be accused of being pushy. (In high school, Kelly nicknamed me "Bossy Becky." I had suggested the 12 girls in our circle of friends or "gang," as we called it, dress up like M&Ms for Spirit Week. "I refuse to be an M&M," I recalled Kelly sternly telling me.)

My leadership and organizational skills sometimes came across as domineering. I liked to take charge, a trait inherited from my parents and developed through years of 4-H and FFA involvement. Those life skills were some of my strongest attributes, but it wasn't my place at the station to carry them out. We moved Toni into the Quarters. I had cleaned up the small room at the end of the caravan for her. She settled in, but continued to scan the area for spiders. I told her not to worry about them, but it was obvious she had a real fear. "As long as I know where they are, I'm fine," she said, nearly breaking her neck looking for webs.

Toni's first job was cleaning and organizing the saddle shed. It hadn't been touched since the last mustering season. Jan and I took an hour-plus walk down to the two-mile bore. I was surprised Jan didn't invite Toni for the walk, but then again, Toni didn't need to walk. It was Jan's birthday. I ordered her out of the kitchen and told her I was going to take care of tea. I made Mom's award-winning red velvet cake, but once again it wasn't up to snuff. My batter was too dark and my icing was more like firm gelatin rather than the fluffy white cream Mom's cakes were famous for. Jan was 51 and although the cake had much to be desired—it was a hit.

Lee and I stayed down in the main house to discuss our employment with Andrew and Jan. She was leaving the next day for a fortnight over East and wanted to get our wages squared away. We were set to leave in ten days to go back to the Blackburns. We had committed to working the Royal Sydney Agricultural Show and I had been commissioned to write some articles at the World Holstein Conference being held in conjunction with the show.

I had been keeping records of every cash payment Jan gave me and deducted phone bills and other expenses. I handed the carefully transcribed document to Jan. She looked a little confused.

"I think you misunderstood me. The $300A per week was not per person, but for both of you," Jan said.

It was one of those times I just wanted to lose it, run out of the room crying and screaming. My stomach was in knots, but I held back the tears, held back my frustration. I felt like the mercury rising to the top of a thermometer readying to spew out the top. I only had one thought, *That's $200U.S or $14 a day for each of us. It was ludicrous. How could this happen? How could I have misunderstood and screwed up so badly? Had we slaved on the fence row in deadly heat for poverty wages? This couldn't be happening to us.*

I held my composure. Jan got out the wages book and showed us what Tricky got paid. We knew since we didn't have a tax number nor a work visa that finding work would be difficult, but the Glenns knew all of that up front and agreed to pay us cash. I had such a sick feeling, I didn't want to try to understand. It wasn't right; we had been working hard and deserved to be paid for our efforts. They said they just didn't have resources to pay us more. Jan was very upset with herself for the confusion, but regardless, something had to be done.

"It's late, we'll work it out tomorrow," Andrew said.

Lee and I said good night and walked out the front door. Just steps from the house, I couldn't keep my anguish bottled up any longer, I lost it. Tears flooded my eyes, my face. Lee stopped and held me, tried to console me. His warm cheek pressed against my tears, his callused hands patted my back. It was my first official nervous breakdown of the trip. I blubbered and tried to speak.

"I, I'mm, I'm tired, I'm tired of all the time spent to find work and then not to get paid properly. I want to go home, I can't do this anymore."

Lee held me tighter, calmed me. "It's going to work out," he insisted. "We're going to be okay."

We walked up to the Quarters and got ready for bed. I deliriously stumbled to the dunny half intoxicated with disappointment. I burst into tears again sitting on the toilet. I didn't want to think about the mixup. Why couldn't things just be simple? I crawled into bed with tissues. I was drained, depressed. I thought a beer would have tasted real good, but we had no beer. I was a subdued zombie.

"Look on the bright side, you have me," Lee said as he curled close to me on my cot. "As long as we have each other, we can get through anything."

Zombie girl heard the tender words, but I couldn't kick the despair that consumed me. I'm an organizer, a leader. I'd coordinated hundreds of trips and programs. How could I have made such a shambles of our outback jobs? I felt like I'd let Lee down. I knew it wasn't my fault, it was nobody's fault, it was miscommunication, but I wanted to blame myself. Stupid thoughts crowded my brain. My thoughts went from the wage war to the new girl.

"Can you do me a favor?" I asked Lee. "I caught you staring at Toni tonight. Could you please not stare at her?"

"Are you PMSing?" he said, sure I was suffering from premenstrual syndrome.

"Probably, but I'm not mad. I just don't want you to let me catch you looking at her, that's all. Really, I'm not mad. Maybe you should stay here and work with Toni and I'll take a bus to the Northern Territory and write stories," I said in a very serious tone, like it wouldn't bother me at all.

"I won't stay at Ashburton without you," Lee said. "I want to be with you wherever that is."

I was pathetic, jealous and negative while Lee was supportive, loving and optimistic. I think he truly believed I was on the edge of a mental crisis. He held me and I finally drifted off to sleep.

216

I didn't get up until 7 a.m. I thought, *Screw it, $14 a day isn't worth me busting my butt.* Overnight it had seemed my once strong work ethic had floated downstream with the flood waters. Part of me was disgusted with the situation and part of me knew I was overreacting. The Glenns didn't have to take us on; it was a huge risk they'd taken—a favor for two desperate travelers. They provided food, accommodations and a really unique experience. And there I was completely distraught about wages. I was PMSing, but I still didn't want anyone taking advantage of us. I was exhausted when I got up. I splashed water on my eyes trying to erase their redness and soothe my puffy eyelids. Down at the main house all I said was "good morning." I just wanted to exist, not communicate.

"Are you okay?" Toni asked.

"I'm fine, I just don't feel good, but thanks for asking," I fibbed.

It wasn't necessary or fair to get her involved. She seemed to be a nice girl. I got my laundry and noticed Jan and Lee having a powwow. She told him she and Andrew were really trying to work something out for us. I spent nearly an hour on the phone to the visa office. A work visa would assure we got paid at least minimum wage. While I made inquiries, Lee sat next to me in the kitchen as beams of sunlight streamed through the windows warming our faces. I knew Lee wanted to be out working, but he insisted on staying for moral support.

"I don't want you to be so unhappy," he said. "We can go and work somewhere else, or we could go home."

"I don't want to go home," I said completely retracting my statement from the night before during my weak lapse of defeat. "That would just be like giving up. I don't want to be a quitter."

Jan called us into the office where she and Andrew had been trying to iron out the dilemma. She discussed the payment schedule pointing at different columns in the wage book. They decided to pay the balance according to our expectations, $300A per person per week. Our balance was $2,240A, but the Glenns said $1,100A in taxes had to be taken out so our balance was $1,140A. That was better than nothing.

Lee and Mick poured cement on the shower floor masking the former mud hole I was accustomed to showering over. The cement slowly flowed into the corner that I used once as my emergency dunny, covering it forever. Men somehow got energized when a new babe entered the picture. Wouldn't want her to shower over dirt like I had done for five weeks.

"I don't know what I would have done if you hadn't been here at Ashburton when I arrived," Toni confessed. "I think the culture shock would have been too much for me—I probably would have left."

Initially, Lee and I had planned to work our way around Australia—heading to the Kimberleys, then to the Northern Territory and across to Mt. Isa, home to the world-famous camel races. Then we'd head south toward Melbourne to pick fruit at an orchard where our friends from the Catoctin Mt. Orchard back home had a "chance seedling" from their own orchard in an experimental testing exchange.

"It will be really hard for you to find work on other stations this time of year," Jan said. "Station owners already have their complete crews lined up. We'd like you to come back to Ashburton. I reckon Lee could be pretty handy."

Nothing was said about my contributions to Ashburton, but that was okay. Lee had made so many station improvements in the previous weeks, they couldn't help but admire him. I was relieved to get paid and relieved to be offered a secure job for the next seven months, but I still felt a little frazzled. I walked to the river. The solitude gave me a refreshed outlook. I'd learned that challenges evolved into opportunity, at least that's what I kept telling myself.

Kangaroos nibbled away in the thriving scrub. Their ears perked in response to twigs crunching beneath my feet. They made me smile. The pinkish sunset filled the horizon like it was filling my heart and soothing my distressed soul. That was about all the smiling I did that day until I called my friends at my old newspaper.

"Hi Becky, how are you? It's so good to hear from you," Ann said.

I only knew Ann from circulation and as the egg lady, who delivered her perfect dozens to the office. In her early days she played softball with my mother, traveling with the All-Star team to Pennsylvania, New Jersey and Delaware. Mom still has a collection of silver dollars she earned for her home-run hits.

Ann transferred me to Linda, editor of the travel section, who was printing my travel stories. The phone track continued with a connection to Mary who had been at the paper for ages. She had given me a knitted crucifix with a prayer folded in its pocket to carry on our trip. My last chat was with Bob. He used to be my immediate supervisor. Although a little intimidating at the beginning of my employment, Bob had become my biggest fan. His words of praise and encouragement could cheer me in an instant as they did that day. I hung up the phone with my heart inflated, my ego boosted.

"Who was that?" Lee asked.

"Bob Harper," I said with a giant grin stretched across my face.

"Bob was the best person you could have talked to today," Lee said.

I tried really hard to be in a better frame of mind.

"Don't worry, everything will be all right," Lee repeated.

Jan left for her trip over East and I took over as head gardener, maid and cook again. Lee helped Mick on the fence row, Toni painted the cattle grid at the station's north border, Tricky worked on a ute and Andrew drove Jan to the airport. Finally, I noticed Toni's imperfections. I thought, *Why do women examine each other?* But then the answer hit me, *To discover their flaws—it boosts our own self-esteem.* Sick really, but true.

Her teeth were a little stained; dirt and humidity gave her pimples and she had enormous ankles and calves that matched her wide hips. I knew I was a bad person to pick her apart in my mind, but I'm sure she picked me apart too. Probably something like—Becky is nice, but bossy, and she really could stand to shed a few pounds. Lee walked in the kitchen and saw my shirt was wet from watering plants.

"Are you lactating?" he asked.

"Wouldn't that just be your worst nightmare?" I snapped.

"I've been thinking it wouldn't be half bad having a kid with you," Lee admitted.

I was momentarily stunned. Lee always had made it quite clear he had no desire to have children. *Wow,* I thought. *Lee must really think I'm on the verge of losing my mind and he's saying anything to make me feel better.* I had to give him credit, he was saying and doing all the right things to placate me. Later that day Andrew and Lee discussed the possibility of our return.

"Well, we can come back if you want," Lee said. "We'll get $300A cash per week plus gear if that's okay with you?"

I had a flush of relief. My big smile filled my face and without a word, I just nodded my head up and down. "Now, that's the smile I love," Lee said.

Lee was excited about our prospective return to Ashburton. He really liked working with the blokes and we both looked forward to mustering season. We packed the Road Toad for our trip south. I fixed dinner. Ted and Joan visited from the gold mine, making eight for tea. They were a cute couple in their 60s. Joan was quiet, conservative and a die-hard Elvis fan. Ted was loud, uninhibited, direct. His flamboyant personality made him a crowd pleaser. My stomach ached from laughing, then Ted topped off the evening. He smiled, gave Joan the eye and said, "Hurry up if you want your Friday night slap and tickle."

I went to bed happy, relieved for the first time in days. I looked at the stars from my outdoor bedroom. The pole building that surrounded our cots was like our own little amphitheater. The poles, roof and three-foot wall formed a rectangle simulating a makeshift movie screen—there was no movie or popcorn, but the night sky was a nature cinema. Stars gyrated like the hips of belly dancers with some star-struck performers exploding through the air as if they'd been shot out of a cannon. They entertained us, entranced us. After three shooting stars I made a wish that our return to Ashburton would be all we hoped.

The following day we completed odds and ends jobs. Lee and I went to the Quarters at 10:30 p.m. after visiting with Andrew. Toni had gone to bed earlier. I made my usual trek to the dunny while Lee lit the mozzie coil. I walked into the side unit about five steps from my bed to grab a drink from the refrigerator then crawled into bed. I watched Lee walk toward the room. He stopped dead in his tracks, right at the door.

"It's a snake, isn't it? It's a snake," I said, already knowing the answer.

"Get in the caravan," he ordered.

"Lee, do you want me to get someone?" I asked.

"No."

"Be careful," I urged.

About that time, Toni woke from the commotion. "What? What's wrong? What is it?" she asked with an alarming pitch.

"It's a snake," I said. "If you come out, come directly to my door."

Lee took a metal fencing picket and approached the reptile. Toni and I watched anxiously. He whacked it four times before it stopped moving and then once more when its jaws opened to impale his leg. Lee scooted it out. It was over two feet long—not a huge snake, but possibly deadly just the same. I had just started to walk around at night a little more casually, not worried about snakes too much. The snake visit changed everything. At breaky the following morning, Lee, the snake slayer, was the topic.

"Hey, mate," Mick said to Lee. "Next time don't completely smash the snake. I can't identify it." Mick determined it was one of two snakes—the friendly python or a guada snake, the tenth most deadly snake in the world.

"I'll tell you what kind of snake it is," Lee said. "If it's not wearing a sign saying, 'I'm a good snake,' then it's going to be a dead snake."

We had two days left. It was busy with lots of tasks on the to-do list before we departed for four weeks. I measured and poured ingredients into the two bread makers as I had done nearly every morning. I had to plan every day's baking when the generator was on. The smell of fresh bread baking reminded me of my mom, who always had cookies or cakes for guests. She was in every sense of the expression "the hostess with the mostess."

After morning tea I overheard Andrew give the day's orders. "Toni, you're going to help Lee today put up fence," he said.

I wanted to say, "Fuck you, Andrew. Lee is my husband, I'll help him with the fence like I've been doing for weeks." But I didn't want to rock the boat, I knew how much Lee wanted to return to Ashburton. Andrew must have thought my only qualities were cooking, cleaning and gardening. I was already accustomed to the heat and the demands of the fence row. I should have been sent with Lee.

"What's up with Toni helping you?" I asked Lee.

"Andrew made the orders," Lee snapped defensively.

"It just hurts my feelings," I confessed.

"I'm really sorry, why don't you come help me?" Lee asked.

"No, I'll just cook," I retorted in a cocky manner.

He knew I was upset. I walked to the two-mile bore. The more I walked, the madder I got—the madder I got, the faster I walked. After my hour walk I passed Lee and Toni making fence. It made me sick! I could have bitten a nail in half. My stomach cramped with anxiety. I was pissed off, enraged, but mostly just discouraged. Didn't Andrew have a brain? How dare he send Lee to the fence row with another woman? It wasn't Lee's fault, but I still wanted to be mad at him.

My provoked mood motivated me to shovel dirt on the lawn, ignoring the heat. I sweated profusely, nearly numbed by heated fury that matched the sun's murderous presence. Why wasn't I in the paddock building fence? Actually, I really didn't want to make fence that day, but it was the principle of the whole thing. I wanted to work with Lee. After all, the biggest reason we left the States was to spend quality time together. So why the hell was I shoveling dirt alone and why was Toni pounding posts with my husband?

The previous week Lee and I had worked less and less together. I think I intimidated Andrew because I was a strong woman with a mind of my own. He preferred quiet jillaroos, not my outspoken type. He thought my talents were best spent at the homestead. *Well, we'd just see about that.*

I recovered from my rage and decided the best course of action was to kill them with kindness. I started the next day rejuvenated. I liked Toni, but she lacked initiative. The simple duties she was given were often never completed. No sense in worrying about Toni, we were leaving—but I knew she'd be at Ashburton when we returned.

The river was still up and we were afraid we might not get out. Two weeks earlier the river had receded enough to get the Road Toad into the homestead. That was a big mistake. Rain storms miles away flushed truckloads of water into the Ashburton River, forcing it above flood stage again.

"The river is too high for the Toad," Andrew said. "You may not get out."

Come hell or high water, literally, we are going to get out, I wanted to say, but kept my lips shut. I couldn't risk our opportunity to return to Ashburton. Everyone headed out to work. I turned to wash dishes.

"Hey Bec, how about coming to the fence row with me today?" Lee asked.

"Why do you want me to help?" I asked.

"So we can talk," he answered.

"Why, you haven't wanted to talk to me for six and a half years—why start now?" I said sarcastically, but really just jerking his chain.

We laughed, but Lee knew there was some truth in my statement. We hoped to get across the river that day, but flood waters were too high and swift. *Oh, God, please let the river go down,* I prayed. Anticipating my prayers would be answered, I showed Toni, again, where all food was stored and coached her in food preparation. She'd be responsible for cooking until Jan returned. Toni admitted not having spent much time in the kitchen, but I told her she'd be fine.

"How long do you cook potatoes?" she asked.

"A long time, but just test them," I said.

"How do you test them?"

"With a fork," I said.

She really was serious about having no cooking experience. I couldn't believe a 26-year-old who had lived on her own didn't know how to cook potatoes.

The caravan was cleaned out and the Road Toad was ready. *Please, please, God, let the river go down,* I prayed again.

The river didn't recede, but Tricky said not to worry. At 4:30 p.m., the theatrics began. Tricky and Lee hooked the Road Toad behind the large grader. A year earlier, the flood waters swept Tricky and a multi-tonned grader over the side. He escaped and the grader was salvaged, but it was a scare, Tricky said. There was no way I was going to ride in the Toad and chance flood waters washing us off the cement bridge that I hadn't even seen yet because it had been flooded beneath a surge of water since our arrival.

He drove the grader, pulling Lee in the Toad. They entered the water. Savage waves hit the vehicle's sides aggressively. I questioned our sanity and decided we should have waited for the river to go down. It was too late. They were halfway across the bridge. Water seemed to be pouring into the Toad, but I couldn't be sure. I snapped photos from shore, hoping that my image wouldn't change to tragedy. The grader reached the bank still tugging the Toad in its wake—they had made it!

Lee parked the Toad up the road, safely away from the river until our departure the following day. We said our goodbyes. I hugged Toni and wished her luck.

"You are coming back, right?" she said in a panic.

"Yes, we'll be back in four weeks," I reassured her.

We drove away looking forward to our job in Sydney, as well as our return to Ashburton. The station had been a real eyeopener. I wondered what our return would be like.

"Toni will struggle the month at Ashburton without you," Lee said.

"Yeah, I know," I said with an evil, self-satisfied grin.

"It's great to be driving you again," Lee said as he patted the Road Toad's dash.

Paraburdoo was in the opposite direction, but we had to collect money and hoped to get some last-minute bargains at the op shop. When we returned to Ashburton it would be winter. We sifted through the racks and piles of clothes looking for sweatshirts and jackets.

"Hey Bec, here are a lot of bras," Lee said, holding a few up. "I know you said you really needed some bras."

I nabbed eight of them and went in a back room. I tried the bras on quickly, knowing we had a long drive ahead of us. I selected four, pleased with my selections. My bras had fallen to bits. I didn't particularly like buying used bras, but new supportive bras were expensive. We handed Shirley our $20 note for our buys.

"I reckon a highlight of Paraburdoo is the op shop," Lee said driving out of town. Little did we know we were beginning a 1,000-mile-"plus" road trip from hell.

What Will You See?

Viewing the world and all of its treasures,
With the eyes of a child reveals life's simple pleasures;

Pause at a pond and you may get a glance,
At a shy little frog performing a water-top dance;

Watch a squadron of swallows display their graceful precision,
Swiftly banking and diving, free of collision;

Toss a coin to the water after making your wish,
See it swim to the bottom like a shimmering fish;

Finding a fossil from a long-ago land,
Preserving its existence right there in your hand;

Western horizon on fire marks the end of a day,
You've seen it before, just never quite this way;

You can search for these things, others will happen by chance,
But what will you see, a frog?... or a dance?

Lee Chaney

More than Bargain Bras

We pulled away from Paraburdoo at 11:20 a.m. in hopes of making it as far as Carnarvon—400 miles. It was 170 miles to Nanutarra Roadhouse, the only gas station we'd pass until Carnarvon.

"Have I told you yet today that I love you?" Lee said shortly into our excursion. "I don't know what it will be like living normal."

We were excited to be on our own again. I celebrated with two beers, but after not drinking for six weeks, they went straight to my head and my bladder. "Honey, can you pull over, please—I really have to pee."

When he did, I jumped out of the Road Toad and stripped off my shorts and knickers, as underwear are called in Australia.

"What are you doing?" Lee said with arched brows.

"Pee always splashes and I don't want to ride down the road with pee-y knickers," I said with a beer-induced giggle.

I squatted and peed. Then, I pranced around the vehicle nearly in the buff like a '70s flower child.

"You better get back in here before a car comes," Lee ordered. But I ignored him, laughed and continued my dance recital in the middle of the Great Northern Highway. I was momentarily possessed by my wild spirit. I ended my Vegas showgirl debut knowing we had a long trek ahead of us. I pulled my knickers back on, then my shorts, and jumped in the passenger seat. Four minutes down the road, we passed a road train. Lee gave me that look, that look that said, *You are absolutely nuts.*

"He didn't catch me with my pants down—did he?" I asked.

Lee just shook his head. Every few miles the landscape changed. We passed a succession of jagged rock ridges that soon changed to rolling hills. Before long we came to stretches of rocky bushland, covered in a carpet of small smooth rocks.

"It must be hell to muster up here," I said. "I bet tires are exploding all the time or horses getting hurt."

Then for miles we drove by remains of cyclones Steve and Olga. Thousands of acres were underwater. Old black spindly trees were drowning in small cyclone-made lagoons. Their gnarled finger-shaped branches extended out like the monster trees that grabbed Dorothy as she skipped by in *The Wizard of Oz.* Their eerie reflections in the flooded pools made them seem demonic. I got sleepy, no doubt a combination of heat and alcohol. I laid my head back and fell asleep.

Bang! The single bolt of noise jerked me awake. It sounded like something had exploded underneath the Road Toad. Lee pulled over; it was 2 p.m. He shimmied on his back under the Toad, examined the situation and scooted back out.

"It's the speedo cable," he said as he stretched it out in front of me. "Some of it wrapped around the drive shaft."

My first thought: *It's fucking hot, the tar on the bitumen is bubbled up and we might be stranded.* My second thought, because I'm mechanically ignorant: *What the hell is the speedo cable?!*

He disappeared again beneath the Toad with only his skinny white legs sticking out. The road surface burned him through his T-shirt. I heard him fidgeting with God only knows what.

"Hey, Bec," he called.

"Yeah, what can I do?"

"Go to the back and push when I tell you to push, and pull when I tell you to pull."

228

"Okey dokey," I said, completely sobered by the drama.

I pushed the Toad forward and then pulled it backward at Lee's instruction, not knowing exactly what the hell the little exercise was proving. Maybe it would have been smart to spend a little more money on a more reliable vehicle or just have taken the bus.

Lee reappeared, blackened in tar, sweat pouring down his face. He said, "I got the rest of the cable unwrapped. What a mess!"

"What now?" I asked. "Are we stranded?"

"I rigged the speedo cable and shaft joint together," he said. "It's amazing what a little piece of rope can do. The Toad should go now."

We hopped in, Lee turned the ignition switch. She didn't sound pretty, but we were moving.

Snap! Crack! Urggh! Bang! A succession of loud, sick sounds forced our surrender less than 20 minutes down the road. I wasn't too worried yet. I had packed four peanut butter and jelly sandwiches, ten packs of biscuits, six apples and oranges, and several muesli bars. And we had water. It took 15 minutes for Lee to adjust his makeshift rope Band-Aid before we were moving again.

"Oh shit," I said as the Toad drifted to a halt after a big five miles. I was restless, dreading the thought of being stranded and missing our commitment over East. I was hot, tired and wanted to get to Nanutarra.

"Don't worry, dear, I'm an ideas man," he said in a cocky, self-confident manner, thinking the words would pacify me.

He readjusted the "fix-it" rope and we started moving at a snail's pace. I could have power-walked past the Road Toad with little effort. It was 3:20 p.m., an hour after the initial breakdown and we hadn't made it a mile. Not one vehicle had passed—we were on our own. But at least we were still moving, even if it was at less than eight mph. Three and a half hours and 26 miles later, the roadhouse was in sight.

The Toad sputtered to a stop, again. We were out of gas. Lee refueled from our jerry can on the back and we pulled into the roadhouse. Gus, the owner, said he could tow us to

Onslow, 80 miles north to the coast, the closest town with a mechanic. The bad part was that Onslow was in the opposite direction of where we were heading.

"We'll have to pay with a credit card," Lee told Gus.

"It's going to cost $1.75A per mile," Gus said. "We'll leave at first light, mates."

We rented a modest room behind the roadhouse. Our room was small, hardly enough space to walk around the double bed, but it did have an air conditioner.

Lee drove the Toad onto the flatbed at 7 a.m. Gus motioned for us to sit up front with him. He invited Kim, a 13-year-old family friend, along for the ride. I still hadn't comprehended our predicament. There was nothing like a real curve ball thrown into the mix. We had to catch a flight to Sydney in five days and weren't sure if we'd even make it back to Perth.

"This is known as Ant City," Gus said, pointing to miles and miles of giant dirt mounds near Onslow.

A few more miles from town limits we passed a cemetery. "Gus, why are cemeteries so far from town and not right in town so loved ones can visit them easier?" I asked.

"It's because of the water table and drinking-water contamination," he said.

"It's so the town doesn't start smelling of dead bodies," the wily boy added.

Gus was originally from Zimbabwe. The 60-something-year-old man told us he and his wife went from place to place working. "Another year at Nanutarra Roadhouse will make five years and it will be time to move on," he said.

We pulled into Rex's Auto and unloaded our sick blob of metal.

"You can pay me now for towing," Gus said.

"Okay, just get your credit card machine and we'll give you our credit card," I said.

"I don't have the machine with me," he said.

"Well, that's all we have," I said.

"You don't have any cash?" he asked.

"No, that's why we told you yesterday we'd have to use a credit card," I explained. "Since we have to pass Nanutarra on the way back, we'll just stop and pay you then."

"You really will stop?" he asked skeptically.

"Don't worry, we will stop," I promised.

I was sure by his reaction that many travelers had never followed through on their promises to Gus. It was no surprise he was cynical. Gus reluctantly agreed. He and Kim pulled away from Rex's garage, probably thinking they'd never see us again.

Rex was a stout man in his 50s. He wore a sleeveless, grease-stained shirt and smoked fag after fag, as Aussies called cigarettes. His lips pinched and his eyebrows raised as soon as he saw the Toad. We knew the rusting Lada Niva might never roll triumphantly down the road again. She was an over-the-hill foreign model; parts could be impossible to get.

"Call me in an hour after I've had time to check it out," Rex said after he delivered us to the local cafe.

We ordered and sat down to relax. There was really nothing to do but enjoy our temporary side trip. It had only been 20 minutes when Rex got back.

"You need a new shaft joint," he said. "I could get the parts in overnight and they should be here by noon tomorrow."

"That sounds great, Rex," Lee said. "Could you recommend a reasonable place to stay the night?"

Rex took us to Ocean View Caravan Park, the cheapest place in town at $20 a night. We moved our things into the caravan. Lee wanted to take a nap, but I had another idea. My idea prevailed! With no privacy at Ashburton for six weeks, it was about time.

Dinner consisted of cold baked beans out of the can. We even scraped the sides like I'd seen hoboes do in movies.

"I can't believe we're eating cold baked beans out of a can," I said.

"Well, we've done lots of stuff because we're on a budget," Lee said.

Other than the Road Toad's fate, my only other concern were the damned mozzies. Onslow's moist climate by the ocean made the blood suckers an even greater epidemic.

"Make sure you have cream to prevent mozzie bites," Rex had warned earlier. "They are really bad here."

I had left my repellent at the station so Rex let me borrow his. The recent floods had ignited a mozzie-breeding frenzy. There were 560 new cases of Ross River Virus in the Pilbara. The TV news reporter reiterated the fact that there was no cure and people contracting the virus suffered the rest of their lives. Mozzies were also responsible for an outbreak of encephalitis. One person was dead and many sick. I hated mosquitoes, but they loved me. Our caravan door was closed, but I still got five bites in the first half-hour. We slept in for the first time in weeks. It felt good curled up beside Lee under the same covers and not on separate cots. With only time to waste until the Toad was hopefully fixed, a tour was in order.

It was a small town. We questioned whether there would even be much to see. But many small places offered the richest history. Onslow was established in 1883 by Sir Alexander Onslow, the chief Justice of Western Australia at the time. In the early days the town served the pearling, mining and pastoral industries. Today, fewer than 900 residents called the coastal community home. Onslow continued to support livestock producers, mainly sheep breeders, and was a popular tourist destination known for its year-round temperate climate, quaint atmosphere and historic interests.

We walked down to the museum and looked at old relics, vintage photographs and rare antique collections. Being a nostalgia buff, old photographs especially enticed me. The images depicted the town's life and heartbeat. The original settlement was 11 miles to the west. In the 1920s it was relocated to Beakon Point where water was deeper and port problems were eliminated. The once-booming tiny inlet town was nearly destroyed by a 1934 cyclone, only to rebuild and be ravaged by a 1961 cyclone. Cyclones were notorious for demolishing coastal towns and Onslow often got the wrath of the storms.

"Why do people even live in Onslow?" I asked the museum host. "You live in constant fear of cyclones."

"Well, why do you live in the U.S? You have those tornadoes," the disgruntled woman snarled back.

Embarrassed by my inquiries, Lee melted into the memorabilia pretending not to know the pert Yankee still flipping through the pages of devastation.

"Well, we don't live where there are many tornadoes," I audaciously retorted. "Lee, come here," I asked. "Lee, Lee." He had assumed the role of deaf and dumb and was no way going to participate in the cyclone/tornado debate.

Back at the caravan park I was again engrossed with cyclone photos adorning the office's walls. The Siviour family owned the caravan park. Five days after they purchased it in February, 1999, Cyclone Vance hit and the town was evacuated. The category-four storm nearly destroyed the township. Families were taken to Karratha by Greyhound buses. Some families, like the Siviours, dared to escape in their own car. Once the cyclone had passed, the Siviours journeyed home. At the last flooded crossing, one mile from Onslow, their car had water up to the door handles and the rear end started to float sideways.

"I was so scared," said Chris Siviour, the mother. "I told my two young children if the car was swept away that they had to crawl out of the window and grab a tree and hang on until help arrived. We made it across, but I'll never drive our own vehicle through something like that again."

Lee and I walked a mile and a half to Rex's Auto to check on progress. He was almost finished. More than $200U.S. later, the Road Toad was fixed. Rex offered us a beer and we enjoyed our visit with the rustic outback character. Rex and his wife were a lot like Gus and his wife. I admired the gypsy-like lifestyle. It was brave to change jobs and homes every few years.

"I've traveled all over Australia to work," Rex said. "My next venture will be up in Northern Queensland where I've never visited or lived."

We thanked Rex for putting us ahead of his other jobs and bade him g'day. There was no sense starting the drive that night—too many 'roos and stray sheep in the road. We set out at 6:30 a.m., rolling through the center of town on a Sunday morning. It was ominous, not a person in sight—for a moment I thought I was back in Tonga. Six miles out of town we stopped at Ant City. The extraordinary reddish brown pointy formations studded the landscape. The creations, formed by the tedious work detail of trillions of ants and termites, came in all shapes and sizes.

It took nearly two hours to get to Nanutarra, where Gus's face lit with surprise as we pulled alongside the gas pump. We paid our towing bill and thanked him for his troubles. Four hours later we were just on the outskirts of Carnarvon, finally. The West Coast community prided itself on its crafted vineyards and fruit farms. We stopped at Munroe's Banana Plantation. I told Lee I wanted to write a feature story, but my secret motive was to devour one of their famed banana splits.

"What about your diet?" he asked.

"Fruit and calcium are good for me," I smiled, shoving another bite in my mouth.

After our lunch break we continued on to Geraldton, more than six hours down the road. The oil gauge dropped to zero. We pulled over. Lee fed the Toad her oil. She was fine—for a while, anyway. The gauge dropped again. Lee pulled off the bitumen.

"Bloody hell, at this rate, we'll never make it," I snapped.

Unlike every other town we visited, Geraldton was finally out of the three-digit population category and boasted nearly 25,000 people. That was civilization! It was known as Sun City and attracted heaps of surfers for the sun, beaches and great sailing winds. We arrived at 8:30 p.m. and checked into a youth hostel by the beach. It was $32A for a private room. Our peanut butter and jelly sandwiches filled our empty bellies and we hit the sack.

Before leaving Sun City we took in part of Geraldton's booming seafood industry, tramping through its rock lobster factory. The next 400 miles were much smoother than the first 600. We stopped for two days at Shane and Mandy's new farm in Beverley. We watched the evening news. Cyclone Siniti, a powerful category four packing 160-plus mph winds, was hitting Broome and was on track to hit Onslow. I was glad we weren't stranded there any longer and wondered what the museum host was thinking at that moment.

After a comical stopover at the Days' we headed to the Blackburns to prepare for our five-hour flight to Sydney. It was good to see Mikey, Josette and Kiana. Kiana's hugs and kisses left little doubt she missed her Uncle Lee and Aunty Becky. Josette and I sat in the yard on a sunny afternoon, catching up and folding laundry. The clothes smelled so fresh. I had pitched my op shop bargains into a load with Nappy Wash, the special disinfectant solution used to launder nappies, the Aussie word for diapers. I showed off my new purchases from the op shop.

"What do you think of these shirts?" I asked. "They were only a dollar."

"Yeah, not bad, aye?"

"And these are my stylish new bras," I said, proudly holding one up stretched from cup to cup.

"Josette."

"Yes."

"Is this a maternity bra?" I queried, examining the undergarment for the first time.

"Yes, that's a maternity bra," Josette answered as she chuckled with amusement.

"I can't believe I accidentally purchased a maternity bra," I said shuffling through the pile of laundry for the others. "Oh, shit, all four bras are maternity! I can't believe it. Well, they'll probably be more supportive so I'm going to wear them anyway."

• • •

Lee had no desire to go to Sydney to work the Royal Easter Agricultural Show. It was my idea and he stubbornly agreed. I had worked for Brown Swiss breeders at the Sydney show in '92. It was a super event and I wanted to share that experience with Lee. We landed and then caught the train to the Sydney showgrounds. The first Agricultural Society-sponsored show was held in 1823 and it had grown to the sixth largest agricultural exhibition in the world—the largest in Australia.

The theme, *The Great Australian Muster,* reflected the country's rich agricultural history and unique outback bush life. It was an impressive show with topnotch entertainment, livestock exhibits and excellent facilities. It was the third year the show was held at the new Homebush Bay site, the main venue for the upcoming 2000 Summer Olympics. One week following the ag show, the Olympic committee took over occupancy. The livestock barns were transformed into the official media center and the main arena took shape as the Olympic baseball field. It was all very exciting to imagine the thousands of people who would be converging on Sydney for the Summer Games and that we had stayed there first.

I checked into the ag show's press office sporting my U.S. newspaper identification badge, knowing a media pass would make the entire showgrounds accessible to me.

"I have an assistant with me and was hoping I could get two media passes," I said sounding very polite and professional, but really just wanting to get Lee in free as well.

"No problem, just sign both of your names here," the young woman said.

We flashed our media tags and strolled through the entrance gates bypassing a long line of paying patrons. I didn't feel bad because I knew I'd be publishing stories about the show. It was my *Frederick News-Post* media badge, my cow-queen smile and some sweet-talking "BS" that got me in the gates free eight years earlier. At $15A a pop to get in, anything was worth a try.

We had a map and set out in the colossal confusion to find the dairy office.

"Hi, I'm Becky Chaney. My husband and I are working for Dean Malcolm," I told the attendant. "He told us to check in here for a key to the cattlemen's sleeping quarters."

"Dean doesn't arrive until tomorrow," she said.

"I know, but he said we could get the key today," I insisted.

"Well, let me see if we have a unit available," she said. "You'll have to sign here. Is that okay?"

"No worries," I said scribbling my name. "Thank you."

The portable sleeping units were lined up side by side like row houses in downtown Baltimore. They sat up against the outer ground's fence. Lee fiddled with the lock, the door opened. It was a gutted box—no cots, no rugs, no furniture. Two barred windows were as fancy as the decor got, but we couldn't complain at $15A a night. We threw our gear in the empty chamber and went to grab a bite to eat. We got sidetracked to the showground pub and partied with the rabbit man. He had exhibited his prized hares for years. We toasted his Netherlands floppy-tailed champion, then toasted Australia and then toasted his champion again.

We stretched our sleeping bags across the cool linoleum floor. The night was frigid. Daylight didn't come soon enough, as I woke shaking. Cows arrived and our jobs began. We worked with Kellie, 23; Waylon, 18; and Vaughn, 17. Dean and his girlfriend, Di, were part of the crew, but stayed to themselves. Waylon and Vaughn came under the spell of my natural nurturing ability when they both started calling me "Mum." We have forgotten the cows in Sydney, but the people made a long-lasting impression. If Kellie didn't have us in stitches, Waylon and Vaughn's mischievous antics pinned us with laughter.

Lee and I moved our things from the herdsmen's units into a feed room in the barns beside the show cattle. We transformed the 10-by-10-foot shelter into our bedroom. The first two nights we slept on bales of hay, tightly spooning each other so the other didn't fall out. As the cattle ran low on hay, our bed slowly disappeared. That left us with the wooden floor. We purchased a single swag, the Australian bedroll. It was a canvas sleeping bag with a one-inch mattress in it. Lee and I squeezed together trying the spoon position again. By morning I had unwittingly pushed him out on the hard floor. We helped take care of 12 animals, 10 of which needed milking.

In the milking parlor I visited the Brown Swiss friends I had worked for in '92. We recalled our initial meeting: I arrived during the announcement of the grand champion Brown Swiss, just minutes after I had sweet-talked my way through the front gate. I congratulated the winners and introduced myself. They were excited to meet me as I was the first U.S. Brown Swiss breeder they'd ever met in person. They made me feel like a celebrity and invited me into the show barn for lunch. Fifteen minutes into our visit Richard asked, "Becky, what are you doing the next few days?"

"I'm staying in a backpackers' hostel at King's Cross waiting for my best friend to catch up to me," I said.

"Well, it's just Max and me taking care of 26 animals," he said. "King's Cross is a dangerous area. How would you like to help us a couple of days? We can't pay you, but we'll take care of all your meals and you can stay here at the fairgrounds."

"Sure, that sounds great," I smiled.

I moved my gear to the fairgrounds. It was an amazing week—I escorted the champion Swiss in the grand parade, was dunked in the barn's watering trough for initiation, and drank my share of Victoria Bitter.

I was blessed to visit the show again eight years after that first trip and make memories with Lee. He immersed himself in the entire experience—staying up late with the crew, drinking, telling jokes and trying to top their show and cattle tales. My body didn't function well on four or five hours of sleep anymore. I went to bed by 10 every night except the last night, when I later admitted, I should have gone to bed early.

"Okay, it's my turn to let loose and have fun. It's the last night of the show," I told Lee, though I would live to regret the decision.

Kellie and I pounded back beer, hopping from one show pub to the next. We hurled down the giant slide on burlap sacks, bypassing the ticket takers, confident we wouldn't be arrested. There were six in our celebratory entourage.

"Honey, you were going really strong, laughing, having fun, and then you crashed," Lee told me later.

He had walked me back to the barns, practically carrying me at times, taking breaks when I needed to vomit. It was the first time on the trip to be sick and it was my last. The next morning I couldn't move, I was comatose. Finally, I dragged myself out of our swag. Lee helped me to the bathroom and shower located near our cows. It was a handicapped unit and that morning I did feel handicapped. The one-person unit was my haven for the next two hours. It was my own fault I was sick; I hadn't eaten dinner the night before. Alcohol on an empty stomach was a lethal combination. I showered, gagging every few minutes. Dizziness forced me to sit on the handicapped seat; I was hung over and miserable.

I was partially dressed when someone knocked at the door. It was my partner in crime, Kellie. I opened the door and she made a beeline to the sink. While she puked in the sink, my head was buried in the toilet. It was a hideous scene, two adults spewing their guts out and laughing hysterically at the same time. We loaded the cattle and said farewell to our new friends.

Peter, a dairy cattle sperm dealer, or bovine semen jockey as I called people in his profession, drove us to our hotel at Darling Harbor. We'd met Peter at the show. He and Lee enjoyed the afternoon at the harbor while I continued to recover.

The famed Sydney inlet was a magnificent backdrop for the global leaders in the Holstein industry. Touted as one of the world's great waterfront destinations, Darling Harbor was a kaleidoscope of colors, sights, smells and attractions. We were invited to stay with Di's mother, Averill, at the conference. The Kiwi native and I partnered up, attending the business meetings while Lee took in some of the local interests. He went to the famous Blue Mountains while I listened to world dairy speakers. More than 500 dairy enthusiasts from 36 countries participated in the international event. Translations were given in six official languages.

I sat midway up in the oval theater and recorded notes. One of the panel members looked familiar. I flipped through the program looking at names. There it was: Dr. Paul Boettcher of the University of Guelph, Canada. Paul was my fraternity brother in Alpha Gamma Rho at the University of Wisconsin-Madison. When the panel discussion ended I walked to the front. Paul immediately recognized me and gave me a hug. *What a small world,* I thought. That wasn't the only unexpected meeting. At the finale dinner I told Lee I knew the man at the next table, but couldn't put my finger on our initial introduction. I finally asked.

"That's Frank Sorraghan," a man said. "He's the wealthiest dairyman in Australia."

Frank Sorraghan—it finally clicked. When I'd had an internship with World Wide Sires in '87, I met Frank. My job for the California-based international livestock-semen-exporting company was to escort foreign guests to nearby farms and popular tourist destinations like Yosemite National Park and Harris Ranch—California's largest beef operation.

My most spellbinding part of the conference was attending the First International Forum for Women in Dairying. Although the keynote speaker had no dairy background, Janine Shepherd had a dramatic influence on the group. Janine was a talented athlete training for the Winter Olympics in Calgary when she was struck by a truck while cycling. Her injuries were horrific. She wasn't expected to live. Despite impossible odds, she fought back, walked again, learned to fly, married and had three children. Her story was nothing short of remarkable and is told in her highly acclaimed book, *Never Tell Me Never.* Janine told the group not to sweat the little things in life and to embrace their challenges to achieve success. "Attitude plus power equals performance," she said.

The gifted speaker set the stage for the thought-provoking and motivational presentations from dairy women. Averill was one of the featured speakers. Her profound message touched our hearts. She took over the family dairy farm eight years earlier when her husband, Don, died of cancer. "I faced an uncertain future, with no home, a block of bare land, and no income," she said. "I'd be lying if I said it wasn't daunting, but I had unfinished business with the dairy industry, and I decided it was just too hard to give up everything I'd ever known."

Averill explained the trials she experienced as a woman on her own in the business. "I've had to tackle some things differently because I'm not as physically strong, or as young as I used to be," she said. "But there is always more than one way to tackle a problem—you just have to find it.

"If someone had told me what my life would be like today I wouldn't have believed them, but here we are," Averill added. "They say what doesn't break you, makes you—and I'm still in the industry I grew up loving."

Averill's experiences riveted the group. I took photos through my tear-blurred eyes.

That evening Lee and I were treated to an evening out in Sydney by our Australian hosts, Ray and Lois Blackburn, Mikey's folks. Wisconsin Holstein breeders Doug and Linda Hodorff, and the Blackburns' mates, Geoff and Rosa Hore, joined us. We took a water taxi across Darling Harbor and viewed the beautiful Sydney Opera House with its unique architecture spotlighted in the night sky. Our destination was Doyle's, a quaint but busy bayside restaurant established in 1885. The Doyle family was in its fifth generation running the business, famous for its delectable seafood dishes. I tried John Dory, a type of Australian white fish caught on the coast of New South Wales. It was delicious. Linda ordered mud crab, far from Maryland's blue crab specialty that I was used to. The Australian mud crab was as big as a medium-sized turtle and its claws were notorious for breaking or snapping off its captor's finger.

The final afternoon of the conference was spent at Belgenny Farm, known as the birthplace of Australia's agriculture. It was a historical site and was established by agricultural pioneers Elizabeth and John Macarthur in 1805. The Macarthurs developed the Merino breed of sheep and the wheat-producing industry, as well as the dairying, horticultural and grape-growing industries of Australia. Descendants of the first Merino sheep still grazed the local pastures.

It was time to go and Lee was especially eager to get out of the big city. We flew back to Perth the following morning and back to Burnvale Holstein Farm. Before returning to the outback I tapped out six stories and e-mailed them along with my digital images to a variety of U.S. newspapers and magazines. The side trip was over, my stories were written and the Road Toad was packed. Lee was chomping at the bit to get back to the cattle station.

Ashburton would be home for seven more months. We were excited about mustering season, having heard the stories of gathering cattle and getting them ready for market. I hoped it would be fulfilling and fun. I knew it would be tough, but I welcomed the challenge, or at least I thought I did. Before departure, Lee wrote a quick letter home;

Hey Mom,

Just got back from the Sydney show and I realize that a city was built to see how fast I could get out of it, as usual, not fast enough for me! We had a good time at the show and really liked "The Man from Snowy River" program that was presented nightly; we only saw it twice! Working the show was okay but I won't be making a career of it. Funny that I have spent more time at shows since I haven't owned cows, it just doesn't capture my interest as much. Staying with the Blackburns and Days for a while before going back north so Bec can get her stories sent in, it will be a good time to get organized and catch up on things.

Civilization has been good but I can't wait to get back to the station and get to work. Despite the snakes, outside toilets, open shower, flooded river, limited access, and lack of 24-hour electricity—it is the part of Australia that I have grown to love and appreciate. This is what I was looking for when I came over, a place where even daily routines have interesting outcomes. Hope all is well there. Time is flying by here so we'll be home before you know it.

Love, Lee

Adversity at Ashburton

I t was the middle of May, we had reached our trip's half-way point. The drive north was long and sultry. For the first 100 miles we drove through Australia's Wheat Belt. The area east of Perth hadn't had rain for ages and the typical amber waves of grain shooting up in the region were only stubbles just popping through the ground.

We passed through heaps of little outback towns, some looking more like the remains of ghost towns. At Goomalling, the green population sign boasted 250, but no one was in sight. We stopped at its only gas station and I slipped into the dunny. Locals took their "business" seriously.

"The toilet paper roll is chained to the dispenser in the dunny," I told Lee as I crawled back onto my burning, sticky vinyl seat.

"The toilet paper must be like gold around this country," he said with a laugh.

Five hundred miles into the journey we came to Meekatharra. Another classic outback town, population 150—and that probably included everyone in a 50-mile radius. Old brick houses and shops lined main street, but that's all there was—main street. The town was "skimpy" inside and out.

Lee parked the Road Toad diagonally on main street and we sauntered into the local pub eager to quench our dry dusty throats with one quick stubby and hit the road again.

Two bar maids were keeping up to the drink orders of three bushmen at the bar.

"Two Carlton Mid-Strengths, please?" Lee asked.

Then I noticed his eyes nearly bug out of his head. The one bar maid was dressed in a string bikini. *For God's sake, we're in the middle of the outback,* I thought. *Who will see her and how many extra tips would it actually generate in such a small town?*

"Okay, let's go," I said as I swallowed the last sip.

"Let's have one more," Lee said, eager to traipse to the bar to order another. There's a reason they say "Sex sells."

After 14 hours of driving we stopped in Newman to stay at Ken Walker's house, our friend from Juna. He was rather eccentric. His shelves were lined with Australian environmental, adventure and literary books. He had used the information for his former bush safari tours. Spears and penis gourds hung on his walls. Ken showed us the flood lines on his walls from Cyclone Steve, the worst storm in the town's history. The night's rest rejuvenated us for the last leg of our drive.

When we stopped in Tom Price to refuel, Lee said, "Did you see those people looking at us? They are so envious that we have the Road Toad and they don't. They're just saying they wish the Road Toad was theirs."

"Yes, dear, those people, I'm sure, are very upset they're not driving this amazing vehicle around the outback," I said rolling my eyes.

He was thrilled to own the Road Toad—don't ask me why. I only hoped it kept going. Twenty miles from Ashburton, the Road Toad wobbled to a screeching halt. We had a flat tire. Lee had the new tire on just as the sun was setting. Near the station we noticed some figures by the fence row; a full moon inched up behind them outlining their silhouettes. It was Andrew and a person we hadn't met before. They walked over to the Toad.

"G'day Andrew, how's it going?" Lee asked.

"Good," Andrew answered. "How was the drive?"

"Good, yeah, real good," Lee answered.

"Hi, I'm Becky," the sheila said.

"Oh no," I said. "You mean there are two of us now?"

Becky Padgham beamed with a bright white smile that nearly radiated in the moonlight. She was a 29-year-old school teacher who had taken off for a year to work on a cattle station. She kept her long dark-blondish hair back in a ponytail and tucked under her bush hat. She seemed really sweet. Barney was also new. He was Becky's younger half-brother. He was 15 and full of himself as many teen-agers seemed to be, no matter what nationality they were. He appeared to be a nice enough kid, but we soon learned he needed adult guidance.

Since it was dark when we arrived at the homestead, Lee and I slept on our usual cots outside at the Quarters. The following day the living arrangements changed.

"I thought we'd leave the young people [Toni, Becky Padgham and Barney] at the Quarters and move the old married folk [Lee and I] across the hill," Jan said.

At first, I was a little disturbed by our abrupt eviction. Lee and I had worked hard to make the Quarters livable. We got bumped over the hill to the area where Tricky lived in a caravan that was parked inside a large dome building. Three other very small tin sheds were near the dome. We picked one. I soon found out that our new home was the old Aboriginal camp decades earlier. *That's really kind of cool,* I thought, *unless native spirits still haunted the area.* Our first day back was devoted to cleaning up and moving into our tin shed or the "Nest" as it was dubbed. It was like a storage shed, a place where one might park a lawn mower, but certainly not live.

The shed was called a humpy, the Aboriginal word meaning dwelling place. Our humpy consisted of four tin-sheet panel walls and a roof. Sun shone through heaps of cracks and holes. A section of the wall was missing where a double window once provided a view to the east. It had been smashed out ages ago. The old wooden door with wire handle was sturdy, but offered little security. The cement floor was layered with dirt, and a rusty metal double cot that took up the majority of space added to the squalor.

On the outside, green netting draped the front section helping to prevent the afternoon sun from turning the Nest into an oven. In the back, under the extended roof, four dingo scalps hung from the rafter. The Australian Department of Agriculture paid $35A per dingo scalp. The wild dogs killed livestock and were considered dangerous. The collection of cut-off dog parts didn't add to the decorating scheme so I moved the scalps to the next humpy out of our viewing pleasure.

Our broom head swirled up cobwebs like Velcro. Sweeping the dirt-covered floor choked me. We salvaged a damaged old curio with four good shelves. A metal post hung in the corner from two pieces of twisted wire. After the dirt was polished from its rusty surface, it became a perfect towel rack. Lee doubled a sheet and nailed it at all four corners over the windowless hole. Sunlight still filtered through the sheet's threads. Most big holes were covered, but cool wind blew through the opened cracks. With a little elbow grease, the shack became our tiny retreat.

For lack of wanting to clean up a mess from the demise of the huge hairy huntsman spiders, we lived with them in harmony. Our first guest was Henry, an arachnid large enough to take on a mouse. Henry's double-yoked, egg-shaped body sat atop long gripping legs that straddled the wall like the space shuttle on a launching pad. Lee thought I was silly when I faced the wall and made house rules with Henry.

"I'll respect your space if you respect mine," I said to the furry brownish creature. "Henry, if you ever crawl on me, especially on my face while I'm sleeping, you will be evicted."

Henry was soon joined by Henrietta and Little Henry. My initial knowledge of the prolific outback spiders was that they were just big and ugly, not poisonous. After months of believing the spiders were harmless, I found out they were venomous, but I still refused to kill them.

After we set up the Nest, Lee hugged me. "Come on, give daddy some lovin'," he said.

He had been really sweet since we returned to Ashburton. He thought I was still a little fragile from the whole wage catastrophe the month before. We fell back into life at Ashburton, back to the fence row and back to helping in the kitchen. Becky Padgham, Toni and I made a pact to always take turns helping at the homestead so one of us didn't always get stuck with it.

One of the first nights back, I joined the gang for a 'roo-hunting venture. Toni drove the ute. I curled up under a blanket on the passenger seat already feeling Australia's winter blowing in. The blokes stood in the back, guns loaded and ready.

"There's one!" Barney yelled. "Stop the ute."

"Don't shoot!" I screamed back. "It looks like a young one."

Barney, who suffered from an acute case of TMT ignored my wishes and pulled the trigger. The shot riddled my eardrums, the 'roo dropped. Toni turned into the bush to find it.

"Hurry, hurry, before it gets up, hurry!" Barney shouted.

Toni pulled beside of the still marsupial. It was by my door. I looked at it, I felt numb, disgusted. I stared at the 'roo while the others chanted, "Good shot, Barney." My eyes zeroed in on the stomach area—it moved. I stared harder, believing I was seeing things. The stomach moved again. *Oh my God, it couldn't be, please God, no,* I thought. The stomach moved again, but then I realized it wasn't the stomach, but something in the stomach.

"Its got a baby in it!" I shrieked in horror.

The little joey in the pouch squirmed deeper and deeper into the mother's protective covering, but the mother couldn't protect her baby any longer. No one told me that baby 'roos were involved. I was so naive. The blokes made 'roo hunting sound fun. I wanted to fit in, so I agreed to go. Mick reached into the mother's pouch, grabbed the joey and pulled it out. It was eight inches long, beautiful and innocent. I watched silently as tears soaked my cheeks. *How precious, a baby 'roo*. I wanted to hold it, cuddle it, take the place of its lifeless mother. Mick walked around in front of the ute and stepped on the joey's head until it stopped breathing. It seemed cruel, but the Joey could not survive without its mother. I regretted being part of the killing spree—I didn't care if the dogs had to be fed—the ordeal sickened me.

"The joey pup isn't dead yet," Toni squealed as she knelt in front of the ute checking the small animal's pulse.

Mick gave it one more fatal knock. It was another rude awakening to outback life. I was a seasoned farm girl, raised with hunters in the family, but 'roo hunting revolted me. "They're rodents," Lee insisted. "Kangaroos are like ground-hogs, they're just larger pests." My 'roo-hunting debut was my last.

Lee was elated to be back at Ashburton—elated to get hot, sweaty and tired. I was happy to be in one place for the next seven months, but still concerned about my role at the station or lack thereof. My original concerns resurfaced quickly one afternoon as Andrew gave everyone orders—well, everyone, but me.

"Mick, Lee and Barney go put in pickets," Andrew said.

"Toni and Becky Padgham go start cleaning the stock trailers."

Everyone just walked out from lunch and left me, left me to clean up and put away food as usual. Did Andrew really think I only had domestic qualities? Was he threatened by my strong female personality? Or was he just a dickhead?

Lee's excitement to go work with the blokes shrouded any thought that I was left behind. It wasn't his problem, but I knew it would put a strain on our relationship. When I was unhappy, camp was unhappy. For lack of wanting to deal with it right then, right there, I said under my breath, "Fuck it" and retreated to the Nest. Everyone else was working, probably sweating. I didn't care. My feelings were hurt. A part of me questioned the rationale for returning to Ashburton. I really liked Jan and Mick. And even Tricky's straightforward persona had grown on me. I was getting to know Toni better and just met Becky and Barney. But Andrew walked to the beat of different drummer. Sometimes he fascinated me with stories, other times he disgusted me with his he-man ego.

I pondered the situation lying on my bed. I scanned the room for redback spiders. Unlike the huntsman spiders, redback spiders did worry me. They were mostly black, but easily detectable by the bright red oblong circle on their backs. They were small and venomous. The redback's poison was lethal. No sign of them in the Nest, yet, but one had a little web in the dunny. Lee could kill it later. I didn't go near it.

Finally, I dragged myself back over the hill to the main house to help Jan fix dinner. I was still pissed, but I wasn't going to take it out on Jan, or anyone else for that matter, not even Lee. The sun had set, it was almost pitch dark. I forgot something and trekked back to the Nest. As I crested the hill, I stopped, dead in my tracks. No, it wasn't a snake, but something vibrant and startling off in the distance. I stared for a few seconds, focusing on the fluorescent tangerine-colored object, not knowing exactly what I was looking at. Then I realized the oval brilliance was the full moon rising beyond the horizon. I just stood there dumbfounded by its dreamy glow.

I had just finished reading *Pieces of Blue,* about a young girl growing up droving cattle across Australia with her three siblings and father. She often talked about the orange moon illuminating the horizon. As I read it, I remember thinking, *What is the author smoking? I've never, ever seen an orange moon. At least not like the one she so eloquently described.*

I felt blessed to have caught a glimpse. Within two minutes as I stood there mesmerized, it rose slowly, changing from bright orange to peach to cream to white. It made me smile and forget my earlier worries. There was still so much to experience in the outback, I couldn't let Andrew or anyone else break my spirit. That night I told Lee my feelings were hurt and Andrew didn't respect me.

"You have to just be ready to leave when everyone is ready and just go with someone," he said.

"You don't understand," I said. "Andrew gives everyone their work instruction for the day, but me. It's like I don't exist."

"There's nothing I can do," he said. "You just have to be assertive and when Andrew tells the other Becky and Toni to do something, just tell the girls that you're going to help."

I didn't know what I expected Lee to do, but he often knew what to say or do to make me feel better. The words never came. Part of me wanted Lee to defend my honor, but I knew it was up to one person and that person was me. Lee and I nestled down in our separate sleeping bags and huddled together with a large wool blanket thrown over us. It sufficed. I slept in leggings, socks and a long-sleeved shirt. I stayed pretty warm, but usually woke up with a cold nose. The morning ritual of jumping out of bed, stripping and putting on my work clothes often had Lee in stitches. He was just as bad grabbing for his pants and shirt as chilly air tingled his bare skin.

The mornings were very cool, but temperatures often reached the mid-80s by early afternoon. We had been warned about outback winters. Cold winds cut through our clothes like a knife. Our primitive humpy didn't have insulation. Gaping holes allowed cold night air, wind and dirt to blow in.

The next day after breaky I was optimistic. Outfitted in my $1 work shirt, $1 jacket, my new Akubra bush hat, and finally, my not-so-tight jeans, I was ready to work. My water jugs were full, my snack bag packed and I held my gloves eagerly awaiting instruction. I refused to be stuck with household duties one more day. Andrew looked at the other Becky and Toni and said, "You girls go put droppers on."

I followed Becky to the kitchen door. She stopped. "I think he means Toni and I," she said.

My heart sank. Was I a disease? Didn't anyone want to work with me? I had worked hard the first six weeks building fence with Lee, but the new crew had arrived; I was an outcast. Becky's comment took me by surprise. She didn't mean it nastily; she was just honest. I gave Lee that look, that bitch look that said, "Do something about this situation or

I'm getting the hell out of Dodge." My daggers worked. Lee turned to Andrew and asked, "What would you like Becky to do?"

I knew I could have said something myself, but I had an "attitude," and it wasn't getting any better.

"She can either come with you and me to eye-up fence pickets or go put droppers on with the girls," Andrew said.

Hell, I wasn't completely sure what droppers were, but it sure sounded better than spending the whole day with Andrew. Toni, Becky and I loaded our equipment into one of the utes and headed to the bull paddock. Droppers were shorter reinforcement posts placed between pickets. I really felt like the new kid on the block, even though I had technically been there longer than both girls—just not in the previous four weeks. I drove while they threw droppers out along the new fence row. Then we had to attach them. The girls showed me the routine. I picked it up quickly. We each used a small instrument, similar to a bottle opener, to clip the dropper with a metal hook to all four strands of wire. It wasn't a bad job at all, except for the continuous squatting. I brushed it off as good exercise.

Three women working together provided a perfect opportunity for a verbal fest. Toni said she'd read an advertisement in the paper about topless bartenders making big bucks. Then Becky told us she had a good friend who wanted to go overseas, but didn't have the money, so she became a topless waitress and made a small fortune.

"And to think I sold Tupperware and Princess House Crystal to help finance my travels," I blurted out.

Our casual chitchat soon evolved into a big bitch session. Toni thanked me for letting her vent. She said she'd been stuck doing really shitty jobs and just in the past week made it out to the fence row. Droppers were on and we started putting tie wires on next. Tie wires were wrapped around every strand of wire on every main picket. We finished up at 5:30 p.m. It felt great to be tired—I actually had made a contribution to the team. I had two cuppas (cups of hot coffee) at the homestead. I'd joined the ranks of Aussie drinkers, consuming three to six cuppas of caffeine daily.

For the second night in a row and the last time on the trip it was there—the same magnificent phenomenon crowning the vista with its majestic orange glow. The moon soothed my soul, giving me an inner peace. The outback's remoteness made me aware of so much more—there were no diversions. I was only temporarily preoccupied by my role at Ashburton. I hoped I wouldn't sour to the adventure or put undue tension on our marriage.

When Becky, Toni and Barney took off for a four-day holiday, I hoped to reestablish myself at the station. Trying to take Lee's advice and be assertive, I asked, "Andrew, do you want me to come put droppers on?"

"No," he said. "Mick and Lee will be all right."

So again, I had been abandoned. I immediately got depressed. I disappeared to the Nest; it wasn't fancy, but it was my refuge. I lay on my bed escaping reality and losing myself in the pages of *Never Tell Me Never*. Part of me wanted to pack and leave, but that was impossible; we needed money. All the other stations had their crews for the season. We were stuck at Ashburton and I had to make the best of it. Later I joined Jan at the main house, but she gave me no instruction. Andrew walked in later.

"How ya goin'?" he asked.

"Well, okay," I said in a sluggish manner hoping to spur a response. Then I'd lash back and tell him what I thought. He said nothing—I said nothing.

Finally, I got up and went back over the hill to the Nest. Lee was lighting the donkie. I vented to him. He listened and consoled me. I wasn't happy and he knew it. Just when I thought he might say something profound and lift my spirits, Tricky rounded the corner.

"I'm going bush," Tricky said.

"What the hell is going bush?" I asked.

"I'm taking the grader out to the bush to make the washed-away dirt roads accessible for the cattle trucks," he said. "I'll see you in a couple days."

The following day I asked Andrew nothing for fear of rejection. I walked out from breaky with Lee and Mick and trailed them to the machinery shed.

"Mick, what needs to be done?" I asked.

"Why?" he queried. "Do you want to work out here?"

"Yesterday, you all left me and I did absolutely nothing when I could have put on at least 50 droppers," I said irritated.

"We didn't mean to piss you off," Mick said. "You can cut tie wires all day. Is that all right?"

"Yeah, I'd love to do that," I answered, content to do something constructive.

That day I thought my age had caught up with me. I labored with every step. The muscles in my legs ached. I had no idea the two days on the fence row attaching droppers, standing and squatting 100-plus times, could have induced such agony. I walked gingerly, putting little pressure on my body.

"You're waddling like a pregnant woman," Lee said.

"That's not funny, ya jerk," I retorted. "I really hurt."

Lee and Mick worked on the road train all day preparing it for Andrew's trip south to pick up hay. They worked a lot together and established a brotherly bond. The duo were so comical on the fence row I referred to them as Forrest and Forrest II. Mick also had a serious side. He was determined, authoritative and liked to make the decisions. Mick didn't take advice well from others, but it was different with Lee. He admired Lee and often asked Lee for his opinion.

An addition to the crew arrived in a rusty blue station wagon. Geoff Proud was the new 30-something horse breaker from South Australia. He joined us older folks over the hill and moved his gear into the Aboriginal humpy next to ours, which had been used years earlier as the kitchen. Dusty shelves became Geoff's makeshift drawers. An enormous cast iron wood/coal stove, that no doubt had cooked up 'roo, bungarra and witchetty grubs decades earlier, crowded the room.

For the first time since we had returned to Ashburton I was sent to the fence row with Lee. We worked hard putting on 500 droppers, but it was fun. My spirit was rekindled. I smiled, laughed aloud. I became a master at attaching droppers and raced Lee for the coveted Dropper Champion title.

"I'm pulling ahead of you again," I said with a chuckle.

"You always have to be, 'Becky one-up-on-you Long,'" he said sarcastically.

"Lee, do you know what you just said? You said Long. That's not my name, remember I married you—I'm a Chaney now."

"You were an icon way before I met you and you'll always be Becky Long to me," he said jerking my chain.

Working with Lee again was like a dose of good medicine that worked in his favor. During smoko (the break for a snack and a cuppa) I sat in the front of the ute. I unlatched the hook on the cup of my infamous maternity bra and pulled it down. My excited nipples darted out, starved for attention. I called Lee over. His eyes lit up like someone had just plugged him in. The baby-feeding apparatus had suddenly turned into a seductive piece of lingerie. Who ever said maternity bras weren't sexy?

I'd hoped my provocative plan would get a reaction out of Lee and it certainly did. It didn't matter that we were parked along the main road into the station, there was no stopping him.

"Honey, would you like me to build fence with you tomorrow?" I asked, teasing him on our drive back to the homestead.

"Let me recover from today first," he said, donning a satisfied grin.

Andrew got back with the road train stacked tight with large round hay bales and other supplies. I told Jan and Andrew about the days of baling hay at The Farm. We sometimes unloaded 3,000 square hay bales daily. It was a sweaty job, but I loved it. It was a family effort; cousins and neighbors often helped. There was nothing like the feeling of rolling down the road on "Big Bertha," our huge Ford tractor, pulling a heaping load of hay. Warm breezes blew back my hair and dried my sweat as the sun tanned my skin. I nonchalantly waved to passersby like I had the most important job in the world. I wheeled into The Farm's lane, making a wide turn assuring the wagon didn't drop into the ditch. I threw the tractor into low gear and climbed the steep barn hill, parked right beside the hay elevator, then started hoisting the bays onto the machine en route to the hay mow. I reminisced a lot about my parents' farm. I guess I wanted to prove that I had done a lot of physical work growing up, although my older sisters, Cindy and Karen, would swear they worked harder since they had to carry milk before milk pipes were introduced. I wanted the Glenns to know I had experience. I still craved Andrew's approval.

Becky, Toni and Barney returned from their holiday. Lee, Becky and I went to the fence row. She shared stories about her experiences teaching at an Alice Springs Aboriginal school. "One time an Aboriginal lady thought I had sights on her man and she stood outside my house with a hulla hulla club to bash me in," Becky said.

"What's a hulla hulla club?" I asked.

"It's just an Aboriginal weapon," Becky said.

"I really loved the kids I worked with," she said. "They dug up witchetty grubs from the roots of trees, but I was never daring enough to taste one. I heard they tasted like chicken with a hint of nut flavor."

"I think I'd like to try the grubs," I said. "But only if they are cooked."

"My students used to bring me honey ants," Becky continued. "I'd suck the honey out of their guts and then spit the ants out. One time the children ran over and asked me if I wanted a bite of their 'roo tail. The kids had snotty noses, and blood mixed with charcoal dripped from their faces. I couldn't try it."

I hammered more nails in our tin shed to hang our jackets and my new $1 bathrobe. The humpy took on a homey atmosphere. The family calendar my sister, Patty, sent was hung. The crucifix my brother, Dennie, had crafted from Palm

Sunday leaves adorned a shelf, along with guardian angels from family and friends.

Our loved ones weren't physically with us, but photos and station incidents often sparked memories of the support team we had in America.

20

Lee Takes on Offsider

To my surprise and delight, life at Ashburton had improved—at least for a few days. I was content, but always felt pressured to prove myself. Andrew told us to unload the spools of barbed wire and the fence pickets on the road train. The spools were painfully heavy. I was sure I had pulled something, but I couldn't stop. Toni lifted them, which meant I had to lift them, no matter how difficult. We both struggled with the awkward spools. Later that day Lee and I worked on the fence row by the homestead yards. Toni helped Andrew in the cattle yards, where they were castrating calves.

"Ya know, Lee, I used to help castrate calves when I worked for Doc Carmen," I said.

He threw his pliers across the flat. "I'm sick of you bitching about Andrew," he said, mad and irritated. "When are you going to give it a rest?"

His quick temper upset me and put me in silent mode. A little later he asked, "Are you angry with me?"

"No, I'm just not happy with anything right now," I said, starting to cry.

I really tried to have a better attitude, but no matter what effort I made, I still didn't feel like part of the crew. I turned my dismay into nervous energy, offering to pound pickets for Lee. The fence row was therapeutic as I pounded my frustrations away. We went back to the homestead. Toni,

Andrew and Becky had saddled three horses to move a mob of cattle. My stressful concerns flooded back like a tidal wave. I wanted to be included—I wanted to ride!

My self-pity was soon muddled by Lee's snake-killing report. He explained, "Our donkie sprung a leak and it was only a matter of time before all of the water would run out. I figured you'd want a warm shower tonight. I found a barrel down by the old sheep shed. When I moved it, a king western brown was under it."

"What'd you do?" I asked.

"I killed it."

Lee's story shot to hell my theory about snakes hibernating in the winter. I had just gotten comfortable walking around in the dark without a torch.

Andrew told Lee to put fence up across the Ashburton River, which had receded from its previous flood stage. Naturally, Andrew gave me no instruction. I stood there on the lawn daft from depression.

"Becky will you help me?" Lee asked. I had wanted to hear those words for weeks. "You can be my official offsider," he added. "When I get a job to do I'll pick a special person and that special person will be you."

It was the coldest day since we arrived at Ashburton, mid-40s and windy. I was dressed warmly, but Lee wore shorts knowing he'd have to wade in the waist-high water to pound pickets into the river's gravel bottom. He was so cold, he shivered and goose bumps raised on every inch of his skin. "If we run those bulls through this water we won't have to castrate them—they won't have any knackers left," he said with chattering teeth.

I was up to my knees in the frigid water. As the biting water absorbed into my pants, the chill went even higher up my leg and numbness set in. We tried to quicken the task, but our bodies were in slow motion. Finally, the fence was up. All I could think of was getting back to the homestead, stoking the donkie, and getting lost beneath the warm waters of our self-sufficient shower. I longed for a bath, but unless I wanted a soak in a cattle trough, a bath was months away.

Since first arriving in the outback, I had toughened up quite a bit. I remembered my first few days at Juna when I always put on makeup and wore my baseball cap to hide my messy hair. It only took a few days to lose the hat and a few more to lose the makeup. At Ashburton my bush hat plastered my hair to my head. I'd take it off, run my fingers through my sweaty hair and go in the house. I guess I had become somewhat of a bush woman, but still had a lot to learn and a lot to adapt to.

I was still adjusting to eating beef every day. Beef was free and accessible. When the freezer got low, the blokes ventured out for a "killer," the next bovine victim destined for the dinner table. We didn't have to worry about being iron deficient.

"I have a craving for a peanut butter and jelly sandwich," Lee said. "I reckon those sandwiches got us through our couple days stranded in Onslow."

"Yeah, the sandwiches and cold baked beans out of a can," I reminisced.

"I wouldn't trade anything on this whole trip for the world," he said.

"I wouldn't either," I added. "I'm sorry I've been so upset and complaining lately."

My non-bitchy remission was short-lived. I was drowning in dissatisfaction and regret. On the way to the fence row we passed Andrew, Toni and Becky moving a mob of cattle on horseback. Tears formed small tributaries down my rounded cheeks, dripping onto my shirt. Lee didn't throw anything, he didn't yell. He knew I was at my breaking point.

"Will you be okay?" Lee said in the compassionate tone I'd fallen in love with.

"Yes, I'm just not happy in my work," I said taking the words right from Herby, the elf in *Rudolph the Red-Nosed Reindeer*. I was Herby, a little lost elf at Ashburton—expected to go with the flow and not respected for my contributions.

Lee stopped the ute and wrapped his arms around me. "Look at it this way," he said. "We are in a foreign country, technically on vacation, spending time together and not spending any money."

I knew he was right, but I was still sad. Was I being selfish? No one promised us the perfect outback job. Much of the whole adventure was the unknown. Part of me wanted to say, "Screw this place." I thought about giving up, taking what funds we had and traveling through the Kimberleys up to Darwin until our money ran out. We'd catch the Aboriginal festivals, view spectacular gorges and Lee could pursue his crocodile hunting obsession. But if I quit, I'd be a failure—not tough enough to stick it out. I couldn't let Lee down, I couldn't let the outback beat me and I refused to let Ashburton crush our dream.

That afternoon something miraculous happened. For the first time in months, Andrew asked me to help him. He, Becky and I moved cattle to another paddock. Finally, I got to ride! Lee was excited for me and thought it would help my state of mind. He was probably hoping he didn't have to commit me. Before we set out with the cattle, Becky told me what little she knew about how Andrew liked to move cattle. She took a stick and drew a diagram in the dirt.

"You have the lead horse here, with someone on the side or the point, and then someone brings up the tail," she explained swirling her stick in the red grainy surface.

It sounded straightforward enough. Andrew took the lead, Becky was on the point and I brought up the rear. It was exhilarating. I breathed in deeply fresh outback scents as I sat confidently atop my mount, Harlequin. I pushed the cattle, turning a few strays back into the mob. It was so gratifying. My shattered soul was healed in minutes. The cattle were moved with no problem. I sat high and straight in my saddle; my strong posture represented the excitement of completing my first cattle task.

"Isn't Andrew interesting to watch?" Becky asked.

"I wouldn't know," I said. "I haven't had the opportunity to work with him until today."

I tried to look at Andrew through Becky's eyes in hopes of gaining a better respect for the boss. I concentrated on the seasoned bushman, the outback cowboy—erasing the fact that beneath the worn Akubra hat there was still a self-centered egotistical Aussie man. Andrew's bush banter was testament of his outback experiences when he decided to share it with us.

"See those cattle tracks?" he asked. "I can tell they're one or two days old. It's not anything I can teach, it's just something I've learned over the years."

The next day dawned a new beginning for me at Ashburton. The phone rang at seven.

"Hello, Ashburton Downs," I said into the receiver.

"Is Becky Chaney there?" the voice asked.

"It's me, it's me!" I said, hardly able to contain my excitement.

"It's Patty. How are you? We miss you," she said.

"Lee and I miss you too," I said.

My sister boosted my injured ego. I told her everything was wonderful and she never suspected I was living a psychological soap opera. No need to worry the family back home. I could handle it—right?

With no more cows to move for a few days it was back to the fence row. The station dogs never missed a day traveling to the scrub with Lee. They'd find a shady tree, lie under the ute and sometimes walk the fence row all day with him. During Lee's water breaks, the thirsty dogs lapped the water from the crease in the top of his bush hat. Their long pink tongues splashed water everywhere.

I had a story deadline and switched my energies to writing. Because of some computer foul-up at Karingal I wouldn't be able to get online at the community center again. Nikki and Shirley suggested I call the Karratha College Paraburdoo Annex.

"Hello, this is Yvonne Quill, may I help you?" said the woman who answered the phone.

"I hope so," I answered, continuing to explain our situation and the importance of e-mailing stories and photos home.

"I'd like to help you, but I can't allow other people to use the equipment," Yvonne said apologetically.

"I just need a telephone line to hook up," I said desperately.

"If that's all you need, just come to my house," she offered.

A sensation of disbelief filled my body—it was that damned horseshoe up my butt again! We were complete strangers and she offered us her hospitality. I couldn't wait until our next trip to town.

Toni wore on me. Some days I enjoyed spending time with her. We'd vent our frustrations to one another, swap dating stories and laugh uncontrollably. Other days she worked on my last nerve, demonstrating her no-care attitude and poor work ethic. Toni and I worked on fence one day and picked up wooden posts for firewood on the drive back. I threw my first post on the back of the ute.

"Look at that!" Toni gasped. A six-inch centipede was crawling on the post I had just loaded. I was so lucky it hadn't bitten me. Centipedes were calculating, multi-legged little monsters in my opinion. We had to be prudent when we killed them. As a defense mechanism, their front end looked like their back end. When predators attacked what appeared to be the head, a centipede often surprised its attacker by doubling its body backward, sinking in a painful sting. Toni and I carefully examined every post after that before loading it. We arrived back at the homestead at the same time the blokes returned. Lee and I walked across the lawn together and glanced into the kitchen window.

"I know that guy sitting at the kitchen table," Lee said.

"How do you know him?" I asked.

"I met him at that ag show I went to with Michael Blackburn. I think his name is Chris."

Wonder boy Lee was right. He had a knack for remembering names and details. Chris was a Harvey Beef representative making his annual station stops to develop cattle contracts. It was the first time the Glenns met Chris. They signed documents promising several loads of steers to the slaughterhouse south of Perth. They couldn't believe Lee knew Chris; neither could I.

After everyone had turned in, Lee and I had a meeting with Andrew and Jan. We wanted to make sure there was no miscommunication about wages. I was nervous, Lee was on edge. He had told me earlier not to get all upset if it didn't go our way. They agreed to pay us exactly what we asked for— $300A in cash and $250A in gear per week. We were certainly not making minimum wage according to U.S. standards, but after calculating in the perks, we were doing well. We had free accommodations (no matter how crude), all the food we could possibly eat, and chauffeured trips to town. Plus, we were having the time of our lives, minus my mental woes.

The Glenns purchased a $1,900A stock horse saddle for Lee and ordered a $2,400A custom-made saddle for me. It seemed ridiculous to have such expensive saddles, but we wanted to get something valuable with part of our pay. Lee had to drive the big red truck to Paraburdoo for supplies. I got to tag along. We'd become the official trucking team, making our third trip to town. Trips were long and bumpy, but I always learned something new about Lee.

"This drive reminds me of 4-H," he said. "Every night when we had a 4-H meeting, I missed *The Dukes of Hazard* and this trip to town reminds me of that show. Just trying to keep this truck on the road is a challenge."

The rear view mirror had been broken off and the side mirrors were tied in place with string and wire. The blinders were missing. Lee had to hold the gearshift in place so the truck didn't jump out of gear. Heaps of springs poked through the top of the seat and all the electrical wires under the dash were exposed. Lee was practically crammed under the steering wheel because the Japanese designer didn't allow enough room for normal-sized people. With all its imperfections, Lee reveled in driving the old truck. He affectionately dubbed it the "Red Chariot."

After everything was picked up, strategically placed on the flatbed and secured with trucking cables, we had one last stop. Lee parked the truck close to the curb right in front of Yvonne Quill's home. Yvonne was in her early 40s and was as sweet as she had been on the phone.

"I'm so sorry I don't have wine chilled," she said, hurrying around the kitchen to offer us refreshments.

"We didn't expect wine," I said. "We are flattered that you invited us into your home."

"It's my pleasure," she said.

"Why did you invite complete strangers into your home?" I asked.

"I traveled alone in South America and many good people helped me. I always told myself if a traveler was in need I would help them. It's a way for me to reciprocate what those folks did for me."

She had two sons—Jack, four, and Ben, six. Her husband, Kevin, like most men in the town, worked for Hamersley Iron. The Quills had a beautiful yard with gorgeous Sturt's desert peas bordering their front lawn. The perennial flower is one of Australia's most recognized flowers. It thrives in drier weather and produces scarlet elongated blooms with a black pod-like center. Their backyard was swallowed by a sparkling sapphire-blue swimming pool. A small trampoline sat by the boys' playhouse. The kitchen's sliding-glass door was covered with colorful drawings from the kids' school projects. Toys, a patio table and chairs were arranged on the slate veranda. The Quills were saving money to leave the country in two years. They were planning to pull the boys out of school and travel around the world for a year. I was grateful for her generosity that enabled me to file my stories.

Darkness fell quickly on our drive home. Unexpected 'roos and cattle made the drive tense. Animals shot across the road, testing Lee's alertness. After lots of near misses, we safely delivered the supplies to Ashburton.

Finally, Lee and I got our first days off. The Glenns were not slave drivers by any means. They had given us other days off, but Lee just preferred to work. I packed a cooler with some food and a couple of stubbies. I was excited to 'roo shoot with cameras. I broke out my zoom lens, but it wasn't quite powerful enough to get really good photos before their giant leaps made them even smaller in my frame.

We visited Ted and Joan at the gold mine and their friends, Marg and John. Ted gave us a tour. It was initially founded by two brothers in the 1800s. They invited their third brother in on the discovery because he was a soldier with great survival skills and bush experience. The two brothers sent their soldier brother to town to get supplies, a four-day ride by horseback. They gave him strict orders to keep the secret. Once in town the brother hit the pub, got inebriated and confessed his sworn secret. Over the next few days, thousands of men converged at the secret claim to seek their fortunes. The gold mine had been known as "Soldier's Secret" for two centuries. The mine's two other names were Wandery and Secret Creek Mine.

The six of us drank beer and exchanged stories while damper cooked, the Australian camp-oven bread developed by drovers in the 19th century.

"Marg and I used to pack up the kids and head off for the weekend," John said. "One time we stopped and Marg had to go to the bathroom. She picked a spot near the scrub and dropped her shorts. Marg said, 'What are you looking at?' I said, 'Don't move. When I say leap forward, leap forward as fast as you can.' A good thing she leaped forward. There was a snake ready to bite Marg on the bum and I sure wasn't sucking the venom out!"

We were treated to 'roo burgers. The sweet meat was tasty, but a little chewy. Marg offered another round of beers. "You can't have bush tucker without a stubby in your hand," she said, smiling.

It was dusk, time to get back to Ashburton before the generator shut off. Scores of 'roos invaded the foliage by the road. A momma 'roo poked her head up from her leafy dinner, allowing me a close-up look at the joey sticking its head out of her pouch. It was an incredible sight.

The evening air turned very cold. Lee zipped his sleeping bag up around his head like a little Eskimo. Air blew hard through the holes in our humpy's walls. I disappeared in my sleeping bag with only enough space to breathe. I snuggled close to Lee, but separate sleeping bags left little hope of shared body heat.

There were still issues at Ashburton that needed to be ironed out, but it was comforting to know we were in one place for several months. Since our U.S. departure seven months earlier, it was always from one place to the next. At breaky, Andrew said he was giving a horseshoeing lesson at 11 a.m. Tools were limited so Lee and I watched during the first session. I engrossed myself in the workshop, observing every detail. I was determined to be a good farrier. Andrew carefully explained the process—trimming the hoof, rasping it, sizing and shaping the horseshoe and nailing the shoe on the horse's hoof.

"Every horse is an individual," Andrew said. "You could track a horse by its hoof print."

Considering Andrew was often a man of few words, he did a nice job explaining the procedure, the dos and don'ts. Becky put three shoes on Popeye, but Andrew had to help her with the last one. Toni was having real difficulty. She wasn't strong enough to handle the hammer and hold a hoof at the same time. Andrew nailed on all of Jill's shoes while Toni watched. Barney shod Daryl quickly, doing a thorough job, but Andrew told him to slow down.

"Andrew reckons Lee will be pretty good at shoeing," Jan said at dinner that night.

"Yeah, Lee will be good and I think I'll be good at it too," I said building my own self-confidence since no one else bothered.

As usual, Mr. Wonderful (Lee) could do anything. I teased Lee about how much praise he got and probably didn't realize at the time I was a little jealous of his numerous talents. I was glad that Jan and Andrew had so much faith in Lee—he deserved it.

Our shoeing debut was put off another day as we were sent to the fence row. Lee banged in 140 pickets. I don't know how he did it. The mixture of slate and rock made it nearly impossible to get pickets into the ground in some places. To my and Lee's astonishment, I pounded a few pickets. I felt really useful and proud of myself. I only wished Lee had asked me to help pound the pickets sooner. It may have saved his hurting shoulders and back. My main job was eyeing up the pickets and holding them while Lee pounded.

Maybe my attitude had changed or maybe I accepted the situation. For days everyone else rode to condition their mustering horses while Lee and I worked on the fence row. It didn't bother me as much. The days passed quickly as Lee's offsider; it was rewarding. We had fun, laughed, worked hard and sweated together. We often argued about the straightness of the fence. Lee was such a perfectionist—the fence had to be flawlessly aligned. He once made me take a picket out three times before it was exactly right.

"We're in the middle of an almost million-acre station, it doesn't have to be perfect," I pleaded.

"We're going to do this right," he said. "If someone isn't going to put in a 100-percent effort then they shouldn't put in an effort at all."

I admired his strong work ethic, but most of all I loved being his offsider. It was why we went to the outback—to experience it together. Lee yelled at me a few times when I got sidetracked from my fencing job to pick up really far-out rocks for my garden. The cruel cool wind tried to pierce through my layers of clothing. I had on a polo shirt, a long-sleeved shirt, a sweatshirt, and my red hooded L.L. Bean jacket. I stood out like a red Michelin man in the middle of nowhere, but I was warm. Lee called me Little Red Riding Hood.

Andrew and Toni drove by after they welded in strainer posts at the end of the fence row. "Do you think it's going to snow?" Andrew said with a snicker.

"I'm cold and I'm not here to make a fashion statement," I brashly responded.

My romantic interludes with Lee on the fence row abruptly stopped when Barney was sent to fence with us. Barney contributed if you kept him focused and gave him instruction. If not, he stood around and watched us work.

"Look, there's a dust devil," I yelled as I pointed to the funnel of dirt whirling toward us.

"That's a willy-willy," Barney said.

"In America we call them dust devils, but I like the name willy-willy," I said.

We worked on the fence row until I finally crested the top of a hill and was out of sight. I had made great progress and took a break. I wanted to do something imaginative and playful. I found a cow skull and a sturdy fallen branch. I secured the skull on the end of the branch. I slid my jacket and gloves onto the branches to form a body. The skull peeked from beneath my baseball cap and sunglasses. I tied my red bandana around the bottom of the skull. The extra Band-Aid in my pocket added a unique touch on the cow's skull. I even found an old brown empty liter beer bottle in the scrub and placed it by my artistic creation.

Barney and Lee thought I was nuts, but appreciated my efforts. The outback was vast and remote, often forcing people to do strange things, like building a ridiculous cow scare-crow. I liked to entertain, be creative and unpredictable—it was my identity.

Lee said he was going to pound in some short end posts to secure the pickets on the hill. He told Barney and me to go back for an afternoon ride. I didn't want to go without Lee, but he insisted, knowing how I longed to start conditioning my horse for mustering season.

No one had officially told me what mustering horse I had, but Barney told me it might be Harlequin. I was disappointed Lee stayed at the fence row; he hadn't even had one ride yet. He was determined to get all the fencing done first.

Barney, Toni, Becky and I rode for an hour and a half. I was stiff when I got off. Forget about conditioning the horses, what about conditioning my own bum? I couldn't even fathom being in the saddle all day during a muster. Earlier on the fence row Barney asked if I'd ridden before. I told him I grew up with horses and showed my horse Kizmit in 4-H. He was fascinated by my stories of playing cowboys and Indians with my siblings in the Catoctin Mountains. He couldn't believe I used to hook a toboggan behind Kizmit and pull screaming passengers over snow-covered fields. Becky and Barney had limited horse-riding experience, but did really well. Toni was an accomplished rider, but was careless, often dropping a rein or putting her horse or herself in danger.

The outback took its toll on my body. My neck was covered in a rash; my ear was infected, no doubt as a result of the dust bowl we lived in; and my jeans rubbed burns on my waist. If it wasn't one thing, it was another. I often asked myself, *Am I too old for this shit?* Sometimes I thought I was too old or not fit enough, but other times I was really proud of what I'd accomplished. I was pleased with the many fence rows and river crossings Lee and I built together. It was a team effort.

The fence row was a place of solitude where the important things in life came to mind or I conjured images of life change. My thoughts were often interrupted by the sights and sounds in the scrub. The wind whispered through the air, changing its tone and pitch as it cut through trees and bushes or scattered dust across the ground. The song of bright-feathered birds joined in the wind's chorus, producing notes that stirred my senses. Brilliant green parrots with black neck bands chirped alongside smaller hazel-colored feathered friends brushed with apricot. Lavishly colored lizards stained in emerald, turquoise, salmon, ruby and saffron scurried off just before my foot invaded their previous resting place. Perhaps I was finding myself, finding my position at Ashburton.

Days of Glory

I stand here slackly reminiscing 'bout days of glory,
There are no real surprises, it's the same old story;

In my prime I stood tall and straight,
I drew the line, no need for debate;

I have covered some miles, seen cattle untold,
But that was my youth and now I am old;

Once people looked to me for where the boundaries lay,
Now they resent my presence and push me away;

Through years of neglect and a cruel turn of events,
Now all people see is a rusty old fence.

Lee Chaney

Tony Hutchings and Lee show off their Rainbow trout.

Lee and Becky after church in Tonga. Atu Luau

Becky mustering sheep in New Zealand. Lee Chaney

All smiles washing her *kaukau* (sweet potatoes) in the Papua New Guinea market.

Lee and his guide, Joe, prepare to climb Mt. Wilhelm, Papua New Guinea's highest mountain.

Kids play in the Highlands of Papua New Guinea. Rebecca Long Chaney

Kiana Rose Blackburn hugs her Uncle
Lee. The Blackburns of Burnvale
Holsteins were one of our many adopted
families away from home.

Stuart Day's guinea pig wears the infamous
Statue of Liberty sunglasses on our
departure day from Juna Downs Station.

Sunset at Juna Downs Station.

Rebecca Long Chaney

The homestead at Ashburton Downs Station.

Aboriginal kids enjoy a pit stop
at the Auski Roadhouse.

The *"Road Toad"* in all of her glory.

Jack Harvey of Mininer Station, the last of the old-timers.

Above, Lee holds a beast
steady during broncoing, an
age-old pioneering practice.

At right, Becky fires up the
"donkie" to provide warm
water for a shower.

Cattle crowd together as the crew broncos at the Cattle Camp yards.

Lee's faithful companions, Livingston and Roy, watch as he strands barbed-wire fence.

Lee and Becky take smoko, Austrailia's midmorning break.

Becky Padgham

Becky and one of her many mustering horses, Maggot, take a water break.

Becky Padgham

Lee contemplates the muster.

Rebecca Long Chaney

Lee chases a bull in his Suzuki bull buggy.

Lee pounds a picket in the "Chaney Paddock."

Becky grabs a Hereford calf to eartag.

The crew on our departure day from Ashburton Downs Station are from left, Barney, Lee, Mick, Andrew, Jan and Geoff.

Windmills, the lifeblood of Western Australia, attract cattle, as well as pink and gray galahs.

21

Hammer, Rasp and Nails

D espite our isolated lifestyle, a TV tower caught the signal for a few channels allowing us occasional glimpses of local and world news. June 8 marked the first day of the Olympic torch relay around Australia. Nova Peris-Kneebone, the Aboriginal track-and-field gold-medal hopeful, carried the torch on its first leg. She started at Uluru (Ayers Rock), one of Australia's most famous natural landmarks, and ran with her daughter Jessica.

Lee and I never had time to follow sporting events or teams in the States, but I always loved the Olympics. It was something about international camaraderie—thousands of people of different cultures and beliefs convening for the passion of sport. They put world politics aside, war-torn lands often declared a temporary cease-fire. Religion, color or race did not prevent athletes from embracing. I was a sap for the Olympics, as Lee reminded me when he saw my glassy eyes fill with emotion during the torch relay. The Games didn't officially begin for two weeks. The Olympics lifted my spirits and on a town run, Jan gave me the biggest compliment since I'd been at Ashburton.

"Andrew reckons you're the strongest rider," Jan said. "After he takes a ride on the newly broken-in chestnut filly, if she's not too bad, that filly will be your second mustering horse."

I could hardly contain my elation. I never knew my love for horses as a child would pay off later in life. We had been at the station a total of three months and Andrew had praised me for the first time (though not directly). Maybe I was, finally, part of the team and valued for my ability. I shouldn't have been upset—after all Jan was the brains of Ashburton and got little appreciation. I really didn't know what Ashburton would be like without her. Jan may have worked herself into a frenzy at times, often making three cuppas before she finished one, but Jan was the heartbeat of the station—she kept everything happening. Not only did Jan oversee the books and make all the phone calls, she was the one who networked off the station, making important contacts and finding most of the equipment and supplies.

As the days passed we got closer to the family. Jan continued to tell us why we should immigrate to Australia. She really thought Lee was the best thing since sliced bread, saying, "I think you and Lee should operate a feed lot for us down south."

"Yeah, and call it Ashburton South," I said with a smile.

"I trust Lee more than anyone and I'd want him to run it," she added.

It all sounded wonderful, but I told Jan there were two problems. First, we couldn't obtain a work visa and second, our family and friends might disown us. The idea of living in the outback for a few years was tempting. We knew it wouldn't be easy, but then look at what we had already endured or should I say, what I survived.

"We have to go back to the States for a while," I said. "But we'll think about it."

"Sometimes you just have to do something for yourself, no matter how hard it is," Jan said.

We were busy finishing up fence, excited about mustering season. Lee and I did a few more river crossings. The steep embankments made them the most strenuous. In between fencing days I kept up with our laundry and helped Jan with hers. There was always something to be done. Jan showed us pictures of their stint at Meentheena Station. She pointed out the orange ute, the beat-up four-wheel drive Lee and I always drove to the scrub. At Meentheena, the orange ute was the family transport.

"The kids would hide in the ute because they were embarrassed to be seen in the beat-up thing," Jan said.

"I used to love riding with Mom and Dad in our big farm truck," I said. "I wasn't embarrassed; in fact, I thought I was pretty big stuff sitting up in the front seat."

The official Chaney trucking team was sent to town again. On the way, three dingoes ran in front of the truck for a quarter of a mile before disappearing into the scrub. Lee had speeded up to run over them knowing they posed a threat to cattle. He told Mick the story later.

"Lee, you should have driven right into the scrub to kill one—a dingo scalp is \$35A and we could have gotten the truck fixed," Mick said sarcastically.

"Mick, I got in big trouble one day on my parents' farm for doing something like that," I said. "I was raking hay for Dad and I saw a groundhog come out of its hole. I knew Dad always tried to shoot the little varmints because their burrowed holes broke equipment. I thought Dad would be really proud of me if I got it, so I proceeded to chase that damned groundhog in circles trying to run it over. I finally gave up, but my nicely raked straight rows of hay had turned into a cluster of misshaped circles impossible to be baled up. Not only was Dad miffed about the mess, I didn't even have a dead groundhog to show for my efforts."

• • •

It was the middle of June. We had to take the Red Chariot to town again. We left at 9:45 a.m. after I'd taken Lee's photo by the truck. Lee was sporting his J Patrick Transport hat. We sent the photo to our American mate, Johnny, and told him we were "J Patrick Transport Down Under."

We stopped at the garden center and purchased a few plants. Plants were not a necessity, but I knew that a flower garden would be aesthetically appealing and improve my mental outlook at the station. Our main mission in town was picking up the furniture Jan had ordered. It wasn't ready to load so I slipped into the local deli for a Diet Coke. I looked at the dark-complexioned woman across the counter as I paid, thinking she might have a trace of Aboriginal blood. I was determined to meet some of the indigenous people. I straightened up and flashed her my cow-queen smile.

"Hi, my name is Becky. My husband and I are here for a couple of months working at Ashburton Downs Station and we're looking for some Aboriginal art."

"Come with me. There's an Aboriginal lady sitting right outside who can probably help you," she said. "She's known as the town medicine woman."

This could be my lucky day, I thought. I followed the deli lady outside and she pointed to the woman at a nearby table. The Aboriginal woman was clad in jewelry and a blue-and-white dress. She had skin darker than coal. She sat quietly and fidgeted with her drink. Although she was seated, I could tell she wasn't a tall woman and like most Aboriginal women I had seen, she was pleasantly rotund. Her round face and flat, wide nose, typical of her race, shined in the morning sun. My first impression, *Now, there's a lady with lots of stories to tell.* I walked over to her table.

"Hello, I'm Becky," I said as I extended my hand to shake hers. "I was wondering if you may know someone who does Aboriginal paintings?"

"My son does," she said.

"My husband and I are here through October working at Ashburton Downs Station," I said.

"My goodness, I was just thinking about Ashburton last night and thinking I need to get out for a visit," she said. "I grew up there about 50 years ago. I was a waitress and my grandmother was the head cook. I'm Lola Young."

It had to be that infamous horseshoe working for me again. Not only did I stumble across a possible connection for Aboriginal art, but someone who could piece together bits of Ashburton history I couldn't find in the library.

"Is the camp still there over the hill with the dome and the sheds?" Lola asked.

"Yes, that's where Lee and I live in a tin shed," I said.

"The shed with the old stove—is that still there?" she queried. "That's where my grandmother lived. We worked for a man by the name of Kelly. I'd like to come out to Ashburton and show you the old burial sites."

At that point I was having a traveling "O"—I was beyond excited. I couldn't believe I'd met Lola. What little information she provided during our initial meeting had my mind churned in a whirlpool of images. I thought about the humpy Lee and I lived in. What history it must have! Visions of Aboriginal ceremonies, customs and rites of passage intrigued me. I promised Lola I would come visit her and perhaps I'd see her at Ashburton for a visit soon. I was ready to burst. I found Lee and shared my chance meeting. He shook his head in disbelief, but he was not surprised.

We drove back to Ashburton and helped get everything unloaded. We had two days off and devoted it to our landscaping project. After all the debris from in front of our humpy was removed, Lee worked up the ground. He discovered a patio beneath six inches of soil. Swirled blue and gray slate faces were pieced together and secured by cement. The name Johnny-1974 was inscribed into the cement. I found out later that Johnny was Lola's son, who had been the head stockman at Ashburton during the '70s.

Lee made two trips to the river and scooped up silty, nutrient-filled soil which wouldn't dry into hard bits as the red clay-like soil around the homestead did. While we worked on the garden plot, Geoff moped around his humpy. I asked him what was wrong.

"I feel really crook," he said.

"Do you have a cold?" I asked.

"I don't know," he groggily said. "It just hit me."

"Hey, what are those marks behind your knee? I bet you've been bitten by a redback spider."

"I just kneeled to light the donkie and felt a stinging sensation under my pants when I got up. A spider must have crawled into my pants while they were hanging in my humpy."

"It probably got crushed between your leg and pants. A redback bite could be serious."

"If I don't feel better by tomorrow, I'll go to the doctor's," he said.

After that day, I religiously shook out all my clothes before pulling them on. I had already killed six redback spiders in our humpy and prayed none were hiding in the creases of my clothes.

Lee and I went to the fence row first thing the following morning. Old wooden fence posts we were digging out would make perfect fuel for the donkie. Lee used the ute's 'roo bar to knock four of the posts loose. A gecko ran around one post, but it was too quick for me to catch and get it to safety. Once the posts were loosened by the ute, Lee wrapped his whole body around the post—pushed and pulled, pushed and pulled, rocking it until he could tug it out. All of a sudden something leaped from the post onto Lee's face. He jerked, but stood there, eyes crossed, starring down at the gecko hanging on for dear life from his goatee. I doubled over laughing, shocked that the creature sought refuge on Lee's prickly goatee. The traumatized gecko took a another brave leap and scurried off. It was those serendipitous moments that I'd remember most about Ashburton—the times the unexpected either had me in stitches or had my adrenaline pumping so hard I thought I might collapse.

Jan asked us to go to town again and Lee pulled up by the Nest to pick me up. "Your chariot awaits."

We zipped from one place to the next gathering supplies. On the way home I opened up a package from Mom and Dad. They had sent elk jerky, news clippings, gum, candy bars, bandanas and thread—all the things I'd asked for, plus a few treats. I reached farther into the mail envelope and pulled out what I thought was a wool scarf. To my dismay, three wool dickies lay perfectly folded in my hand. I detested the old-time neck warmers Mom made us wear as kids. I couldn't believe it. I had specifically asked Mom for a small scarf because the cold mornings were often unbearable. She knew I hated dickies, how could she send them? I couldn't complain, she sent them halfway around the world, after all. And I wouldn't dare tell Mom she'd sent the wrong thing—I'd hate for her packages of goodies to stop coming.

The next morning it was bone chilling. I trembled from the nippy air as I slipped into my work clothes and laughed at Lee, who acted as though we were waking up in an igloo on the tundra. It wasn't freezing in our humpy, but some mornings we did see our breath.

"My thing is going to fall off if it's exposed to the elements much longer," Lee said voicing his disgruntlement of the cold breeze blowing up his boxer shorts.

We got an early start to what I hoped was the final bit of fencing. We pounded in 50 pickets. Lee made me pull out several pickets and redo them—they were all of a half inch off. "I hope one day to aspire to the great fencing of Lee Chaney," I teased.

We were reinforcing a fence a so-called "professional" had put up two years earlier. In Aussie terms, it was a shit-house job. So the official Chaney fencing duo was called in. The fence was a mess. "I would rather put up brand-new fence than try to correct other people's mistakes," Lee said.

We made steady progress until we came to a territorial ant colony. I attached one tie wire on a picket and retreated, dancing and swatting at the ants. Lee attempted to finish the job.

"Lee, the ants are on your boots, now they're going up your pants leg," I shouted with delight watching him shake his legs violently while he attached tie wires.

"Damn, they're in my boots!" he cursed.

"Oh shit, an ant is biting my butt," I squealed, running around hitting my rear end.

"At least he knows where the sweet meat is," my smart-ass husband replied.

I retired early to the Nest, but wasn't too beat to notice our new houseguests. Two more hairy huntsman spiders had found refuge on our wall. They had darker markings than Henry, Henrietta and Little Henry, our first eight-legged roommates. I gave Homer and Horace the same lecture I'd given the others to make sure they knew to respect my space.

"Who are you talking to?" Lee asked when he walked in the door.

"Oh, just our two new guests, Homer and Horace," I answered, pointing to them on the wall.

Huntsman spiders stayed completely still as a defense mechanism. Some days they'd be in the same spot all day. I'd come to the conclusion they were dead and when I'd go to touch one, its quick movement almost gave me a panic attack. Less frightening was Gilbert, the resident gecko. I liked Gilbert and hoped he feasted on the smaller bugs that made me crazy.

Lee wished me a happy third anniversary as soon as he woke up that particular morning. I gave him a Leatherman tool in a leather case since leather represented three years of marriage. Lee's Leatherman was much like a Swiss army knife, but with lots more gadgets. He immediately attached it to his hobble belt. Barney and Mick also wore hobble belts which were originally designed to hobble horses and camels, but the blokes wore them to carry their Leatherman tool and penknife. The thick, leather belts hung on their hips, lower on one side.

As I watered our garden later I noticed Lee walk over the hill at dusk. I could only make out his bow-legged silhouette. He had his Wranglers on, hobble belt, boots and his Akubra hat. I felt a little randy like I did the first day I met Lee more than seven years earlier at my parents' cattle dispersal. He had a little ponytail and wore a Drizabone, and baseball cap that day. He was a "hotty" according to my friends. He stood quietly at the back of the sale tent giving his subtle bids—he was mysterious. Lee purchased the high-selling cow, Long View Jade's Raisin, for $4,000 and later told me it was a lot of money to spend to get a date with me.

The weather turned colder. I took back all the non-appreciative comments I had made about the dickies Mom sent. I learned to love them and valued their warmth around my neck. If it warmed up in the afternoon I just slipped the dickie over my head without having to remove any other piece of clothing. I hated to admit it, but maybe mothers did know best.

I rode with Mick to Mininer Station to pick up 48 head of Ashburton cattle that had crossed the station border. I met Wendy Harvey and her boyfriend, Peter. Wendy's parents, Jack and Dorris Harvey, had established the half-million-acre station from scratch 50 years earlier. The Harveys' son pursued a city career and Wendy helped her father operate the station. The Harveys didn't have TV and just got telephone service in 1988—shocking really.

"Getting a telephone was great," Wendy said. "I can call and order stuff quicker and we can call our neighbors and whinge."

We delivered the cattle back to Ashburton. It was time for Lee and me to shoe our horses for mustering. Lee picked up Duck's hoof. The chestnut mare stood quietly. Sweat rolled down Lee's face, his shirt stuck to his back and his armpits were drenched, but he completed the job.

I had to shoe Kate, a liver-colored, five-year-old mare. I clipped off the excess hoof, rasped and shaped all four hooves. Then I hammered and crafted each horseshoe for its respective hoof. It was a difficult and tedious task; each horseshoe had to be shaped precisely. I held each hoof tightly between my knees and carefully pounded each nail, hoping the mare wouldn't jerk her leg and catch the nail in my flesh, ripping it open. I wore a leather farrier's apron, but it always seemed to creep up above the hoof, offering me little protection. My hands were raw from accidentally rasping them, my legs hurt from squeezing the hoof between my knees and pain shot down my back. I remembered Jan telling me months earlier that Andrew expected employees to shoe their own horses and at that time I said under my breath, "There's not a chance in hell that I'm ever going to shoe my own horse."

I underestimated my capabilities. What a feeling of accomplishment when I had completely shod my first horse! Lee and I wobbled into the Nest later like two crippled zombies.

"I reckon changing a tire on a semi with a spoon is easier than shoeing a horse," Lee said exasperated and exhausted. I couldn't help but find humor in our discomfort. If mustering season was going to be anything like shoeing our own horses, we certainly were going to have our work cut out for us.

Time to Muster

Fences are up, horses are shod,
Crates are completed and given the nod;

Yards stand patient, strong and steady,
Tires are mended, buggies are ready;

Green horses are started, gotten used to the saddle,
More of an understanding, less of a battle;

Mills have been fixed and tanks have been filled,
Patch up the holes so the water's not spilled;

With a good meal in our bellies we turn in for the night,
Do some reading and writing before we turn off the light;

Wait for the word from the boss and the laying of the wind,
Not 'til all these are done will the muster begin.

Lee Chaney

22

The First Muster

Excitement, fear, anticipation and relief swelled inside me as Andrew announced our first day of mustering. Cattle roundups we'd read about or heard about sounded fascinating, fun and dangerous.

I'd had a restless night thinking about our inaugural muster. I laid my mustering clothes out the night before to limit the time my tender skin was exposed to the morning elements. I woke groggy-eyed, but eager. I squeezed into my jeans and wove my leather belt through the loops. My dickie and long-sleeved shirt would keep me warm and protect my skin from the sun's rays and wind's sting. Of course, my Day Radiance foundation was smoothed on my face for the same reasons, to screen my skin from the weather. I had been a devout Mary Kay cosmetic user for 20 years. Rarely a day went by I didn't blend on my creamy fawn beige foundation, or Day Radiance as Mary Kay called it.

For months I had stopped wearing makeup—a pretty bold move. I wanted to be all natural in the outback, makeup-free, but Jan told me foundation would help protect my skin from the wind and sun. Sounded like a good reason to me. After I blended in my Day Radiance, I fastened my bandana around my neck. I felt like I was about to rob a bank, but Jan insisted bandanas were a must because cattle stirred up constant dust storms. She didn't want us to get station lung, whatever the hell that was.

I pulled on my special Aussie riding boots, famous for the tabs on the front and back of the boot's ankle piece. My leather riding gloves were snug, and last, but not least, I positioned my Akubra hat with a black braided chinstrap secured under my throat. A southwestern-looking band wrapped around my brown Warrego hat, purely for fashion. It held the guardian angel pin Mom and Dad had given me. It seemed like a complicated process to go chase cattle, but necessary garb.

At 6:30 a.m. Andrew gave us each a radio. Lee's was attached across his chest by an old rein called a bandolier strap. My radio was in a leather band fastened around my upper arm. I spent opening day on Harlequin and my new saddle. Lee was on Duck, Mick rode Sox, Toni was on Jill, Becky Padgham had Popeye, Barney was on Daryl and Geoff was on one of the young geldings, Mac. All the horsemen except Mick rode out the dirt road to the river paddock. Mick rode through the horse paddock to check a few gates.

"Andrew, I've just had the biggest fuckin' stuff-up," an agitated Mick radioed. "I was closing a gate and my horse bolted away with a mob of other horses."

I had two thoughts: *Poor Mick* and *Better him than me*. It didn't take long for Mick to catch Sox and join the group. Although Mick was disgusted by the incident, I thought it gave our first muster a certain melodramatic effect.

Jan and Tricky were each in a bull buggy, a four-wheel-drive Suzuki. Andrew piloted the plane. Riders headed toward the starting point. Andrew's fancy plane maneuvering and engine revs scared cattle from their hiding places. Before we knew it, a coach mob of about 75 were gathered. The idea was to steady the initial mob, or coach mob, and continue to muster more cattle. Lee, Toni, Barney and I surrounded the coach mob and waited for more cattle. Andrew quickly rectified the quandary of two Beckys on the crew. His system was simple, really, and worked. I became known as Becky America and the other, Becky Kimberley, since she was a native of Australia's Kimberley Region.

"Becky America, go out and bring those four in," Andrew commanded through static on the radio. "Becky Kimberley stay with the mob."

The cattle did well as they stood quietly and grazed in a disfigured oblong circle. Tricky and Jan made rounds with their bull buggies making sure everyone had a drink and a snack. I had a headache and took two aspirin. The day's excitement and pressure from my Akubra stressed my brain. I focused on one goal—impress the boss. I tried to anticipate every move of an animal—to cut them off, turn them and keep them steady. I chased two beasts through the scrub.

"Becky America, stop, stop, don't run," Andrew scolded after he spotted me from the plane.

No one had ever told me not to chase any cattle while the mob was just forming. Chasing them only got them more worked up and less cooperative. Since we had very little instruction, I reckoned it wasn't my fault, but counted it as a good lesson.

"Mick, you and Becky America go to the river and bring those cattle up and the rest of you start taking the mob toward the double gates," Andrew ordered from the sky.

My early chasing must not have irked him too much. It felt good being singled out by Andrew. It meant he had confidence in my ability to ride and work cattle. Finally, after three months, perhaps I was getting some recognition. It boosted my ego and Ashburton started to feel more like home than a prison I couldn't escape.

Mick and I crossed the river. The horses were up to their bellies in water. I held my legs high trying to keep my boots dry. The horses' laborious splashes still nearly soaked them. We found a small mob and started to move them, then they bolted. Mick and I galloped through the wooded area, darting in between trees trying to stop them. We had to get them across the river and toward the double gates, but they ran the wrong way. We eventually got them back on track. I doubled back to check for strays.

"Hey, Mick, I found a mob of cattle, but they're on the other side of the river," I radioed.

"Well, what are you waiting for, mate? Go get 'em," he answered.

Harlequin slid down the steep river bank on his rear end, I leaned back in the saddle almost horizontal before we splashed in the river. The cattle started walking in the right direction, but kept bolting for the scrub. I took off on Harlequin, fast and furious, to turn them toward the double gates. Hell, after the tenth run of turning back stupid cattle, I was exhausted, or stuffed, as Aussies would say. Poor Harlequin panted, but gave everything he had.

I joined back up with Mick and we moved the 50 misfits homeward. While Mick went to help the others with the big mob, I held the smaller group. I raced from end to end keeping the cattle under control. The beasts tested my ability and Harlequin's speed. Finally, I saw the big mob coming. Dust drifted above them as they plodded along behind Becky Kimberley on the lead horse. Lee was on the right point. The lead horse was just that, a walking, living target up front for the cattle to follow.

We held the mob and waited for Andrew. His "TMT" kicked in big time during mustering season. He had to be part of everything—micromanagement at its finest. Andrew landed the plane, jumped on his black stallion, Nomad, and rode out to orchestrate the river crossing. Ironically, while we waited for Andrew, Lee—who had worked on fence more than anyone—unwittingly walked Duck right into a mess of wire.

"I knew Duck was in the wire before Duck knew he was in the wire," Lee said later. "I didn't know if I should try to jump off or what." He held Duck steady and, remarkably, walked out of it. Lee was lucky—it could have been a disaster since most horses don't react well when tangled in wire.

Andrew told us river crossings were critical and cattle had to be pushed hard or they'd turn and stampede the wrong way. The first few cattle hesitantly placed their front hooves into the cold water. We pushed; Andrew cracked his long black plaited leather whip from atop Nomad's back. The beautiful stallion stood motionless as Andrew snapped his whip over and over again, urging the cattle across. The cattle steadily crossed the river and climbed the opposite bank. Some cattle were sidetracked up a near-vertical hill and stopped.

"Is anyone going up there?" Andrew said, looking at his group of greenhorns.

No one responded. It looked totally impossible for a horse to navigate, but if Andrew thought it was safe, then it must be safe—right? Still, no one moved. "Becky Kimberley, put Popeye into four-wheel drive," he ordered.

After two refusals, Becky kicked again and Popeye shot up the steep bluff. He leaped forward, front legs bent, his flank and rear end muscles bulging. Becky leaned forward in the saddle, practically lying on Popeye's neck. I prayed she'd make it and not pull Popeye back, tumbling backward down the embankment. They crested the top and moved the cattle.

"That was a great climb," I told Becky later. "I was very impressed."

"Thanks, Bec," she said quietly.

Becky Kimberley was not a confident rider. I often complimented and encouraged her—she did the same for me. We moved the cattle through another set of gates and down the fence row to the cattle yards. Mick, Barney, Andrew and I followed the cattle into the yards.

"Becky, once the cattle are to a gate just stop and wait until they start going through on their own, then push," Andrew advised. How typical of Andrew—to give instruction after we'd already screwed up. I guess there were worse teaching methods, but I wished we had completed a few hours of Mustering 101. I was knackered after eight hours in the saddle. My body ached when I stood up from a late lunch and headed back to the yards. *Oh, God,* I thought, *we still have hours of work to do.*

Lee, Toni, Becky and I helped Andrew draft the cattle, sorting them according to gender and age. We were stationed by the five gates surrounding the round pen. Andrew operated the swing gate. He let one beast in the small round pen at a time. "Cleanskin!" Andrew yelled, followed by "Bush!"

A sequence of cleanskin, bush, bullock, steer, continued, only interrupted by a few shouts for Mininer, Rock Lea, Wyloo or Pingandy—the strays that had wandered over borders onto Ashburton property. Cleanskins were cattle never ear tagged or earmarked; bush represented cows, calves, weaners, heifers, and young steers destined for the bush to graze; bulls, steers and bullocks were drafted out to send to market.

I was in charge of the bush gate. The first couple pens went okay. Then Becky Kimberley went to help Andrew push the cattle. That gave me the bush and bull gates. I always kept a close eye on the bulls. I knew farmers who had been killed or maimed by bulls. I was afraid of them. I soon realized bulls were not our only threat. A young horned cow scrambled into the round pen.

"Cleanskin!" Andrew shouted.

I walked toward her to shoo her through the cleanskin gate. The crazed beast charged. I scaled the metal fence faster than you could bat an eye. I thought she'd pierce my legs with her sharp curved horns as I hung from the top panel, but she couldn't reach me. Then she turned on Lee and he shot up the fence.

A little later another cow came at me; I retreated to my safe place on the top panel. There were blind animals that nearly toppled over us. I embraced the idea that every animal was dangerous. I teased Toni about the plastic pipe she used to direct cattle in the round pen.

"Sheep people tap the ground, not cattle people," Andrew told her.

Toni didn't have a clue about working with cattle, but she seemed to want to learn—or at least at first she did. At 5:30 p.m., Andrew called it a day.

"Were you worried when that first cow came at me?" I asked as Lee and I hiked over the hill to the Nest.

"No, looked like you were climbing that fence pretty fast," he chuckled.

Back at the Nest, our garden bursting with color relaxed me after our 11-hour day. I sprinkled every bloom with water. "I really thought everything would just die," Lee confessed. "But you have a beautiful little garden. I'm proud of you."

The three poinciana trees had taken root, as had the poinsettia bush and rose bush. Lee built four wire cages and attached shade cloth to protect the small plants from the harsh winter breezes. Forty petunias bordered the garden and three flowering vines had started to spread. I hoped the sunflower seeds and the Sturt's desert pea seeds would pop through the soil soon.

Lee found six flat pieces of gray and black slate that made a perfect path into the garden and patio. I made a little metal sign, *The Chaneys, Tidy Nest Award, 2000,* and put it in the flower bed. I got the idea from the Tidy Town Awards that charmed many outback towns.

I had put in long hard days building and tearing down fence, but that first day mustering was grueling—every muscle in my body protested my involvement. I almost feared what was to come. I peeled off my dirty stinky clothes and looked down at my body. "Bloody hell!" I said aloud. Not only did it feel like I'd been run over by a beast, but I looked like it. There was a massive blue-and-purple bruise on my upper inner thigh that rolled like a tennis ball under my skin when I touched it. The insides of my knees were purplish-red and black.

At tea time Andrew highlighted my mustering mishaps. I appreciated the constructive criticism and was more determined than ever to be the best ringer in the crew. Ringer was the name given to cattle drovers a century earlier. "Stockmen used to take cattle in continuous circles until they were quiet," Andrew explained. "Because of the circular motion, the cattlemen were called ringers."

The following day it was back to the cattle yards. At breakfast Jan told me, "You're the testicle girl."

"What's the testicle girl have to do?" I asked.

"When Andrew marks [castrates] the calves he just throws the testicles everywhere. It makes a mess and the meat ants come into the yards. Count the testicles and make sure they are all thrown in a barrel." I thought, *Great, my claim to fame at Ashburton is the official testicle girl—won't my parents be so proud?*

"Mum, I always chuck the testicles," Mick said.

"I've been chucking testicles for more than 30 years and ya can't teach an old dog new tricks," Andrew added. Through the day I retrieved the scattered bloody balls and tossed them in the barrel.

We processed bullocks next. The aged steers had escaped musters for years. They reached intimidating proportions and grew irregular-shaped horns. One huge bullock broke through the locked crush (chute). If any of us had been standing in front of the crush, where we always stood, we would have been trampled to death. The new hydraulic ram snapped. I held it while Andrew welded the broken bits back together. For the first time at Ashburton, I was Andrew's offsider—I couldn't believe it. We fixed it and started moving bullocks through the crush again.

The following day we processed bull calves again. I gripped each bull's tail tightly and bent it back until the animal seemed controlled. Andrew grabbed its testicles, squeezed, sliced, popped, cut and chucked. Next, I put nose leads in the beast's nostrils and tugged its head to the side and held it steady for Andrew to dehorn. Andrew placed a two-handled device over each nubby horn and clamped it shut, cutting the horn to the skull. Toni clipped in a yellow ear tag as she shied from its wild swirling head. We took turns with the earmarker. The instrument cut shaped notches out of the top and bottom of the ear. If the animal's plastic tag was ever lost, it could always be identified by its earmarks. I liked yard work. It was physical, dangerous and exhausting—and it burned away calories.

I admired Andrew's talents—a sign he had grown on me, or perhaps I had softened. Little did I know the new respect and appreciation for Andrew wouldn't last. Jan had been upset because she'd been stuck inside with office work. She wanted to be in the yards working cattle. She always thought she had to prove herself and made occasional appearances at the yards.

"Jan, you don't have to prove anything," I said. "We all know you're capable and have done it all before. Take advantage of us while you have a crew and get your office work done."

My advice was ignored, but I couldn't blame her—I'd rather be out working with cattle than managing an office too. Jan was no stranger to cattle work or difficult times. She certainly didn't have to prove anything to us. For years she and Andrew did most of the mustering and processing themselves. However, Jan knew the importance of maintaining the business aspect of Ashburton. Andrew didn't have the business savvy and people skills Jan possessed. She was an amazing bush woman. I admired her strong persona and grew to love her soft, gentle nature. I wished she realized how much people appreciated her.

After processing 114 cattle, we moved them to the airstrip paddock via the cooling paddock. The cooling paddock was about a quarter of a mile long, which allowed cattle the space and confinement to walk out of the yards slowly and quietly without stampeding—at least that was the theory.

Andrew unsaddled Nomad and walked to the horse barn. I dismounted at the saddle shed as I always did. The bridle slipped smoothly over Harlequin's big furry ears. He jerked back, the bit clanged between his teeth and he jerked again, leaving the bridle in my hand while he trotted off.

This is not happening to me, I said to myself, shaking my head in disbelief. It had been one crisis after the other that day. My $2,400A saddle was still tightly girthed to the runaway. I felt like an idiot—a real rookie, especially when Harlequin ran in the barn right behind Andrew and Nomad. Andrew just smiled, reached out and slipped a lead over Harlequin's neck.

"Thanks, Andrew," I said with an embarrassed flush of red to my face.

"Can I have a go in your saddle?" he asked.

"Sure," I said, relieved that I didn't get another lesson in horsemanship. In Australia, saddles are to bushmen as cars are to Americans—a personal extension of one's self.

"It's got a nice seat," Andrew said as he dismounted.

"Thanks," I said. "I reckon I'll keep it."

Lee, Mick and Barney put 15 bulls through the crush to tip their horns. The bulls were big, agitated and mean. Their horns were cut back to a regulated length to make the animals eligible for shipment. The tipping procedure was bloody and demanding. The blokes used hydraulic dehorners. The heavy-handled chopper was positioned over the horn, a button was pushed, the hydraulic blades closed and the horn dropped. The crunching sound was loud and disgusting. Blood squirted from the top of the horns, showering everyone with a dotted pattern of dark red.

Lee and I beamed when Jan told us she had named the new bull paddock the "Chaney Paddock" in honor of our tireless hours constructing a majority of that fence. Our departure wouldn't be the end; the Chaney Paddock would be a constant reminder of the months we spent at Ashburton.

All the cattle from our first muster were processed and moved out of the yards. Andrew called it our practice muster. It was time for the first big muster. Lee, Mick, Geoff and I spent the night at Lightning Flat, where Lee and Barney had constructed a portable yard with metal panels. It was an hour's drive from the homestead. Lee and I drove the Red Chariot with four horses on it. Geoff followed with two more horses in the horse float. Mick drove the three-sectioned road train.

I stumbled around the flat with a torch collecting old branches and built a fire. We warmed up water for cuppas and ate cold baked beans and spaghetti out of cans. Nine falling stars shot across the night sky before I drifted off beneath the warmth of a double swag we'd borrowed from Jan. I nestled close to Lee as the temperature dropped. Brisk morning air helped shake our sleepiness away before the sun had even reached our part of the world. We filled the nose bags that fitted on each horse's head with its breakfast at 5 a.m. They needed time to digest their morning meal before their long mustering day.

The fire crackled as I threw on more wood. We sipped our hot coffee and chatted about the day's muster. The rest of the crew arrived at 6:30. Eight horsemen rode out of camp at 7 a.m. It was an hour's ride to the location where we would start gathering cattle. The Glenns had hired Butch, a professional helicopter-mustering pilot. He was actually Barney's father and Becky Kimberley's stepfather. Butch and his helicopter were one in the same with every swift motion. He could drop nearly to the ground in seconds to stop a bolting beast or circle around a mob encouraging them onward. His high- and low-flying aerobatics were nothing short of incredible and just as frightening to watch.

Butch moved the first groups of cattle from the scrub to the flat where steeds and riders were stationed. The coach mob had been formed. We held them steady, waiting for more. One completely feral cow kept trying to escape. Tricky had the wheels of his bull buggy almost touching her. She turned and rammed her horn right through his passenger door. Her horn broke and blood streamed down her head. That was the day the deadly mustering stories I'd heard finally sank in. Angry bulls and irritated cows could easily take the flesh out of my horse's side or my leg. I had a new appreciation for mustering. It was more demanding and more dangerous than I'd ever imagined. I chased a dozen escaping beasts and brought them back to the mob. It wasn't easy. The cattle were clever, daring and quick.

"Females return to the mob sweaty and tired," Andrew said. "That's when the bulls pick up her scent and go for her."

Several of the females got repeatedly raped by the bulls. It was one of the most horrible things I'd ever witnessed and there was nothing we could do. I asked if we could draft the victims out and let them go, but that risked losing the entire mob. The females were brutally attacked and often collapsed. The cow that put the hole in Tricky's passenger door was back in the mob. Her foamy lathered hide and blood-covered face produced a sweaty stench, making her an easy target. Nine bulls mounted her in a hormonal relay that disgusted me. She lost all strength and fell to the ground. She was lethargic, panting with her tongue hanging from the side of her mouth. I turned my head and concentrated on the other cattle as Barney and I pushed the mob toward Lightning Flat. I felt helpless, as if I had abandoned her, but there was nothing I could do.

Bang, Bang! Two shots rang out echoing through the valley. Tricky put the animal out of her misery. It was sad, but her suffering was over—the bulls' abuse was over.

Lee's second muster on Duck was impressive. Every time he rode he improved. He went after a few beasts, his unsteady seat bouncing with every stride. He scared me to death, but I admired his willing nature. Lee and I pushed up the rear of the mob. Mick and Andrew were both in front sharing the lead. A 1,500-pound horned bull continued to charge them. I tightened my reins with dread every time I watched the bull charge, not sure if Mick and Andrew would get hurt. They often just escaped the deadly points of the bull's horns. I studied their reaction, technique and strategy—I wanted to learn how to handle bulls, or at least how to save my ass.

My hands shook with excitement each time I chased an animal. Sometimes when a beast bolted and a horseman was in pursuit, Butch swooped in with the helicopter to help. At that point the horseman backed off to prevent a helicopter beheading and served as backup. We held the mob for half-hour breaks every few miles which aided in the education process, conditioning the cattle to remain calm and cooperative. The area we mustered hadn't been touched for two years, so it was no surprise the cattle were toey, the Aussie expression for skittish and nervous. The mob grew to 600 and Andrew was concerned they wouldn't fit in the yards.

"Lee, tie Duck to a tree and hop in with Butch," Andrew radioed. "I need you and Butch to fly back and enlarge the yards."

"Righto!" Lee said.

Jan was amazing in the bull buggy. She took on all the bulls, big or small, as well as unruly cows. She was gutsy and didn't seem to be afraid of anything. We got the mob to the yards at 5 p.m. That explained why my bum was so sore—I'd been in the saddle ten straight hours. We pushed the cattle into the yards and called it a day.

The following morning we all drove back to Lightning Flat to bronco. It was raining, totally unusual for July, which is typically very cool, windy and dry in Western Australia.

Broncoing was done with determination, speed and strength. It was an outback station practice developed more than a century ago as the only way to brand and castrate cattle. While broncoing was often seen as an anachronism, Jan and Andrew were keeping the tradition alive. For them, broncoing was a management tool adopted at almost every set of yards. The homestead yard was the only one with a race and crush. In pioneering days, cattle were pulled up to a tree to be branded and castrated, but the Glenns used stationary bronco panels. Ashburton was the only station in the Pilbara Region that still broncoed.

A successful day depended on the broncoing team, including the horse. The bronco horse rider selected and slipped a lasso over a beast's head and pulled it to the bronco panel. The bronco panel was designed to allow the rope to slide up, and then down, between two poles which helped secure the animal's head. The rope remained firm around its neck until ropes were attached to the animal's two offside legs. The ropes were then wrapped around the bronco panel and the animal was tipped to its side. The neck rope was removed and the bronco horse rider departed to lasso the next victim. Two people held the leg ropes while another pulled back the other rear leg to immobilize the animal. The person on the shoulder held down the front leg. Once the animal was immobilized, the rest of the broncoing crew stepped in to ear tag, earmark, castrate and dehorn.

One of the stars at Ashburton was Fatty, the bronco horse. A strong, dependable bronco horse made the difference between an efficient day and a long day. Once the beast was lassoed, Fatty knew it was time to pull. He dug his hooves into the ground, leaned to the side and carefully, but forcefully, pulled the selected animal to the bronco panel. Not only were calves and weaners processed, but many large cows and cleanskins were identified or had their horns tipped. Andrew rode Fatty, Becky Kimberley held the rear leg rope, Toni held the front leg rope, Barney had the shoulder and Lee tipped the beast over and held the rear leg back. Lee had the most demanding position—if the leg slipped from his grip, it risked a serious injury to the others. Mick dehorned and castrated and I ear tagged and earmarked. Lee's pants were covered in mud as he handled each animal with authority.

"You really like this, don't you?" I asked. Without a word, but donning the biggest smile, he shook his head up and down like his whole being had culminated into his greatest adventure yet. He was in his element—rough, filthy work. He loved making fence, but broncoing entranced him. Perhaps he envisioned stockmen before him who still held a place in Australia's rich pastoral history—the Duracks, Kidmans, Tysons, Falkiners and McCaugheys. Lee had just finished reading the Australian classic, *Kings in Grass Castles,* which depicted the epic Australian journey of the Durack dynasty. Lee was living a part of history and loving it.

"Ahh, shit," Lee said as he limped toward me. "I just popped my knee out."

"You'll have to let someone else on the rear leg," I urged.

"Naw, it'll be fine," he said returning to his broncoing position. Pain crossed his face, but nothing diminished his stamina and conviction.

While the bronco team tired, Fatty continued relentlessly. With graying hair and distinctive scars of his triumphs and struggles over the years, there was no beast that could beat the 19-year-old horse. Referred to as a legend in his own time, Fatty captivated us. The horse had been part of the family for 15 years and rarely missed a muster. They had purchased him for $400A as a four-year-old quarter horse.

"Fatty's real name is Tobun," Andrew said. "He got the name Fatty because he eats lollies [sweets], corn beef sandwiches, chocolate, dog pellets and meat, but he likes his meat cooked."

During the Glenns' time at Meentheena Station, Fatty was noted for pulling supplies over flooded waters year after year to bring necessities to the family. He was a valuable asset to them. Fatty's precarious capers, everything from unlatching gates to stealing lollies, assured him a place in Ashburton's history.

My brain was in overdrive. We had digested so much information and experienced so much in a matter of days. The crew was compatible, working like a team. Life was good. It was the calm before the storm.

I'm Going to Die

The day after our broncoing introduction, the plan was to draft out bulls and steers to truck back to the homestead yards. Becky Kimberley, Toni, Andrew and I saddled up. We didn't have the efficiency of a round pen and several gates like the homestead yards. The objective was to walk in front of the cattle coming out of the yards, making sure they settled in the fenced-in lane way. The gate was opened and we proceeded slowly in front of the anxious animals.

They walked faster. As the cattle increased their pace, my heart's tempo accelerated. A young heifer shot out between Andrew and me. When she escaped, the whole mob wanted to bolt. We continued to hold them, reining our horses back and forth to cut off possible runaways. I looked back at the opened gate where cattle were starting to rush, running and pushing the beasts in front of them. It was a domino effect. The faster the cattle moved, the more edgy I became.

"To the end, to the end, block up, block up!" Andrew shouted. Hell, I didn't even know what block up meant, let alone what to do. It was another example of having no instruction and just winging it. I guessed block up had something to do with stopping the cattle. Intuition told me to go for cover, but there wasn't any. I was trapped with 700 stampeding cattle coming toward me. I raced Harlequin to the end of the fenced-in lane way and held him steady, trying to stop the bolting mob. It was hopeless. The cattle ignored Harlequin and me as they leaped through the barbed-wire fence on both sides of us. I shook, I could hardly breathe—we hadn't discussed the possibility of a stampede. Thousands of pounds of beef with trampling hooves ran wildly, often missing us by just inches. I had two thoughts: *I'm going to die* and *This is going to hurt real bad!*

Harlequin shuffled his legs in place nervously as the beasts practically crashed into him, but he held his ground. I prayed silently, *God, please let Harlequin keep his composure.* I knew if Harlequin lost it, it could mean my death warrant. I hoped the gray gelding's years of mustering experience would help us survive the ordeal. The cattle ran a mile from the yards. It took two hours to muster them back into the lane way. No one was hurt, the mob was saved, and boy was it exciting!

"You don't need drugs in the outback when you have highs like that," Jan said as she passed me in her bull buggy.

To sum up mustering, it was physically and mentally draining. We drafted cattle for the remainder of the day. Drafting out bulls and steers on horseback was a lot more challenging than just opening gates in a round pen. Every time I challenged a bull I'd cringe, thinking he was going to call my bluff and charge. We moved about 100 bulls and steers into the yards to load. The other 600 head remained in the lane way. Only 12 bulls were left to load when the loading ramp shifted.

"Lee, could you run around to the orange ute and get the tire jack?" Andrew asked. "We can probably jack this ramp back into place."

"Righto," Lee said.

I watched Lee move slowly toward the ute, being careful not to disturb the cattle in the lane way. He was 200 yards from us. I saw some dust filter into the air, but didn't think anything of it. Lee ran back to the yards. His face was wrinkled with anguish and the whites of his eyes looked stunned.

"They're gone!" Lee gasped, out of breath.

"What do you mean, they're gone?" Andrew asked.

"I mean the cattle stampeded and they're gone," he said.

"Grab your horses," Andrew shrieked.

It was 6:30 p.m.; the sun had already set. The stamped-ing cattle had torn down all of the barbed-wire fence Lee and Barney had repaired that morning after the first stampede. It was like a slow-moving film; it had to be a dream, but it wasn't—it was a nightmare. I ran to the gate and fell on my face, tangled in wire hidden in the darkness. I scrambled to my feet, untied Harlequin and climbed on. Like a streak of lightning we galloped across the flat.

Every stride intensified my immense body pain. After several days of riding, muscles I hadn't used in ages pro-tested with a vengeance. It was almost unbearable. I wanted to stop, but pride masked the soreness and commanded my quest. Darkness was prevailing; we had to save the mob. My sure-footed steed sprinted courageously through the scrub; I ducked just before a limb took off my head. I thought about my girlfriend, Becky, back in the States, who I trail-ride with. She once told me her little girl, Jessica, would ride an old mare named Meg. Becky was always amused by Jessica's confidence in the horse when the seven-year-old would say, "Mom, Meg takes care of me." I seized hope from that story and thought to myself, *Harlequin, please take care of me!*

The cunning cattle tested my ability and skill. Several bolted for the scrub, but I stayed in hot pursuit, racing un-der trees, over bushes and jumping across creek beds. The night blackened. Our only light was reflected by the moon. It was a frenzy of blinded effort. I'd heard adrenaline often does strange things to a body and was sure that's what induced my unalloyed courage that evening. I also put great faith in Harlequin, praying he would be my salvation.

A single muster with a helicopter cost an average of $3,500A, depending on hours a pilot was paid and number of horsemen and bull buggy drivers on the crew. It was vital to save the mob—losing 600 head would be a great financial loss. We got them back to the lane way, but before we had them in the yards, they bolted again.

"Oh God, no, this can't be happening," I said aloud, as if Harlequin understood my words of anguish.

My body just couldn't take the pain and Harlequin was stuffed. My heart beat so hard I thought I'd done the running instead of Harlequin. After the fourth stampede that day, we got the mob into the lane way. *Praise the Lord, we had them—* or so I thought.

"Do you reckon you all can hold the mob until Mick and I get back?" Andrew asked us three girls on horseback and Lee, who was driving the ute.

"Yes sir," I said quite sure that it wouldn't be a problem since the cattle were back in the lane way.

Mick and Andrew rode their horses back to the truck to load the last bulls so the cattle in the lane way could be herded back in the yards and gates could be chained. For ten minutes the cattle remained calm—then all hell broke out. Suddenly we saw a cloud of dust and what sounded like a row of heavy dump trucks rolling toward us. Something had spooked the mob—again. We blocked them up for a couple of minutes, dashing from side to side like the cutting horses I'd watched on TV. Harlequin amazed me, placing his body right in the path of a beast. The cattle were forceful. They bolted in all directions; we couldn't hold them. We raced farther back and tried to block up again. We screamed, trying to scare them back, to no avail. It was only me on one side. I tried to block up, but it was so dark I could only see shadows rapidly approaching straight for us. They didn't dart around Harlequin and me until they had almost run us over. I was sure an animal was going to slam into us at any moment, knocking us to the ground, where we'd be tromped on by the others. After a few seconds, the dust settled. I raced out across the flat, again, to cut off the stampede.

I got to the front and Becky Kimberley struck out wide to turn a group back. Cattle ran right by Toni. She didn't make an attempt to bring them back. I'm not sure if she had any idea what to do or was just tired of chasing cattle. I didn't care about her ignorance, someone needed to jump-start into action. My body thumped with pain, I was exhausted, but I knew we had to save the mob. Toni still did nothing—it was up to Harlequin and me. It all happened so fast, my physical well-being wasn't a concern. I was focused on one thing—stop the cattle. I was in dense scrub when ten stupid animals split in different directions.

Harlequin leaped into the path of a confused heifer; she turned back toward the mob. I shot through the scrub ducking under branches and swerving around trees and bushes, often nearly losing my balance chasing more escapees. Harlequin and I worked hard—we were partners.

"Did you just get that whole group back?" Mick asked, a little surprised.

"Yeah, mate," I answered.

We got the mob almost back to the lane-way gate and a cow bolted, Andrew and I both took off after her. After Andrew realized I wasn't going to let up, he turned back. I had to prevail. Harlequin ran alongside the cow, nearly bumping her, until she finally surrendered and ran back to join her buddies.

"Did you get her back?" Andrew asked as I trotted back to the mob.

"Yeeeess," I gasped, breathing like I'd just finished a 10-K race.

"Good on ya," he said.

Could this be the same man who thought I could only cook and clean? Andrew had given me a compliment—I was elated. We got the mob into the yards and locked them up. The final count: we had saved the mob five times that day, four of which were during the three-hour fiasco in the dark.

"That's probably the most excitement in one day that I've had in my life," I told Andrew.

"And we have months of mustering to go," he responded.

Jan, Barney and Geoff had gone back to the homestead earlier in the day. It was 9:30 p.m. and I knew Jan would be sick with worry. On the drive home, Jan met us halfway. She thought someone was hurt and couldn't be moved, which very well could have happened. Barney and Geoff greeted us at the horse shed at 10:30. They sent us in to eat and told us they'd take care of the horses. They could tell by the looks on our vacant faces and fatigue in our lethargic bodies that we had had an unprecedented day of mustering warfare. We walked into the kitchen. Jan was still frazzled, but so were we.

"That was quite an experience for you," she said.

I couldn't answer, too many emotions filled me. I thought, *Yeah, it was quite an experience, but I'm not sure I want to experience that much danger again.* It was exciting and I was very proud of myself and Harlequin, but we could have been killed.

"I'll never leave a muster again," Jan said. "I should have been there."

"Don't blame yourself Jan," I said. "Thank God we're all okay."

Exhaustion nearly numbed me; every step was torture. There were months of mustering left—how would I survive?

In the morning I helped Jan prepare lunches. She was much better and more relaxed. That was one of Jan's greatest attributes. She could explode from worry or rage, but be fine in a matter of hours.

"I heard you were quite a ringer last night," Jan said.

"Well, I did what I thought I had to do," I said, flattered by the compliment, knowing "ringer" was only used to describe top station hands.

We went back to Lightning Flat to draft more cattle to haul back to the homestead. It was almost a boring day—no stampedes, no near tragedies. A baby calf escaped from the yards, running and jumping like a circus clown. Andrew, Becky, Toni and I were in a bull buggy trying to lasso the tiny beast as we rolled by. Andrew went over a bump. We all bounced high in the air and I crashed back down on the spare tire, right on my tailbone. Pain surged up my back—I tried to ignore it. We got the calf back in the lane way, but it bolted again. We pulled ahead of it and cornered it. I jumped out and by that time, Lee had joined the capture squad. We all walked toward the clever calf. I pounced on it like a cat leaps on a mouse. I pushed it up against the barbed wire and pulled it down to the ground. The 85-pounder fell on top of me and pain pierced my tailbone. "Lee, help!" I pleaded. "I can't move."

He pulled the calf off and I rolled to my side. That's all I needed—another injury. My shoeing and riding bruises had faded and my fencing cuts had healed to scars. I squirmed to my feet and limped to the bull buggy for the long drive back to the homestead. I lit our donkie, anticipating the eventual flushes of hot water tumbling down my lifeless body. I collapsed in bed.

The next day the cattle at Lightning Flat were processed and ready for renewed freedom. We walked the cows and calves 300 yards in the scrub and held them for an hour.

"A lot of stations just throw open the gates and the cattle rush for the scrub," Andrew said. "The more cattle are worked in a calm manner year after year the easier they are to handle every year. It's all part of the education process."

Back at the homestead yards, we drafted the bulls and steers we had trucked home. I became an expert at scaling panels in seconds to escape pointy horns. The crew laughed, but I didn't care. I wanted to stay alive.

"If you're on the ground and a bull comes at you, never turn your back and run because they'll have you for sure," Andrew explained. "Run at them or step to the side." Not this cat! If a bull came at me I was going to run and climb. I had heard too many horror stories of deaths in the outback by the horns or hooves of angry bulls and cows—I was not going to be a casualty, or at least I hoped not.

The following day, Mick, Becky and I worked in the yards. We processed more than 200 head, making sure they were ear tagged, earmarked, dehorned and castrated, if necessary. I learned how to use the hydraulic dehorners and was even more disgusted by the crunching sound when I actually held the massive tool. Completely dehorning or tipping horns was crucial. Not only did horns pose a threat to humans and other cattle, but they often grew around and back into the animal's skull. The self-inflicted wounds, so to speak, were serious and eventually cost the animal its life if not found and treated. Becky and I ear tagged, earmarked and dehorned while Mick castrated. We watched him with curious eyes.

"Now, you have a go," he said, looking at me.

"Are you sure, Mick?" I asked.

"Yeah, mate, have a go," he encouraged.

I'm not sure if it was eagerness or shock intruding my consciousness when Mick thrust the sharp knife in my hand. I nervously, but confidently grabbed the calf's gonads and squeezed the testicle hard to the bottom of the scrotum. I started slicing into the animal's skin, but barely made a cut.

"You have to cut harder," Mick instructed.

I put more pressure on the knife and it pierced the sac. I made a two-inch incision, squeezing the right testicle until it popped out. I steadied my hand and started slicing again gently over the outer layer until the purple-veined testicle was in sight. I squeezed again, popping it out of its protective covering. I held the soft slimy organ in my hand and scraped back with my knife until the testicle fell free in my hand. I chucked it across the yards like the blokes did. Blood dripped from my fingers. I wiped them on my pants and proceeded to cut out testicle number two.

"Good job, mate," Mick complimented.

"Ya know, Mick, Lee is going to be very jealous that I learned how to castrate before him," I said. "He'll probably be afraid of me."

I operated on five sets of knackers. After we processed animals we walked them to different holding paddocks or areas to graze. The bulls and steers were put in the Chaney Paddock awaiting market. Cows and calves were bushed, usually back to the area they were initially mustered. Weaners were trucked to windmill ten until they reached market potential.

At windmill ten, we walked the weaners 40 minutes to a lagoon. It was centered in what looked like an outback Club Med for cattle—their own little paradise. Milky puffs of white clouds splashed across the aqua blue sky.

Cattle lazily reclined under the huge hanging branches of uniquely shaped white gum trees scattered along the bank.

Occasionally, the beasts wandered down to the billabong for a drink. It was one of the most stunning landscapes I had seen in Australia. I was swallowed up by the divine aura, freed of my station worries.

Despite my exhaustion, I felt more at home at Ashburton, more accepted, more of an asset. So long ago were the days of my station insecurities and gloominess. I once had vowed not to ever cook again at Ashburton, but preparing meals for the crew had become as much of a challenge as mustering. Jan spent 10- to 14-hour days mustering with the rest of us. It wasn't fair that it was her ultimate responsibility to feed us too. I pitched in more and more, often ordering her out of the kitchen to give her a break.

When we moved a mob of bulls to the Chaney Paddock, Andrew commanded, "Toni, you bring up the back. Geoff, you and Becky Kimberley take the sides. Becky America, I want you on the lead with me." Andrew was recognizing my cattle sense and riding skills. It was amazing what a little appreciation could do for a person's soul.

The bulls started out pretty quietly. We walked them up the fence row about a quarter of a mile, then they had to turn right and follow a path. "Okay, Becky America, you're the leader now," Andrew said as he backed off, taking the left point position. I almost panicked. I'd never been in the lead by myself, let alone for a group of bulls. I paid attention, knowing many eyes were judging me. I slowed down when the bulls slowed down and walked faster if the bulls speeded up, always maintaining equal distance between me and them. I quickly opened the river paddock gate from atop my mount and walked through. The bulls followed, no problem.

"Most stations never move a mob of bulls. They reckon it's impossible," Andrew said.

"Stockmen I know don't think bulls can even be worked with horses," Becky Kimberley added.

"Just from how we've handled them in the yards, fed and watered them, they've been educated," Andrew added. The bulls grazed happily in their new paddock and we rode back to the homestead.

I was worried about Jan. She seemed distressed. The woman worked her guts out in the office, on the phone, picking up supplies, cooking and mustering. Andrew was just kind of blase about what she did, not realizing a little respect and appreciation would have made Jan's day. Andrew wasn't strange, it was human nature to take important relationships and loved ones for granted. Many of my best friends in America liked to come to me with their troubles. They said I always had a worse story that would cheer them up and help them develop a better outlook. I tried desperately to think of a worse story to share with Jan to lift her spirits. I told her my parents had a very tough life. Years of economic hardships on the family farm plagued by family issues put tremendous strain on their marriage.

"At times the arguing was so bad when I was a kid, I cried myself to sleep and prayed they'd divorce," I said.

"How are your parents today?" Jan asked.

"Remarkable, they're inseparable most of the time. They've weathered the storms and have been married 43 years."

I suggested Jan discuss her concerns with Andrew. I told her men often had an unusual way of showing their feelings and Andrew fit the stereotype perfectly. Andrew and Lee were similar—quiet-natured, reserved personalities. I often had to drag information and conversation out of Lee, as Jan did Andrew.

Quiet or not, I knew I was blessed to have Lee. He had a subtle, but poignant ability to show me respect and appreciation with little gestures. Andrew was a rugged station man dedicated and determined to pull Ashburton out of debt and to prosper. He wasn't the most sentimental man, but he had some good qualities. For the most part he was respectful to the employees and answered our questions. His many stories of outback life intrigued us, kept us on the edge of our seats. I hoped he would share some of that positive energy and enthusiasm with Jan and his stepson, Mick. Andrew would probably never admit it, but Jan and Mick were the true backbone of the station. Ashburton had such potential, but it was going to take a concerted effort from the three of them, plus the crew's dedication. From my two decades of growing up on The Farm I knew commitment was needed by the whole family and the employees to keep the operation afloat.

I didn't want to stress about the station, I wanted to embrace life's challenges. I had learned so many new things about Lee on the trip. The extra time together allowed us to get to know each other all over again. Even the mishaps along the way and our disagreements had made us stronger, had made our relationship more secure. The next three months at Ashburton would test both our physical strength and our mental endurance; and although our marriage seemed stronger than ever, the work and other "workers" would strain our relationship.

Smoldering Embers

Thoughts I have denied, plans and desires,
Glow like embers, an unextinguished fire;

Long they have lain in the bed of my mind,
Kept putting them off, just didn't have time;

Left ignored and untended they would last not much longer,
But with the fresh breath of change their flame grows even
stronger;

No wish to jump into the flame and play the part of a fool,
Just want to admire its beauty and provide it with fuel;

Show no respect for the flame, you're gonna get burned,
But it can cast an insightful light on lessons to be learned.

Lee Chaney

Trigger and Me

It was mid-July and we were deep in Australia's winter. Cold night air blew through our humpy. Many nights the generator went off before I had my long hair completely dried. Fearing I'd get pneumonia from the chill breezes in our tin hut I got eight inches of my brunette hair chopped off to shoulder length.

My whole attitude at Ashburton had changed. The newly expressed appreciation had transformed me from a human form of existence to a daring package of self-worth. I loved the long, hard mustering days, followed by the three to five dusty, arduous days in the yards.

Another muster was scheduled at Lightning Flat, but from the opposite direction of the first one.

Everyone camped out the night before. Jan set up the camp table—it looked like we had everything except the kitchen sink. The raging campfire illuminated the area. A crippled-looking tree held a lantern, rope, tea towels, garbage bag and a roll of toilet paper on its disfigured branches. Hot embers were shoveled onto three piles, one for the stew I had made the day earlier, one for the pan with Andrew's steak (naturally he wouldn't eat any stew) and one for two billies (tins) of water. Swags were pitched in different locations; Lee and I found a discreet place by two large bushes.

Morning came early—5:30 a.m. The fire warmed our bones after a brisk night while we had a cuppa. Andrew took a piece of firm wire and bent and twisted it until he had created a makeshift toaster. He had many innovative outback surprises for us. He handed it to me and I popped a slice of bread into it and held it over the fire. It was almost like roasting marshmallows.

Andrew flew the plane while Toni, Barney, Geoff and I rode across the hills to start moving the cattle. Immediately two mickey bulls (young males) bolted in different directions. Barney took off after one and I went after the other. It was my first muster on Kate. The young horse tromped across the flat trailing the mickie bull heading straight for a forest. I was galloping about 30 mph. I pulled Kate up, fearing we'd crash into the trees, but nothing happened. Kate had no idea the pressure on the reins was signaling her to stop. I imagined Kate taking me full speed through the wooded area and leaving me hanging from a limb or plastered up against a tree trunk. I didn't need anymore scars—I had to stop her. I took a deep breath, pulled as hard as I could and turned her head to the right. She slowed to a trot.

Kate responded quickly to my "go" commands; she was just clueless about stopping. We galloped alongside the river and oddly, Kate stopped without my signal. She stood still. I looked down and she was tangled in wire. Horses and wire were no combination. I was shocked the inexperienced horse didn't bolt, buck or go berserk—she didn't move. The wire was wrapped around her hind legs. I dismounted and gently picked up Kate's hind legs, one at a time, freeing her. I patted her neck, jumped back in the saddle and back to moving cattle.

It was our third muster and Andrew put me at the right point, one of the critical positions. Andrew's confidence in me had grown. I had to deliver the goods and perform at peak level if I wanted to maintain my key role. Lee was on Harlequin and was just behind Mick at the left point, which was also an important position. Lee's riding had improved, but he was still not as confident on musters as he would have liked to have been.

The mob came in much smoother with the airplane. The helicopter got cattle back quicker when they bolted, but the helicopter was often responsible for stirring them up. After nine hours we herded the mob into the Lightning Flat yards. Lee, Barney, Andrew and I were nominated to stay at Lightning Flat again. Lee and I were in charge of dinner. He shoveled embers on two piles, one for the leftover stew and one for Andrew's steak.

It was a brilliantly peaceful night. We watched a lunar eclipse that eventually camouflaged the bright moon until the sky of the Southern Hemisphere was completely dark. I snuggled up to Lee, smiled and stared into the blackness. "This is incredible," I said. "Good night, I love you."

"I love you, too."

When I awoke, Lee was already by the fire having a cuppa with Andrew. Once daylight struck, we drafted cattle and loaded bulls, steers and weaners on the road train. Mick trucked them back to the homestead while the rest of the crew broncoed.

"Becky, do you want to ride Fatty today?" Andrew asked.

"Really?" I asked, thinking he was kidding.

"Fair dinkum," he answered.

"I'd love to," I said.

Other than Jan and Andrew, no one else rode Fatty. Broncoing was dangerous. It took a lot of stamina and concentration. I lassoed calf after calf and pulled it to the bronco panel. "Now, you're getting daring," Andrew said as I started to rope larger calves. I thought riding the bronco horse looked easy, but it was hot and tiring. After I'd caught 50 calves, Andrew relieved me. I took over Andrew's job, castrating calves. One calf's testicle became mush in my hand after I'd made my incision a little too deep—blood poured from the opening.

"Will he bleed to death?" I asked.

"He'll be fine," Mick assured me. "You're doing a good job."

One more day of broncoing under our belts. I rode back to the homestead in the Suzuki bull buggy with Lee—that was a mistake. The doors didn't open. I jumped in over the side like race car drivers do. There was no passenger seat. I piled jackets on the vehicle's rusty floor. Lee drove like a maniac, nearly losing control in sections of the road laden with five or more inches of soft dirt, or bulldust as Aussies called it. The bull buggy was open. The only thing over the top was a roll bar—like that was going to save me when I didn't even have a seat or seat belt. It was the dustiest damned trip of my life—I was a walking dirt ball. Bulldust was embedded in my face, neck, clothes, bush hat and even my bra. I couldn't even shake it out. Lee laughed, knowing full well it would be a long time before I'd ride in the bull buggy with him.

It ranked right up there with a '92 bus ride from hell in India. Thinking we had gotten the ultimate bargain ticket, Kelly and I boarded the ancient-looking passenger mobile. The sweltering day made the inside of the bus a boiling pot for the five-hour trip. Windows were down, but the only thing that blew in was dirt. We closed our eyes hoping to arrive in one piece. The bus stopped. We struggled to open our eyes, nearly pulling our eyelids apart. Dirt layered our skin. We persevered because it was all part of the adventure. The difference was that economics dictated India's poor conditions; I didn't know what Lee's excuse was other than a mentally deranged driver. I showered and got ready for bed.

"Look at your skin," Lee said. "There are still patches of dirt."

"Yeah, ya jerk, I couldn't even scrub it out, it's so deep."

• • •

The next challenge was hosting 40 students from Paraburdoo High School for an overnight station camp. Becky Kimberley and I were nominated to work with the kids because of our youth experience. She took one group to the yards and explained how cattle were processed while I led a two-hour walk around the homestead. I revealed the significance of the buildings, their ages and uses during the past century. I showed them Patrick Bresnahan's grave, a rounded tombstone surrounded by an immaculately designed, sunburnt black wrought-iron fence. I told the students about his tie to Ashburton and the events surrounding his untimely 1889 death.

My station research provided a wealth of information to the students. In the afternoon, Becky took her group to teach them about shoeing and to give horse rides. I took a group down to the river to swim, but only seven kids braved the cold water. Jan prepared five roasts. The kids had never eaten fresh homegrown beef. They loved it and lined up for seconds. The group, including five teachers and volunteers, camped in tents on the front lawn.

In the morning I took a group on a walk to the two-mile bore. We found Baby, the camel. Something spooked her and she nearly trampled one of the teen-agers. That would have just been my luck. I envisioned the newspaper headlines, "Camel crushes kid at Ashburton." Thank goodness she wasn't hurt, just frightened. The students departed after lunch.

Station duties overwhelmed Jan and she appealed for Andrew's support. They worked hard and made a good team at the station, but their union was focused on business.

"No other woman would put up with Andrew, anyway," I told Jan, trying to lift her spirits. "My mom would have killed Andrew a long time ago." It wasn't that my mom was a hard ass, she just expected people to carry their own weight. The next morning Jan confided in us, tears running down her face. She was working herself into a depression, but I knew she'd survive—she was a fighter. "It's going to be all right," I said as I hugged her. "We love you."

"I don't know what I'd do if you and Lee weren't here," she said.

Jan felt comfortable sharing personal information and emotions with us, probably because we were the only other married couple. I told her life was funny—when we feel bad, we sometimes try hard to think of more bad things in order to feel as miserable as possible. Jan was physically and emotionally burned out. Andrew expected her to be super woman, taking care of the business as well as household and mustering duties. She asked Becky, Barney and Toni to start having all their evening meals up at the Quarters. She needed a break.

"Lee and I can eat at the Quarters, too," I said.

"No, Becky, I want you and Lee here with the family," she said.

The Quarters crowd was fine with the request except for Toni. She was immature and inconsiderate. "How will I know what time to be at work if we don't come down for dinner?" she asked. "How will I know what we're doing?"

I didn't respond. I wanted to slug her and say, "You selfish bitch, Jan really needs our support right now and all you can do is think of yourself, as usual." I bit my tongue instead.

"This is really going to mess up my eating schedule," Toni added.

"Why is that?" I asked not being able to contain my anger.

"Tea was ready every night and I was eating really healthy, now I won't eat properly."

"Well, that's no one's fault but your own," I said. "There's a whole freezer of meat and a walk-in refrigerator full of food."

She didn't say a word. I was shocked a 26-year-old woman was pouting about cooking for herself. I knew Toni was spoiled, but I never realized how dependent she was on others.

Jan's changes went further than eating venues. She decided to ride again on musters, sure it would boost her spirits. Lee was promoted to the bull buggy. High winds and a horse breakout canceled our next muster. Andrew never flew if it was too windy and the great horse escape was due, no doubt, to Fatty and his gate-unlatching talents.

I helped Jan with household chores. We cleaned the walk-in refrigerator. It was revolting. Dried blood was splattered across the walls and on the floor where fresh "killer" had hung for days. We filled bags with moldy spoiled food. Jan took a load of rubbish to the tip. She returned with a grimace of disbelief. I asked what was funny.

"It's difficult to find good staff," she said. "Barney has been putting all the rubbish beside the hole at the tip instead of in it."

"You're kidding me, right?"

"No, I couldn't believe it."

Every time I thought Barney was maturing and taking on more responsibility, he'd do something stupid. He was a good worker, but needed constant supervision.

A butcher arrived to cut up two more killers to restock the freezer. He unscrewed the mincer (grinder) to clean it and found it full of maggots. The last butcher hadn't cleaned it.

"Don't worry, it's just like a little more protein chopped up with the beef," said Mick, who always had something funny or shocking to say that usually caught us off guard.

The wind had surrendered and we were off to muster. My new mustering horse was Trigger, the tallest horse at the station at 16.2 hands. It was Lee's debut in the bull buggy, or the "Suzi" as he called it. Lee had much more control in the buggy and didn't miss riding. Toni gave me a boost up on Trigger. I thought, *If I fall, it's a long way down and if I get off to pee, how will I mount again?* It was always bad to think the worst because the worst happened.

"I need two horsemen to ride over the hill and push the cattle out of the forest," Andrew radioed from the plane.

Toni and I trotted over two hills and spotted cattle in a very dense forest. We pushed our way through, breaking limbs and toppling over logs and bushes. Cobwebs covered my hat. Trigger struggled through the overgrown foliage, hesitant of his footing. Without warning, he went berserk, leaving me on the ground in his wake. It happened so fast I didn't know if he had gotten tangled in logs or sensed a snake. I wasn't mad at Trigger. I knew I had asked a lot of the big horse on his first day of mustering. I tried to get to my feet, but was thrown back by a severe twinge pinching my tailbone. I hoped my tailbone wasn't broken. Trigger stood nearby quivering. I struggled to my feet and limped slowly toward him, talking to him, reassuring him. If he took off and left me, I'd be lost. No one knew exactly where I was and my radio was dead.

I pictured Trigger galloping across the flat without me on his back and everyone wondering if I was dead or alive. I patted his neck, then found a large fallen tree to aid my re-mount. Trigger stood still, but continued to shake. He was just too big to work in such a tight area. I took two painkill-ers from my fanny pack. I hoped they'd kick in fast. We walked slowly through the jungle of trees and bushes and caught up to the cattle.

A mickie bull broke away from the mob and Jan went for him on Harlequin. Lee immediately backed her up in his Suzi. He bumped the beast a couple of times trying to "educate it." Finally, the mickey turned back to the mob. "Good job," I radioed to Lee. He seemed to really get the hang of bull buggy work.

A group of beasts bolted between Toni and me. We both took off after them, creating a "lane way" situation which gave the animals nowhere to turn.

"Are one of you going to turn them in?" Mick yelled over his radio.

"These beasts aren't going to beat me," I said under my breath, gritting my teeth.

Toni turned back. I raced Trigger over and around bushes and major clumps of buffel grass. According to Tricky, buffel grass was native to India and when camels and their drivers were sent to help with the transportation needs in Australia's outback country, the cameleers brought their own saddles— stuffed with buffel grass. After decades of seeds sieving out of the saddles near watering holes, buffel grass has exploded all over the country. It's hardy, drought resistant and is a main food staple for livestock.

But for me, the massive patches of Indian vegetation only slowed my direct path to the stupid beast I was chasing. Trigger galloped alongside the animal's shoulder. The faster it ran, the faster we ran and the harder I pushed Trigger into the heifer's shoulder. She finally knew she was beaten and turned into the mob. I was out of breath and trembled like Trigger had trembled in the woods. It was the first time I had shouldered a beast and forced it back into the mob at a flat-out gallop.

"Good job," Andrew said as I rode past.

"Good on ya, y'all," Mick praised. Mick not only called me his American Mum, but called me "y'all," ribbing me about my southern Yankee accent. It was a name I earned at the University of Wisconsin-Madison from my Alpha Gamma Rho fraternity brothers.

Andrew was on the lead horse. Mick and I were at the point positions. Toni, Jan, Tricky and Lee backed us up and Becky and Barney brought up the rear. We moved the mob a little farther and a few high-strung beefers broke out of the front. Andrew went after two and Trigger and I took off after a mickie bull. We stopped the bull, but in the process the bloody thing ended up under Trigger's tall gangly legs. Trigger bolted to the side, almost losing me again. The mickey took off and I chased it toward the scrub. I heard a bull buggy closing in. As the beast ran into the heavy scrub Lee took over the pursuit, plowing through the foliage like a bulldozer.

I followed them through the scrub and back to the road. The mickey stopped and stared us down. I was four feet from Lee, helping to block the animal's escape route. In a second the bastard charged Trigger and me, ramming our side as we retreated. The impact didn't drop Trigger, but it jarred us and gave me a scare. The bull threatened my safety and that pissed Lee off. He zoomed his Suzi into the bull and dropped him. It was as if Lee said, "Hey bull, don't mess with my woman." I was quite flattered by Lee's immediate protective response.

"Andrew, this bull just charged Becky," Lee radioed.

"Becky, come back to the mob," Andrew said. "I'll send Tricky and his bull buggy over."

Andrew told us that when animals were all worked up, horses were of little use. Lee and Tricky's combined "Speed Racer" antics got the bull back to the mob. We yarded cattle up at sunset. I rode back with Jan to help prepare tea.

"How was your first day in the bull buggy?" I asked Lee later that evening.

"I like it and feel more useful," he said. "Now, Andrew isn't afraid to send me after a beast."

Lee and I were both finding our niche at the station. I felt better than I'd ever felt. I'd enjoyed making fence, but felt more valuable mustering.

Rise and shine—our alarm rang at 4:30 a.m. Jan wanted me to stay home and nurse my injured tailbone, but I insisted on mustering. I popped some pain pills and hobbled down to the horse shed. Trigger was sore so I rode Murray, a bay gelding. Becky and Mick went into the scrub first to push out cattle.

I asked Toni to help me look for my lost radio, but she couldn't be bothered. I really couldn't figure her out. I was always nice to her, complimented her and taught her things. I was coming to the conclusion that she was a user and only did something if it benefited herself. It was sad, really, as there were many times I enjoyed her company. But I couldn't worry about Toni's irresponsible character; I had cattle to muster. Mick chased a bull through the scrub and into a riverbed. He went up the steep bank and his horse got trapped in a log and fell back on top of him. Lee jumped out of his buggy to help, calling, "Are you all right?"

"Yeah, mate, but she's really heavy," Mick said with a grunt as his horse lay on top of him.

He was lucky he was not seriously injured. Station workers were hurt and killed every year during mustering season—horses crushed riders, buggies flipped on drivers, pilots pivoted to their death and bulls maimed their captors. Mick was a key player in the mustering crew and the entire operation. Ashburton wouldn't survive without him. Lee and I admired Mick's determination and assertiveness.

A cow bolted from the mob, giving Lee an excuse to drive the Suzi through the scrub like he was competing in a "Hell Drivers" competition at a county fair. He could have put them all to shame. Lee loved his new challenge and was pleased with his new mustering talents. The Suzi's front fender poked out of the scrub, then Lee appeared. Blood dripped from his forehead.

"What happened?" I asked.

"I ducked, but a branch whacked me anyway," he said.

"You're driving too reckless," I scolded. "You're going to get hurt or killed."

He rolled his eyes. I might as well have talked to the moon. Lee was on a mission, a mission to stop any bolting beast, no matter what the outcome. I applauded his devoted work ethic, but his bull buggy conduct was extreme.

Once we were near the cattle yards at Parry's, I walked up the opposite side of the lane way and got off my horse. The painkillers had worn off and my aching tailbone needed relief. The others moved the cattle up the other side and into the lane way. I walked my horse slowly, thinking about Parry, the cameleer from decades earlier who had frequented the original hand-dug watering hole to water the thirsty beasts of burden in his camel train. Years later station owners turned the watering hole into a major bore to support hundreds of livestock and continued to call it Parry's. Although camel trains are a thing of the past, nearly one million wild camels still roam the continent and are descendants of those first animals that helped open up the Australian frontier. My historical daydreaming ended when Andrew and Mick noticed a mob of cattle grazing near the yards.

"Becky America, just come up slowly on that group in front of you," Andrew radioed.

I painfully got back in the saddle and started moving the small mob. A horned bull charged me like a freight train heading down the track. I spurred Murray; he leaped in retreat. My hat flew back and the chinstrap jerked my head, but we escaped the bull's horns. I walked back toward the mob. The bull charged me again. My heart beat faster, my heavy breaths inflating my shirt. I walked up again and another bull charged me—I ran.

"I'll come over and sort him out," Andrew radioed. He rode over and when the bull charged, Andrew cracked his whip. The bull withdrew his threat, but charged him again.

Andrew cracked his whip again and the bull backed off. Then the son of a bitch charged me again. I turned and bolted. "Don't run!" Andrew yelled, reprimanding me like a child.

I wanted to say, "Listen here you jerk, I don't have a whip and I'd rather not go home with horn holes in my leg or Murray's side."

Andrew told us later we shouldn't run from bulls, that we should always stand up to them. He assured us they rarely called our bluffs. My only thought, *In his dreams was I going to stand up against a horned bull. I did plan to see my family again.* Sometimes retreat is the wiser part of valor!

I was a bit miffed because once again Andrew had not given us any instruction on how to deal with bulls and then I got yelled at. I was disappointed with myself and wished I was more daring.

"I thought you were very brave," Becky Kimberley said.

"Thanks, Bec. I appreciate that."

Jan drove me home so I could rest my hurting tailbone. We laughed a lot on the way home, a welcome tonic.

"My back really hurts from riding Duck," Jan said. "She has such an unusual gate. I want 'quality' between my legs. I'm never riding Duck again. I have no idea how poor Lee rode that horse."

The next day Jan, Mick and I left for town at 8 a.m. I quizzed Mick for his driver's test for a class B tractor-trailer license. Once in town I ran into Gill Herbert of Hamersley Station, the station where we were originally supposed to work, but couldn't without a work visa.

"Hi, Gill, how ya goin'?" I asked.

"Hello, Becky, what are you and Lee still doing up here?" she queried.

"We've been at Ashburton Downs for more than four months. We really like it."

"Well, my dear, if you two can hang on at Ashburton, you're doin' really good."

I guess everyone in the Pilbara knew Ashburton was a developing station and "rough-as-guts." Shoot, I took it as a compliment and it only reaffirmed the Glenns' commitment to making Ashburton the most prosperous station in the region. Rough or not, we had come to know it as home.

After running errands in Tom Price we drove to Paraburdoo. I had become a regular in the post office and Emily and Rose let me use the back room to check e-mails. I still stopped at the Quills when I could, but the post office was more convenient. I e-mailed a query letter and eight photos to *Outback* magazine, the flash magazine in Australia with more than a 120,000 readership. I thought since we still broncoed at Ashburton it would make an interesting story. My philosophy was, "It never hurts to ask."

The following day Becky, Toni, Andrew and I worked in the yards. We processed steers and bulls. The bulls were big and irritated by their captivity. We used Stockstill, an electrical charge that immobilized them for a minute, so we could ear tag, earmark and dehorn them without getting hurt. Two metal ends clamped onto the animal's body, one on the bum and the other to the cheek or neck. The electrical current was turned on until the bull stopped fighting. The procedure caused a limited amount of discomfort to the animal, but nothing compared to the damage the bull could have inflicted on us.

We processed more than 200 head. I had to show the girls how to use nose leads before the instrument popped our eyes out. I used nose leads growing up when I prepared my dairy animals for exhibitions. Becky and Toni had never seen the tool, let alone used it. I tried to be diplomatic in my instruction, only offering my suggestions if they wanted them. I knew if I was too bossy, I'd upset the apple cart.

"This is how we did it on my parents' farm and it should work here and be safer than what you're doing if you want to try it," I said.

"Sure," Becky Kimberley said.

"Clamp the nose leads in each nostril and squeeze," I explained. "Don't ever let up the slack on the rope or the leads will come back and whack you in the face."

Lesson time was over and it was time for smoko. We walked to the main house.

"Guess who I talked to this morning?" Jan asked.

"Who?" I said.

"Paul Myers from *Outback* magazine," she said. "He wants a short story and lots of pictures for a photo essay about broncoing. He is even sending you over film."

I was so excited I could have jumped out of my skin. If I got something published in *Outback* magazine, it would be my greatest accomplishment as a professional journalist.

Andrew told us he was going to let the air out of the Road Toad's tires because he didn't want us to leave in three months. I guess that was a pretty sure sign of his admiration for us. Andrew's change of heart was all quite ironic.

"When I told Andrew I had hired an American couple to work at Ashburton, he had one response," Jan said. "'Bloody tourists, they'll be here a few days and nick off.'" We were entering our fifth month at Ashburton and we hadn't nicked off yet.

I'm Not Afraid of Bulls, Right?

I t was August already and we'd been mustering for a
month. The days were physically and psychologically taxing. Even though there seemed to be personal drama every day, nothing took away from the excitement and danger
of mustering. Each time I rode out of camp it was as if God
had given me a new lease on life. I left my worries by the
campfire as I trotted through the scrub. I melded into my
horse's gait, hypnotized by the magical surroundings. Mustering locations were diverse with unique topography. Rivers
snaked through hills and valleys, mountain peaks and cliffs
shadowed dingo dwellings and tropical rain forest teemed
with exotic birds and other creatures.

Tiny almond-colored wrens with a distinct orange ring
around their necks played in puddles, while rainbow lori-
keets seemed to be in a breeding frenzy. I almost forgot about
mustering as I was dumbstruck by a lorikeet's blue head,
orange breast and green body. Golden orb spiders wove their
intricate handiwork from branch to branch and tree to tree;
the deep yellow-colored threads often glistened in the sunlight.

Despite my turbulent beginning, I came to love Ashburton
as much as Lee did. I loved mustering and cattle work. I
loved our garden—my own private sanctuary. It made our
humpy feel like home. Each time I walked over the hill our
garden's vibrant floral reds, pinks, purples, whites and yel-

lows made me smile. I felt blessed by our experiences and surroundings.

We had a 4:45 a.m. start. I made 12 sandwiches for the crew and got the esky ready. We loaded the horses and left at 5:30 a.m. It was another chilly morning, 10 degrees Celsius (50 degrees Fahrenheit). We were mustering in heavy scrub and it was easy to get disoriented and lost.

"Andrew, could you fly over and tell me where I am and where to go?" a confused Lee asked from his bull buggy.

"Righto," Andrew said. "You're not far from a huge roan bullock. Go to your left and you'll nearly run into him, about 100 yards. If you push him down the creek bed, you'll run into the rest of the mob. Lee, I think that's the bullock that gets away every year. He's about a ton—watch him."

Lee found the bullock and started moving him down the creek. His buggy got stuck. When he finally got unstuck and back to the mob, the buggy was full of branches and debris and he'd lost the bullock.

"Andrew sends Lee into places he never would have sent me," Jan said.

Lee had the strength to get out of difficult situations and the mechanical savvy to fix just about anything. The crew worked pretty well together the first four weeks of mustering. Becky Kimberley gained a lot of confidence. Barney got so much negative feedback for his station goof-ups that I often gave him positive reinforcement on musters when he earned it. He was a good kid, but he lacked initiative and a strong work ethic, as did Toni, but Toni was an adult and had no excuse. Her lackadaisical attitude often put other crew members in danger. One day she'd work hard and the next day she didn't care. Mustering depended on a 100-percent effort by everyone. When someone didn't try or got lazy, it risked injuries to the crew and the horses and it risked losing cattle. We all stuffed-up occasionally, even Mick and Andrew, but those stuff-ups were not from lack of trying.

We continued to move the mob minus the lost roan bullock. I was on the left point, Andrew was in the lead and Mick was on the right point. A red-and-white bull with threatening horns challenged me several times. I ran at him and he turned back to the mob. My bluffs worked. Andrew bolted after a beast. The lead position was vacant. No one had ever told us what to do in that situation so I used common sense. The cattle needed a target to follow so I immediately assumed the lead position. The cattle continued to walk steadily. Kate did a super job and understood the stop command much better. Andrew told me I had done exactly the right thing by taking over the lead. Three hundred head were safely walked into Parry's yards.

We split the crew to work the homestead yards and Parry's yards. Mick, Barney, Jan and I drafted animals at the homestead and the others drafted at Parry's.

"Mick!" I screamed as a bull charged him from behind. He scaled the fence just in time. We hadn't had a serious bull incident yet, and I hoped it stayed that way. It was a miracle no one had been seriously hurt yet mustering or working in the yards. We had completed five musters and gathered more than 2,000 head. All cattle were processed and either released to the bush again or herded to the Chaney Paddock to await their market destiny.

Jan received an order for 150 bulls for Indonesia. We had to muster them to the homestead yards to get the proper inoculations for shipment. It was the first time for us to muster the bulls back in and I had no idea what to expect, except to encounter the same mean bulls that had charged us in previous musters. While the rest of the crew stayed at a midway point, Mick and I rode to the end of the paddock to herd the bulls toward the homestead. I was nervous. It was no secret—bulls worried me. There were too many bull tragedies to feel any differently.

"I'm not afraid of bulls, I'm not afraid of bulls, I'm not afraid of bulls," I repeated to myself aloud as we entered the far-end gate. My philosophy was, "It never hurts to psyche yourself out a little."

"The bulls should be much better since they've had time to be educated," Mick reassured me.

Most of them still had their horns, but they were tipped to regulation length for shipping. The sharp points were gone, but the six- to seven-inch stubs were still intimidating. Andrew started to scare bulls out of hiding places with his low-flying daredevil stunts. Mick and I gathered the growing mob and started to move them.

"Okay, Becky, you just keep taking them down the fence line," Mick said.

"Where are you going, Mick?" I asked, feeling unprotected.

"I'm going to the other side to move bulls. Don't worry, you'll be fine," he said, still trying to reassure me.

"Okay, Mick, I can do it."

But I really thought, *Oh yeah, right, 33 bulls and I'm supposed to move them by myself?* I was overwhelmed at first, but then I made the conscious decision that those testoster-one-packed beasts were not going to embarrass me. I was giving Kate a rest and hoped Murray didn't let me down. I galloped him around to the front, turning the lead bulls back in toward the fence. They were determined to return to their refuge in the scrub. I galloped back and forth, turning the lead into the fence and pushing up the rear. It was tough, but I could be as stubborn as those bulls—they weren't going to escape on my watch. An hour passed before reinforcement arrived.

"How have you kept them together and moving?" Becky Kimberley asked. I explained my technique, adding "I just used my cattle sense, but it sure hasn't been easy."

All the bulls behaved and not one threatened me, but my heart raced all day. We mustered in 180 bulls, steers and bullocks and pushed them across the river to the homestead. Max, Graham and Peter arrived from Wesfarmers, the main bull-buying conglomerate. Max had been buying cattle for world export since 1966. He sold from 80,000 to 100,000 head annually. Max stood by the round pen and as each bull entered the closed-in area, its fate was determined.

"Ship!" Max yelled. "Bush! Put that one in the 'maybe' yard."

He had specific criteria and if a bull didn't meet the requirements it was sent back to the bush for more conditioning. Andrew drafted the steers and bullocks for Harvey Beef, the slaughter house near Perth.

Everyone admired the way Lee worked cattle in the yards. He was calm and the cattle responded to his ease. My jumpy nature probably made the cattle more temperamental. Although Lee was always composed, he did have a scare or at least it gave me a fright. A bull charged him and butted him, lifting him off the ground up against the panels. He brushed the beast away like it was a bug.

"I really like the way Lee works the bulls, he's so calm and it shows in the reaction of the bulls," Becky Kimberley said. "They stay calmer, too."

"I know, doesn't it make you sick?" I said sarcastically.

"I want to be like him when I grow up," Becky added with a giggle.

We needed a few more bulls to make the shipment and had to muster the rain-forest area the following day. On every muster two or three horsemen were sent out early with Mick to start moving the cattle spotted by Andrew or a hired pilot. The rain forest was thick with impenetrable foliage in many places. Often I found myself in areas I'd have to back my horse out of because I was trapped. In partial clearings I followed Mick as he swiftly trotted through the tropical oasis. It was a challenge just keeping up with him as we flew through bush and trees and up and down riverbanks. I felt like I was in a sulky race and the trotting would soon burst my insides.

Clouds cloaked the sky, completely shutting out the sun, but I still wore my sunglasses to protect my eyes from branches as we crashed through the forest. Thousands of sticky golden orb spiderwebs blanketed my bush hat. I often caught a glimpse of something moving on my hat, only to focus in on a spider that had taken up residency on my hat's rim. I got so used to them crawling on my hat, jacket and horse that they stopped frightening me. I just nonchalantly brushed them off. The cobwebs on my Akubra earned me the nickname Spider Woman.

I wish I could blame the webs for blinding me when I got completely lost, but I really don't know how I got so disoriented. I looked at the sun's position, pretending I was some directional genius and could determine the way to Parry's yards. I came to a dried riverbed and thought my best bet was to follow it. I found two cows, two calves and a cleanskin. As I moved toward the cattle yards—what I hoped was the right way—I picked up 11 more animals. I walked them slowly and quietly. *No one will believe this,* I thought. *I found my own little mob and was moving it solo through the forest.* Barney eventually found me and helped move them into the yards. I was shocked I had made my way back.

While most of the crew processed cattle the next few days, Jan, Mick and I left for Meat Profit Days, a two-day beef conference in Carnarvon on the West Coast. We stopped at the Auski Roadhouse for dinner and Mick drove a few more hours. It was hazardous on the highway at night with 'roos and cattle meandering on the road. We pulled over to sleep in a field at 10:30 p.m. We threw our swags on the hard, stony ground and said good night. I crawled into my swag only to discover that I had forgotten my sleeping bag. The swag had two light blankets in it, but it was really cold that night. I curled up and pulled my swag over my head. I got warm enough to fall asleep, but woke up shaking in the middle of the night. I was too cold to sleep and too embarrassed to wake Jan.

I was tired when we arrived in Carnarvon, but a shower revived me. The conference was interesting and I met a lot of people. I had attended hundreds of conferences in the States and a few overseas. I was truly in my element. Lee didn't call me a social butterfly for nothing. I knew how to work a crowd—it was a talent I nurtured as a journalist. I was glad Jan had encouraged me to go. It was fun and I learned more about Australia's beef industry. We were inspired and amused by the keynote speaker, who was an herb farmer from New South Wales. In her presentation she mentioned the problem with

LOMBARDs in the world, describing someone with 'Lots of Money, But a Real Dickhead.' The crowd roared with laughter.

The conference was a good break, but we were happy to return to Ashburton for mustering. It was windy and cool. Someone had told me June and July were the coldest months in Western Australia, but by my accounts, August had them beat.

I told Andrew and Jan there was confusion on every muster because we never had an overview plan. We were always just dropped in a location and trotted off. In the previous muster, it was total mayhem with cattle sprinting in all directions. There was a major communication failure, but even our overview plan didn't work on the next muster. Another horseman was needed and Lee was nominated to ride Murray. He was stationed at the end along with Tricky in his buggy.

"Lee and Tricky, here they come," Andrew radioed. "You've got to stop them." After they'd successfully stopped the mob, he added, "Perfect, that's good, now hold them."

The radios were silent. Then I heard an "Oh crikey!" I couldn't distinguish the voice, but it didn't sound good. Evidently, Tricky had moved his buggy, scared the mob and they bolted.

"You would have been proud of me, I was going flat-out on Murray," Lee said excitedly later. "I got ahead of the mob and cut them off."

We pushed the mob into the yards at bore 29 just as the sun disappeared. Days later Lee confessed another episode he hadn't shared with anyone. "I was riding Murray flat-out and nearing the scrub and forest area when all of the sudden Murray stopped and dropped his head."

"What happened?" I asked.

"I went flying over his head," he said. "I never lost the reins. I got up, looked Murray in the eye and said, 'All right Murray, you son of a bitch, now that we have that out of the way, let's get some work done.'"

The following day we mustered the bull paddock. Lee and Mick missed the muster because they took the road train to bore 29. They loaded cattle to truck back to the homestead yards to be processed. Lee told me while loading, the dust was blinding, like a continuous willy-willy stirring up the dirt.

"In all of the dust a bull ran right toward me and I thought, 'This is really going to hurt,'" he said. "The bull skidded and stopped right at my belly and went the other way."

"How big was he?" I asked.

"A full-sized bull with horns," he said.

I could have done without hearing that story. There was no other way to load the cattle other than walking toward the cattle on foot, pushing them to the loading ramp. I thought Lee took unnecessary risks, but that day I almost got myself killed.

Once the bull paddock was mustered, Toni, Becky, Andrew and I drafted 133 animals. We put 18 bulls in the holding pen. One by one we moved them up the race into the crush. A huge white bull hesitantly walked into the crush. It was the one from the previous muster that bolted from the mob five times and charged us repeatedly. He was nasty and aggressive. While he was in the crush, we clipped two holes in his left ear, pierced his right with a bright yellow tag and diminished his prized horns to four-inch stubs. He snorted and pawed the ground. Blood trickled out of the holes in his horns like a tranquil fountain and stained his cottony white hair. He dropped to his knees, flopped his head on the ground and one hoof inched out of the front of the crush.

I lifted up the bar on the crush, releasing the pressure around the animal's neck to free him, but he didn't move. His back end dropped to the ground, he lay motionless in the crush. Little did I know it was a ploy. We yelled, jabbed his sides—he wouldn't move. He seemed to be stuck, wedged in the crush somehow.

"Becky, will you hold the crush open, please?" I asked.

"I'll be the decoy and coax him out," I said, kidding the crew because I was sure he was stuck.

I walked three feet in front of the opened crush. The enraged beast burst from the crush and went for me. I hurdled the fence in one mighty leap and went ass over head to the other side. Becky Kimberley, Toni and Andrew couldn't stop laughing.

A. Was I mental? B. Did I lack common sense? C. Was I just stupid? Yes! All of the above! I had no right to talk about Lee's careless acts, as I had nearly gotten myself maimed. I tried to regain my composure around the bulls, but I was a nervous wreck. The bulls went from the crush to an open pen, where they charged us from behind. Everyone was climbing fences. One time I climbed the fence only to be charged by a bull on the other side, butting the bottom of my boot. They came at me from all directions. It was one of the times I asked myself, *What the hell am I doing here?*

We had mustered and prepared 150 bulls for shipment. The road train was loaded and Andrew hauled them to Port Hedland to join 14,000 other cattle bound for Indonesia. Andrew left for his 450-mile trek at dawn and Jan and I left to run errands in Tom Price. I met three little Aboriginal girls in the library. They wore dirty clothes and had matted hair and snot-filled noses, but were cute and polite. They had an innocence that drew me to their happy smiles. I later sent Beanna, Ronetta and Shaunola the photo I'd taken of them. I wondered how their lives would go.

I joined Jan in the grocery store and we filled three carts, packed the eskies, and drove home.

"We've had incredible times here," Jan said on the drive home. "It's been very, very difficult."

"It's not easy living in the outback, is it?" I replied.

"No it's not, but we've managed so far," she said. "There's been a lot of blood, sweat and tears."

It was obvious Jan's bush life had been marked with many good times as well as bad. Lee and I had crossed the paths of so many people on our trip, but it seemed our fate was to end up at Ashburton. It taught us a lot about ourselves, about tolerance of others, as well as each other.

Tomorrow

Does tomorrow exist or simply today?
Mischievous recluse remains a sunrise away;

Search for the rascal by morning's first light,
Master of disguise changed masks in the night;

Tomorrow becomes today, effortless perpetuation,
Attempting to seize tomorrow, no excuse for procrastination;

Squeeze each precious drop from the finite time we're given,
Careful to observe the balance held between planning and living;

Tomorrow knows no magical answers, absent of a mind,
Solutions are found with action and thought... Wait for tomor-
row, waste valuable time.

Lee Chaney

26

Where is Lee's Hobble Belt?

A bull was chasing me, he almost had me. I was frantic, afraid I was going to meet my maker. I jerked, not from the bull, but from my horrible nightmare. Bulls weren't only charging me on musters and in the yards, they also charged their way into my dreams.

I rode Kate to muster the steer paddock. We veered right, then made a sharp left at high speed. I went to zig, but Kate decided to zag. I stayed in the saddle, but twisted my hip. Just one more ailment for me to nurse. Five months at Ashburton had conditioned me to pain and suffering. We gathered 200 animals in the steer paddock and held them steady. They seemed pretty "educated" so I radioed to let everyone know I was taking a bush break. I needed someone to cover my position. Kate and I jogged to the scrub to find a porta potty—I mean a large enough bush to shield my big bare behind from the world.

First order of business, I extracted my tampon. On musters far from the homestead I buried my tampons or disposed of them beneath a bush; they were biodegradable, after all. But the steer paddock was too close to the homestead and I feared the dogs would drag the remains of the feminine-hygiene product home. I wrapped it in the extra toilet paper I always carried for emergencies and hid the tightly wrapped torpedo in my fanny pack. I re-armed myself and went back to the mob of cattle.

A calf had been abandoned by its mental mother. Orphaned calves were not a priority at the station since there were more than 10,000 other animals to worry about, but she was different. She was healthy and vigorous. Lee put her in Jan's bull buggy and back at the station he got the calf bottle his mother had sent from the States and fed the rescued baby. Jan knew my childhood job on The Farm was raising calves, so I became the calf's adopted mother.

She was a gorgeous Hereford calf. Her soft red-and-white hair shimmered in the sunlight. Round red spots circled each eye and crowned the top of her nose. There was no calf milk replacer powder, so Jan and I concocted a mixture of sweetened condensed milk diluted in warm water. I named her Spanky because she reminded me of the kids and dog on *The Little Rascals*. She immediately became my pride and joy—my special project. We put Spanky in the old wire chook house, as they called chicken coops Down Under. She had shelter, shade, fresh air and a dry, warm place to sleep.

One night was short. No bulls chased me, but horses disturbed me by their clanking outside. I got up to protect my flower bed. They had already eaten some of my precious blooms days earlier and I refused to allow them to destroy anymore. As I investigated I found Roy and Livingston, Lee's faithful cattle dogs, keeping watch outside our humpy. They spent every night inside or outside our humpy. I had to pee, but was afraid to walk to the dunny in the dark. I dropped my pants by the humpy. Something moist lapped my cheek and I don't mean the one on my face. I jumped, spraying pee down my leg, afraid it was a snake. That damned Roy had sneaked up behind me and licked my bum. He followed me back into the nest and lay on the floor by Lee's head. They were his devoted mates. I would have declined the company of mutts in my bedroom, especially ones snoring right beside me, but I knew they'd protect us from snakes, or at least I hoped.

Jan's eldest cattle dog, Joy, tried to protect the homestead, but could only gum trespassers to death. The old dog barely had any teeth left and walked around with a growing tumor under her belly. She was a sweet dog and Jan's constant companion. When Jan worked in her office, Joy lay by her feet and when Jan visited the yards, Joy was right on her heels. The tumor grew until the softball-sized growth burst and stinking puss oozed out of it daily.

"Lee, could you please soak a hole?" Jan asked. "I think we'll have to put Joy down."

The hole soaked for days, but Jan never had the heart to give the killing request. Then a vet from Wesfarmers came out to check cattle and Jan asked him to look at Joy.

"That tumor can be removed and she'll have five more good years," he told her. That's all Jan needed to hear. She called and scheduled Joy's surgery later in the week. Like people, Jan would do anything for Joy.

After my morning cuppa, I prepared Spanky's breakfast. She aggressively sucked the bottle's nipple, a good sign in a newborn calf. I'd raised hundreds of calves for Mom and Dad. I knew symptoms and signs of sickness. I'd saved many calves over the years through early detection of problems, though several others I lost. My brother, Dennie, was a genius at giving calves a second chance at life. Some calves the vets gave up on, Dennie would give an I.V. followed by a series of special shots. In days the sick calf would thrive. I didn't have my brother's talent, but knew I was a good calf raiser.

Barney and Becky's mother, Robin, visited for a couple of weeks along with her younger son, Josh. Robin was a short woman and wore her hair in pigtails. She photographed outback scenes and sold 1,000 photograph cards annually. "I don't get rich, but I enjoy it," Robin said. "I make enough to cover my supplies." Robin was excited to hear I might get something published in *Outback*.

The next few days were filled with catching up with homestead chores. I worked in my journal and on feature stories. Lee helped Tricky repair a windmill. Tricky hated heights so Lee climbed to the top of the windmill, gripping tight as bouts of wind shook the structure.

"Too bad you weren't there," Lee said. "It would have made a good photo."

Lee got roped into running errands to town with me. He was not thrilled. Not that he didn't want to spend time with me, but because he'd rather work, at least that's what I told myself. Lee even shaved for the outing.

We packed a few snacks and drinks for the drive. "I can't help you today, Tricky," Lee said. "I have to drive Miss Daisy to town."

We stopped at the Wakuthuni Aboriginal Community near Tom Price and visited Lola Young. She was as chatty as the day I had met her a month earlier. She told us about her days growing up at Ashburton and working from 3 a.m. to 8 p.m. "We wasn't paid, ya knows," she said. "We's run away sometimes to fish and swim, but they's find us and give us a hidin'. Da white woman was mean."

She reminisced about the life, times and hardships five decades earlier. Lola was in her 60s and remembered well her childhood days. "We's have to go find da goats and milk 'em. We was very scared of da boogie man."

Lola wrote a book about the medicinal uses of plants, flowers and bark that her Aboriginal ancestors used and which are still used today. The book serves as an educational resource for Aboriginal children. She shares stories and cultural history with youth to regenerate their indigenous spirit.

"Where to now, Miss Daisy?" Lee teased.

"You know you're real funny, ha, ha," I said. "You could at least pretend you're having fun with me."

"You know I'm just kidding," he said. "I know just how to pull your strings."

Back in Paraburdoo getting groceries, we bumped into David Cox. I had seen him many times before, but never met him. He was the elder from the Bellary Aboriginal Community on the outskirts of Paraburdoo. David was dark, tall, neatly dressed and wore a cowboy hat. He drove a yellow pickup truck. We asked David if he could make us four boomerangs for our nephews at home. He said he would make four hunting boomerangs from the wood of the minnirichie

tree, the same wood his ancestors used. His project acceptance topped off a good day.

"Are you ready to go home, now, Miss Daisy?" Lee asked.

"Yes, Miss Daisy is ready."

Back at the station I resumed my duties. Spanky continued to grow stronger. "Did you miss mommy?" I asked as
I nuzzled my nose to hers.

"You know, you're mentally disturbed," Lee said, shaking his head.

Everyone concentrated on station improvements and
homestead work for a few more days. Geoff was working with
four young horses. "I was on Dutchman in the scrub yesterday," he said. "I heard a rustling noise and looked around. It
was a king western brown coming for Dutchman. I kicked
Dutchman in the guts and took off." Every snake story made
me flinch. They must have been waking up from their long
winter's nap. I found myself jumping at the sight of long sticks.

I gave Spanky her afternoon feeding and found a little
foal halter in the shed. It fit Spanky perfectly. She followed
me to the front lawn as I coaxed her with my fingers. It was a
trick I learned growing up. Calves thought they'd eventually
suck milk from my finger tips. I played with her for an hour.
Spanky was my escape from outback isolation. I still loved
mustering, but the baby bovine somehow had added a special element to my place at Ashburton. Spanky broke the
"sameness" for everyone. They asked how she was and
laughed when I talked to her. Spanky always responded to
me in her own mumbled animal language.

Jan went to Port Hedland for a few days to get supplies
and to get the two-way radios fixed. She returned with a few
surprises. She brought a bag of milk replacer powder for
Spanky and a double mattress for Lee and me. "You can start
working on baby Ashburton," she said with a smile.

"Thanks, but you don't have to worry about baby
Ashburton," I replied. "It's hard enough living in the outback
without being pregnant."

Our first night on the double mattress was special. After
months of spending every night in separate sleeping bags on

separate mattresses, it was great to sleep next to my husband under the same covers.

The following day Mick, Lee and I took the road train to pick up Ashburton cattle that had crossed the borders on two other stations. First, we picked up four at Mt. Vernon Station, then stopped for 75 at Mininer Station. I finally met the famous Jack Harvey. I'd heard he was tough, though reserved. He invited us all in for morning smoko, but I was a little afraid.

Jack's hands were rough like leather, weathered by seasons of severe outback conditions. Graying hair swept down from his balding head. My edgy feeling soon dissolved as Jack's intuitive character warmed me. The 71-year-old bushman had the spirit of a young bloke going on his first muster. He moved a bit slowly, but he was steady and determined. He helped with all aspects of mustering. His outward appearance, although distinguished, told of his toil over the years. His inward personality was kind, witty and genuine. He was the most fascinating person I had met on the trip and I hoped I'd get to visit him again.

Geologists camping for several weeks in the area to retrieve soil samples stopped for evening tea. Dane, the head geologist, had quizzed Jan about Lee and me the day before. She said, "Yesterday, Dane asked me if Lee was mute because you never hear him speak. I told him that Becky just doesn't let him get a word in edgewise."

We bubbled with laughter. Poor Lee took such abuse for being quiet. The crew, of course, blamed me because my mouth runneth over at times. "Lee doesn't have much to say," Jan said. "He's quiet, but when he speaks, it knocks your socks off. It's profound and meaningful."

Jan, Robin and I drove to Paraburdoo for groceries and airplane fuel. We stopped in one of the only two delis in town, chatted with the owners and ordered lunch.

"Are you Becky America?" the lady asked, slapping together our sandwiches behind the counter.

"How do you know I'm Becky America?"

"I read all about you in the school newsletter," she said. "They have stories from the students' overnight visit to Ashburton and it often refers to Becky America and Becky Kimberley. When I heard your accent, I guessed you were Becky America."

She was curious about the year-long trip we were on and said, "My husband and kids just returned from traveling around Australia for a year."

"Is that typical?" I asked.

"Yeah, a lot of Aussie families go on the road for a year," she said.

High winds canceled mustering again. It was a good break. My tailbone felt better, bruises faded and cuts healed. Just when I thought I was getting a day of R&R I had to re-shoe Kate. Hooves were to be trimmed and re-shod every six weeks. I straightened the nails in Kate's hooves and got both front shoes taken off in ten minutes. Last time I shod Kate she stood beautifully. I thought it was going to be an easy day—I was so wrong! I secured her rear hoof between my legs and started straightening nails to remove the shoes. She pushed with all her weight, almost knocking me down. She did it again and again. Andrew saw me struggling and came to my aid.

When Kate was finished I held Bo Derek, a bay mare, for Andrew to shoe. Bo Derek would also be my mustering horse. Everyone at the station had their own "plant" or group of mustering horses. My plant was Kate and Bo Derek, at least for a while. Lee spent the entire day working on the new black bull buggy. He welded on a bull bar and a roll bar.

Thursday was a big muster. We started by gathering a small coach mob.

"Mick, Barney and Becky America, I need you go into the scrub for some scattered cattle," Andrew radioed. Minutes later Lee was called out. We brought in 25 more animals.

"Did you see me go airborne in the bull buggy?" Lee asked with a wide grin. "It was really cool."

"I think you're really dumb and you're going to get hurt," I snapped. I didn't want to nag him, but I didn't want him to die either. He had stopped wearing his seat belt because it bruised his shoulder and chest. Lee didn't miss riding at all; the bull buggy was a challenge and he loved it.

We moved the mob farther down the dirt road. I was on the right point when a big heifer bolted. I took off going wide and closed in to cut her off. She turned back toward the mob for the moment, then suddenly the bitch stopped, looked at me, dropped her head and charged! Before I could react she slammed into my horse. She pissed me off and I called her bluff. Kate and I retaliated and ran straight at her. She didn't falter. The heifer dropped her head, charged and hit Kate again, nearly knocking us off balance. Jan spun around in her bull buggy to take over. The feral heifer had no respect for Kate and me. Jan got her back to the mob.

Nearly 400 cattle were pushed into the yards at the end of the day. I dismounted, threw my reins to the crew and jumped into Tricky's bull buggy. He was the fastest driver. The idea was to get me back to the homestead quickly. I made dinner and Tricky lit everyone's donkie. I thought Lee's driving scared me, but Tricky's terrified me.

Musters were starting earlier. The alarm sounded its annoying ring at 4:45 a.m. We were mustering the rain-forest area again. Becky, Mick, Barney and I rode off to start gathering the coach mob. I was on Bo Derek, my sixth horse. She was a deadhead and had an unusual gait.

"Mick, could you watch Bo Derek a minute while I canter?" I asked. "Her gait feels funny."

"Hey, Becky, she's lame," Mick said. "You'll have to take her back to the truck."

Crikey, I thought. *I just didn't have any luck with horses.*

"Becky, you can ride Harlequin," Robin said. "I'll ride in the bull buggy with Jan."

"Are you sure you don't mind?" I asked.

"No worries, mate," she said.

I tied Bo Derek to the truck and took off on Harlequin. I was a half-hour behind the others, but eventually found them.

We were moving cattle up the creek bed and eight animals bolted. Becky Kimberley and Geoff went after them. I saw them and tracked the cattle from 15 yards away. I did what you're not supposed to do when bringing a fresh mob in at the beginning of the muster—I was chasing them. I thought I was far enough away that I wouldn't scare them and at the same time wouldn't lose them. The forest floor was thick with growth that made the quest difficult as Harlequin maneuvered through the trees. I had no idea what had happened to Geoff and Becky. I focused only on the cattle. Then I heard chatter on the radio. I held my arm closer to my ear as I reined frantically with the other.

"We've lost that small mob," Geoff radioed Andrew.

"I'm still with the mob," I said almost breathlessly into the two-way.

"Do you have them held up?" Andrew asked.

"No, but I'm trotting alongside of them."

"Where are you?"

"I have no idea, but I see a clearing up ahead."

"Good job, good job," Andrew said as he flew the plane over me and spotted my small mob. "Try to bend them a little and head them to the road."

I had them walking slow and steady. I knew Andrew was impressed and even if he wasn't, I sure was proud of myself.

"Lee, there are two bulls over on the clay pan, bring them to the mob," Andrew said.

"The bulls keep separating," Lee radioed back.

"Just try to bring one in."

"He's giving me a lot of trouble and keeps going back toward the scrub," Lee said.

"Knock him down and tie him up," Andrew ordered.

"How exactly do I do that?" Lee asked.

"Run the buggy in to him and knock him down, park on top of him and tie him up with your hobble belt," Andrew instructed.

I listened closely to the commentary and tried to imagine what was going through Lee's mind. I could picture it. Lee slamming into the bull, setting the parking brake, jumping out, whipping off his hobble belt and tying the bull down. It sounded like a rodeo competition, but it wasn't—it was real life and real action in the outback. Uncooperative bulls often brought chaos to the mob and danger to horses and riders. Difficult ones were tied up. They lay bound on the ground until the blokes dragged them onto the horse float at the end of the day and delivered them to the yards. The biggest problem was that cattle were typically not yarded up until sunset and it was too dark to find the bulls. That's what happened with Lee's first bull catch. We pushed cattle into the makeshift six-mile yards at dusk; the search would have to wait.

First thing the next morning we took two vehicles out to find Lee's bull. We searched for hours. There was no sign of hoof prints, Lee's tire tracks, or a barren spot where the bull had been left. It was as if it never happened. Andrew reckoned he had escaped. Jan promised to order Lee another hobble belt. It had been part of his daily garb.

August showed no signs of the approaching spring. Some mornings plummeted to 6 degrees Celsius (43 degrees Fahrenheit.) I traded my leggings in for the flannel pants my sister sent me and cuddled up beside Lee on our new double mattress. The shared body energy did wonders combating the cold air creeping through cracks in our humpy.

The lifestyle was alien but we had adapted to it, even reveled in its primitiveness. Friends e-mailed us:

> *You're a much better person than I am, there's no way I could live like that.*
> *Just got the photos of your modest outback home—Wow! You are tough.*
> *Better you, than me.*
> *What an experience you're having.*
> *You're crazy, but we admire your guts.*
> *My husband never reads e-mails, but he reads every word of your e-mails.*

I wasn't sure if the monthly e-mail updates kept family and friends consoled, entertained or really afraid for us. Their support was always affirmation of our decision to go on our self-discovering journey. What I once thought was disgusting, evolved into no big deal. What was difficult, had become part of everyday life; and what seemed totally unthinkable, transformed into uniqueness.

27

Taking the Lead

The search was on a second day for Lee's bull. Andrew flew over the area—there was no sign—the bull was gone. We abandoned the search and rechanneled energies to trucking cattle from the six-mile yards back to the homestead. Right before we started to load I noticed a newborn calf. Its mother had disappeared in the confusion. The calf was wobbly and delirious. Calves and mothers often got separated in the yards. There were too many animals confined in limited space.

"Mick, can I get her out before she's trampled to death?" I asked.

"Okay, but remember it's just a calf."

I carried her to a bush and laid her in the shade. Her mouth was dry and full of dirt. I was sure she hadn't nursed her mother—that was bad. If a calf didn't get its mother's first colostrum which was packed with anti-bacterial fighting nutrients, the calf usually died. But I was a professional calf raiser, I could save her—right? I took my water bottle and squirted drops into her mouth throughout the day. I named her Hope because my morbid thought was she didn't have much hope of surviving.

I caught two calves that had squeezed out of the yards. I put them inside to find their mothers. Lee was upset with me for fussing over the babies. In the outback most people believed it was easier to put orphaned calves down rather than go through the effort and headache of trying to save them. With limited resources, raising calves was not economical or practical. In my mind every saved calf meant money—either as a mother one day producing offspring or per pound when it was grown. I just couldn't turn my feelings off to the suffering young animals—I had to try to save them. Lee and Barney carted Hope back to the homestead in the back of the ute.

"Did you see her nurse her mother?" Jan asked.

"No," I said. "I don't think she did."

"I doubt if she'll survive."

"I know, but before you shoot her, can we put her in the yards tonight and see if she finds her mother?"

Jan nodded her head reluctantly. I was sad about the whole thing, but kept telling myself it was business—it was life in the outback. I still had my Spanky. She jumped, butted and danced in circles every time she saw me coming. I'm sure it was the milk that created her happy mood, but perhaps she was attached to me as much as I was attached to her.

Geoff, Tricky, Lee and I had happy hour after a baking, choking day moving cattle. It was nice being over the hill away from the main house. We had a little privacy. The four of us shared stories, jokes and talked about life at Ashburton. Tricky's true story outdid them all.

"My great-grandmother died and on the way to the cemetery the horse buggy driver ran into a post and it knocked the coffin," Tricky said. "It gave my great-grandmother such a jolt, it woke her from a coma—she really wasn't dead. This all happened in the late 1800s. She lived for seven more years. When my great-grandfather paid to have her buried the second time he gave the buggy driver an extra English pound and said, 'This time don't hit any posts.' It's true, that really happened."

For evening tea, our entree was meat, again. I thought I would have gotten sick of meat every day, but homegrown Ashburton beef had such flavor. I did, however, miss pork in my diet. Mainly older boars were processed in Australia and the meat had a strong, unpleasant taste. How I longed for a tasty tender pork chop.

The next day I fixed Spanky's bottle and headed to the shed. I walked around the corner and to my amazement found Hope lying in the calf pen with Spanky. It gave me such an incredible feeling, I teared up. All my common sense told me not to get attached to the calves, but I couldn't help it. Hope looked up at me with her sparkling little eyes. She had similar markings to Spanky with tiny red circles around each eye and two small red dots on her nose. I walked down to the yards.

"Jan, what happened?" I asked.

"I found the calf and couldn't kill it," she said. "I took her up to the calf pen."

"Thanks, I'll do my best to keep her alive."

Jan, Robin and I mustered a small paddock while the others worked in the yards. I had to ride Daryl, Barney's horse. Kate and Bo Derek were lame.

"If you went through men like you do horses, I would have been gone a long time ago," Lee jested. I couldn't believe my misfortune with Ashburton horses. My count was up to seven different horses, though my final steed count would reach 12. I reckon Lee had a point.

That evening there was a new addition to my family. Jan named a little Hereford calf Faith and put her in the pen with Spanky and Hope. Lee helped me with the evening feeding. I gave them each a kiss good night. "Mommy loves you," I said, leaving my babies for the night.

Lee had worked wonders on the bull buggies, improving the safety features and their running ability.

"Your husband is bloody amazing!" Jan said.

"I know, he can do anything," I said.

Jan, Lee and I rolled hay out in the dark. It was so peaceful under the black canopy that stretched across the sky, stars flickered like far-off fireflies. The outback ceiling was vast—different from other night skies. No airplane lights flashed overhead and there was no brightness illuminated from towns. We were in the middle of nowhere, isolated from the rest of the world.

We ducked beneath our covers early that night. I shut my eyes and had just started falling asleep. Something heavy hit my pillow. I reached above my head and felt something cold and clammy. My heart pounded. *God, is there a snake in our bed?* I leaped on top of Lee, looking for safety.

"Get the torch, get the torch!" I shrieked. "Something is on my pillow!"

I switched on the torch. Gilbert, the resident gecko, ran across the cement.

"Shit, Lee, it's just Gilbert," I said with a huge sigh of relief. "If he had fallen on my face, I think I would have died."

Although I was restless after that, I managed to get a few hours of rest before the alarm sounded at 4:15 a.m. I had yet another mustering horse, Magray, but everyone called him Maggot. The dapple-gray gelding was a former polo pony and responded quickly to my neck-reining and stop commands. We were doing a cleanup muster near the six-mile, hoping to collect the cattle we had missed the week before. We mustered cattle to a watering hole where there was a heap more battling for a drink. As the cattle moved out we noticed a bull hopping along. *It was impossible! It couldn't be Lee's bull—or could it?* The bull Lee had tied up five days earlier was struggling along with its front legs still bound by Lee's hobble belt.

"If we ever have kids and I have to spank them with my hobble belt, I'll have a good story to tell them," Lee said.

Though the bull had been hobbled for days, it hadn't educated him at all—he continued to break from the mob. Andrew said, "Knock him down again, Lee, and tie him up."

"Righto, this time I'll make sure he can't escape," Lee answered.

The mob was toey and made several attempts to escape, but we always stopped them. It was so fulfilling to stop an aggressive mob. We learned new rules, techniques and responses on every muster. We had become a more efficient, dependable mustering team. Andrew and Jan said one of their biggest challenges was working with a different crew each year, but that we were their "best crew to date."

"Becky America, do you want to take a gallop?" Andrew asked.

"Yes," I said excitedly, as I pushed the send button of my two-way radio.

"Catch up to Mick and move the cattle out of the scrub," Andrew instructed.

"Lee, there's a mickey bull out to your right—roll him," he added.

"Righto, Andrew."

"Is he going to stay this time?" Andrew asked.

"He's tied as good as last time," Lee answered.

Lee took off after another bull, oblivious to the terrain. He concentrated on one thing—stopping the beast. He hit a ditch and went airborne again. The sun's light streamed beneath the vehicle's wheels. Lee's eyes were probably bugging out of his head. The wheels finally touched down like an airplane coming in for landing. Lee's short flight didn't deter his persistence to bring the bull back to the mob.

We held the mob while strays were mustered back. Sometimes holding the mob was monotonous—standing, waiting, watching, monitoring. Although we didn't want breakouts, the animals that bolted kept us alert and focused. During the silent waiting and watching time, Lee recited his new poem. It was brilliant, as usual.

"You know, you are bloody amazing," I said with that first-date twinkle in my eye.

We yarded up at dusk. The sunsets continued to enthrall me. The blending of soft colors was like a silent window blind that God pulled down every night. Such sunsets are often missed in America because there are so many other distractions, but in the outback nature and the environment rule—it is a timeless land some 100 million years old.

Sunrises and sunsets were daily pleasures, but there was no rest for the weary. We were doing musters back to back. We drove an hour to the Kooline Station boundary to start the next muster. Butch was back, wooing us with his piloting genius—up, down, left, right, backward, forward. I rode Sox, Mick's horse. She was fast, but had Kate's problem of not wanting to stop. A blister rubbed raw on my hands from fighting to hold her back. The cattle steadily moved along the river, except for one large bull. He'd stop, turn and charge. Eight horsemen were held at bay not knowing what to do— there was no bull buggy in sight. The game of cat and mouse went on for 15 minutes until Andrew had a bright idea.

"We're all going to run at him," Andrew said. "If he charges, it's likely he'll only get one of us."

I thought that was the most ridiculous plan I'd ever heard, but I had to go along with it or look like a coward. We all galloped toward the bull. The intimidation tactic worked; the bull retreated, running toward the others. It was our biggest muster yet. We had gathered about 1,000 head and held them.

"I'm putting you in the lead today," Andrew said.

"Righto," I said, flabbergasted.

Andrew put me in the lead of the largest mob we'd ever gathered. I could hardly contain my enthusiasm. It was a huge responsibility and I couldn't stuff up. There was no room for error. If I didn't control the lead and they bolted, I'd risk losing the entire mob. Sox and I took our position and led out the cattle. Being on the lead horse was incredibly satisfying. There was a never-ending river of cattle trailing me, a vapor of dust blurred the air above their backs, I couldn't even see the end of the mob. It was a remarkable sight, one I'll never forget. I led the cattle for three hours until we were a half-hour from the homestead, when Jan radioed, "Becky Kimberley and Josh need a break, they're exhausted from pushing up the tail."

I didn't want to give up the lead, but I knew pushing up the tail was bloody hard work. "No problem, I'll go back and switch with Becky and put her on the lead," I said. Becky Kimberley deserved to take over the lead; I admired her effort. We herded the mob across the river and they started walking through the paddock gate. Horsemen maintained their positions. I relaxed on Sox's back, watching the cattle and reflecting back on an incredible day. Sox dropped to the ground, leaned to the side and was about to roll.

"Get up, get up!" I screamed as I kicked Sox as hard as I could in her sides.

Instinct told me to jump because Sox could have crushed me, but I had to protect my saddle. Everyone looked at me like I was nuts and I was momentarily—crazed by the thought of Sox destroying my expensive saddle. My hysteria worked. Sox leaped to her feet. I had saved my saddle and myself.

I was buggered at the end of the day. I still had to feed my three babies and fix evening tea. I walked into the shed and found Hope stretched out, motionless. Tears welled up in my eyes. The little calf draped limply over both my arms like a cooked noodle hanging over a pan. I carried her to the ute and laid her on the back. She couldn't even lift her head. I found Josh and asked him to put her down. I couldn't bear to see her suffer. Josh, like his brother, Barney, was gun happy. Not that they liked killing calves, but it wouldn't faze them a bit. It was more humane to put Hope out of her misery than to let her suffer through the night.

We were caught up for a day at Ashburton. I was going to fly to Mininer with Butch to take photographs. Lift-off was at 6 a.m. and it was my first helicopter ride. There were no doors—it was totally open on both sides. I hoped the seat belt was enough to keep me from my first "free fall." We sailed over the flat. The closer to the ground we were the faster it seemed we traveled. I felt like I was in a virtual reality theater that made me believe I was really flying, but I really *was* flying. The sun was just popping over the horizon. The rays hit my face, warming my cheeks while the rest of me was frigid. I wore my baseball cap, gloves, a scarf and jacket, but cool air fingered its way down my neck.

The Ashburton River wound across the semiarid plain. Debris left behind after flood waters receded scattered the riverbank. Heavy vegetation flanked the river, though nearby it was sparse scrub and barren ground, evidence of the dry season. Cattle dotted the landscape, their crisscrossed trails leading to the river or to the windmill tanks that were strategically positioned throughout the station. Cattle stayed close to a main water source. 'Roos nibbled the early dew-covered buffel grass. The terrain was flat, but occasionally interrupted by hills, ridges or rock faces. As we flew I got lost in the surroundings, lost in the moment—Lee and I had experienced so much.

It only took 20 minutes to fly to Mininer—by road it took two hours. Butch started pushing cattle out of the scrub until we landed at 9:30 a.m. to chat with Wendy and Jack about the day's strategy. While they organized a plan, I shot photos. I lost my camera cap. Jack spotted it. I rewarded him with a kiss on his cheek—he beamed.

Butch scared more cattle toward Wendy and Jack, who were moving the cattle with their bull buggies. Jack had three flat tires that day and changed them all himself. For a man in his 70s, he was amazing. I rode with Wendy in her buggy part of the day. She was fast and furious. She could back up 20 mph to cut off a beast and speed forward to cut off another. Wendy chased down one uncooperative cow and rolled her for a little "education." I realized why Lee loved driving a bull buggy so much—he could drive like a total maniac without getting a traffic violation. We made it to the house at 4 p.m.

"Did you get a few pictures of my Red Devons?" Jack asked.

"I sure did," I said, knowing I made his day.

We had a cuppa and then Butch and I had to go. Jack gave me a great big hug good-bye, saying, "I got a kiss today when you lost your camera cover. Next time lose your whole camera."

"Don't worry, he's harmless," Dorris said.

On the flight home Butch and I chatted. He admired Lee and me for being brave enough to leave our home country for a year.

"Robin and I are talking about doing something different for a year," he said.

"I think you should," I said. "Come to America if you can."

"Did you ever see the movie *Thelma and Louise*? he asked.

"Yes, it's one of my favorite movies," I said.

"Remember the part where they go off the cliff?" he asked.

As I went to answer we flew off a hidden mountain bluff, I totally lost my belly. Butch looked at me and laughed.

"You know, I was just about to tell you I hated that part of the movie," I said.

I enjoyed Butch's company. He proved my whole theory about Aussie men wrong. Butch was a gentleman and polite. He adored Robin, his wife of some 15 years. He often tipped his hat to the ladies at the station. "When a man tips his hat, I go weak in the knees," Jan often said. We all looked forward to Butch's visits. He brought us news from other stations and thrilled us with his helicopter expertise.

Butch and I landed back at Ashburton and Jan asked if I'd drive to Port Hedland with her for supplies. We left at 2:45 a.m. Two hours into the trip, Jan was tired. I was wide awake and took over the helm. We arrived at the Auski Roadhouse at 7:30 a.m., and refueled.

Bushfires were burning near Port Hedland. Black and gray plumes of smoke swelled in the sky. Flames licked like wild tongues hungry for the oxygen that fed their fury. No one battled the bushfire that stretched for miles. Unless bushfires closed in on towns or livestock stations, wildfires just burned, destroying millions of acres of scrub and bushland annually. It rejuvenated the land, but destroyed everything in its path.

At 10 a.m. we were at Port Hedland's town limit. First stop was a car dealership. Jan was so excited to pick up her new Toyota Land Cruiser. It was the first new vehicle in her life that had more than two seats. For years, Jan, Andrew and Mick had squeezed in the front seat of their ute. We drove the new Land Cruiser on errands. Instead of getting a room in town we drove to Pardoo Station, a cattle operation 100 miles northeast of Port Hedland.

"What we are doing is real Australian," Jan said as we pulled out of town.

"Do you mean driving 200 miles out of our way?" I asked.

Pardoo Station was in the opposite direction of Ashburton. It was the only opportunity for Jan to visit her friends. The station was located right along the North Coast on the Indian Ocean and supported 5,500 Santa Gertrudis cattle. Owners Pam and John Leeds also operated a tourist business welcoming thousands of folks annually. The Leeds seemed busy and stressed, but were wonderful hosts. They served us steak, lamb and a salad for tea.

"Becky, I think you called here in February looking for a job," Pam said.

"You're right, I did and you told me to call back in a few months, but we found work at Ashburton."

"Ha, ha, we have them, and they're the best employees we've ever had," Jan chimed in.

We stayed in one of the Leeds' tourist units and left at 8 a.m. the next morning. Menstrual cramps kept me up most of the night. I was tired and sick in the morning. I tried to sleep a little on the way back to Port Hedland, but Jan and I were always eager to talk.

"I know Andrew has heaps of potential, I just need to get the spurs into him sometimes and nudge him up," Jan admitted with a giggle.

"I nudge Lee a little too," I said.

"You and I are a bad combination," Jan said referring to our ability to get along and talk about anything. We were a bad combination, but in the best sense of the word. We enjoyed each other's company, shared personal stories and served as a sounding board for the other. It was going to be very hard when Lee and I had to leave Ashburton.

I felt sicker mile after mile. *How was I going to tell Jan I didn't think I could drive the ute seven hours back to Ashburton?* She was depending on me. We departed Port Hedland at 12:30 p.m. Jan drove her new Land Cruiser and I bucked up and drove the old ute. We arrived at the Auski Roadhouse. There were two carloads of Aborigines. I asked a woman if I could take pictures of the kids. They were polite and playful. I didn't see any of the negative behavior I had heard about. The kids looked healthy, not like the gas-sniffing, brain-burned young-sters Lee and I had heard about.

Jan pulled out of the gas station, I followed. I was start-ing to feel a little better. I popped in the new Aussie cassette she had given me. It was old-timers' music and poems. I got lost in the words, concentrating on their meanings, visualiz-ing their descriptions. Then I focused on the white vehicle I was tailing.

"That's not Jan!" I said aloud. "Oh God, where the hell did Jan go?"

The Land Cruiser I was following was full of Aborigines. I freaked out and started talking to myself, "What should I do? Should I go back to the roadhouse?" I speeded by them. There was no sign of Jan, no sign of any vehicle. *Had Jan turned off? Had she pulled over? Did I just drive past her? Was I going the wrong way?* On the verge of turning around, I noticed a white Land Cruiser in the distance. I speeded up, finally catching it—it was Jan. We rolled into Ashburton at 7, unloaded and I went straight to bed.

We mustered the following day. Jan was so tired, she had worked herself into a tizzy. When she was in a good mood, she was so much fun, so happy. When Jan was ex-hausted or stressed, her personality changed. I couldn't blame her—too many people expected too much from the woman. "We women are different cattle," Jan said. I had to agree.

It was good to be back. Good to see Lee, and, of course, good to see Spanky. I think she missed me. Faith had died while I was in Port Hedland. Spanky was still healthy and spirited. I weaned her from the bottle and graduated her to a bucket. She was so rambunctious at feeding time. She rooted and butted her head in the bucket, splashing milk all over me. Then she slurped, rooted and butted again. She gave me a fit, but I couldn't help but love her frisky nature. I let her out of her wire cage to run in the larger horse pen. Spanky bucked, kicked and ran like she'd been released from jail. She was a nut. I sat on the watering trough watching her and laughed. She'd run to me, stop, twist around and play some more. Every time I fed Spanky I talked to her. As soon as she heard my voice she licked her lips. Spanky was even better therapy than my garden. She always brightened my moods and made me smile.

It was time again to muster my favorite place—the bull paddock. We saddled the horses and Barney and I drove them to the Ram Creek gate. As I rode Maggot through the gate, I noticed a limp. *Not again,* I thought. I stopped, hopped off and picked up Maggot's hoof. A piece of wire was stuck in his hoof. Mick arrived and dug the wire out with his handy-dandy Leatherman tool. It was deep; Maggot would be lame for days. We loaded Maggot on the horse float and I drove him back to the homestead and turned him out. My choices were limited and I radioed, "Andrew, the only other horse in is Franky."

"Saddle Franky and head out as fast as you can," he responded.

After two hours of riding "Franky" and thinking, *Wow, Franky is fast,* I was totally embarrassed when Jan informed me, "Becky, that's not Franky, it's Ferrari."

I felt like such a dummy, I thought I knew all the horses. Ferrari was Mick's horse. We mustered the bulls into the homestead yards and Becky Kimberley sprinted off to the dunny.

"Hey, somebody, there's a snake!" she yelled. "There's a snake coiled up in the corner."

Mick grabbed a shovel, but the snake disappeared before he got there. *Just great, I always used that dunny.* I just couldn't conquer my snake affliction.

Lee helped process over 200 bulls the next two days. He enjoyed working with the cattle, especially the bulls. Working in the yards was rare for Lee. He was usually called out on other duties because he was one of the only people who could do them.

"Becky and Lee are leaving the 18th," Jan told Andrew.

"Of October, right?" he asked.

"Yes, but what are we going to do, sell the place?" Jan mused, making it quite clear that our role at Ashburton had been valuable.

We loved it at Ashburton. I couldn't explain it. It was rough-as-guts, but something tugged at our souls, lifted our spirits, even clouded our thoughts of home. Quite a change from my previous state of mind. Would we extend our stay at Ashburton? Would we immigrate and become Australian citizens? All we did know was that Ashburton had provided an incredible opportunity—one that still had many smiles to share and unfortunately, many tears to wipe.

Rebecca Long Chaney

Mustering Madness

Well before dawn it all begins,
Buggies are fueled, horses are in;
Weathered hands rub the last bit of sleep away,
It's gonna be a big muster, gonna be a long day;

The crew sets out, leaving the homestead behind,
The air is brisk, the weather fine;
Out near the flat where the mob will soon gather,
The pilot swoops low and radios chatter;

Lead cattle walk out with a push from above,
Bullocks and bulls more reluctant, those lords of the scrub;
Horsemen get around cattle spotted from the air,
Pick up a few here and a handful there;

Out on the clay pan the mob is quiet and steady,
But you can't fall asleep and must always be ready;
Restless cattle look to the scrub as they turn,
It's no laughing matter and good cause for concern;

"Block up, Block up!" The call is repeated,
With skillful riding of ringers the rush is defeated;
Cattle stood up to calm and settle in,
Then the order is given and hours of riding begin;

This time is crucial, no room for mistakes,
Push up the tail and turn back the breaks;
The river of cattle moves off, but not all have conceded,
One error in judgment is all that is needed;

The mob has been quick and crew has been right,
Day near to the end and yards are in sight;
As the tail pushes in and sky turns to night,
Head stockman's words ring clear, "We draft at first light."

Lee Chaney

28

Tragedy Hits Ashburton

I t *was Spanky's one-month birthday. Her personality made* me laugh and brought pleasure to my lengthy work days. Finally, I was working with Lee in the cattle yards processing weaners. Lee castrated, Mick dehorned and I tagged ears. It was fun working with "Mutt and Jeff"—the duo kept me in stitches.

Jan had found Spanky another pal. The nearly solid deep-red calf was small, but alert and energetic. I named her Promise.

Jan walked around the house in half a daze. She was rundown and fatigued. She was always up before anyone and was the last to go down at night. She put other people's needs before her own. She drove Becky Kimberley six hours to Carnarvon to the doctor's; she slipped Toni to Tom Price to get medicine; she drove seven hours to Port Hedland to get supplies, radios fixed and to visit Andrew's parents in a nursing home; she bought little gifts for everyone on the crew; she monitored Joy's recovery and checked her stitches; and she made a point to keep in touch with her loved ones on the East Coast. Her demanding schedule, stubborn character and heart of gold were going to kill her. I told Jan to go take a shower and have a rest.

"I think I will, thanks," Jan said accepting my advice. "I was thinking about you and Lee leaving."

"Let's not talk about it," I said and shooed her on her way.

I didn't want to think about leaving. Lee and I weren't ready to leave our new "home."

Lee drove the road train to deliver weaners to windmill ten. He was full of himself again. Jan threatened to buy him a singlet (Aussie tank top) and pair of real short cutoffs just like the Aussie truckers wore. Lee filled with such pride when he was behind the wheel of a road train—men and their big toys.

Spanky followed me on a walk. She paraded around the lawn on my heels, excited by her temporary freedom. We relaxed by the flower bed and fended off curious cattle dogs. I returned Spanky to her pen. I moved Promise to another small pen, fearful that her diarrhea would infect Spanky.

Jan was overwhelmed with office work and I offered to make tea again. I'd become the main cook in addition to all my outside duties. My culinary skills gave Jan a break and that made the extra responsibility worth it to me.

Lee walked with me to the shed that evening. Promise sucked a fourth of a bottle of warm water and electrolytes. She didn't look good. When I finished I stopped to talk to Spanky. I didn't touch her for fear I'd transfer a virus from Promise. I bent down by the mesh fence.

"Give momma a kiss," I said.

She stuck her snout up by the wire and we touched noses.

"You know you are a weirdo, but I love ya," Lee said.

He knew I had a strong affection for Spanky. I always told him of her progress and escapades—she was my little sweetheart.

"Lee, guess what?"

"What?"

"I got on the cattle scales today and I weighed 138 pounds," I said elated by my achievement. "I haven't been in the 130s for ages."

"I liked you fine at 165, there was just more of you to love," Lee said. He looked at Jan and added, "Is that what I'm supposed to say?"

He was such a shit, but almost always knew the right things to say. We both had attributes that attracted us to the other. We also discovered traits over the years we'd like to change. I'm sure Lee would like to shut me up at times, probably as much as I begged him to talk. I wished he spoke his mind more often to me and others. He wished I wasn't so straightforward and that I'd stay out of controversial situations. He allowed others to take advantage of him. I had a dynamic personality and naturally voiced my opinion or gave unsolicited advice. They say opposites attract and I guess with us that was true to a point, but our shared love was agriculture. It's what brought us together in the first place.

At first light I fed Spanky and attempted to get some fluids into Promise's sunken-in belly. Her mouth was cool and clammy, her ears were cold. Those were the first symptoms of a sick calf that Dad had taught me when he turned the calf raising over to me when I was nine years old.

"Jan, Promise is cool in the mouth and going downhill fast," I said.

"Can you go shoot the sick calf, please?" Jan asked Barney.

I stayed in the kitchen to have my morning caffeine fix. As I stood by the sink rinsing my cup I saw Lee and Barney walking with a steady pace toward the house. *Boy, they must really be on a serious mission,* I thought. Never in a million years had I imagined what was about to unfold.

"Come here, Becky," Lee said as he opened the kitchen screen door.

"Just a second, I'll be right there," I said drying my cup.

"Come out of the kitchen," he insisted pulling my arm with the most steadfast gaze I'd ever seen on his face.

I thought I had really stuffed up and Lee was going to warn me before the wrath of Andrew came down on me. But Andrew wasn't even home, he had taken 150 beasts to Harvey Beef's slaughter house. No one else at the station scared me.

Andrew didn't scare me, really, he mostly just pissed me off sometimes. Lee walked me to the side of the house and looked into my eyes. "Barney shot Spanky," he said. "It was an accident, he thought Spanky was the sick calf."

I broke down in a torrential downpour of tears. I couldn't explain the emptiness that immediately struck me. I walked away from everyone and went into the lounge and collapsed on the sofa. I buried my face in my hands; tears cascaded down my cheeks. Lee sat beside me, but didn't say a word. His rugged hand touched my back letting me know he was there and that he understood my loss. Lee, more than anyone, knew my connection with Spanky. She had been my baby for over a month, I'd forged a bond with her.

Why was I so emotional? I tried to tell myself it was just a calf. But it wasn't just a calf, it was Spanky, full of spirit and spunk. I adored Spanky for the added joy she brought to my station life. I loved her, but she was gone. She had depended on me to feed her, play with her and protect her. *How did she end up with a bullet in her head?* I just couldn't believe it—I didn't want to believe it. I was gutted.

I sat in the lounge for what seemed an eternity bawling until I thought there weren't any tears left. Lee never left my side, his silent presence comforted me. Finally, I straightened up and tried to speak, tried to compose myself. I struggled to see through clouded eyes and to pronounce my garbled words. "How, how d-did Barney accidentally kill Spa-Spanky?"

"He didn't see the calf in the other pen and assumed Spanky must be the sick calf," Lee answered.

It had to be a nightmare. Spanky had bebopped around her stall that morning full of life. It was impossible for Barney to get the calves mixed up, wasn't it?

"Cooould you pa-please get my shoes?" I whispered to Lee. "I want to go se-see her."

"Are you sure you want to do that?" Lee said as he peered into my red and swollen eyes.

"I'mm sure, it's something I ha-have to do."

I knew it probably wasn't the best idea, but I had to see her. I had to have closure, if that was possible. I exhausted myself with emotion and walked slowly toward the shed as Lee steadied me with his arm intertwined in mine.

You would have thought I'd lost a loved one. In the outback you cling to each other and to a few of the animals. It's the only way to survive the isolated life. When that formula loses an element, your heart is ripped out. I walked into the shed as I'd done everyday for weeks, but that time I didn't hear Spanky's unequivocal bleats of "maaa...maaaa," waiting for her milk. I didn't see the adorable way she lapped her pink tongue across her nose in one steady sweep.

What I did see was Spanky lying still on the ground. She was such a precious calf. How could her life have been stripped so needlessly? I knelt down and held her head in my arms as I stroked her soft hair. I laid my head on hers and uncontrollable tears spilled out of my already strained eyes. Spanky was still warm as I clutched her tightly to my breast. I felt like I had let her down. I rocked her in my arms, "Momma is so sorry. I'm so sorry, I love you."

No doubt, Lee thought I had cracked up, but he stood quiet and supportive. He knew I was sentimental, but I could usually control those emotions to a point. That day in the shed I felt helpless, lost. Spanky's head rested in my arms. I looked into her little face and saw the bullet hole square in the middle of her forehead. A piece of cold metal had ended her life. Blood streamed from the fatal wound, matting her soft white hair in clumps and seeping into my clothes. It was a horrible death. I pictured Spanky peering up at Barney with her big brown eyes, hoping for her bucket of warm milk and she got a death blow to the head instead. The accident had a tremendous effect on me.

Finally, I pulled myself away from Spanky and stood up. Barney was behind me. I wanted to hit him, yell at him, tell him what a dumbshit he was for shooting a healthy calf. He was crying. Barney knew he had stuffed up. He was in his own pain. I embraced him—we cried together over Spanky's lifeless body.

"I'm so sorry, Becky," Barney sobbed.

"Barney, it's okay. I know it was an accident and you didn't mean it. Spanky was a pain in my butt sometimes, but I really enjoyed her," I said trying to offer a little smile to reassure Barney that mistakes happen.

There was little sense in pointing blame at Barney, he was suffering his own hell. I asked Lee and Barney to take Spanky to her final resting place, but I didn't want to know where it was. I returned to the house.

Jan was beside herself. She felt responsible because she gave the killing orders. She only specified the sick calf, not the red calf next to Spanky's pen. I told Jan not to blame herself, what was done was done. Spanky's death upset the whole crew. Jan wanted to fire Barney because of his many screw-ups. The day earlier he parked a vehicle on the hill by the house and didn't have the brake on. It popped out of gear and rolled down hitting two gas tanks—lucky for him, empty tanks. Four days before that he crushed his hand in the cattle yards being careless. And two weeks before that he changed the tires on the ute and didn't tighten the lug nuts properly. Someone noticed the loose lugs in town and tightened them for Jan and me. We could have been killed.

I changed my blood-stained shirt and bra and resumed my station duties. I didn't want to mope, but I couldn't help it. The once jovial, wisecracking Becky America had vanished. Her zombie replacement spent the next two hours washing the kitchen floor. I wiped, scrubbed, then cried; wiped, scrubbed, then cried. Toni walked in and gave me a hug. Becky Kimberley kissed my head while I sat nearly comatose on the floor. The crew was wonderfully supportive.

"Becky, why don't you come to the fence row with me," Lee suggested later that afternoon. "It will help to get out." We went out and dropped pickets. My tears dried, but my heart didn't mend. I eyed-up pickets while Lee pounded them. On the ninth picket a swish of strong air brushed across my face. It grew stronger. Lee grabbed his hat, dirt swirled in our eyes. I was blinded and reached out frantically to find Lee in the flurry of wind, dirt and chaos. I grabbed Lee's shirt before the wind whipped me back in its clutches. It was like a small tornado. The wind tunnel came up on us so quickly, it scared me. The noise faded, the gusts mellowed and I rubbed the dust and filth that layered my face.

"That was a willy-willy, wasn't it Lee?" I said, still stunned by the natural phenomenon.

On the drive back to the homestead I told Lee I'd come to terms with Spanky's death. I said, "I think God took Spanky and it's supposed to be a message to Barney. I'll get through Spanky's death knowing it's part of God's plan. It should get Barney's ass in gear before he seriously injures himself or someone else."

I skipped tea that night. I didn't feel very sociable. I was emotionally exhausted. My eyes hurt. I had cried more tears that day than I had during the year. I put away all my calf buckets, bottles and milk replacer—I removed all reminders of my baby.

We got up at 5 a.m. to muster the two-mile paddock where we had put a heap of cows and calves from two previous musters. We hadn't had time to process them yet. Nearly 500 were herded back to the homestead cattle yards. Many of the cows had been missed for years. Horns curved around, some piercing the skin and growing back into the skull. Those horns were sawed in half and the tip was pulled out of the animal's skull. Anti-bacterial solution was sprayed on the wound as maggots tumbled from the hole. It was repulsive, but necessary.

After smoko one morning we handled baby calves in the round pen that were too small to put through the crush. Mick and Barney threw the little beasts to the ground, Andrew castrated, Toni marked ears and I tagged. Mick and Barney huffed and puffed; the calves were feisty. I thought I'd have a go and my alter ego, *Xena*, warrior princess, took over. The first calf I threw was small and not a problem. The next two were a bit bigger, but I got them down. I huffed and puffed too, but the rough work energized me, improved my self-confidence. I was dirty and bloody, but possessed a new sense of toughness and skill.

My newfound enthusiasm was stimulated more that afternoon when I switched on the TV and watched 100 Australian stock horses gallop into the Olympic stadium for the opening ceremonies. Although the host city, Sydney, was some 4,000 miles away, it was electrifying to watch thousands of athletes from more than 200 nations proudly walk into the stadium carrying their countries' flags. I sported my U.S. T-shirt and did every job possible in the house that afternoon to catch portions of the ceremony. I baked a cake, did laundry and worked on tea. I was a die-hard Olympic fan. Almost everyone at the station had disappeared.

"Mick, do you know where Lee is?" I asked.

"He's getting his truck ready to move cattle," Mick said.

"Okay, thanks, mate."

Lee was ebullient when I told him Mick referred to the Scania road train as Lee's truck. Other than Mick and Andrew, Lee was the only non-family member trusted to drive the road train with cattle. Ashburton had become Lee's passion. I grew to share that passion, but was still plagued by my snake phobia and I cringed at the sight of redback spiders. I also continued to climb fence to escape the dangerous horns of bulls and feral cows. But my greatest fear was Lee not wanting to leave Ashburton. He had already talked about returning the following year for another mustering season. "There's still a lot of fence the Glenns need built. I'll have to come back." I worried he might forfeit his ticket back to America and if so, what would I do?

I went over the hill to do a few things in the humpy and to gather our filthy clothes. I threw Clyde's strap over my shoulder, had three bags in one hand and a basket of laundry in the other. About 25 feet from the Nest something twitched on my shoulder. It was heavy and it sure wasn't my ponytail. I tried to shrug it off thrusting my right shoulder forward. It fell. I scanned the ground, it was Gilbert, our live-in gecko. He scurried across the dirt a few feet, stopped and looked around as if saying, "Where the hell am I?" He ran back to me and put his tiny webbed claws on my pants like he was going to climb up my leg. Then he retreated under the small space of my boot between my heel and the ball of my foot. I laughed, startled by my temporary passenger. I moved my foot, threw a shirt over him and gently carried him safely back to the humpy.

How could Gilbert have fallen on my head without me feeling it? Finally it dawned on me that Gilbert hadn't fallen on my head. He must have been on the floor, got scared by my footsteps and ran to the highest point, which was the top of my head. Someone had told me when Aborigines hunt goannas and bungarras they surround the reptile while one Aborigine stands in the center of a circle. To escape, the animal runs to the highest point, which is always the head of the Aborigine who is stationed in the middle of the group. Then they catch it.

I didn't believe the story at first. I was notorious for being gullible. I shared Gilbert's caper with everyone, but they were skeptical. "It happened," I insisted. "It gives credit to the Aboriginal myth."

If it had been a giant huntsman spider dangling from my hair, I may not have been so willing to save the little hitchhiker. I'd seen a huntsman rear back and jab its two front legs high in the air, signaling combat. There was no chance I was going to take the hairy creature on. So far the huntsman spiders had respected my space. The same certainly couldn't be said about Gilbert's escapades. First he fell from the ceiling, practically landing on my face in bed, then he was a stowaway on my head.

Thursday we were up at 4:30 a.m. to muster the bull paddock. The sunrise was brilliant. The orangish red fireball ascended slowly, coloring the surrounding sky with a glow of lilac, crimson and gold. *That's really beautiful,* I thought, and breathed a deep sigh of admiration while I sat comfortably atop Maggot.

He'd recovered from his punctured hoof and his spunk returned. At the river crossing, the bulls turned and stampeded back at us. All 300 beat us, but they hadn't gotten far before the majority of them were mustered back to the river and pushed across. Lee had put a new motor in his Suzi and had more power, though he probably didn't need it. He was doing fine crashing through scrub, running down beasts and flying over ditches.

"Lee is great, he's got a new motor and a big red bull," Andrew radioed to everyone at the start of the day.

Two bulls charged me in the yards. Did I try to stop them? Hell no!

"No worries, mate, I would have moved too," Mick said to make me feel better. "It's better to move and live than get the bravery award and be dead." Mick's words meant a lot.

The Olympics continued to electrify me. I watched the individual equestrian three-day event. Andrew Hoy of Australia was exceptional and won the silver after having a super jumping program. Kiwi Mark Todd took the bronze and was also named the Three-Day Eventer of the Century. America's David O'Connor, originally from Maryland, my native state—took the gold. How cool was that?

There was something about the Olympics that made my patriotic spirit come alive: the individual sacrifices, the unmatched determination and stamina of the athletes and the fellowship between teams. I'm not sure if it was Olympic stimulation or true love, but Lee surprised me with a fence around our flower bed. I finally could put away the barrels, tires, chairs, metal cot, string, water containers, eskies, pots and pieces of wood that had served for months as a barricade protecting the precious plants from the jaws of hungry horses and cows.

He used wooden sheep-fence posts that were 100 years old and stretched large wire mesh fence between the posts. He left a small opening where the slate path lead to the patio. Our flower bed's colorful charm always put a smile on my face and warmth in my heart. There was much I'd miss at the station and a few things I'd be happy to bid g'day. The Glenns had become our family and Ashburton our home. *How were we going to say good-bye?*

29

Bulldust and Danger

O nly one month was left at Ashburton, but a lot of cattle needed to be mustered before our departure. Nights were still cool, but days turned baking hot, as if I was stuck in a kitchen with my mother canning 100 jars of green beans using a pressure cooker. Australia's winter was on the way out and summer had been dumped into our laps.

We mustered near Stone Hut and it was Andrew's first ride on his new $10,000A stallion, Super Loop. He was 14.2 hands and had black velvet hair. Super Loop's jet-black silky mane and tail blew with the breeze across his muscular frame. If he'd pass his athletic ability on to his progeny, they would be great mustering horses.

Butch had mustered a large mob out of the scrub toward the horsemen. As the mob came closer, all the horsemen were in a semicircle to hold them up. A bull bolted and it took both Lee and Jan in their buggies and Butch in the helicopter to bring him back. Lee and Jan zoomed their buggies over the rough and bumpy terrain, cutting off the beast, throwing their vehicles in reverse and circling around him again. It was always entertaining to watch a chase unfold, and scary too. The bull finally succumbed to their efforts and ran back to the mob, but he was a troublemaker the rest of the day. Cattle moved up the path smoothly. Andrew was in the lead and Mick and I were at the points. The mob looked pretty calm so I got our video camera out of my new belt-on camera carrier. The camera's long strap fit around my neck. If the camera slipped from my grip it wouldn't crash to the ground, just jerk my neck.

One of the lead bulls bolted on Mick's side. Mick leaped in front of him. The bull started running to my side. *Oh shit,* I thought. I had the camera in one hand and the reins in the other. I dashed to cut him off. He stopped for a moment and bolted again right by me. The 1,400-pound Hereford thought he'd escaped until Jan rolled her bull buggy in front of him. I caught Jan's quick and skillful performance on video. We arrived at the yards and held them for an hour—educating them. Then it was time to yard up.

As we pushed the mob, beasts tried to break out. We worked hard to turn them back to the mob. One huge, horned bullock, which would have tipped the scales at nearly a ton, bolted from the mob along with a mickey bull. The bullock had an intimidating horn span of four feet, one of the largest set of horns I'd seen at the station. Bullocks' horns grew differently from all the other cattle. A cow's horns typically curved, turning back toward the animal's body. A bullock's head trophy grew long, straight and sometimes curved up slightly on the end. The unique growth of their horns made them more dangerous than any other animal on the station. All the buggies were on the opposite side.

There was no help in sight; it was up to Maggot and me. We took off after the bullock. I raced up to the beast and galloped along his right side like we were in the final turn of the Indianapolis 500. Synchronized to the animal's gait, the parallel position was critical to prevent the animal from skirting behind or in front of me. I remained two feet from his side, aware that at any second, if he bolted to the right, his horn could hook into my leg or Maggot's stomach. My legs trembled, my hands quivered, my heart pumped like a steam engine. I'm not sure if it was excitement or fright, but it was one hell of an adrenaline rush. Blown off during the chase, my hat hung around my neck, the string choking me. My mouth was dry from dust. I didn't get paid enough for that dangerous shit, but for some reason Lee and I couldn't get enough.

My effort paid off and the bullock turned back to the mob. I immediately put my attention on the mickey bull, cutting him off and pushing him back with the rest. I had a real sense of accomplishment and a real sense of *Thank God, that bullock didn't take me out!* Barney gave me an astonished look. I guessed he didn't quite believe the action he had witnessed. His boggled stare reaffirmed my mustering talents. He nodded as if saying, "Wow, that was all right, Becky, good on ya."

We continued to push as cattle rounded the outside of the yards toward the gate. We hoped they would all walk calmly through the gate, but that day nothing went according to plan. Suddenly, a couple three-quarter-ton bulls made a break for it. As they escaped, cows and calves tried to join them. It was chaos—beasts ran wildly, dust was blinding and bull buggy drivers and horsemen were in pandemonium. My mouth was not just dry from dust anymore, but particles of dirt crunched in my mouth as I gasped for every breath. I choked for air, but continued to cut off escaping beasts. I had one thing on my mind: save the mob.

It was a race against time, a race against numbers and a race against the circus of fleeing animals. It looked like they'd beaten us. Butch swooped here and there, stopping the unruly beasts in their tracks only for them to dart off in another direction. I looked across the flat, barely focusing through the brown haze of dust stirred up by thundering hooves—it was bulldust at its finest. Lee closed in on a bull, bumping it—the bull tumbled. Lee's buggy tipped on two wheels. Through the screen of dust it looked like Lee's buggy continued to tumble over.

My heart sank below my stirrups. *Oh God, Lee flipped, he's not wearing his seat belt!* I was sickened with fear. *Was he hurt? Was he dead?* The dust settled. Lee was upright. The heavy anchor that weighed down my heart lifted. We gained control of the mob again, at least most of the mob.

Amazingly, only seven animals had gotten away. It was an exciting ten minutes of action.

"That was big fun," Geoff said as we loaded the horses. I'm not sure if it was big fun, but I was glad no one was hurt. While the gang processed the defiant group, I flew to Mininer with Butch to help muster. The Harveys rarely asked for help and almost never needed help, but they needed another bull buggy driver for a big muster. Everyone nominated me since Jack liked me so much. I thought Lee should have gone; he was the one with bull buggy experience. I'd never driven a bull buggy, but it was just racing a four-wheel drive around the flat like a lunatic—or at least that's what I thought. We landed at one of the outer cattle yards and I greeted Jack with a big hug and kiss.

"You just can't stay away—a good thing your husband doesn't get jealous," the rugged, but sweet, bushman said.

"I know," I agreed with a giggle. "I flew off with one man to see another."

Jack and Wendy got me set up in my big white beat-up bull buggy. I was nervous—nervous about the muster, nervous about stuffing up the bull buggy and nervous about letting Jack down. I was nearly in a panic about a possible flat tire. I'd helped change a few in my life, but never ever had a flat tire while I was by myself. I didn't want to tell anyone that I'd never changed a flat tire—I was too embarrassed. They might think I was a real idiot.

In the first 20 minutes I managed to get bogged in sand. *Oh shit, this isn't going to be my lucky day, I just know it,* I thought. Wendy helped me let air out of all the tires and she used a shovel to dig me out. We got the ute out and Wendy offered to switch vehicles. Her buggy was smaller, lightweight and easier for me to drive. We arrived at a windmill where Wendy and I held the mob. A few times I couldn't get the bull buggy in reverse fast enough and almost lost several animals. Lee often joked that I had a five-speed car at home and still didn't know how to drive a stick shift. I guess there was a good reason Dad never allowed me to drive The Farm's truck. I just sometimes had problems with my gears.

During that full day of mustering in a ute, I developed a new appreciation for bull buggy drivers. It was a lot harder than it looked. Deciding where to drive and where not to drive, cutting off cattle without crashing into trees, and conquering the technique of reverse at high speeds was difficult. An hour and a half into the muster Butch radioed that something was wrong with the helicopter and he couldn't finish the muster. It was only 8:30 a.m. We had already gathered 300 Red Devons and without Butch we faced a great challenge getting them back to the cattle yards. We moved the cattle up a fence row. Jack was up front on the left point, Wendy was on the left side and I brought up the tail.

"Wendy, I think the ute is getting hot," I radioed. "The temperature gauge is up."

"Stop and turn off the engine," she said. "Pour water over the radiator."

I used to do a lot of things growing up on The Farm, but mechanics was not my forte—I was usually with the animals. "What the hell does the radiator look like?" I said aloud, as if some little fairy would appear and direct me to it.

I never cared what was under a car's bonnet. I succumbed to my mechanic ignorance and called Wendy on the radio. "Wendy, I'm not real familiar with engines," I explained, no doubt sounding pathetic. "Could you please tell me what the radiator looks like or where it is located?"

"Becky, it's the black thing on the left with yellow caps," Wendy instructed. "Use a jug of your drinking water."

I found the radiator, I thought, and poured water over it hoping it cooled the engine. I sat there waiting for the temperature gauge to go down and laughed as I thought to myself, *What is Lee going to say? What is Dad going to say? I couldn't believe I didn't know where the radiator was located.*

Cooled and ready to go, I fired up the motor and caught up to the mob in minutes. Wendy had to navigate heavy bush on the side and we switched vehicles again so her smaller, more agile vehicle could maneuver better through the difficult scrub. I putted along in my big white ute and leaned high and forward in the seat to make sure I didn't run over the baby calves that lagged in the back. I felt confident, even arrogant. I was a big shit mustering at Mininer Station. Then it happened—my worst fear of the day materialized: I had a flat tire. Wendy and Jack were going to find out what a block-head I really was if I couldn't change my tire.

"Wendy, I have a flat tire so I'll catch up as soon as I change it," I radioed, thinking I'd probably catch up to them in two or so days after I figured it out.

"I'll come over and give you a hand," Wendy said.

It was a blessing to my ears. "Oh yes, there is a God!" I yelled into the air.

Wendy pumped the jack, screwed off the lug nuts, jerked off the tire and in minutes had a replacement tire on. From what I'd heard about Wendy, she was an amazing bush woman, right up there with Jan and Mandy. Wendy did the station's electrical repairs, welding, fencing, mechanic main-tenance and cattle work—you name it, she did it. She wasn't just tough, she had a warm side, full of fun and flair. She loved reading, gardening and painted wildflower portraits.

I took my position behind the wheel and turned the key. Nothing happened, my ute was dead. I jumped in with Wendy on the passenger side. For five minutes we pushed cattle until Wendy asked, "Would you mind walking behind the cattle to bring up the tail?"

"No, I don't mind," I cheerfully said. What was I think-ing? It was hot, and dusty and I was on foot. Thank goodness I had a bandana over my nose and mouth to filter the dirt I couldn't help but suck in. I hadn't worn my bush hat be-cause I thought I'd be driving all day. My baseball cap shielded some of the sun's harmful rays, but they beat down on my back. I often ran at the cattle, yelling, throwing my arms in ridiculous antics to turn beasts back into the group and speed their pace. When we got them back to the homestead I was covered in a film of dirt. We had hot tea and homemade choco-late chip cookies while we waited for an engineer to fly in from Broome to fix the helicopter. The phone rang. The pilot had gotten lost and he'd be at Mininer at first light.

A sand trap, an overheated radiator, a flat tire, a dead truck, and getting stranded all in one day—wow! Dorris and Wendy fixed me up with a new toothbrush and clothes to borrow. Dorris gave me a brand-new pair of knickers, white with delicate lavender flowers. Very pretty, except they were granny panties, ones like my mom wore. I couldn't be picky— it wasn't like I could slip in to town. Dorris prepared a single cot in their library. The Harveys' extensive library was a magical collection of hundreds of books and videos. With all the literary works they owned, they never missed not having a TV or radio.

Dorris spent her days inside except for short stints outside to water the garden and to feed the poddy calves orphaned by their mothers. Poddy derived from the calves' pod-like bellies after they've drunk their milk. My first impression of Dorris was that she was domineering. I discovered one-on-one that Dorris was a soft, kindhearted woman longing for outside communication. I enjoyed chatting with her and shared stories and even station gossip. She corresponded with 150 pen pals from 25 nations. She had a pen pal in New Zealand she'd met for the first time when Dorris was her wedding attendant. They still wrote to each other, but hadn't seen each other since the nuptials more than two decades earlier.

Initially, I was scared by stories that exceeded Jack's reputation. He quickly won me over with his natural charm. Bush life had taken its toll on Jack. His wrinkled skin was testament of his days building, developing and running Mininer Station. His funny stories sometimes had us in tears. Jack was passionate about reading, loved poetry and was happy to discuss his favorite books. He provided more history for me about Ashburton, more than I'd even read in history books. Jack's biggest love was his Red Devon cattle. It was not a breed of choice in the Pilbara, but that hadn't stopped Jack from pursuing his dream. He had bred and developed a quality herd of the dark roan-colored cattle.

"Becky, every year I wonder if I'm going to make it an-other year mustering, but I reckon every year is a bonus," he said. "I'm the last living old-timer."

Jack Harvey was truly a legend in his own time—I'd truly miss him. Dorris fixed us cold baked bean and butter sand-wiches for lunch. It looked odd, but it was very tasty—a new sandwich idea I'd take back to America. As I enjoyed Dorris's famous cookies, one of the cats ran into the kitchen. It had an unusual-looking mouse clamped in its jaws. It looked like a kangaroo mouse, that's if kangaroo mice existed. It had big rabbit-like floppy ears on its tiny body and a long pointy tail. It was a bilby, a rodent-sized marsupial. Although they are protected, there was no getting the bilby away from the clutches of Jack's favorite kitty. Australia has to have some of the most interesting creatures, I knew it had some of the most dangerous.

Wendy, Jack and Dorris waved bye to me as the repaired helicopter stirred up mounds of dirt on takeoff. Back at Ashburton, plans were under way for another big muster the following morning. I was exhausted. I wanted a day off, *needed* a day off, but that wasn't in the cards. I pushed myself like the others did. We got up at 4 a.m., made lunch, loaded horses and drove out to Cairn Hill.

"Lee, how exactly do you tie up bulls?" Jan asked.

"Like this," Lee answered, taking Jan's hands and throw-ing a rope around her wrists.

The two were like little kids on a playground. Jan had been so stressed, it was good to see her laugh. It was thera-peutic for all of us. As Dad always said, "When Momma ain't happy, ain't nobody happy."

The bulls were unusually disruptive that day. Lee ended up rolling and tying up five bulls. He was really proud of himself and so was I. The outback cowboy chased one bull through a riverbed and his bull buggy got bogged sideways in the sandy bank. The bull stopped, looked at Lee and de-cided to give him a little nudge of revenge. He tipped Lee's buggy right on its side.

"I wasn't worried about the bull tipping me over. I was worried about all of Becky's gear falling on me and crushing me to death," he told everyone later.

He always complained about the stuff I made him carry during musters. I couldn't carry it on my horse so Lee had to pack it in his buggy. Lee hauled my camera gear, water bottles, jacket, treats and extra toilet paper—there was no time to drip dry.

As we moved cattle toward the Cairn Hill yards, they rushed. Sod flipped in the air as animals sprinted to freedom. Butch attempted to cut them off with his fancy flying aerobatics. Mick and Andrew were like cow rustlers in the wild West determined to stop the stampede. Nomad fell in a hole and toppled over on Andrew's leg. Horse and rider were fine, but the fall cracked the tree of Andrew's brand-new saddle. The accident was a reminder of how dangerous mustering was and how quickly something could happen. Andrew's leg or Nomad's leg easily could have snapped.

We lost about 30 head, but the other 400 were yarded up with no problems. On the drive home, the sun was setting. Tints of blush pink, baby blue and pearl cream stained the early evening sky. The dramatic sunset was heightened by the contrast of sherbet and fire-orange finger-like rays extending down to the horizon, like a meteor exploding through the earth's atmosphere. I relaxed back in my seat, wonderfully intoxicated by God's creation. My body seemed to float from the buggy as I thought, *This is breathtaking, peaceful. What a way to top off a great mustering day! We're so blessed to be here.*

My out-of-body experience and outback high were short-lived. At the house we got serious news from home. My sister, Patty, had had a bad seizure at the Frederick County Fair. She lay in an aisle on the cement floor of the fair's cattle barn fighting for her life. She went into shock, was blinded. The paramedics couldn't find a pulse. Finally, they found a faint one as she struggled for every breath. The ambulance crew stabilized her and rushed her to the hospital. Patty had one or two attacks a year, but they were getting worse. It was the first attack since we had left on the trip. For more than a decade she'd battled a condition that specialists could not diagnose. Even during her five-day stay at John Hopkins University Hospital physicians couldn't pinpoint the problem. Patty lived in constant fear of when another attack might occur, what might bring it on. It broke my heart, but how could I help her if the experts couldn't help?

I got more unsettling news. The same week of Patty's attack, one of my best friends was diagnosed with cervical cancer. Sally had an emergency hysterectomy and had to undergo radiation and chemotherapy. Sally was voted best all-around in high school. Her grounded, jovial and friendly personality drew people to her. Why did God pick her? Question after question garbled my mind. I didn't want to believe the news. She was a devout Christian, loyal wife and dedicated mother of three. It didn't seem fair.

On my next trip to town I mailed Sally a card. I didn't know what to write. I felt guilty. I was in Australia having the time of my life and Sally was fighting for hers. I had to get over the guilt and send words of love and encouragement. Sally was one of the strongest people I knew and if anyone could beat cancer I knew she could. I promised in my letter to be at her disposal when I returned in December. It made me think how Lee and I had unwittingly taken friends for granted over the years because our jobs took priority. I wanted to rectify that and prayed God would give me the chance. Sally and Patty were at the top of my prayer list—they just had to get better.

The year away from family and friends was not easy. Ironically, the separation was a blessing. It made us realize the importance of loved ones. The transformation started about halfway through the trip when e-mails, letters and occasional phone calls ended with, "We love you and miss you"— words often neglected. I monitored e-mail transmissions, answering the more than 1,000 we received. Lee's responsibility was snail mail. He wrote letters to parents and siblings. His notes had me nearly doubled over with laughter so

I guessed the recipients enjoyed them too. Here are some excerpts from Lee's letters to my parents;

Dear Mom and Pap Long,

>*It seems hard to believe that we have been gone for six months, time has really passed quickly. I find myself constantly thinking about things at home that have happened at different times in my life and I never seem to think of bad times, only good. So I guess our memories are what we make them.*
>*Becky and I love you both and can't wait to see you.*

• • •

>*I thought if I got Becky away for a while she would relax and not have too many projects. I was wrong, wrong, wrong.... She now has projects spanning the globe: Ashburton Downs social director, Paraburdoo project planner, tour guide, art agent and freelance writer/photographer for no less than four publications through the U.S.A., New Zealand and Australia. If she keeps up at this rate I will be able to take early retirement!*

• • •

>*Becky and I have less than two months left on our trip so this may or may not be the last letter I write. Anyway, we have been very busy mustering and shipping cattle out. I don't think that we have covered half of the property yet and the weather is starting to turn hotter.*

• • •

>*Jack from Mininer Station next door has grown very fond of Becky, but at 71 years of age his wife said he is harmless. Becky has made a lasting impression on everyone in Paraburdoo and my claim to*

fame once again is that I am Becky America's husband! Oh well, I suppose she is likable enough and I think I'll keep her.

You have seen Becky handle a group of unruly kids so all you have to do is imagine her on a horse being very authoritative and loud, loud, loud! That is Becky mustering cattle!

As for me I am doing a little of this and a little of that...driving road trains, fixing tires, welding, mustering, windmill work. On our last muster I rolled three bulls and strapped them. One of the bulls thought it looked like fun and rolled my Suzuki buggy. After I put her back on her wheels we got even! That same bull took me almost an hour to find the next day. He was close to where I left him but it's a big country and he was in some heavy scrub. We also got three flat tires getting him out—all in a day's work.

Enjoy the pictures and say hello to everyone.

Love, Lee & Becky

Kindergarten Breakout

Maggot had the day off and I saddled Kate. We were moving 300 cows and calves from the yards to the two-mile bore. The mob moved quietly along the fence row. Andrew was in the lead, Geoff had the right point, Jan was in her bull buggy and Becky, Toni and I brought up the rear. Twenty-seven baby calves dawdled at the back. We considered leaving them to fend for themselves, but knew they couldn't survive without their mommas, who at that point were way ahead and didn't give a hoot where their babies were.

The calves tired, moving even slower, often stopping to duck under a bush for shade. One calf was blind. We yelled at it and pushed it forward with our horses' chests. I felt sorry for the sightless animal and wanted to carry it on my horse, but that would have been another drama. An hour passed and we struggled to keep the baby beasts walking. They had been confined in the cattle yards sucking in dirt, blinded by dust, and, no doubt, traumatized by being dehorned, ear tagged, earmarked and castrated. It was midmorning. The sun sizzled their delicate hides and soft pink noses. They panted trying to keep up to the mob.

It seemed cruel to demand such an effort from one- to five-week-old calves, but I knew the water trough was only a quarter of a mile away, they could make it. Geoff galloped toward the back of the mob and motioned for me. I thought he wanted me to take over the right point position. "Becky, there's something I think you'd like to see," he smiled. "You won't see it in America."

I followed him, knowing Becky and Toni would be fine to cover the tail during my short break. I glanced back and Toni tagged behind me. No big deal, the calves plodded along and would be no problem for Becky.

Geoff pointed near a bush. My eyes widened, my dimples creased with excitement. It was an impressive six-foot-long bungarra showing off its yellow, copper and jade square-patterned skin that was accented by stripes down its back. It placed its web-like clawed feet gently on the ground and seemed to move in slow motion. It shuffled along, dragging its enormous tail and scanned the ground with its forked tongue. Bungarras rarely attacked and usually only did so if threatened. They fed on carcasses. If a station dog or person was bitten, bacterial infection was high.

The horses remained calm. I was entranced with the movement of the outback reptile. Geoff returned to the right point. Jan drove over to shoot some photos. Suddenly some commotion pulled our eyes off the bungarra back to the rear of the mob. Some of the sluggish baby calves had gotten a surge of energy and were trying to escape. Becky Kimberley cut them off. Toni went to help. They were just babies; the girls didn't need me yet. I was still engrossed with the bungarra. A minute later the little shits bolted again. I galloped back to the rear to help the girls gather the escapees. Then suddenly the calves erupted with spunk like a bell had just signaled recess.

A kindergarten breakout! A dozen calves determined to play tag with each other and the horsemen, and the calves definitely outwitted us. I never knew calves could run so damned fast. I wore shorts that day for the first time, but it was the last time I ever made that mistake. The faster we chased the calves the faster they ran, darting through the scrub much easier than we could. As soon as I thought I had one, the four-legged fugitive shot like a missile in the opposite direction. More daring runaways joined in the ridiculous game. I had chased and been charged by wild bulls and feral cows, but it didn't compare to the frustration those calves created.

I kicked Kate into high gear, racing between bushes and branches that scraped and cut into my bare skin. I was determined to stop those stupid calves. Jan joined in the chase, but even in her buggy, the attempt was futile. Finally, some of the calves had been retrieved. Jan and the girls returned to the main mob. There were still ten calves on the run that I refused to lose. I was a conditioned jillaroo—a bunch of snot-nosed baby calves weren't about to make me look like a rookie.

I chased, turned, backtracked and chased some more. I made it back, back to the cattle yards that is. I couldn't believe it. I sat there on Kate and laughed uncontrollably. Trails of cuts, scrapes and blood marked my legs and arms. I had just shaved my legs the night before for the first time in five months. Yes, Lee was rather frightened at times by my furry limbs, but it had been too cold during the winter months to take time to shave my legs in the open-air shower. There was no one I needed to impress. Lee loved me, hairy legs and all. It was just my luck that once my legs were shaved and presentable that they looked like they'd been in a battle with barbed-wire fence.

Mick, Lee and Barney were processing bulls in the yards. Mick noticed me standing by the gate on Kate surrounded by ten panting baby calves. He walked over to inquire. "Can you explain this?"

"Well, Mick, see, these really mean bulls, they made a break for it and bolted from the mob," I said, hardly able to talk through my laughter.

He knew I had made the story up because there were no bulls in the mob. I confessed about the bungarra and he helped me push the calves into the yards. I headed back to the mob. I didn't care if Andrew or anyone else was mad. The episode was too funny not to enjoy and I continued to laugh as Kate and I walked down the track. Jan drove her buggy back. I composed myself, not knowing how mad she might be by the whole upset. As soon as I could focus on her face I saw her huge smile. We laughed again until we cried.

"Glad you're all right," Jan said. "The last time I saw you, you were flat-out like a dog on a bone."

"Ten calves are back in the yards," I said.

"I told the girls to tell Andrew that the bungarra ran right through the middle of the mob and caused the calves to bolt," Jan said hoping the story sufficed. I agreed to the little fib, not knowing Geoff had already told Andrew what really happened.

"You and I are to load the calves on the horse float and take them out to the two-mile," she added. "The rest of the crew is holding the mob until we return."

Lee hooked up the horse float and helped us load. He caught three baby calves and pushed them onto the float. Jan watched the ramp. One calf got back out. I got inside the float to hold them as Lee continued to pitch them on board. Sweat ran down his face. The calves continued to escape and continued to piss him off. All Jan and I could do was laugh. I drove the float out to the two-mile. We unloaded by the watering trough facing the mob so the calves would search for their mommas.

The kindergarten breakout was the beginning of an eventful day. Mick shot a king western brown in the shed. It still wasn't the eight footer we had all seen slithering around the homestead. I prayed I'd never encounter it.

• • •

We were caught up on mustering for a few days and Lee and I flew to Perth for the Royal Agricultural Show. We were supposed to take care of the Blackburns' show cattle, but they didn't go. Ray was recovering from knee surgery and Mikey and Josette had just welcomed baby Tullia into the world.

We arrived at the show at 3 p.m. We found the Blackburns' locker they had reserved for show tack and feed. It would be our tiny living quarters at the show. Mikey told us to find Leon Giglia if we had any questions. We threw our gear in the locker and strolled up the aisle between two rows of Holstein cattle. We saw the Giglia sign and noticed a man clipping a cow.

"Hi, I'm Lee Chaney and this is my wife, Becky. We're mates of Michael Blackburn."

"Blackburn—well, any mates of Blackburn's ought to be all right. I'm Leon Giglia."

"How many head do you have in the show string?" I asked.

"Twenty-seven," he said.

"We're here at the show through Sunday and we're staying in the number two locker of the Blackburns," Lee said. "We'd be happy to give you a hand if you need it."

"Do you know how to clip?" Leon asked.

"No, I have mates at home that do that," Lee said.

Leon managed the Herd Improvement Society of Western Australia (HISWA), a dairy cattle company that provided milk testing and semen. He also owned his own cattle and kept them at his Uncle Lou Giglia's farm. We met Leon's wife, Kerry, and their two kids, Ashleigh, 13, and Michael, 11. The first afternoon Lee and I walked around the showgrounds, knowing we wouldn't have time later. We returned to the barns at 7 p.m. and everyone was gathered near the center area of the livestock barns. We investigated. Every year at the show, beef and dairy exhibitors joined forces on Thursday night for a fun and friendly competition.

The theme was the Olympics in tribute of the Games that had just concluded in Sydney. Events included synchronized dirty wheelbarrow dancing, couples' cross-country riding obstacle course, the shit-put throw and the dinkydoodle dash. Lou Giglia, who was also the show's president, took top honors in the wheelbarrow contest with his suggestive gestures to music. In the shit-put competition, reserve champion cattle exhibitors had the chance to fling cow dung at the grand champion exhibitors.

Four married men hoisted their wives on their backs to navigate an obstacle course in front of the 100-plus spectators. They stumbled over buckets of water, tripped over a row of plants, and one husband nearly lost his wife over the hay jump. Capping off the evening was the dinky-doodle dash—the most shocking race of the evening. Four selected male exhibitors donned vegetables shaped like their genitals. The blokes ran the length of the barns barefooted with their tubers and "company" dangling wildly. It was all good fun, but under no circumstance would the event be allowed at a livestock show in the States; Americans are way too uptight. We could take some lessons from the Aussies on relaxing, kicking back and having a good time once in a while. The fun Olympics gave exhibitors a chance to forget about the real competition in the showring and provided much entertainment.

Lee got up early Friday morning and helped Leon with the cows. I wandered out about 7 a.m. The Giglias had the grand champion Holstein and the supreme champion. There were extra helpers show day. We met Ian, who also worked for HISWA, and his daughter, Tanya. Rebecca, Lou's daughter, had flown in from London. It was a real family affair.

Down south at Perth it was still cold, not like the recent heat wave that had hit Ashburton. Lee and I cuddled close in our single swag on the cement floor, but by morning I had unknowingly nudged poor Lee out.

Mandy was at the show. She had recently been elected as a director of the Australian Stock Horse Society. Lee joined her in the arena on Saturday morning to set up for the campdrafting competition. Campdrafting fascinated me. A horse and rider demonstrated their mustering skills by running a beast around a sequence of three trees in a triangle formation and across a finish line. It was similar to the American version of barrel racing, except an animal had to be herded around the formation as well. That afternoon was the grand parade, the largest exhibit of champion species at one time in the world.

"Would you like to lead one of the Holsteins?" Ian asked.

"Sure, I'd love to," I said.

I had no idea he'd give me the supreme champion cow. Winners in America got small ribbons and occasionally champion blankets. In Australia, they decorated the animals with long sashes tied around their girths and necks; my cow sported four. She was restless and I thought I'd have to ask for Lee's help before she dragged me across the arena and provided some surprise entertainment for the crowd. She was headstrong and shoved and pushed me. After one walk around the arena she calmed down. When we got around to the grandstand area, Leon was decked out in a suit as the show's chancellor, greeting exhibitors as they passed with their prize winners. He looked at me as though he had known me for ages.

"Becky," he said as he walked over and gave me the traditional Italian greeting—a kiss on both cheeks. He was handsome and his Italian flirtation always came out. Leon was a social butterfly, much like me. Cattle were released and most exhibitors packed up and left Saturday night. Leon found us a vacant exhibitor's unit. The small units only had bunk beds, but that was better than the cold cement floor. We spent the evening with the Giglias down Sideshow Alley, the equivalent of a U.S. fair midway. Since Leon was a board member, he had free dinner tickets and free ride tickets. We got on the Hurricane and another twisting, turning, high-speed ride that nearly made me lose dinner.

"I had forgotten how much I like rides," Lee said. "I haven't been on rides for fifteen years."

Lee got on a swift three-story ride with Ashleigh and Michael, while Kerry, Leon and I laughed at their mischief in the air.

"Ya know, Lee is like a big kid," Leon said.

"Yeah, I know," I agreed.

"Michael thinks Lee is a legend," Leon added.

"What do you mean?" I asked.

"Earlier today Michael said, 'Ya know, Dad, Lee is a bulldogger from a station in the outback. He's a real American cowboy,'" Leon told me.

"Lee's going to love to hear that story," I said.

After rattling our bones in the bumper cars, we said our good-byes. We showered and packed our gear for our trip back to Ashburton.

The next morning we walked to the closest train stop. The train dropped us in Perth's city center and we caught a bus to the airport. Our flight back to Paraburdoo was on time and we were eager to return to Ashburton. Becky Kimberley picked us up.

We had received a package from Patty, containing several items I had requested. The outside of the box said it had been opened by Customs. The letter inside said, "Due to Australian tobacco regulations the six tins of oral snuff have been confiscated." Lee had gone the first eight months without a "chew," then Patty surprised him with a couple tins. She tried to surprise him again, but Customs ruined it. The idea Customs took $25 worth of Copenhagen really ticked Lee off.

Most of his disappointment didn't stem from the fact he had missed out on some chew, but rather that we were scheduled to leave Ashburton in ten days. We weren't ready to leave and the Glenns weren't ready for us to leave. It was a dismal subject around the station. We were part of the team, part of the family. It didn't seem right to leave before mustering season was finished. We didn't have a choice. Lee had committed to milk cows for Ray Blackburn while he judged a cattle show in New Zealand and attended an ag show in Canada. We adored the Blackburns and knew it would be a good time. It would be back to civilization, 24-hour power, indoor plumbing and a store two miles away. We should have been elated about the move, but we were sad—Ashburton for a time had become our life.

It was hard to fathom, really. Our initial employment at Ashburton was for three weeks. We were asked to stay on and were nearing our eighth month at the station. Our last week and a half would be some of the most heart-pounding days at Ashburton.

Lee scribbled his last letter home;

Dear Mom,

It was good to hear your voice on the phone today. Being so far away from friends and family I now realize how much I really missed out on when it was all right there.

The time that Becky and I have been able to spend together over here cannot be replaced by, or compared to, anything and although we haven't always agreed, we have learned how to tackle just about anything together. I have been given the best family in the world—from the wife who put her plans on hold just because I wanted to go to Australia, to the family at home who puts a smile on my face every time I see a picture, hear a voice or read a letter. Most of all I am lucky to have you to let me make my own way and mistakes, accepting me for nothing more, or less, than your son.

This trip has taught me that you are more likely to regret not doing something than you are doing something no matter what the outcome may be. I'm sorry I couldn't tell you all of this on the phone but I always seem to stumble over the words before I can get them out so I hope this letter makes some sense and brings a smile to your face.

Much love,

Lee

31

A Tearful Farewell

D uring our final days at the station I daydreamed about Jan's many stories and recounted both her wise and witty statements. She often said it took unique people to live in the outback. I wholeheartedly agreed. It wasn't easy for a visitor, let alone someone spending their entire life in the bush.

"You really have to love the outback," Jan said. "There's no glory in living in isolation."

"Isn't it exciting when you sell a big load of cattle?" I asked.

"When the cattle are shipped out sometimes it's sad because I get to know some of the cattle. The biggest thrill is when the cattle leave the yards behind a lead horse with a horseman following up the rear and the mob is moving real slow and quiet. That's exciting."

Jan had endured so many trials and tribulations over the years that she had to love the outback in order to continue living in it. I guess she and Andrew were like my folks— no matter how rocky the boat got, they kept sailing. I believed it had something to do with an inborn obsession for agriculture, a respect for the land and a compassion for livestock— all things my parents had ingrained into my being. It had only strengthened during our stint at Ashburton.

Lee and Barney carted beasts all day back out to Cairn Hill. Lee was going to miss driving the road train. I told him he should think about getting his class-A license if he liked big trucks so much. One thing I definitely was not going to miss was centipedes. I had a visitor in the shower that day and it wasn't Lee. My hair was full of suds, but I constantly cleared my eyes to scan the floor. Snakes, spiders, centipedes—I had to be prepared for anything. A five-inch centipede almost crawled over my bare foot and disappeared beneath the wall. I quickly rinsed my hair, having an eerie feeling I couldn't shake. The centipede came back under the panel and was headed right for my feet again. I grabbed my shampoo bottle in one hand and my conditioner bottle in the other. I attacked it with both bottles, not sure where its stinger was. I dismembered it. Lee said he had killed a six-inch centipede in the dunny that morning and earlier in the week he had found a two-inch centipede on our bed. They were everywhere!

Wendy called from Mininer. A bushfire was threatening their station. The fire was only 70 miles from Mininer and they were worried that if the wind picked up, the fire could be at Mininer in hours. To reduce burn risk, Wendy picked up everything at the station that was a potential fire hazard. The bushfire was in the hills near Turee Creek Station and two and a half miles east of Windall Gap. The blokes at Turee Creek were working on a firebreak. The fire also posed danger to Ashburton. Our scheduled muster at Hay Stack was canceled.

"If the wind direction changes and the fire hits the river, it could rip right through where we would be mustering and trap us all," Andrew said.

Although I was excited about the Hay Stack muster, I had no aspirations of dying in a bushfire. We anxiously waited for a call from the Harveys summoning our aid. If the bushfire neared Mininer, we were all prepared to go build firebreaks and help the Harveys save their homestead. Fire really scared me, but I thought the world of the Harveys and would do anything to help them, just as I knew they'd do anything to help the Glenns.

A Tearful Farewell

I felt tension build in my body; my stomach was queasy. It was excitement mixed with fear. I envisioned the bushfire eerily crawling along the flat, burning everything in its path. We had heard many heroic stories of bush folk saving their stations, as well as the tragic tales of millions of acres lost and thousands of cattle killed by the flames and heat. Even with the bushfire a considerable distance, smoke darkened the sky to a screen of gray. The bushfire was spreading, a dull stench was in the air. The Harveys called back with news that the fire was contained. The second firebreak had worked, but Turee Creek was destroyed. They did, however, save their homestead. My God, I thought. *How do these people cope?* If it wasn't the floods, it was the heat, and if it wasn't the deadly creatures it was bushfires, drought or low market prices.

Andrew confirmed our muster for the next day, well, actually in five hours. Our battery-operated alarm clock rang at 3 a.m. I dragged myself from beneath my covers and dressed. I always prepared my mustering garb the night before. Bush hat—check. Gloves—check. Bandana—check. Long-sleeved shirt—check. Jeans—check. Riding boots—check. Fanny pack filled with toilet paper, camera, painkillers, gum and Chap Stick—check. And last but not least I covered my face in Mary Kay's Day Radiance to protect it from wind and sunburn. In the house I made 25 sandwiches, two for everyone in the crew, plus a few extras. Our new pilot was Donald. He was 42, tall and polite. He sported shorts and a shirt with cutoff sleeves. He crunched down in the helicopter seat and flew to the Hay Stack yards.

It was a two-hour drive by car and we arrived at 6 a.m. Andrew spit the dummy because most of the crew forgot to grab their radios. It was the first time I'd seen Andrew lose his temper. He accused the crew of not being responsible. His wrath didn't faze me; I had picked up *my* radio. Part of me thought Andrew's outrage was justified; part of me thought it was uncalled for. The radios could have been one responsibility for Andrew. We all had our separate jobs before musters. Tricky and Lee did bull buggy maintenance, Toni, Becky, Mick and Barney caught horses and fed them. Geoff took care of the young steeds. Jan and I prepared all the eskies with sandwiches, snacks, fruit and filled water jugs and thermoses. We all took turns loading the horse gear and loading the horses. What was Andrew's job? Nothing, but I guess that's the benefit of being the boss. It didn't seem fair when Jan busted her butt preparing for a muster and Andrew did very little.

We rode out of camp toward the mountain top Andrew had pointed out. But once again that was the only instruction we had. We weren't advised what to do once we got to the mountain or what direction we would be moving cattle. It was a situation the entire crew had to accept and just do the best we could. Toni and I ended up in an area with lots of cattle, but had no idea where we were. "What direction are we pushing them?" I asked anyone who was listening on the radio.

"Toward the windmill," Donald answered from the air.

Well, that's just dandy—if I knew where in the hell the windmill was! I thought. Windmills were relatively tall and as far as I could see in any direction, there was no bloody windmill. "Could you give me a direction?" I asked.

"I can't until I know where you are," Donald responded.

"Yes, you can—just tell me north, south, east or west. I can figure it out by my watch," I said in an irksome tone. Mick had shown us how to figure out direction by using the sun and the 12 hand on our watches in case we were ever lost.

"Northeast," Donald finally said.

Toni and I had the bizarre feeling we were in the wrong place and galloped toward the chopper to a faraway ridge in hopes of finding more horsemen. We made it to the ridge and waited 20 feet apart. I asked, "Toni could you please come over and take my picture?"

"Come over here and I'll take it here," she replied.

"But I want the landscape directly behind me," I said. "Why don't you want to come over here?"

"I just can't be fucked," she said.

It was the same immature and raw remark she often used that reflected her lazy personality. I held my tongue and thought I'd try to kill her with kindness. "This is my last muster and I won't bother you again. Please take my photo over here on Maggot?" I begged. She reluctantly toddled over on her horse and snapped my photo. Just when I'd start forming a better opinion of Toni, she said or did something so shocking I was zapped back to the reality of her inconsiderate nature.

We still had no idea what was happening and no one had called for us. We continued toward the chopper and finally found the coach mob. In the first five minutes it was nonstop action, chasing beasts bolting for the scrub. The tail bolted but Maggot's quick response had them turned back toward the mob in seconds.

I only lost one and Lee turned her with his bull buggy. She bolted again and I went after her. She was a dark burgundy heifer, about a year old with a serious set of horns and an attitude to match. She charged me several times, and several times I just barely escaped the points of her sharp weapons. I'd become very bold in the past seven and a half months, but not bold enough to take on a head rack like that and certainly not bold enough to risk my life over one heifer. Even my attempts to bluff her failed. Lee, my hero, came to the rescue once again.

About 600 head had been gathered and we moved them around the ridge. A mickey bull bolted over the rocky hill and I took off. It was a hillside blanketed with small smooth rocks. Sparks flew when Maggot's steel shoes slipped on the rocks as I galloped him over the difficult terrain. I ran shoulder to shoulder with the beast, leaning Maggot in to him to turn him back toward the mob. At that stage, one thought entered my mind, *It's my last muster and we leave in five days. If Maggot slips on the rocks he'll most likely fall on me, break my leg, and the Royal Flying Doctor Service will have to come.*

Jan watched me and said later she'd had the same vision. But her image was that I'd be hurt so badly, I'd have to recover at Ashburton. The bull stubbornly pushed farther over the rocky ridge; Maggot skidded on the rocks as we tried to turn him. We retreated. It was one of the only beasts I'd given up on all season, but Maggot's safety was more important to me—and honestly, my safety was too.

Andrew had me on the right point and we continued to gather cattle. We estimated the mob at between 1,200 and 1,500 head. It was huge. Maggot trampled over tangled wire on the ground, but maintained his cool. The riverbank crossing was so steep it was difficult to find a safe place for animals, horsemen and buggies to cross. Lee's buggy tipped to the side and nearly rolled down the bank. Jan's buggy had to be pulled out. Once across the dried riverbed, Andrew pursued a smaller group of cattle, hoping to add them to the already massive mob. When he left the lead, eight beasts dashed for freedom. They were on the right side where Toni had the point position. She took off after them and then suddenly stopped.

What was she doing? I assumed that since no one told her to bring them back, she was going to let them escape. I had a head on my shoulders and could make my own decisions. I knew if that group got away, it would influence others to do the same. We had a large mob and couldn't risk it. My heels just nudged Maggot's sides and he took off like someone had dropped the green race flag. We ran through the scrub, leaving a trail of dust and broken debris. Dried spinifex and buffel grass crushed beneath Maggot's powerful strides. We got in front of the cattle and turned them back to the mob. It was another very proud and satisfying moment. I patted Maggot's neck gently. "Good boy, good boy," I said and then trotted over to Toni. "Next time radio me for help, don't just stop."

She'd hardly ever worked the point and frankly she didn't have a clue. After more than three months of mustering the girl should have had more cattle sense and should have known what to do, but she didn't. We arrived at Hay Stack only to realize the yards were too small. We herded the mob in as far as we could and stationed bull buggies and trucks to form a barrier until the yards were enlarged with extra stationary panels.

If the cattle didn't fit we would have to stay with them all night—not my idea of a romantic evening in the outback, but a challenge I welcomed. The cattle barely fit. It would be impossible to process them. The following day we walked the mob to the yards at Cattle Camp, ten miles away. It was an all-day journey. Friday the 13th and over 1,200 head to move sounded like a lethal combination. I wasn't superstitious, well, not a lot. It was another 3 a.m. start. The Hay Stack gate was opened and as usual the mob bolted. It was a few minutes of mad riding, yelling and swearing, but the cattle were turned, calmed, and started on their way.

"Becky turn the wing in," Mick radioed about an hour into the walk.

"Do you mean Becky America?" I asked.

"Do you see anyone else?" he answered very cheekily.

"Okay, smarty pants," I said with a laugh.

We continued to move the mob, Mick in the lead, me on the right point. The mob was stretched out for a quarter of a mile. There was more distance between riders and buggy drivers than on any other muster. It was critical to pay attention and stay alert. I sat high in my saddle, spine erect and shoulders back scanning the mob—front, back, front, back. The cattle moved calmly, cooperating for once.

I glanced back to monitor the mob and saw a kangaroo leap from the scrub and bolt right for them. I had one thought, *Oh shit, this isn't going to be good!* I wanted to warn Mick, but there was no time, it happened too fast. The 'roo hopped right through the middle of the mob, igniting a stampede. Hundreds of cattle ran straight at Mick—the ground rumbled. Mick and I worked frantically to bend the mob. My heart almost beat out of my chest—hooves and dust flew. The thundering noise deafened me, but Mick and I saved the mob.

"What happened?" Mick asked when it was calmer.

"It was a bloody kangaroo," I roared, nearly falling off my horse.

It could have easily been a disaster, but I couldn't help but find humor in it. Donald mustered up a few hundred more head and added them to the growing mob. As we neared Cattle Camp the animals passed two water tanks. They licked the moisture from the tanks' walls and licked the mud that surrounded each tank—they were parched. They hadn't had water for a day. We yarded them up. While everyone unsaddled horses for the two hour-drive home, I hopped in the chopper with Donald. It had become routine for the pilot to fly me back to the station to prepare dinner for the crew.

Months earlier I would have hated it, but fixing evening tea had become my signature at the station. It wasn't as fulfilling as mustering, but I was pleased to have both talents. Supper was on the table when the crew arrived. After tea, we visited with Donald, who had mustered at many stations. "Stations get a lot of couples, but usually one is good and one is a mongrel," he said, suggesting his surprise that Jan and Andrew had found a pretty grounded couple like us.

Most of the crew headed back to Cattle Camp at sunrise. During the night the cattle broke the water pipe and all the water drained out of the water tanks. The cattle had been without water for two days. It was a critical situation; cattle would start to die soon. Mick hauled water most of the afternoon, but only got 250 animals watered. Well over 1,000 head hadn't had a drop. Lee stayed up all night to help Andrew cart water.

"If we don't get them watered, we'll have to open the yard and let them go," Jan said. "They get to the stage where they don't want it anymore. I've seen them shake and die on the tracks—I've seen thirsty cattle."

It was weird not having Lee beside me in the humpy that night. I missed him. I did have guests for the evening, Roy and Livingston slept by our bed. They were never used as cattle dogs, but they were great companions. Three-thirty came early—sometimes I thought I was back on The Farm getting up to milk. We got to Cattle Camp at 5:30 a.m. Lee was on trough watch and Andrew was tucked away in his swag. It was a near-sleepless night for the pair, but they saved the cattle.

We drafted all day. I had the steer and bull gate. The legendary Mammoth walked calmly into the round pen. We all stood silent. This 2,000-pound-plus gigantic bullock had been at the station for years, even before the Glenns took over ownership. He was beyond massive and his long threatening horns threw shadows on his roan-colored hide as he tilted his head. Mammoth towered over all the other animals, even the bulls. He was a brilliant-looking beast. If Andrew said "steer gate," it signaled Mammoth's fate to become hamburger at Harvey Beef.

"Bush!" Andrew said.

We all jumped, excited and pleased that Andrew saved the station icon. I always knew Andrew had a heart, he was just reluctant to express his feelings. We finished drafting with a total count of 1,745 head. Wow! I couldn't believe it. I knew it was a large muster, but had no idea we had brought in so many. Bulls and steers were hauled back to the homestead yards. We broncoed all the calves and a dozen cows that had missing tags, horns curved into their skulls or wire wrapped around their legs. We hadn't broncoed since *Outback* requested a story and photos. I shot five rolls of film and sent them to the editor. I hoped I had captured the quality photographs the color magazine was famed for. Lee handled some of the castrating and spent most of the day on the rear leg. There were few station jobs that Lee didn't enjoy, but brocoing topped the list—it was painstakingly filthy and challenging.

We had heard a bull at another station horned a bloke and ripped his testicle out. *Ouch!* He got stitched up and was supposed to be okay. Not sure if okay meant one, two or no testicles, but I wasn't going to ask. It was another reality check to outback dangers. I told Lee to protect the family jewels.

We had two days left. Lee and I counted our blessings. Our time at Ashburton could have easily ended in misfortune with all the close calls we'd had. We respected the danger, but somehow always found ourselves faced with it.

Another 3:30 a.m. start and we arrived at Cattle Camp at 5:30. Broncoing was finished by 1 p.m. We walked five miles to release the 600 cows and calves to freedom. The sweltering heat sapped what little energy we had left.

That evening at the house Lee and I presented the family with a collage of 30 photos and three outback poems Lee had composed. Jan and Mick teared up and hugged us tight. For months the crew had been asking to see all the photos I had taken. I always had some lame excuse, but I didn't want to ruin their surprise. I made little photo albums for Mick, Geoff, Tricky, Becky Kimberley, Barney and even Toni.

The day had at last arrived, October 18. It was time to depart Ashburton. Lee and I hadn't packed at all, there was never time. We filled four boxes with all of our $1 items from the op shop. No sense in lugging it back to the States. We told Jan to hold on to them because we'd be back some day.

I watered our garden one last time. It had provided much joy and beauty over the months. "Oh God, I can't believe it!" I said aloud. My Sturt's desert pea had bloomed for the first time on our final day. Sun shimmered on the tears slowly creeping down my face. Everyone said it would never grow, that it was the wrong time of year. Perhaps the red bloom was a sign, applauding our outgoing nature and adventurous spirits.

The Road Toad was as packed as she'd ever been. We stopped at the cattle yards to say good-bye. There were a lot of tears and shiny eyes. I think they were really going to miss us—I knew we'd miss them and we'd miss Ashburton.

Was it a fluke or fate that we ended up at Ashburton? I'd say fate. We had learned a lot at the station and took away great personal accomplishments. We also left behind our own teachings that the crew might draw upon during the rest of mustering season, perhaps throughout their lives.

I didn't bawl the whole way down the road as I had expected. I knew deep in my heart that Lee and I would return to Ashburton—in six months, a year or ten—I knew we'd be back.

Origin of Thought

The air is still and dry, absent is conversation,
It is not a midsummer drought, but the seed of concentration;

Time to unearth the fragments of thought your practical self
    negates,
Assemble all the pieces you believe to be one to reveal what
    they might create;

Numerous finds lay intact, buried beneath the sand,
But many more are fragile and broken, demanding a skilled
    artisan's hand;

These wondrous relics offer no instruction or drawing of design,
But the only blueprints truly required are etched, there in
    your mind;

Joining the rubble is a task of frustration, like a puzzle obscure
    and worn,
But the shapeless pile yields to your efforts and the fragments
    take their full form;

The priority turns to preserving the site against inevitable winds
    and rains,
Before the sands of your mind reclaim and destroy the insight it
    now contains.

Lee Chaney

32

Road Trip from Hell

O ur outback adventure was over. We hit the bitumen
and were well on our way, or so I thought. Twenty
miles into the drive the Road Toad shook, snorted
and slowed.

"We've lost fourth gear," Lee said.

"Oh no!" I said. "Will we make it?"

"Do you want the good news or the bad news?" he asked.

"Just give me the news," I retorted.

"The bad news is that we won't make it to Geraldton to
see a movie," he said. "But the good news is, that at least the
Road Toad is still going and we might make it."

That was Lee's way of turning a bad situation into a hopeful one. What a disaster. We still had almost 1,000 miles to
drive and only had three gears. It was going to be a long trip.
I tried to soak up Lee's optimistic outlook. He was right, after
all—we didn't have to be towed. Our pace had only been
slowed, but we were still powering along at 45 mph. Several
hours later we were at Carnarvon's city limits. A young female in her early 20s, clad in a long pastel-flowered dress,
tried to flag us down. Lee passed slowly. "Should we stop to
help?" he asked.

"Yes. Who knows when we might need help."

Lee turned around and went back. They had a South
Australian license plate. The girl's boyfriend had his head

buried in the bonnet of an old yellow station wagon. The pair of free spirits had all the props of hippies.

"Are you all right?" Lee asked.

"Our bonnet keeps blowing open and we have nothing to latch it with," the soft-spoken girl said as her long dirty blond hair tangled in the wind and her dress swirled up.

"I think we have some emergency rope," Lee said.

Lee gave them half the rope just in case we needed the rest. That rope had saved us once before.

"Thanks, we really appreciate it," she said.

Another 150 miles down the road we rolled into the Overlander Roadhouse. Lee revved the motor trying to get to the pump, but the Road Toad conked out anyway. An elderly man stood and stared at our unusual-looking vehicle. Lee stepped out to push.

"She's good on the open road, but she's not a town car," Lee told the man.

"Why didn't you just start her again and pull up to the gas pump?" I asked.

"Well, dear, the starter has problems and she doesn't have that many starts left."

This could only happen to us, I thought, *We've lost fourth gear, we're about to lose our starter and we're not going to make it back to the Blackburns'.*

Once in Geraldton, our midway point, I had a craving for McDonald's food. I was far from a fast-food junky, but since I hadn't had it for months, I got some hot salty fries and a cold coffee milk shake. I relished each bite of my fries and was in true ecstasy with every sip of my shake.

Two hours past Geraldton we pulled over at 11:30 p.m. We slept alongside the road again. Lee had driven 750 miles straight without a break. I leaned over and lay my head in his lap. If he wanted to keep driving, he could. He was like the Energizer bunny—he could keep going and going and going. It was still dark when we woke up at 4:45 a.m. Lee turned the key and the Road Toad started—thank goodness! We initially had planned to sightsee on the drive south, but our vehicle problems axed that idea. We promised Mikey we'd arrive in time to take the show cattle to the Harvey District Agricultural Show.

About 9 a.m. we drove through Perth, slowed by many stoplights. Lee's face was tight and tense. His eyebrows sloped inward in confusion. He gripped the gearshift with conviction.

"Work with me, work with me," he muttered, staring up at the traffic signals.

Every time he had to change gears or slow down, the remaining gears were jeopardized. The Road Toad refused to stay in third gear. Lee held the gearshift with his foot, preventing it popping out. At 9:30 a.m. we were a little south of Perth in Armandale, with Lee's foot still firmly on the gearshift. The area around the gearshift started to smoke. Clouds of gray fumed between us.

"Oh my God!" I said frantically. "Lee, we're going to catch on fire."

The situation looked dismal. We approached one of the busiest intersections—16 lanes of traffic, four each from all directions. The light turned red. We were forced to stop. The light turned green, but the Road Toad wouldn't budge. My body stiffened, I was fidgety, jerking my head around looking for oncoming cars that were going to plow into us or over us. The Road Toad was stuck in gear; we were at a standstill. Lee pushed and pulled and knocked the gearshift. Blue veins popped out on his neck. The gear would not shift back in. I wanted to jump out and run for safety, but I knew Lee didn't need a hysterical wife on his hands. Horns blew. I stuck my arm out of the window and motioned for vehicles to go around us. The light turned red. *Oh God, help us!* I prayed silently.

Lee jerked, pushed and pulled some more until finally the Road Toad popped into gear. We slowly rolled through the intersection when the light turned green again.

"Do you want the good news or the bad news?" Lee asked again.

"Just tell me," I said, still overcome by the intersection drama.

"The good news is—we're moving," he said. "The bad news—we've lost third gear."

Rather than our final 30 miles taking an hour in third gear we putted along two and a half hours in second gear. Impatient drivers speeded around us tooting their horns. How dare they? We weren't on a Sunday afternoon drive, we were only trying to get home to the Blackburns'. The best medicine for that kind of situation was laughter and that was just what we did. If we had learned anything in Australia, it was not to sweat the little stuff and not to worry about the things we could not change.

We couldn't change the fact that the Road Toad was falling to pieces so we might as well enjoy the moment. Aussies were typically much more laid back than Americans. It was a trait I'd like to pass on to many family and friends at home who overwhelmed themselves with worries that they had little to no control over, but shoot, I'd have to make sure I lived by my newfound rule first.

We coasted down some hills in neutral. We actually increased speed from 25 mph to almost 40 mph using pure gravitational pull. Lee assessed the situation: "Since we left the station 48 hours ago, we have lost our turn signal, windshield wiper, third and fourth gears. The radio crapped out, the master cylinder for the brakes is going, the tachometer broke, the starter is sick and we had to put a brand-new battery in. But other than that, she's running good!"

The boy really cracked me up. At the beginning of the trip I had questioned our compatibility on the road together. I reckoned we'd shaped up into pretty good traveling partners. We'd had a rocky start, but as Lee said, "We had to figure out how to drive each other."

"Listen to her purring. Hear that? I'm telling you, Becky, you could write a whole saga on the Road Toad," Lee said, still putting humor into our calamity.

"I need to call Karen Marsh tonight because she sounded upset in her fax," I said totally off the subject.

"That's the difference between you and me," he said. "You're thinking about solving the world's problems and I'm just concentrating on getting an hour down the road." Lee called it my "shotgun" personality. I'd be in a discussion about one subject, and in midsentence, I'd go completely off-track. My shotgun personality made him laugh—and made him crazy.

"Becky, stop!" he often said. "Now, finish your first thought before you start telling me about anything else."

The remoteness at the station had been good for our relationship because we only had each other. We had developed a closer, more intimate union. We shared more feelings, more concerns, more dreams.

As we got closer to the Blackburns', the Road Toad's engine just quit. Lee fiddled with the ignition switch as we coasted down the highway. We slowed to a crawl and the motor finally turned back on. We arrived at the Blackburns' at 11:40 a.m. Although she was on her last roll, the Road Toad had miraculously carried us more than 5,000 miles. All afternoon we unpacked everything on the lawn.

Kiana had graduated from the nursery to make room for her baby sister, Tullia, born four weeks earlier. Kiana's new room was the old guestroom—our old room. It moved her to the bumblebee room, decorated in black and yellow, adorned with bee drawings and crafts. Kiana was happy to see her Uncle Lee and Aunty Becky.

The next morning at 5:30, Lee and I followed the truck with the Blackburns' four show cows and three heifers. The Harvey Fairgrounds was already teeming with action. Exhibitors unloaded cattle and gear and others scrubbed their cattle in the wash rack. The temperature was 20 degrees cooler than the Pilbara. It was a cold morning to wash cattle. Cows swished their wet tails in my face and neighbors accidentally squirted me. Lee scrubbed, I rinsed, but it looked more like the cows had given me a bath.

The Blackburns asked me to show most of their cattle and I changed into my show attire, white shirt and black pants. I led six in the competition and won the reserve grand champion sash with the Blackburns' old cow. Everyone thought she might be grand, but once again, "Always the bridesmaid, never the bride." (That was the joke for years at home. Many times the cows I exhibited came in second best and I was a bridesmaid 15 times before I walked down the aisle with Lee.)

During the show, Don Fry, the Jersey breeder we had met at the Perth Royal Show two weeks earlier, was the announcer. When I was showing the first cow, Don was busy chatting on the microphone.

"We are graced with the presence of an international strapper today," he said. "I won't say who it is, but you can probably figure it out. She's the best-lookin' one out there. Becky and her husband, Lee Chaney, are dairy breeders from the States and they just got some good news that their family bred the grand champion Brown Swiss at World Dairy Expo. We're very happy to have them with us today."

Long View Jetway Oprah had achieved the top dairy recognition in America. Ironically, Oprah was purchased by Edwin Genasci, whom Lee and I had visited at the onset of our trip. Edwin showed us Oprah and I snapped a few pictures. We had no idea she was going to go all the way. I beamed in the showring, unable to hide the pride I felt for my parents, my siblings and the friends who had worked with Long View cattle over the years.

After the show we drank a few beers with everyone at the show office. After two cans I was too cold to have anymore. I had coffee and visited with the older folks who helped with the fair. It was a two-day event and featured a small carnival. Kiana was in the Little Miss Show Girl competition and donned her little jean dress, hat and Aussie boots. Her blond hair had grown and soft curls reached her shoulders. She would be two years old in a month and loved her new baby sister. "Mikey you're good for one thing and one thing only," I teased. "Producing beautiful little girls."

Kiana was really attached to Uncle Lee and the duo loved to spend time together playing and reading. That night she wouldn't sleep and asked Josette if she could see Uncle Lee. He tucked her in. I believe it was Kiana who changed Lee's mind about becoming a father.

I was both excited and apprehensive about our final four weeks with the Blackburns. Lee and I had adjusted to outback life. We had accepted the rough-as-guts living conditions and learned to love it. It was so foreign, it intrigued us, humbled us. We'd gotten accustomed to working with a crew, watching out for each other. We sadly had left our outback stint to see what civilization had to offer.

I welcomed the inside bathroom—no more scary trips to the dunny or squatting on the ground at night. I welcomed the hot shower fueled by a hot water heater, rather than wood we had to gather. I was happy not to scan the ground for snakes and centipedes, although Mikey told us to watch out for the poisonous and aggressive tiger snake. There was just no escaping the deadly creatures. I welcomed modernization, but missed our happy rustic days in the humpy.

My biggest concern was Lee. He would milk at the Blackburns for a month while Ray and Lois were away. I knew the last thing in the world he wanted to do was milk cows, but he had promised Mikey. I would care for show calves and Lois's immaculate garden. I feared it wouldn't be enough. If Lee got discouraged with milking or I went through mustering withdrawal, it would affect our relationship without us even realizing it.

We had had the experience of a lifetime, filled with ups and downs. I hoped our jobs at the Blackburns' farm would cap off the trip and not diminish our journey.

33

The End?

We took up residency in Ray and Lois's house, next to the dairy and a five-minute walk from Mikey and Josette's. Lee milked and I fed my show heifers, mucked out behind them and tried to train them to lead. I worked daily to prepare them for another agricultural fair on Saturday in Brunswick, another nearby town. Two Holsteins did well in the education process, but one was still psycho. I was committed to training the heifers, but was more worried about Lois's prized landscape.

Lois gave me instructions on house care and the sacred floral vista that wrapped around their brick rancher. I monitored hundreds of flowers, plants and little garden plots. I watered the thirsty foliage and went back to the barn and untied my next victim. I tugged on the heifer and got her as far as the milk house, just as Lee walked out of the dairy door, which spooked her. The heifer leaped to the right and pulled me down. I hit the ground with a heavy thud. A stone gouged my elbow. Pain shot up my arm, but I never let go of the blasted heifer.

"Are you all right?" Lee asked.

"Do I look all right?" I snapped from my horizontal position.

From my harsh reaction I think Lee was afraid I was going to spring to my feet and rip his head off. Lee grabbed the lead rope for me. I lay on the ground.

"I quit, I quit!" I yelled both from pain and frustration. A moment later I collected my thoughts and my confidence. "That shittin' heifer isn't going to beat me."

I stood up and tried to concentrate on the task at hand and tried to forget the painful thumps in my arm. *Mind over matter—that's it,* I kept telling myself. Lee handed the stupid animal back to me and I walked it back to the hay shed. That was enough for one day. I took my first bubble bath in nearly a year. It was wonderfully soothing! The little things in life we so often take for granted. Lee sat in the bathroom on the floor and talked to me while I enjoyed my warm bubbles and an icy cold beer. Oh, civilization was grand!

We adjusted to society again. Small gestures for each other helped fill the void we felt not being at Ashburton. I'd have a beer chilled at the end of the day for Lee. He'd surprise me with a four-leaf clover, as he'd been doing for years. The secret to our relationship was unexpected surprises.

We looked forward to going back to America, but had a few reservations. Lee was a bit of a lost soul. He couldn't pinpoint exactly what he wanted to do, but he was sure he did not want to milk cows. He realized that working outdoors was his passion and he had become fond of beef cattle. I hoped he'd find a job that would use his talents and challenge his skills, making him excited to go to work every day. As far as I was concerned I was going to write and I could write from anywhere. No sense in fretting about it—we wanted to focus on our final days in Oz.

A letter from Aunt Libby arrived at the Blackburns'. She had written to us several times during the trip, but the last letter touched a fragile chord. Since we'd left the States I'd ignored the fact that Dad and Mom were selling the family farm. I knew it was the right thing to do, but part of me was already having separation anxiety. Whether I was at college in Wisconsin, at my first job in Minnesota or halfway around the world—I always knew home was The Farm. Aunt Libby reminisced about her days growing up there, chasing her nine younger siblings around, including my mischievous father. Tears filled my eyes, both sad and happy. Sad because "home" was being sold and happy because my folks would be unburdened and wouldn't have to suffer the financial roller coaster they'd been living for years. I knew it was the best thing; Mom and Dad could start living again and enjoying children, grandchildren and great-grandchildren, but finding out The Farm was being sold did break my heart.

Other than maintaining Lois's botanical oasis, I fed the cattle dog Kep, the house terrier Sox and a little yellow canary. I gave daily scraps to the chooks and gathered eggs. It was no big deal, but I detested the feathered egg layers for the most part. When I was eight, a rooster cornered me in the chook house, holding me captive for hours. I crawled up the side and clung to a ceiling rafter. The more the rooster hopped in the air and flapped its wings trying to flog me, the more I screamed and cried. I went on chook boycott after that. Lois didn't have any roosters, so that made my job easier.

I realized that night what I had missed about normal life. I relaxed on the couch, watched my favorite TV flicks and didn't have to swish away bugs or mozzies or worry about a generator turning off any second. It was great, and although I wondered how I survived without such modern conveniences, part of me still hungered for that vivid station life.

"This is the closest we've been on our own since we left home almost a year ago," Lee said.

"I know, it's a little weird isn't it?" I said.

My intense heifer-training week didn't payoff. The day before the Brunswick Show, the largest heifer got away from me three times. She knew she could pull right away and I wasn't getting paid enough to be dragged. Actually, even if I was getting paid a fortune, it wasn't enough for me to get dragged behind the churning hooves of a blockhead bovine. Been there, done that!

The alarm went off at 3:45 a.m. *Crikey, was it time to muster,* I thought, wiping my tired eyes. Reality check, we're not at Ashburton, it was show day. The truck arrived at 5. We loaded six heifers and three cows. One was the cow Lee had just put a halter on for the first time five days earlier. He had worked with her throughout the week. Lee and I were in charge of the show string. Mikey did the home milking and came to the show later.

I showed three heifers and two cows. Lee was busy in the barn keeping the cattle clean, fed and watered. He was also the pooper scooper. The grand champion Holstein I showed was also named the interbreed champion. The judge was from New South Wales.

"How many calves has your cow had?" the judged asked.

"Five," I said.

"Do you mean five or fiiiiivvve....?" he asked teasing me about my Yankee southern twang.

"I mean fiiiiivvve," I said with an embarrassed red face.

"I know you're from America," the judge said. "I'm mates with Ray Blackburn."

After the show Lee went home to milk. I offered to go, but he told me to stay and enjoy the after-show gathering. He didn't have to tell me twice. I joined the dairy and beef cattle exhibitors at the show office for happy hour and special award announcements. Everyone had a stubby in their hand. It was a great way to top off a busy day showing animals. Livestock folks in the States had private parties in their aisles, but there was never a show-committee-sponsored activity. For the most part, alcohol was banned from county, state and national exhibitions in America. Socializing was part of Australia's fabric. I admired the Aussie breeders for their friendly competitiveness and their hospitable events. I sat with Mikey, Leon and his mate, Bradley. We drank and laughed. Mikey and Leon received the top show awards.

"I'd like to thank my wife and daughters for making all of this possible," Mikey said, accepting his award. "And I'd like to thank Americans Lee and Becky Chaney for getting the cattle ready and bringing them to the show."

I wished Lee could have stayed to hear Mikey's praise and, of course, to enjoy the party. Lee and Mikey celebrated the supreme champion honor that evening at the home dairy while I fixed evening tea. Sometimes I avoided Lee when he was chatting with others. It gave him more of an opportunity to talk and me time to give my motor mouth a break.

We only had three weeks left and they passed quickly. Lee's days were filled with morning and afternoon milkings, feeding baby calves and making hay. I concentrated on finishing stories, updating my journal and battling Mikey. I always had to be ready for his wisecracks and often tried to beat him to the punch.

"Has anyone seen the dummy?" Josette asked, referring to what Aussies call a baby pacifier.

"No, Josette, I haven't seen Mikey anywhere," I answered with a big smile, knowing Mikey was just in the next room and could hear me.

Our comical ribbing was a daily ritual, but he was such a good mate. I especially adored Josette and the girls. Once a week I went to swimming lessons with Kiana and played netball on Josette's women's team. Six players were on a team. It was basketball minus bouncing and other specific rules, like only one shooter and only two net defenders. My competitive nature made me too aggressive. I leaped through the air to intercept a ball and accidentally plowed into a woman.

"I'm so sorry," I said.

"That's okay, I'm just not used to American gridiron," she answered with an irritated tone and expression.

A few times a week we'd walk to the Cookernup Store. "Watch out for the magpies, it's nesting season," Josette warned.

"Do they really swoop down and attack?" I asked.

"There's a territorial one on the way to the store and we have to keep an eye out for it," she said.

The black-and-white birds made national news at the Olympics when they started diving down and whacking people in the head at outdoor venues. "Don't wear any shiny hair clips," I remembered the TV reporter announcing. "Wear a hat and sunnies (Aussie sunglasses) to protect yourself."

Magpies are the most widespread bird in Australia and have the most notorious reputation. My walks to the Cookernup store were always hiding under my baseball cap and subtly carrying a stick in my hand.

The Cookernup Store was a small country shop that was a combination feed store, hardware store, post office, video store and grocer. I purchased little 50-cent bags of candy for Kiana on every visit and collected our mail.

We got our last package from Mom and Dad. Mom had sneaked in two tins of Copenhagen. They made Lee's day. She also sent a photo of her and Dad at her class reunion. They looked happy and healthy and certainly didn't look 67 and 68 years old, respectively. Mom bragged in the letter that her classmates said she was the prettiest girl at the reunion. I only hoped I could age as gracefully.

I called home and found out they were in North Carolina visiting Aunt Evelyn, who was losing her battle with cancer. Doctors gave my Mom's sister one to three weeks to live. My next call was to North Carolina. I wanted to talk to Aunt Evelyn if she was strong enough. I knew it might be our last conversation and I wanted to have closure in case something happened before we made it home.

"Hi, Aunt Evelyn, this is Becky," I said.

"I miss you, Becky," Aunt Evelyn said.

"I miss you, too, and I love you," I said.

The following day I went to the chiropractor with Josette. I didn't have any back problems, but thought the specialist could tell me something about my occasional headaches. The doctor said my shoulders were crooked, my pelvis was tilted and I should have been to a chiropractor five years earlier. He adjusted me, but frankly, it was disgusting. I thought he cracked all the bones in my neck, but he said it was just air crackling between the bones. I found out my neck was responsible for all my headaches over the years.

Lee and I visited Don and Lorelle Fry at their nearby dairy farm. We helped milk their 240 head in their double-20 rapid-exit setup. Don and Lee talked about cows as they changed milkers. Lorelle and I sprayed and wiped udders.

"Lee, are you familiar with Holstein sires?" Don asked.

"Lee bred a reserve All-American Holstein," I said to Don before Lee had a chance to answer.

Don's eyes got big, he was stunned for a moment. "That's huge, that's really big, I'm impressed," he said. "I never knew you were such a legend." I don't think Lee really knew what he had accomplished in the dairy industry until that very moment.

We grilled hot dogs on the barby and slugged back a few stubbies—only a few more days to enjoy Aussie beer. Don and Lorelle looked in the little photo albums we carried of family, friends and cows.

The editor of *Outback* called. He said my photos turned out well. I was numb with excitement. My feature article and photo spread was pegged to run in the January/February issue. I knew that having work published in *Outback* would have great ramifications for my career as a journalist. I radiated with pride. Lee was happy for me, but a little depressed he was stuck milking cows.

"I'd rather chase bulls through prickly scrub on a push bike than milk cows," he said.

The situation had nothing to do with the Blackburns; we adored them. He had milked in the States for nearly half his life and just didn't want to do it anymore. He yearned to be back in his bull buggy. He missed his bulldogging days, crashing through scrub, flying over ditches, chasing bulls, knocking them down and tying them up.

We took a two-day jaunt to the Days'. Mandy's birthday was the perfect excuse for celebrating. I surprised her with a birthday cake and flowers from Lois's garden. Shane had to work on Saturday, but the rest of us drove into Beverley. It was a very small town. We stopped at the airplane museum, the only tourist attraction. Lee read about gliding and saw the adventurous people flying through the air. "I think I'm going to go gliding," he said.

"You just can't get enough of dangerous sports, can you?" I asked.

We drove to the airport and Lee registered. Paragliders had no motor so there was no way I was going up. I was edgy, but Lee loved the adrenaline rush of taking risks. He scooted down into his glider in the front seat. An instructor sat behind him. A motorized plane pulled them down the runway and into the air. High in the sky, I watched the plane detach from the paraglider and thought about Lee's face lit-up with excitement. I'm not sure if he breathed a sigh of relief when he landed, but I sure did. Our visit with the Days was fun and we planned to see them at our farewell barbecue in a week.

One day I lined up a surprise for Lee. I walked into a small hair salon in Harvey. I put the fate of my locks literally in Catherine's hands. "My husband's brother is getting married in two weeks," I told her. "They haven't seen us for a year. I want Lee to escort me to the wedding and for people to think he is with another woman."

I was hoping with my new do and my 25-pound weight loss I would surprise a few people. Catherine went to work, chopping different angles. For the first time since I was 12 years old, I got all my hair cut off. Catherine bobbed it in the back and left my bangs long, running down along my jaw bone. She dyed it burgundy to hide my gray hairs, ones I was sure I'd earned mustering.

I showed the ladies the bite I had on my shoulder. It was red and swollen. Their eyes widened, their brows raised. "For sure, that's a redback bite," one woman said. "You have to go right to the doctor's. I was bitten by a pregnant female and couldn't breathe within ten minutes."

They scared me to death. I wasn't sure it was a redback bite, let alone a pregnant one or not. My only fear was that I was going to have baby spiders hatch out of my shoulder and start crawling up my neck. A doctor saw me for two minutes. He asked a few questions, took my temperature and blood pressure and diagnosed me. "It's an insect bite, but not a redback bite," he said. "There's really nothing you can do." I guessed that meant that it was not life threatening, although the comment was a little vague. I paid the $36A fee and drove home.

We had spent a lot of time with Mikey, Josette, Kiana and Tullia. They had been good to us. I hoped we would have the opportunity to reciprocate one day. We spent evenings mastering new lawn games, playing with the girls and enjoying each other's company. Josette invited us up for our final evening together. They had a wedding the following afternoon and we departed the day after that. We exchanged gifts. Lee wrote a poem inspired by Kiana. We framed the poem, along with photos of Kiana with her Uncle Lee and Aunty Becky. Eyes teared up—we were going to be lifelong mates.

Ray and Lois returned home that evening. They were exhausted from their cross-continental flights. They were pleased the house and garden all looked intact. I only lost two tomato plants. (I never said I had a green thumb.)

On our last full day in Oz, many emotions overwhelmed us. I had been tired for days. Insomnia attacked me with a vengeance and when I did finally sleep, nightmares disturbed my slumber. I was nervous about returning home. Nervous about our future. Nervous about seeing people. Lee tried to console me, but I knew he was having his own inner turmoil, trying to determine his next path in life.

Lee milked and Ray went out to help him finish up. Ray was happy to be back in his element, working with cows. Mikey and Josette left for their wedding. Lee reluctantly agreed to drive Miss Daisy around on our final day doing last-minute errands.

That night Lee and I stayed up to check a pregnant cow we thought might need help delivering. We checked her at 11 p.m. and the front hooves were poking out a little. We returned to the house and set the alarm for 1 a.m. Ray, Lee and I went back out to check her. The feet were out a few more inches, but the cow had made little progress during her two hours of labor since we first checked her. We used a pulley to help get the calf out. I pulled off my rings and inserted my fingers into her vulva trying to stretch her skin, relieving the pressure of delivery.

Memories of calf deliveries when I grew up on The Farm filled me as we stood under the dark Australian sky. A full moon peered down, aiding us with its subtle glow. There was something special about bringing life into the world. I had helped deliver hundreds of calves at my parents' farm. I remembered one time when Dad and I delivered twins. They weren't breathing.

"Leave them, they're dead," Dad said.

"Dad, let me try to save them," I said as I proceeded to give them mouth-to-nose resuscitation.

I held one little calf's mouth shut and covered one nostril as I tried to blow life into the other nostril. My lips were smashed up against the newborn's slimy nose; afterbirth covered my face. I continued the bovine CPR until I had saved the twins. Dad couldn't believe his eyes. "Those two calves are yours, you saved them."

I had a tremendous feeling of pride. It was that same feeling I got that final night at the Blackburns, our final night in Australia, our last night of our year abroad. The shoulders of the calf finally squeezed through the mother's vulva, then the calf gushed out in one laborious effort. We dragged the wet bull calf under the mother's nose for her to begin cleaning it. "Good job," Ray said to Lee and me.

The emergency delivery somehow seemed to reflect our entire trip. The new life paralleled our own rebirth. A renewal of our souls, our relationship. Our trip was not only a physical journey, but an inner odyssey that had changed our lives forever. The calf's birth was like the beginning of the new chapter in our lives about to unfold.

Kiana

She's growing up quickly, she's growing up fast,
These precious moments, wish they would forever last;

Like the first time you held her and she fell asleep in your arms,
Lulled by your heartbeat, sheltered from harm;

Her first solo steps and you watched all the while,
Enchanted by the look of pride on her face and mischievous smile;

She spoke her own language, full of words garbled and bent,
You never mastered the words, but you knew what they meant;

She is still growing quickly, she is still growing fast,
Be part of these moments before they are passed;

And though one day she will have a child of her own,
You will remember the little girl that helped make your house a
    home.

Lee Chaney

A Bittersweet Homecoming

A farewell barbecue followed by a sad good-bye at the airport brought the international aspect of our story to a close. What started out as an idea, the hope of working abroad, had evolved from a dream into reality. Our adventure was over. We felt so blessed by our experience, but were in limbo about our return home. We landed at LAX and rented a car for our cross-country drive.

We stopped to visit our mates, Bill and Lynn Vanderham, outside of L.A. They hosted us before our trip departure, as did Bill and Libby Clark, Verne and Polly Adams and our friends at World Wide Sires in Central California. I couldn't believe it had been a year since our earlier visits. We were so lucky to have such wonderful people in our life, in the States and around the world. After a shower and a quick meal, Lynn fixed us a bag of homemade muffins and other treats for the drive.

Lee drove 14 hours straight to my Aunt Carol Ann and Uncle Dan's house in Bisbee, Arizona. Aunt Carol Ann drove us across the Mexican border. We sipped on margaritas and devoured spicy Mexican specialties. My dad's sister was the youngest of the ten siblings. I wondered sometimes about our family and my chance arrival into the world. First, Mom told us she almost didn't marry Dad. "Pappy Leatherman warned me to stay away from your father," she said. Pappy Leatherman had told her, "The Longs are heavy breeders."

Obviously, she didn't heed the advice, being the mother of six. When she had Patty, her fourth child, the nurses could not find Mom's pulse. "Peg, absolutely no more children," Dr. B.O. Thomas Jr. cautioned. "You could die." Three years later in a January blizzard I popped into the world, followed by my brother, Dennie, 23 months later. So, were the Longs heavy breeders? Well, maybe.

I wanted to stop at Geronimo's monument where the famous Indian signed the peace treaty. I wanted to slip into a pub in Tombstone, Arizona, and slurp back a cold one, but Lee had one thing on his mind—home. He was like a horse that could smell hay in the barn. He did surrender to stopping in San Antonio, Texas, to have dinner with my friend, Adriane, who was stationed in the army.

As more miles disappeared, sheets of rain pounded our car. There was little to see through the thumping raindrops so I got lost in a recap of our trip. It seemed ages ago that we had drunk kava with the natives in Tonga, welcomed in the new millennium in New Zealand and hiked through the highlands of Papua New Guinea. But Australia was still fresh in our minds, fresh in our hearts. We already missed our friends, missed the outback, missed mustering.

We learned so much on our journey—patience, flexibility and the willingness to negotiate and compromise. Our transition from very little time spent together to practically being attached at the hips actually went pretty smoothly. Our personalities and compatibility were tested on many occasions, but we passed—not always with flying colors, but we passed. Those trials of discouragement or disagreement simply reinforced our commitment to each other. We were thousands of miles from home, yet we were a team and had vital roles in keeping that team happy and safe. We had to find a happy medium or risk the whole dream.

And a dream it was, an incredible dream. I looked over at Lee, his hands tight on the steering wheel, pushing through the storm. We were different people. We had a greater respect for each other and a greater respect for family and friends who had always taken a second seat to our careers.

"Honey, can we stop for a day in New Orleans?" I asked. "I've never been there and that would be really cool."

"Are you nuts?" he asked. "That's over 1,000 miles out of our way."

"So, you like to drive," I said.

Well, my horse was not about to sidetrack for a day in greener pastures, he was making a beeline for Maryland. After 32 hours of near-undisturbed driving, Lee agreed to a dinner break. The Cracker Barrel restaurant looked good in Birmingham, Alabama, and we knew they'd have a Thanksgiving Day special.

It was a celebratory feast. We were so grateful for our experiences overseas and grateful we made it back to the States safely. After dinner I called home to extend holiday greetings and to let them know we were just a few states away. "Hi Dennie, Happy Thanksgiving," I told my brother over the phone.

"Hi Becky," he said with a somber voice.

"What's wrong?" I asked.

"It's Dad," he reluctantly answered. "They're flying him to Washington Hospital. It could be his heart."

"Dennie, we're in Alabama and we'll drive all night. Dad is going to be all right. I love you," I said very composed and hung up the phone.

My calm, passive persona was all an act—an act I had mastered over the years during tragedy and controversy to keep others grounded. But as always when the phone call ended, so did my Oscar performance. Tears cascaded down my cheeks like waters tumbling over Niagara Falls. "Lee, it's Dad. They're flying him to Washington Hospital. It doesn't sound good. Oh my God, he may die before we get home."

"He's going to be okay," Lee said as he held me and tried to comfort me. We walked quietly to the car. I put my seat belt on and broke down again, hyperventilating from the trauma.

"Jesus Christ, girl! Stop wishing your father dead," Lee retorted.

"I ca-can't help it, Lee," I said, barely getting the words out in my borderline hysteria. "I'll never forgive myself if Dad dies before I see him."

Hour after hour the silent miles melted into the dark night—Alabama, Tennessee, Virginia.

"Becky, it's 5:30," Lee said, exhausted after driving all night. "I'm pulling into this gas station for fuel and coffee; you need to call home."

"I don't want to call home," I said. "I'm afraid."

"It's going to be okay," he said. "Call home."

I was dazed. I can't remember if I used change, called collect or used a calling card. Time stopped. I dialed Mom and Dad's number.

"Hello," a groggy voice said.

"Mom?" I said. "Sorry it's so early."

"Are you almost home?" she asked.

"Yes, but how's Dad?" I asked hoping for the best, but fearing the worst.

"He's stable and he's at Washington Hospital," Mom said.

"Oh my God, Mom, what happened? I was so scared. Sorry I'm not there with you."

"They think your father had an allergic reaction and then the medication at Frederick almost put him into a heart attack. That's when they medevacked him out."

"But, he's okay, right?" I asked nervously.

"Yes," Mom said.

"Lee's been driving more than 30 hours straight," I said. "We can take a break at Kelly and Blane's house or drive straight to Washington Hospital."

"We don't know when your father is going to get released so why don't you stop at Kelly and Blane's."

"Okay, Mom, I love you and tell Dad I love him."

I walked back to the pump. "He's stable," I said, starting to cry again.

"I told you he'd be okay," Lee said, embracing me again.

We were prepared to drive to Washington, but were relieved to get a break—Lee needed one. We turned into Kelly and Blane's lane and were welcomed by a sequence of signs based on the "Burma Shave" advertisements—*No snakes in the dunny / No spiders on the walls / No bulls to muster / Welcome back—we missed ya!!!*

The sun hadn't come up yet. I'd hoped we wouldn't wake everyone. Kelly answered the door in her robe; she was up for a morning feeding with six-week-old Brady. It didn't seem possible I'd missed my best friend's entire pregnancy, but I vowed to make up for it.

"It's so good to see you," she said. "I've missed you so much. How's your Dad?"

"He's stable at Washington Hospital," I said. "I'm going to call him later."

"You two look beat," Kelly said. "I have the guestroom ready for you."

"First, let me admire that beautiful little boy," I said.

Brady was tiny with black swirls of hair. He had his father's eyes and nose and his mother's lips and chin. He was precious, but according to Kelly, he was a hungry, demanding little man. Lee and I stumbled into the guestroom and crawled into bed when most folks were rising for the day. We woke at 11 a.m., rested and rejuvenated, and I wanted to talk to Dad.

I was more relieved making the call, knowing that if his condition had changed, someone would have called me at Kelly's. When his feeble voice answered, I said, "Dad, it's me, Becky."

"Hi," he said.

"Why did you give me such a scare?" I kidded him.

"Bec, it scared me, too," he said as serious as he's ever talked to me. "I really thought I was on the way out. Your mother thought I was too. She gave me a kiss and told me she loved me before they put me in the helicopter. I knew it was serious when your mother did that. She didn't think she was going to see me alive again."

"Are you feeling better?" I asked.

"Yeah, I hope I never experience that again."

I thanked God for watching over Dad and couldn't wait to see him. Lee and I spent the day sharing our adventures with Kelly and Blane. Kelly told us about her sleepless night, dirty diaper and breast-feeding dramas. I was anxious to get home to give Dad and Mom big hugs and kisses. I was excited to see all the folks who had been so supportive.

The sights and the experiences will always be a highlight of our odyssey overseas, but one thing will especially stick out in our minds—the people we met and the friends we made along the way. People not only opened up their homes, but they opened up their lives, their hearts and imprinted on us forever their infectious smiles. We will forever be indebted to their hospitality. The trip, like life, was never about the destination, but rather the journey—and the journey is the reward.

Our visas expired, it was time to bid our saga g'day. We have our memories—memories to last a lifetime. I'll remember the smell of fresh bread baking at the station, the incredible taste of Ashburton homegrown beef, my first glimpse of the enchanting orange moon, and the people who not only became our mates, but our family—relationships forged by fate, friendships flourished by circumstance.

The Reply

I am at peace with myself, the calm is astounding,
Body not weary, head not pounding;

The worries of yesterday lay in my wake,
My greatest concern is which path will I take?

Along the way mistakes will be made,
But that's part of the journey, the toll to be paid;

I will weigh my options with meticulous care,
And search through myself knowing that the answers are there;

This time in my life has not been a chaotic revolution,
But a subtle process like my own evolution;

I'm at peace with myself, my life has new balance,
I don't fear the future, I welcome the challenge.

Lee Chaney

Epilogue

Sometimes it seems weird to be home and not waking up chilled in our little humpy only to be fried by midday. Our trip taught us so much, but especially our stint at Ashburton Downs Station. We're more laid back and more attuned to the real priorities and joys in life. I'm a firm believer that every experience, whether good or bad, can have a positive influence on your life. I once heard world-renowned speaker Zig Ziglar give one of his motivational presentations at a National FFA Convention. He said we should dare to be different, take risks, pursue our dreams and reach for the stars. All failures are building blocks to success. These weren't Zig's exact words, but I'll never forget his message as long as I live. His inspirational remarks encouraged the audience to be themselves, seize the moment and take advantage of life's opportunities—and that's just what I've tried to do.

Lee and I were fortunate that our careers were not affected by our sabbatical. If anything, the trip set in motion a series of events that my mother refers to as a "miracle." A week after arriving home, Lee got a job as assistant manager of a Virginia beef operation and I worked on my book. A year later Lee got a call from George Randall, a family friend and local businessman. George and his wife Betsy had just purchased my parents' farm. George asked Lee if he'd like to become the manager of Randall Land and Cattle Co. and oversee a herd of registered Polled Hereford beef cattle. I'm now living back in the house I grew up in—I'm truly back home on The Farm.

Miracles do happen and dreams do become reality. Our trip abroad will always be one of the most enticing, engaging, incredible, and, yes, challenging, and dangerous, life-altering events of our lives. Would we do it again? You betcha, mate!

Fresh Pages

Resilient old book tattered and worn,
Illustrations faded, pages torn;

Lift open the cover with calm reservation,
Print captures my eye and demands concentration;

Fact mingles with fiction each turn of a page,
Tale of a journey, a coming of age;

Savoring passages seasoned by imagination,
Feasting on each word with hungered anticipation;

Appetite at bay, I paused briefly to think,
Only then I noticed a difference of the ink;

At the outset, letters were foggy and bleeding,
But the print became crisp through the course of my reading;

I also observed, not that it mattered,
Illustrations focused and bolder on pages much less tattered;

The story grew more familiar with every passing line,
Ink became even fresher, unaffected by passing time;

The journey was still unfolding, but print abruptly ceased,
Remaining pages lay vastly open, from razor edges to their crease;

I wasn't given an ending but with my second look...
Discovered inside the back cover a handwritten message:
"Pick up a pen and finish the book!"

Lee Chaney

Kelly Hahn Johnson

Rebecca Long Chaney lives in Maryland with her husband Lee and Australian Shepherd dog, Bode. Chaney is a freelance writer and photographer, teaches travel writing at the community college and coordinates state, national and international dairy events. She also helps her husband with the registered Polled Hereford beef cattle operation he manages.

Chaney is a 1987 graduate of the University of Wisconsin-Madison with a Bachelor of Science degree in agricultural journalism. She's also a 1986 graduate of the University of Maryland's Institute of Applied Agriculture where she studied agricultural business management.